# HIGH CRIMES
### AND
# MISDEMEANORS

# HIGH CRIMES
# AND
# MISDEMEANORS

## The Term and Trials
## of Former Governor Evan Mecham

# Ronald J. Watkins

William Morrow and Company, Inc.
New York

Grateful acknowledgment is made for permission to reprint from *People of the Lie*. Copyright © 1983 by M. Scott Peck. Reprinted by permission of Simon & Schuster, Inc.

Recognizing the importance of preserving what has been written, it is the policy of William Morrow and Company, Inc., and its imprints and affiliates to have the books it publishes printed on acid-free paper, and we exert our best efforts to that end.

Library of Congress Cataloging-in-Publication Data

Watkins, Ronald J.
   High crimes and misdemeanors / Ronald J. Watkins.
     p.  cm.
   ISBN 0-688-09051-6
    1. Mecham, Evan.  2. Corruption (in politics)—Arizona—
History—20th century.  3. Arizona—Politics and government—1951–
I. Title.
F815.3.M4W38  1990
979.1'053—dc20                         89-49125
                                              CIP

Printed in the United States of America

First Edition

1 2 3 4 5 6 7 8 9 10

*To my mother,*
*Helen,*
*who always believed,*
*and*
*for my wife,*
*Jo Ann,*
*who made it possible*

# PROLOGUE

*Are you Jewish?*
—Evan Mecham *to author*

> Whenever I'm in my house or my office, I always have a radio on. It keeps the lasers out.
>
> —EVAN MECHAM

> Don't ever ask me for a true statement again!
>
> —EVAN MECHAM

> Ev has become an ethical pygmy.
>
> —STAN TURLEY,
> senate president
> and fellow Mormon

# JUNE 1988

Superior Court Judge Michael Ryan was attending a lunch-hour conference in a meeting room off the Maricopa County courthouse cafeteria on June 16, 1988, when his bailiff arrived and handed him a note.

Everyone at the conference knew that Judge Ryan was presiding over the most celebrated criminal trial in Arizona history. The trial of Evan Mecham, the state's impeached governor, was the first in Arizona, and the first in the nation, to be publicly broadcast live, statewide, gavel to gavel.

The note from the jury's foreman read, "We are ready to announce our verdict at 1:30 P.M."

The jurors had begun deliberation only the day before. The bailiff had taken them to lunch shortly after 11:00 A.M., an unusually early hour, Judge Ryan noted. Altogether they had deliberated just over four hours.

Throughout the trial the court had been the focus of unprecedented media attention. Every day Judge Ryan's staff received calls from a European wire service, New York newspapers, and all the national television networks in addition to local and individual media outlets.

The assistant attorneys general who had prosecuted the case, Barnett Lotstein and Michael Cudahy, were having lunch with two other state prosecutors at Ruth's Chris Steak House some distance from downtown Phoenix when they received word. Lotstein, whom Mecham had taken to calling Loathsteen during the trial, had reported to court for jury verdicts in criminal

9

trials more than one hundred times but always experienced butterflies at
the prospect. This time was no different.

Though he expressed no concern, it was widely held that his and Cudahy's careers and especially those of Attorney General Bob Corbin and his
chief assistant, Steven Twist, were riding on the outcome. It is one thing
to indict a sitting governor; it is another to convict him. "When you strike
at a king, you must kill him."

He and Cudahy had presented a straightforward case. It had contained
none of the hyperbole, drama, or extremism of the past eighteen months
though Mecham had certainly given them plenty of ammunition. They had
gambled that a jury of eight, faced with the devastating simplicity of an
essentially paper case, would bite the bullet, draw a deep breath, and deliver
the only possible verdict.

When Evan Mecham received the call, he was seated at his desk in
Glendale in the office of his "government in exile," as he termed it. He had
just enough time to pick up his wife, Florence, and drive the fifteen miles
to the courthouse. Mecham is a spare man, five feet six inches, weighing
138 pounds. His hairpiece is not readily apparent but fits better on some
days than others.

Throughout Arizona television sets were turned on, radios switched to
news stations. Whether for or against the controversial ex-governor, everyone recognized that a momentous event in state history was about to occur.

Just ten weeks earlier Mecham had been removed from office, becoming
the first American governor in fifty-nine years to be impeached. Not since
Henry S. Johnston of Oklahoma, who in 1929 had called out the National
Guard to surround the Capitol and prevent the legislature from convening,
had a governor faced this indignity.

The impeachment had been for Mecham's performance as governor.
America adopted impeachment from England, where the impeached official
could be imprisoned or even executed, in addition to being removed from
office.

The Americans viewed this as one more excess of the English system.
In the United States impeachment became an entirely political process where
all three branches of government came together in what was inevitably a
traumatic experience. The legislative branches charged and tried the official.
The chief justice of the state supreme court presided over the process.
Punishment was restricted to loss of office. In its simplest terms, impeachment was an elaborate job performance hearing.

Because of this difference from English impeachment, the American
system allowed the official to be criminally charged in the courts as well.
Some of the traditional impeachable acts of a chief executive, such as abuse
of power, are not violations of criminal law, and it is possible to be impeached

and removed from office without committing a chargeable crime. But many, perhaps most, impeachable acts, such as misappropriation of state funds, are also violations of the law.

Impeachment is intended to protect the government and safeguard the public from the abuses of the chief executive. Mecham had been impeached for allegedly concealing a large campaign contribution, for misusing state funds, and for obstructing justice by ordering the head of the state police to refuse cooperation to the attorney general in a criminal investigation.

At the same time Mecham was indicted and placed on trial. It is unusual for a governor to face both at the same time. A number of states, including Arizona, allow citizens to compel an unscheduled, or recall, election, an American vote of confidence. Recall of governors is extremely rare.

No governor before in American history had been criminally indicted, politically impeached, and scheduled for a recall election. Not until Evan Mecham. Every lawful means to oust Evan Mecham was in place by the anniversary of his inauguration. The only steps not taken were armed insurrection and assassination.

Mecham had been indicted for allegedly concealing an illegal campaign contribution of $350,000 from controversial attorney Barry Wolfson, then being investigated by the attorney general along with his partner, Hubert V. Gregan, for an alleged arbitrage scam. Under the terms of the agreement Mecham had written Wolfson a letter stating the arrangement would remain "confidential." Wolfson had wired the money into a special Mecham campaign bank account created solely for these transactions. That contribution, coming as it did in the final days of the campaign, had made Mecham's victory possible, according to one of his closest campaign aides and later a special assistant to the governor, Donna Carlson.

She did not then know the source of the money, nor did she know that Mecham would not report it on his campaign finance disclosure forms; but when she heard that there was such a loan and that it was being processed through a special bank account to conceal its source, she had remarked to another key Mecham aide, "That sounds like money laundering to me."

Carlson was not alone in her opinion that the Wolfson money had won Mecham's election. Without that money Mecham would have had great difficulty running the televised endorsement obtained from Barry Goldwater, and without Goldwater's imprimatur Mecham would have been unlikely to attract the mainline, conservative Republican vote in Arizona, a vote crucial to any hope for victory.

This had been Mecham's fifth bid for governor. In 1982 he wrote that his inability to raise money at the last minute had cost him the election in 1978. It appeared that in 1986 he was determined that would not happen again.

On November 23, 1986, after Mecham had won the election, the *Arizona Republic*, the state's largest and most influential newspaper, reported Mecham's ties to Wolfson but not the existence of the secret loan. The next day Mecham's brother and campaign treasurer Willard Mecham, prepared a receipt identifying the $350,000 Wolfson money as a personal loan to the campaign from Evan Mecham. On December 5, 1986, Evan Mecham filed his campaign contribution report without listing Wolfson, as the law required, and instead "lumped" the $350,000 together with a legitimate loan from Western Savings and some of Mecham's private money.

In early February 1987, shortly after taking office, Mecham filed his personal financial disclosure statement. He did not list Wolfson or his money. By his concealing the loan when he first filed, the rest followed as a cover-up, or so the attorney general argued. Had his name been linked to either Wolfson, or any "fat cat" for that matter, he would have lost.

Since all the documents were filed under oath and since the $350,000 did not appear in either the campaign or Mecham's personal report, it was not disclosed anywhere; such secret sources of funds were illegal in Arizona.

Mecham had managed to repay a hundred thousand dollars shortly before assuming office, but the balance had remained outstanding. Not until October 1987, when *Republic* reporter Sam Stanton disclosed its existence, had the loan been made known. The attorney general had launched a grand jury probe that led to the governor's indictment. Many believed it was as simple a case of campaign finance fraud as one was likely to see.

There had been no bombshells during the criminal trial. The prosecution had treated Mecham with respect even though he had vilified it, even though Michael Scott, his attorney, in the heat of his closing remarks, had branded Cudahy and Lotstein, who was Jewish, "guards at Auschwitz" obeying orders from Republican Attorney General Bob Corbin and his minion, Chief Assistant Attorney General Steve Twist.

Scott had scrambled, accused, and diverted. He had pleaded and begged, working, many thought, as much for a hung jury as for acquittal. He had attempted to place the prosecutors and others on trial, anything to escape the accusing finger of the notarized documents bearing Mecham's signature. One courtroom observer thought Scott had gone out of his mind.

It was widely believed that Mecham was guilty. Judge Ryan had been concerned about the ability of any Arizona jury to give Evan Mecham a fair trial.

Now the unanimous verdict was in. No one had held out. Mecham's desperate pretrial request for his followers to lie if necessary to get on the jury had apparently not worked.

Judge Ryan's bench was in one corner; the jury box, in the other. There were small flags mounted on the beige walls behind the judge. It was summer, and the spectators were dressed in bright colors or pastels, pinks and whites, the men in short-sleeve shirts with ties. The reporters who covered the story sat immediately to the left, behind the prosecution, since the similar area to their right was occupied by the Mecham family.

There was Sam Stanton credited with covering the governor as no Arizona reporter had before. He fielded a telephone call on his mobile phone as he waited. Beside him was Laurie Asseo, one of the two Associated Press reporters in Phoenix. Beside her was Michael Murphy, Stanton's longtime rival with the Phoenix *Gazette*, the state's second-largest paper, the capital's afternoon daily, owned by the same parent corporation. On the end was *Gazette* columnist John Kolbe, the famous "non-person," as Mecham had declared him early in his administration.

Lotstein and Cudahy waited in chambers with Judge Ryan until Michael Scott, his assisting attorney, Norbert Settle, and Willard Mecham's attorney, Joe Keilp, arrived. They then filed into the courtroom from the front, hands folded, looking very solemn. The state's attorneys sat at their table, hands folded again in front of them.

As Evan Mecham entered the courtroom, the normal grimace that passed for his smile was gone. A small, even petite man of sixty-four, until this day he had held himself erect and assured. If there were private doubts or moments of anguish, they had never been publicly displayed.

Now, as he sat with his attorneys, he looked every bit his age, thinner, haggard, weary—and fearful. His nervous facial tic and blinking eyes were busy, and he moved as if in a daze. Today even Mecham looked braced for conviction.

Mecham no longer scratched notes in his leather folder. He clasped his hands and sank in his chair as if by will he could disappear. His angular jaw was bunched with tension. He no longer looked arrogant, no longer angry. He was now very alone and visibly shaken.

His older brother Willard, the invisible codefendant during the two-week trial, looked as if he wished he were sitting in the gallery giving moral support to his brother rather than facing the jury with him.

Willard Mecham and his attorney suddenly rose, then after a moment sat back down. The buzzing of the crowd stopped. In the silence coughing spread from spectator to spectator. The jury filed in.

Shortly after 2:00 P.M. Judge Ryan took his place behind the bench. The gavel sounded twice.

Judge Ryan looked to the jury. "Ladies and gentlemen, have you reached a verdict?"

"Yes, sir, we have."

It had been a long road to this moment, a long road for Evan Mecham

and for Arizona an even longer one. The election of this governor after four
failed attempts and his subsequent administration typified all that was good
and all that was bad about the state.

Before Mecham was removed, careers were destroyed, reputations
were in tatters, and his own party was catastrophically fractured. It is not
unreasonable to say that the face of Arizona politics was made over because
of him.

There is a mystique to Arizona that no other state possesses. The Old
West is alive and well there, and what took place when Evan Mecham
became governor more closely resembled a western shoot-out than a political
process.

Seven times the *Wall Street Journal* editorialized on the events in
Arizona. In September 1988 it lamented that "we never felt throughout the
impeachment process that we had read anything adequately explaining what
was going on in Arizona politics."

Every lawful means had been used to oust Evan Mecham. And if the
*Wall Street Journal* was unable to decipher a reason to remove this man, a
majority in Arizona believed it had a cornucopia of abuses from which to
pick.

Yet Mecham is quite typical of that brand of opportunist who migrated
to Arizona following the Second World War, and his success as a businessman
is a mirror of their own.

In many ways his supporters, who in the year following his removal
stood at 25 percent of the electorate, are stereotypical Arizonans. The state
has always attracted the disaffected along with those seeking an escape
from the social structure of the East and new opportunity. To understand
Mecham's rise and fall is to understand the state and the mystique that
surrounds it.

In the Old West the good guys wore white hats; the bad, black. In
modern America, in its large cities, in its corporate offices, you cannot see
the hats or witness the conflicts with clarity.

But in Arizona you do.

The story behind the bizarre events of the Mecham administration is
the story of modern Arizona. It says a great deal about all of us, about what
we expect from politicians, about what we give, or do not give, of ourselves.

It should not be assumed that Mecham stood alone or that he spoke for
an extremely narrow constituency or that those who support him are limited
to Arizona. In many ways Mecham speaks for a certain brand of the common
man nationwide. His effective, if grammatically flawed, English announces
he is one of them. There were, and are, many in and out of Arizona who
admire Mecham.

To understand what happened in Arizona, you must understand Evan
Mecham and his roots. He called himself a conservative and was elected

governor largely because of his conservative stands. Yet it was conservatives, members of his own Republican party, who were instrumental in his removal.

And to understand what happened to Evan Mecham, you must understand Arizona, who lives there and why.

This is a story of America, stripped of artifice, free of camouflage. It is a story of fundamental conflict, where the line was scratched clearly across the dirt street, where sides were chosen, the guns were drawn, and the gunfight took place for all to see.

# PART ONE

*I had no idea he was insane.*
> —Colonel Ralph Milstead
> *director, Arizona Department*
> *of Public Safety*

> *Some of my best friends are black.\**
>                    *—attributed to*
>                        EVAN MECHAM
>
> *As I was a boy growing up, blacks themselves*
> *referred to their children as pickaninnies.*
>                    —EVAN MECHAM
>
> UNPICK A NINNY—RECALL MECHAM
>                    *—Mecham recall*
>                    *bumper sticker*

# 1

U tah is hard country, and the tribute paid its Mormon pioneers is well deserved. One third of the land is desert; much is mountainous. The rest is too high and too dry to be properly farmed. But by channeling the mountain streams, by hard work in digging ditches, by careful raising of crops, and by lowering expectations it was possible to have a life largely independent of outside influence.

A religion acquires a communal wisdom based on its group experiences, wisdom that is passed on to its adherents. The Mormons had a history of unpleasant relations with their neighbors almost from the beginning in the 1830's in upstate New York. The founder, Joseph Smith, Jr., led his followers first to Ohio, then to Missouri, and finally to Nauvoo, Illinois, which they quickly transformed into the largest city in the state—three major relocations in just fourteen years.

Everywhere the sect settled the experience was the same. In those days the church of several thousand was comprised entirely of zealous converts who believed the Second Coming of Christ would occur in their lifetime.

---

*Evan Mecham denies ever saying this. The quote is attributed to Mecham by the Reverend Dr. Warren Stewart, Sr. It was reported as said during Mecham's meeting with local Arizona black leaders in November 1986. Mecham's press secretary Ron Bellus points to this misquote as an example of press deceit. The correct quote, according to Bellus, is: "As far as this other, I have friends that are black, and they know I'm not a racist."

Their leader, a modern prophet of God, received direct revelations, which he passed on to his flock both orally and in written doctrine. God concerned himself with the intricate affairs of the church, from the giving of its name, the Church of Jesus Christ of Latter-day Saints (LDS Church), to chastising individual members.

Though hardworking and devout, the early Mormons had a reputation for arrogance and clannishness. Their proselytizing was always viewed with disfavor. And some of their teachings were strange to mainstream Christians. Not a small part of the hostility was generated by envy since the Mormon sect was a conspicuous economic success.

In the final few years of his life their young prophet, charismatic, handsome, gifted, appeared taken with himself and overcome by his success. He built the largest militia in Illinois, the Nauvoo Legion, which he commanded; was installed as leader of the local Masons; tolerated no contradictions from newspapers; and ran as a presidential candidate, the first American religious figure to do so. In 1844 at the age of thirty-nine he was murdered by a mob while in jail awaiting trial on charges of rioting and treason.

The sect became an established church under its second president, Brigham Young. Following a two-year period of strife and internal dissension Young was recognized by most of the members as the new prophet. The lesson of persecution with Gentile neighbors was not lost on him, and in 1847 he led the church westward, across the plains into Zion, the valley of the Great Salt Lake. In a series of migrations the Mormons moved to their new home, selected by God, a haven from the outside world.

The similarity of this new land to ancient Zion was not lost on the pioneers. Just as Israel had a Dead Sea, they had the Great Salt Lake. Just as Israel had the Sea of Galilee, they had what was to be named Utah Lake. The connecting river was named Jordan after its precursor in the Old World. These were not accidental similarities to these people of faith. God had willed it and made this place. At last his chosen people were home.

Young took a name from the Book of Mormon, Deseret, and gave it to this new territory. The land at first was under the ostensive control of Mexico but within the year had passed into the hands of the United States. By organizing the Mormon Battalion to fight in the Mexican War, Young transferred three hundred fifty young men west at government expense, earned hard currency for the church, and demonstrated the church's loyalty to the United States. For a time Deseret was left in peace.

Nevertheless, the United States refused to bring Deseret into the Union. In 1850 it established Utah Territory with Young as the first governor. While the new territory was not as large as Young envisioned Deseret, it was larger than the modern state. Now Young ruled the temporal government of the territory as well as the spiritual government of Deseret.

Young sought to occupy every corner of this new land. As parties arrived, they were organized into settlement companies and dispatched to new home-sites. Whenever possible, each settlement was a day's wagon ride beyond the last. He sent settlers north into Idaho and Canada and south into Arizona and Mexico.

Each Mormon settlement of about two hundred people was led by a church-appointed leader. Deseret was administered as a theocracy from Salt Lake City outward. It was successful beyond imagining.

In their western sanctuary there was no need for secrecy. There is a dispute between the two main branches of Smith's church on whether or not their founder practiced polygamy. Whether he or Young originated the practice, the church went public with it in Utah, and the secret temple practices introduced by Smith became accepted practice of the church.

The combination of complaints by non-Mormons and miners and the troublesome practice of polygamy led to Young's replacement as governor in the late 1850's. Believing Utah was in a state of insurrection and enforcing the assumption of office of a new Gentile governor, the federal government sent an army to occupy the territory.

When the United States locked itself in mortal civil war, it was certain that these were truly the last days and that the corrupt outside world would destroy itself as prophesied. The removal of federal troops from the territory to fight in that war was just one more assurance that God was on their side, but the enmity created by their presence remained.

With the end of the war the nation's attention was focused westward on California. The new challenge was to link the East and West by rail and to settle the vast continent in between.

As Nevada, Wyoming, and Colorado were organized, portions of Utah were incorporated into each. In each new territory, once again, the Mormons were a minority. Until 1890 the federal government viewed the Mormon Church with increasing suspicion and hostility, a point of view fully returned by the Mormons. Federal troops were returned.

Polygamy was the most conspicuous practice of the church for which the largely Christian nation as a whole expressed its disapproval. It became a litmus test for both sides. The Christians of the East, through the instrument of the federal government, were determined to rid the nation of this ungodly practice, and the Mormons were equally determined to continue it.

A practice begun in secret and never popular with or practiced by the majority became the instrument of contention between the church and the national government, which finally resorted to seizing land and disincorporating the church. In the end, to the bitter rage of the church, Washington won.

The Mormons eliminated the practice of polygamy in 1890, and statehood for Utah followed five years later. There were those who could not accept this heresy, and there emerged excommunicated cults that practice polygamy to this day. Those already married—sealed, as the Mormons called it—were allowed to remain as they were, and as late as the 1930's trios of a husband and two wives were common sights in Mormon communities in Utah, Idaho, and Arizona.

But the communal experiences of the church in its earliest days, the deprivations in Utah at the hands of Gentiles, and the indignities forced upon devout Mormons almost until the turn of the century were not forgotten. The children, grandchildren, and great-grandchildren of those who had suffered were taught the lessons in infancy and bear the scars today.

The first settlements in Utah had been south, then north of the lake, along the foothills of the Rocky Mountains. In the decade following the turn of the century, canal and reservoir companies were formed to make productive the Uintah Basin in Duchesne County in northeastern Utah. Mormon couples from other parts of the state looking for land of their own would settle 160 acres under the 1862 Homestead Act.

Brigham Bovee Mecham and his wife, Lydia, were such a couple. The seventh of their twelve children was Adelbert, born in 1897 in St. George in extreme southwestern Utah. When Adelbert was thirteen years old, the family moved to Boneta Precinct in the Uintah Basin.

Willard and Agnes Hanberg moved nearby in 1913 to Mountain Home. Their eldest of six children, born in 1899, was Ina.

If Utah Valley by the Great Salt Lake was hard land, it must have appeared as paradise to these hardy settlers. The land of Duchesne County is only marginally productive. Most of it receives no more than sixteen inches of rain a year. It is high country, five thousand to sixty-five hundred feet, and it is only just possible to support a family on a homestead.

Except for the spectacular view of the Uintah Mountains to the north it was a desolate sight to these newcomers. Only a people certain God had named the land Zion would have attempted to farm it. There was no immediate water. The land was covered with large sagebrush and boulders. During the first years the new settlers, more often than not young couples in their late teens and early twenties, saw long lines of Indians pulling their belongings strapped to two poles dragging behind their horses. At night there was the wind and coyotes.

There was no money, rarely new clothing, and never plentiful food. Distant neighbors shared what they could. At least there were summer vegetable gardens. No one starved, no one prospered, but slowly, in time measured more in decades than in years, life improved and the tents and wagons were replaced by two-room cabins wallpapered with newspapers.

In 1916 Adelbert, now nineteen years old, and Ina Hanberg, age seventeen, were married. They were later sealed for "time and all eternity" in the Salt Lake Temple. The couple had five sons and a daughter. Born in 1924, Evan Mecham was the youngest of the boys.

These were hard times made all the harder by Adelbert Mecham's rheumatoid arthritis. Evan Mecham does not recall a time when his father was healthy and able to work on the farm.

Ina Mecham made many of the family clothes. Barter was a common method of exchange. The Mechams were not impoverished, however, and there was at least a single prosperous year, for Mecham proudly recalls the day in 1928 when his father brought home a new Chevrolet with windows that rolled up, the first of its kind in the area.

In 1936 Adelbert Mecham moved his family from Mountain Home ten miles southwest to the old homestead near Mount Emmons. They lived two and a half miles from the small town of about twenty houses. The sixty or seventy families in the immediate area all went to church there. There was no mayor, just the local bishop to organize affairs.

The Mechams raised alfalfa, wheat, barley, and a little corn. They made a living from twenty-five purebred Holstein cows. Because of Adelbert's infirmity, the family relied entirely on the five sons, the baby daughter, and their mother. Every morning the boys milked the cows by hand in the dark.

Mecham's hands are those of a man who has known work. When he says that as a child he was "taught to appreciate hard work," you can believe him. There are today Mechams throughout Duchesne County, and it is said, "If he's a Mecham, you know he's a worker."

As the boys grew up, they left home, and the work fell more and more to the younger sons. Evan went to Altamont High School, which served eight local communities. There were perhaps two hundred students in attendance, and his senior class was about thirty.

Evan did well. He ran the mile in track for his school, a slow mile. He jokes the school was too small for a football team: "All we could support was a basketball team and track."

He is remembered as being shy, and he earned a reputation for devoting himself to his studies. According to one classmate, Mecham's nickname in high school was the Guv.

He was the best student in his class until his senior year. Now only Evan of the sons was left to do the work, along with his younger sister and their mother.

He missed most of his fall term that senior year as he harvested the family crops and most of the spring as he did the planting. Every day, seven days a week, before dawn, he got up, milked the cows, did the chores, and, when he could, attended school.

When he was graduated in 1942, he approached the prospect of college with mixed feelings. Although his father had only a third-grade education, his parents had encouraged college. He had done well in the Future Farmers of America and won a Sears, Roebuck scholarship that would cover tuition and books. His brother Arnold, just one year older, had won the same scholarship and was a student at Utah State Agricultural College (now Utah State College), in Logan.

Going to college meant leaving his mother to do the work. The family sold most of the cattle, reducing the herd to a size the elderly woman could manage, but this resulted in a decline in the family income.

Today, a lifetime after the events, Evan Mecham does not speak of leaving home for college easily. He does not speak of leaving his mother behind lightly. He is overcome with emotion as he tries to talk of it and cannot continue.

Despite his reservations at the prospect of leaving home, Mecham was excited about attending college. He remembers it as having about thirty-two hundred students.

A college campus, even a small one such as this, was a world apart from the life he had known. With his brother Mecham went to work for the college dairy herd, earning thirty-five cents an hour. For the first time he used electric milkers.

Their mother canned and bottled goods for her two sons and stocked the apartment they had rented "for a pittance." Mecham applied himself to his college studies with renewed diligence.

As it turned out, he stayed only a few months of that first year. He had always dreamed of flying, had dreamed about it even before the outbreak of World War II. Now with the crushing need for pilots the requirements were changed. In January 1943 Mecham says he begged his mother to let him enlist. Because he was only eighteen years old, he claims he required her permission and she reluctantly agreed.*

Mecham went on active duty at the end of the quarter. Altogether three of the Mecham boys served in the Army Air Force during the Second World War.

He traveled to various parts of the United States for different phases of his training—Nebraska, California, Kansas. Like many of the men who relocated to Arizona following the war, he took flight training there, at Wickenburg; at Marana, outside Tucson; and at Williams Field, near Phoenix.

Upon graduation fifty pilots were allowed their selection, and Mecham chose the P-38. There was more training, and it was not until November

---

*Parental permission was not required of eighteen-year-old men to enlist in the service during World War II.

1944 that he was transferred to England, only to enter training again, now in instrument flying.

The P-38 was so fast it was the plane of choice for reconnaissance flights, and in December Mecham began flying over Europe. By this time the Germans were operational with jets, and the P-38's were suffering losses of 10 percent a mission. Mecham switched to an armed P-51 so he could shoot back. It was in a P-51, flying escort on a photoreconnaissance flight, that he was shot down by a jet, on March 7, 1945.

In his treatise *Come Back America* Mecham provides a description of how he bailed out of his flaming plane, was captured and threatened with "a switchblade knife," how he kicked the man with the knife in the stomach and wrenched free of the one holding him. He was interrogated and held prisoner for twenty-two days. He had injured his knee in bailing out and was in considerable pain. This account is dramatic and intensely patriotic.

But when he speaks of the same events, it is done lightly, with nonchalance and humor. From Mecham's perspective his captors were following the book when it made no sense for them to do so. As they moved him around, oblivious of the collapsing fronts, east and west, Mecham lived "a charmed life." At one point a British POW doctor X-rayed his knee, after which Mecham was escorted away by burly guards weighted down with grenades, pistols and submachine guns. It struck him as a ludicrous waste of manpower needed elsewhere.

He was taken by rail to a hospital and recalls fearing American planes might strafe the train. One morning the guards were gone, replaced by Germans with Red Cross armbands. Not much later a group of war correspondents arrived in jeeps with Army drivers. "I was liberated by the press," he says, adding with a smile that not everything about the press is bad.

Evan Mecham had dated Florence Lambert of Altonah, Duchesne County, Utah, while in high school. She was one year younger than he. They were engaged while he was in the service.

After his liberation Mecham was flown to a hospital in France, where he stayed for six weeks. In May 1945 he sailed back to the United States. During his sixty-day leave he married Florence in the Salt Lake Temple. On V-J Day he reported for duty at Luke Air Force Base near Phoenix. He applied for jet fighter training but instead was assigned as an instructor of Brazilian students.

The following December Mecham's father died. After an emergency leave Mecham put in for his discharge. He sold insurance in Utah for a time while Florence worked as a secretary, but by the fall of 1947 he had returned to Arizona, enrolled in Arizona State University, and begun selling cars. Mecham liked selling cars. "It was a business in which you could be honest, offer fair value, if you really wanted to, and work at giving people a good deal," he writes.

In 1950, just sixteen hours short of a degree, he says, he used savings and money borrowed from his mother to purchase a Pontiac dealership in Ajo, Arizona. There is surely no bleaker, no more physically desolate corner of earth. The population of Ajo was, and is, largely Hispanic. At that time it was supported by a copper mine and was in every way a company town. Mecham sold Pontiacs—Mexican Cadillacs, as he liked to call them—from a dealership that appears to have been a converted garage.

He had two children by then, served his church as Scoutmaster and as Sunday school teacher, and also was a district councilman. In 1954 he acquired the Pontiac dealership in Glendale and moved his family.

At that time Glendale was a sleepy farming community located about fifteen miles from downtown Phoenix. It was larger than Ajo, greener and part of a metropolitan area. For the next thirty-three years Mecham was to make his living from this dealership.

He adopted, almost from the beginning, his trademark motto: "If you can't deal with Mecham, you just can't deal."

He remained active in his church. He served on the stake (diocese) high council, as a counselor in the stake mission, and as a lay bishop from 1957 to 1961.

He appeared regularly on television, in thirty-second spots, eighty-three words, hawking his cars. He had a pleasant and easy manner. He looked directly into the lens, and the viewer felt as if Ev Mecham were speaking personally to him. He was soothing and calm, a polished huckster. As the city grew, as Glendale became part of the Phoenix suburbs, the dealership did well.

Until 1960 there was nothing to separate Mecham from that brand of men searching for opportunity in Arizona following the Second World War. Some had failed, others had prospered more than he, but he was as much a part of the Arizona economic success story as they.

It could have stayed that way.

> *I understand Sam [Steiger] hired [Donna Carlson] because she gave the best head he'd ever had.*\*
> —EVAN MECHAM
>
> *I didn't think Ev knew what head was.*
> —SAM STEIGER, special assistant to Governor Mecham
>
> *People who are not prayerful in life like to point fingers at those who are.*
> —EVAN MECHAM

# 2

Surely there are others who have pursued public office with the same tenacity as Evan Mecham, but these are men confined to the outer fringes of the political process, not men who actually achieve high office.

Those who knew him best, former U.S. Congressman Sam Steiger for one, say Evan Mecham believed with absolute conviction that God was guiding him. His mentor, W. Cleon Skousen, associate professor of religion at Brigham Young University and founder and director of the National Center for Constitutional Studies, once vowed to a predominantly Mormon gathering that "God foretold the gubernatorial candidate that he would attain the governorship to help save America from going to hell in the hand basket of socialism." Skousen called Mecham "a modern-day Isaiah." Others say

---

\*Sam Steiger denies ever making such a statement, "unequivocally." He and Donna Carlson, both of whom were single during the Mecham administration, have been friends for many years and acknowledge dating but agree that it was very casual and occurred prior to either of them joining the Mecham campaign. Though they occasionally attended functions together rather than acquire separate escorts, these appearances were matters relating to their positions. Each of them dated other people during their period with the campaign and when they worked as special assistants for the governor. Though offended, Donna Carlson has graciously consented to the use of this quotation. Finally, Carlson was hired by Mecham, not Steiger.

that Mecham knew that if he were true to his beliefs, he would receive the strength from God he needed to endure.

Sam Steiger, who served with Mecham as a state senator for two years in the early 1960's and later as his gubernatorial assistant, tells of going to see Evan Mecham on the Ninth Floor. As Steiger approached the closed door of the governor's office, he could hear what he describes as "a conversation" coming from inside.

Steiger thought the governor had not finished with his meeting and moved away from the door. Mecham's secretary told him to go in. Steiger entered and found Mecham alone.

Donna Carlson, another gubernatorial assistant, says that it was apparent to her that Mecham believed he obtained office by divine right. She believes that accounts in large part for why he cared so little for the feelings of others; they just did not matter in the greater scheme of things. A reporter who covered him almost daily for two years says that Mecham believes God talks back to him, and Barry Goldwater has said that Mecham believes he has an 800 number to God.

Evan Mecham first ran for elective office in 1952, when he lived in Ajo and was twenty-eight years old. A *Republic* article in August 1952 identifies Mecham as an Ajo businessman, owner of Mecham Pontiac Garage, and reports he "holds a degree in business administration." Mecham ran as a Republican for the Arizona house of representatives and he was defeated.

If you ask him when he first decided to run for public office, he becomes fuzzy on the details but can clearly recall his single term in the state senate.

Evan Mecham never actually says the first time he ran for office was for a state senate seat in 1960; but that is clearly the message in his literature, and it is widely reported and believed in Arizona to be true.

His literature also omits that he ran for the chairmanship of the state Republican party in 1962, just months after his defeat by the venerable Senator Carl Hayden for the U.S. Senate, and that he was again defeated after Barry Goldwater flew from Washington to appear on the platform with Congressman John Rhodes and Governor Paul Fannin for the sole purpose of endorsing his opponent.

It fails to disclose that Mecham announced he was running against Barry Goldwater, the popular figure in Arizona Mecham likes to call his "old flying friend," for the U.S. Senate in 1964.

Paul Fannin, a Republican, was elected governor in 1958. At that time rural Democrats controlled the legislature. When Mecham announced for the state senate in 1960, the same year of Fannin's first reelection as governor, Mecham stated it was his desire to "turn back the tide toward socialism that has been sweeping America the past twenty-five years."

At that time each Arizona county elected two state senators to the legislature.* Mecham finished second behind a Democrat but still won a seat in what was later described as "a hard-hitting campaign." He was one of four Republicans in the twenty-eight-member senate. Sam Steiger was another of the Republicans. Besides opposing creeping socialism, Mecham was in favor of tax equalization. Tax issues always figured prominently in any Mecham campaign.

During his two-year term Mecham established a reputation as a frequent critic of the senate leadership. Harry Rosenzweig, longtime political confidant of Barry Goldwater and Arizona state Republican party chairman from 1962 to 1976, says that Mecham was "very negative" during his single term as a state senator and that he was a "crappy" legislator.

The "most powerful politician in Arizona" at this time was Senator Harold Giss of Yuma. In those days most of the state legislators stayed down the street from the Capitol at the old Adams Hotel, where the lobbyists maintained rooms. The legislators were wined and dined and provided with company if that was to their liking. Giss did not want acrimonious scenes on the senate floor, so differences were hashed out in the Adams's bar. Debate and voting down the street were generally perfunctory.

If you were part of the system, it worked for you. Mecham was not part of the system. Before the end of his first term Mecham had already set his sights on the U.S. Senate seat coming up for election in 1962.

Democratic U.S. Senator Carl Hayden was an Arizona institution. He had been sheriff of Maricopa County, the last sheriff during territory days. Upon statehood he ran for Arizona's only congressional seat. Several years later he switched to the U.S. Senate. In all he served fifty-six years.

In 1962 he was president pro tempore of the U.S. Senate and wielded substantial influence for a state largely dependent on federal largess. He was so valuable that even though he was a Democrat, the established Republican party was not interested in defeating him.

He was also eighty-five years old. His influence was largely due to his seniority, and he was regarded as the ultimate example of what small states must do to have power in Washington. It is widely accepted that Hayden was virtually senile by this time and totally dependent upon his staff.

The state GOP chairman was Stephen Shadegg, who had worked as Goldwater's campaign manager in 1958 and later managed his elections in 1974 and 1980. Shadegg had just written a book, *How to Win an Election*, that had received national attention and he was viewed as a comer in Arizona politics. Barry Goldwater, according to Shadegg, expressed concern that

---

*Arizona is now divided into thirty districts, each of which elects one state senator and two state representatives. These districts are not the same as those used for seats in the United States Congress.

Hayden might die during the campaign, and though the Republicans did not want to beat him, they wanted to have someone in the wings just in case.

After meeting with Hayden to explain that he did not really want to defeat him, Shadegg announced his candidacy for the Republican nomination for the U.S. Senate.

Mecham was already talking about himself as a candidate. According to Shadegg, Goldwater thought that Mecham's positions were extreme and also that Mecham while a state senator had not cooperated with Governor Fannin. Goldwater did not welcome Mecham's candidacy.

Mecham portrays the election as a choice between a socialist superstate or the freedoms penned by our Founding Fathers. He was again identified by the *Republic* as holding a degree in business administration from Arizona State University in 1950. Mecham charged that "the planners of the socialist one world regime are trying to put Republicans on the defensive. . . ."

In April 1962 he stated, "This nation was founded on Christian principles." In the same speech he said that "one worlders are going to get the job done if we don't do something about it." A troupe of young women, identified as "Mechamettes," traveled and made appearances on his behalf.

Mecham won the Republican primary in an upset. He is proud of having ended Steve Shadegg's political career "before it started." According to Shadegg, Mecham "and his supporters circulated the story that my first child . . . was illegitimate" in order to defeat him.

Mecham believes he would have defeated Carl Hayden in the general election if he could have forced the senator out to Arizona to campaign. In the last days of the election Hayden checked into Bethesda Naval Hospital. Mecham learned there was no temperature chart being kept on Hayden and concluded from that that Hayden was "either dead or not sick." Some of Mecham's supporters claimed that Hayden had died and his aides were concealing the fact so Arizona would be tricked into electing a dead senator and deny Mecham the election.

Mecham blames his loss on Eugene Pulliam, publisher of the *Arizona Republic* and the Phoenix *Gazette*. After his defeat he told United Press International, "You can't beat the Pulliam press." He also blames his loss in part on advertisements in which Goldwater praised Hayden. Mecham ran a better than expected race but still lost by a substantial vote. Mecham says he lost 48 percent to 52 percent. The *Republic* reports he received 45.5 percent of the vote.

At this time the state Republican party chairman was working to pull the John Birch Society back into the regular organization of the party. The society in Arizona rebelled against the effort because it perceived that its candidate, Evan Mecham, had received tepid party support during the general election.

Bernie Wynn, the respected *Republic* political writer, reported in 1965 that Mecham's wife, Florence, was a member of the John Birch Society. Mecham's campaign coordinator in Maricopa County was later a coordinator for the John Birch Society in several western states. Mecham enjoyed the active support of ardent Birchers, one of whom said of the 1962 election, "The kind of people who belong to the John Birch Society were in the fight Mecham made."

Shadegg says that he first met Mecham at a function in Mesa where Mecham was "recruiting converts for membership in the John Birch Society. He told us Dwight Eisenhower was a conscious Communist. He said Richard Nixon was a far-out liberal."

Later Mecham said, "I've never been a member [of the John Birch Society], and I've never paid that much attention to it."

During this period Mecham was taking voice lessons. One student recalled thinking of him, "What a cold, removed person. He seems as if he lives in moth balls."

In 1962 a former attorney general of Arizona and defeated gubernatorial candidate who blamed his defeat in large part on the *Republic* started a new daily called the *Arizona Journal*. In early 1963 Mecham learned of its financial difficulties. There are those who say that Evan Mecham is at heart a frustrated publisher. They see in Mecham's attacks on the "Phoenix Newspapers" an expression of envy and what they feel is Mecham's belief that newspapers truly control affairs by influencing the public. They point to his newspaper experiences and to the tabloids that have formed a part of nearly all his campaigns. Steiger says, that Mecham "really believes he's a publisher and that he knows a great deal about the newspaper business." Steiger considered the tabloids used in 1986 and 1987 to be amateurish even though Mecham worked extensively on them.

A competitive paper, especially one he would control, appealed to Mecham. Not long after the *Arizona Journal* went out of business; Mecham purchased the presses and started his own paper, initially called the *Evening American*, "A Straight-Shooting Newspaper".

He says, ". . . I didn't want the news to be anything but straight-down-the-line-news. . . ." The paper was published as an afternoon daily and "was lively and informative. . . ." He blames the *Republic* for keeping advertisers away. He states, "In the car business we had tough competition and knew that we were just going to get a part of the business and didn't hate our competitor because he got some, too." Later he held a very different view when a competitor tried to open a car dealership near him.

Mecham claims a maximum circulation of 27,000 for his paper in *Come Back America*. When he testified before the U.S. Senate Subcommittee on Antitrust and Monopoly in 1967, he claimed a circulation of 185,000. The *Evening American*, however, took on many manifestations during its operation. It was a daily for only a relatively short time. He tried to expand into some of the smaller cities with weeklies and published in Tucson briefly. He was not willing, he says, to be an "also-ran," so he sold out.

The *Evening American* and Mecham's other aborted newspapers were not held in high regard. Jim Garner, a longtime newspaperman and the editor of the *Pinal Ways* magazine, recalls Mecham's newspapers and views his claim that he knows a news story because he was once a publisher as "terribly amusing." He calls Mecham's papers "a joke." He says, "The pages of his papers were crammed with stories so slanted it defied description. The columns were written by cretins whose political leanings put them to the right of Genghis Khan. . . ." When Mecham could not sell papers, he gave them away. Garner concludes that on the basis of the *Evening American* and his other papers Mecham should have been cited "for impersonating a newspaper publisher."

In May 1964 Mecham sent Fannin a letter and asked him to probe "immorality in state government" and to check into possible conflicts of interest. Mecham was assumed to be preparing to run against Fannin, but weeks later he announced as a candidate against Barry Goldwater in the Republican primary. He termed himself a "friendly candidate" who would run only if Goldwater were not nominated for President. After some speculation about his true intentions Mecham announced "finally and irrevocably for the record that I am in the U.S. Senate race to stay. . . ." Four days later, when Fannin entered the Senate race, Mecham switched to the governor's race.

No sooner did Mecham enter it than he launched into an attack on fellow Republican Paul Fannin's record, saying that under Fannin Arizona had deteriorated to "the category of unclean states of the nation." He charged Fannin with failing to seek out graft and corruption.

During the campaign he came out in favor of desalinating seawater to solve Arizona's long-term water problems. He favored the repeal of the state property tax.

Mecham's primary opponent was Richard Kleindienst. Mecham says he entered at least in part because of the cavalier manner with which Kleindienst announced, as if he had been anointed to take over the governor's spot.

The *Gazette* reported in July 1964, "During a question period following speeches, Mecham declined to identify the persons whom he charged were 'pulling the strings in the state.' " One week later Mecham attacked the *Republic* for slanting its news coverage.

Mecham demanded that Kleindienst "be specific" in his allegations against him. Mecham also opposed recalling elected officials because recall does not punish the people who collaborated with the officials.

In the final weeks of the campaign Mecham challenged Kleindienst to join him in disclosing their financial backers so the public could judge for themselves which of them might "have selfish interests in the race." Mecham stepped up his attacks on Kleindienst to such an extent that Goldwater endorsed Kleindienst.

By the end of August Mecham was campaigning so vigorously against fellow Republicans it was causing real concern. Mecham distributed a tabloid fact sheet attacking Fannin and his appointees. Fannin, in the race for U.S. Senate, was not helped by these constant attacks from one in his own party.

Kleindienst had been active in the party for more than a decade, had worked on Goldwater's national campaign, and had been state party chairman. Mecham, on the other hand, was on the outside, at war with his own party as much as with those in office. In August 1964 he published a quarter-page ad with the headline WHY "BOSSES" OPPOSE EVAN.

Mecham's conduct infuriated the party regulars and members of the state legislature. On August 26, 1964, twelve Republican members of the state house and one Republican state senator published "A Response to Mr. Evan Mecham."

The response was prophetic in many regards. It begins: "We are compelled . . . to repudiate Mr. Mecham's candidacy." It cites his "unreasonable and often untrue statements . . ." and says "his conduct reflects unfavorably on our entire party. . . ." It states that "he seems poorly acquainted with the processes of state government. . . ." It points out that when he served as a state senator, he voted against Republican Governor Fannin's own bills twenty-seven times, that Mecham was not present for thirty-five bills and had a high absentee rate. Contrary to Mecham's claim that the party gave him no support in his bid to unseat Carl Hayden, it reported he had received twenty thousand dollars from the party. Finally, it charges him with "sheer obstructionism . . ." and with a "pattern of negativism. . . ."

The *Republic* noted, "In rapid succession Mecham . . . attacked practically every GOP leader in the state . . ." during his campaign.

In the final days before the election Mecham called for the creation of a state bureau of criminal investigation and identification.

Mecham blames his defeat on "the disjointed times we were in." He says that "we could never get a good grip on the issues." He saw no evidence that Kleindienst went on to lose because Mecham's supporters opposed him. He makes it clear that during this election he was not "going to be the source of any blood-letting vendettas within the party." He had run, he says, to hold the party together.

He does not mention that he supported the Democratic candidate, Samuel P. Goddard, Jr., in the general election.

Mecham dropped out of politics for a decade after this defeat. Most of this time he was occupied with publishing the *Evening American* and with running his car dealership. He appeared regularly on local television with his ads. He did not work in the party, nor did he actively support alternate candidates.

In May 1974 Mecham announced he would run again for governor. He says he entered the race because he did not like those who were running. Bob Corbin was also a candidate in that primary. The *Republic* noted that now Mecham was wearing a toupee and that it had improved his appearance.

Once again Mecham came out in favor of repealing the state property tax. In July he supported the recall of lenient judges and again called for the desalination of seawater to solve Arizona's water problem. He ran against Washington and in favor of local control of government, popular positions in Arizona.

This was the height of Watergate. In early August Mecham called for President Richard M. Nixon to resign.

Later that month Mecham addressed the National Organization for Women in Arizona and called for the defeat of the Equal Rights Amendment. He was hooted and jeered.

He has little to say about this campaign. If he had thought that he would emerge fresh after a ten-year hiatus, he was mistaken. He finished second in the primary.

To understand the elections of 1978 and 1982 and in part Mecham's conduct when he did take office in 1987, it is necessary to appreciate his feelings for Bruce Babbitt. Babbitt came from an old Arizona mercantile family. They were largely from northern Arizona but were a part of the recognized traditional powers of Arizona.

Babbitt was everything Mecham was not. He was tall, bright, articulate, a Harvard graduate, and blessed with uncommon good fortune in politics. Babbitt had handily won his first try for public office when he was elected attorney general. Toward the end of a successful administration he succeeded to governor upon the death of the incumbent. As he entered the race for reelection, Babbitt was popular. There was also little support for removing him from office and replacing him with a fourth governor in just over one year.*

Mecham acknowledges that Babbitt had everything going for him, but Babbitt was a liberal Democrat and, to Evan Mecham, very likely a socialist. Mecham believes that the "pre-sell of a landslide victory robbed" him of

---

*Raul Castro, a Democrat, had resigned to accept an appointment as ambassador. Long-time Secretary of State Wesley Bolin succeeded, then died in office. Interestingly, because she had been appointed to replace Bolin, Rose Mofford was passed over under the provisions of the constitution. It was the attorney general who became governor. Later, when Mecham was removed from office, Mofford, who had now been elected in her own right, succeeded and became governor.

financial support. He utilized the unusual strategy of railing against inflation during most of his car commercials, then praising Pontiacs for the final seconds.

By this time Mecham had developed a political philosophy and call for action he called "The Plan." He first touted it during the 1978 election and later published it in 1982 as *Come Back America.*

Significantly, in light of future behavior, Mecham blames his loss in 1978 on his inability to get his message out. "We had planned a strong TV presentation of my issues for the six-week period before the general election," he writes. "Because we couldn't raise the money for it we finally started a reduced schedule three weeks before election. . . . We were gaining rapidly and could have closed the gap for victory had we had the funds to operate as we planned."

It was during this campaign that *Gazette* columnist John Kolbe, an astute and articulate observer of Arizona politics, quoted Mecham as saying, "I wanted to raise about $300,000 but I found out we didn't need to, and if we did, we probably couldn't have."

Mecham blasted Babbitt for putting cronies and campaign workers into the Office of Economic Planning and Development and "building a personal political machine at the expense of taxpayers." He called for dismantling the office.

He issued a tabloid and used direct television commercials to great effect. His defeat of conservative Jack Londen in the primary was a surprise.

Once he had the nomination of the party, Kolbe reported, "Mecham's biggest problems [in 1978], Goldwater said, will be 'the memory of Republicans that he supported Sam Goddard back in 1964.' "

Mecham campaigned against big government and taxes, and called for a constitutional amendment to eliminate the Environmental Protection Agency. Though he had not spoken to Mecham for ten years, Goldwater was persuaded to endorse him.

Even though the director of the Department of Public Safety (DPS) had a term fixed by law, Mecham called for firing its director, Vernon Hoy.

Mecham lost an election that turned out to be far closer than anyone had expected.

By now it was apparent that Mecham simply could not win elections that counted. He divided the party, weakened candidates who survived primaries, and spread dissension. In his campaigns he had often opposed the consensus candidate of those who worked for the party. He was more likely to attack a Republican than a Democrat.

He viewed Democrats as hopeless causes not worthy of his attention, but Republicans were treated as apostates who had rejected their true faith. Mecham apparently believed that if he could not win, no other Republican

should win in his place. He did not support the party, and his followers
were not party activists. Every few years he would show up, wreak havoc,
then disappear back to Glendale until the urge to run came again.

In 1982 the Republican party decided to short-circuit divisive primaries.
The leadership appointed an ad hoc committee to interview those interested
in running for governor and selected Senate President Leo Corbet.

Mecham disavows any early desire to enter the race, but he did not
believe Corbet could defeat Babbitt and believed that he could. He wrote
*Come Back America*, a political tract, reflecting neither the quality nor length
to be properly considered a book, for use in the 1982 election. He paid to
have twenty thousand copies printed. The book was used as a replacement
for his usual tabloid. Mecham appears to have been convinced that now that
he had "The Plan" in book form and could get his message out, he would
win the election. He had forty thousand more copies of *Come Back America*
printed and in the last days of the primary campaign had them dropped off
along with other literature at the doors of registered Republicans.

About *Come Back America* Corbet said, "Some parts of it are kind of
stupid."

Mecham accused the *Republic's* editorial writers of being "surrogates"
for Babbitt. He called for reducing the Department of Public Safety by 250
people. Mecham called for repeal of the five-cent state tax on gasoline. He
said that if Babbitt's department heads "repented" of past management sins,
he might keep them on.

But a sign of how little attention was paid to Mecham occurred in June,
when he appeared with three other candidates at a public forum and was
the only candidate not asked a question.

When the *Republic* endorsed an opponent, it stated, "Were [Mecham]
to be the state's chief executive, he would be locked in constant and fruitless
battle with the state legislature and the rest of the state. . . ."

Just before the primary the Equal Employment Opportunity Commission found that Mecham had fired a woman employee solely because she
was a woman. Mecham's manager, who would not talk to reporters, was
quoted as having said, "I'm sorry, kid. I'm going to have to let you go,
because Mr. Mecham doesn't want any women selling cars for him." Mecham
denied responsibility.

Following his defeat even Mecham seems to have realized his days as
a candidate were over. Interviewed after the loss he said, "I've got lots of
plans, but they don't include politics. This is it. You can set that in cement.
I had a lot to offer Arizona, but the people didn't want it, so I'm liberated."

# 3

The Spanish called it Apachería. For 150 years the nomadic Navajos to the north and the marauding Apaches to the south stopped Spanish settlement into what is modern Arizona.

None of the first forty-eight states was a United States territory longer than Arizona, and the origin of the state's animosity toward the federal government is founded largely on that experience.

When Evan Mecham was first assigned for flight training in Arizona, he arrived during the decade that separated modern Arizona from the old. Before the war Arizona was an indolent backwater; since the war it has been the one of the fastest-growing states in the Union and has come to epitomize the term "Sunbelt."

The northern three fourths of the state were acquired from Mexico as a consequence of the Mexican War, the same war that brought Brigham Young's Deseret within the jurisdiction of the United States. The lower fourth, that part of the state below the Gila River, which includes Tucson, was purchased from Mexico shortly thereafter. To this day some native Arizonans from Phoenix disdainfully claim that Mexico begins at the Gila. Though this land was owned by the United States, it was not organized as a territory for fifteen years, in 1863, and then primarily to counter the Confederacy's claim to it.

During the westward movement Arizona was largely overlooked, though from 1849 through 1851 more than sixty thousand Americans crossed southern Arizona en route to California. When Anglos did begin living in the territory, they came from California as the goldfields played out. As a result, an oddity of Arizona's history is that it was settled from the West, not from the East, as were the rest of the western states.

Apaches and transportation were the two most formidable difficulties these early miners faced. For more than twenty years goods were brought into the territory, primarily by riverboat and barge, up the Colorado River from the Sea of Cortez in Mexico. Once the goods were off-loaded at river ports, enterprising merchants drove overland wagons into the interior to provision the scattered mining settlements.

Michal and Joseph Goldwasser, later renamed Mike and Joe Goldwater, were two such merchants. They had fled Konin, Poland, via England and met with mixed business fortunes in California. A merchant looking to be a success found his best opportunity in the uncivilized desert of Arizona, where the market was unclaimed and lucrative.

These merchants were as rugged as the miners. Massacres of and by Indians were common occurrences. In 1872 the brothers were attacked by a band of Mohave-Apaches. Mike received two bullet holes in his hat. Joe was hit in his lower back during the running fire fight. He was transported to a ranch some miles away for primitive surgery, then another twenty miles the next day for treatment by an Army surgeon.

The territory was desperate for federal protection despite the fact that by the early 1880's 20 percent of the United States Army was stationed there. From incorporation into the United States until the capture of the last warring band of Apaches in 1886, a period of thirty years, Arizonans never felt the federal government did enough for them during a time when the vast mineral wealth of the territory had been transferred to the country at large.

During the territorial years Washington appointed Republican politicians to run Arizona. From 1863 to 1912 all but three of the seventeen territorial governors were Republicans, and the quality was largely substandard. Barren, hot Arizona never appealed to potential federal officials of quality. One governor was removed from office after leaving the territory and not returning.

If the officials were Republicans, the residents were Democrats. The territory was primarily occupied by southerners. In addition, the electorate voted a Democratic assembly to counter the appointed Republican officials.

From the food the soldiers and miners ate to the clothes they wore, even the hay for their mules and horses, all of it was hauled across incredibly rugged terrain under hostile weather conditions and savage attacks. The price in human life was appalling; the expense was astronomical.

In 1867 John W. Swilling, a former Confederate soldier, noticed the wild hay that grew along the banks of the Salt River and contracted with the Army to provide it to them. He, along with others, excavated a portion of the abandoned Hohokam irrigation system and established what became known as the Swilling Ditch. Two years and one hundred residents later, according to the most accepted version, Darrell Duppa, an English expatriate, climbed atop Indian ruins near the river during a picnic and delivered a drunken oration in which he proclaimed, "As the mythical phoenix bird rose reborn from its ashes, so shall a great civilization rise here on the ashes of a past civilization." As a consequence, instead of Salina, the new city became Phoenix.

The Salt River valley, today generally advertised as the Valley of the Sun, overnight became the bread basket for Arizona. By the 1880's two transcontinental railroads had opened the state to easier travel and relatively low-cost goods.

By the turn of the century cattle ranching was nearly statewide, mining for the copper that had replaced silver was flourishing, and farming along the Salt River was well established. The two most serious problems facing the territory were its inability to achieve statehood, and with it control of its own affairs, and the erratic flow of the Salt River, which caused only one year out of three to be truly productive.

Arizona was the first state to profit from the National Reclamation Act, and in 1911 Roosevelt Dam ended for the next century the water supply and flood problems of central Arizona. Almost at the same time the territory, after a frightful brush at joint statehood with neighboring Hispanic and Republican New Mexico, was admitted to the Union, the last of the lower forty-eight to enter.

Arizona has always appealed to those seeking a new start. People who were discontented with their lot tended to be those who moved to the territory. Because of poor national communication, the demand for any person of education or ability, and the need for Anglos to act in unison against the common threats of the environment and Indians, men and women were accepted for what they presented themselves to be. A man's word was his bond, and God help him who failed to keep it.

The racial mix of territorial Arizona was a spirited brew. Jews, Englishmen, Irish, Welsh, Germans, Chinese, Mexican, eastern Americans all came to work the mines, tend the fields, or start businesses. Arguments were settled face-to-face, and if a rancher found a rustler, no one questioned his right to hang him on the spot if that was his desire.

Tucson, which for most of the territorial period of Arizona was the largest city, was identified in 1864 as "a place of resort for traders, speculators, gamblers, horse thieves, murderers and vagrant politicians," many of whom "were no longer permitted to live in California." Tucson itself was described as "a city of mud-boxes, dingy and dilapidated . . . littered about with broken corrals, sheds, bake-ovens, carcasses of dead animals, and broken pottery; barren of verdure, parched, naked, and grimly desolate. . . ."

This rough-and-ready attitude tends to present an image of territorial Arizona as a lawless land when that was not the case after the 1870's. By that time men were generally judged by juries, mining claims were settled by courts, and once the Indian problem had been resolved, Anglos, including unescorted women, could travel unmolested almost anywhere.

Despite its reputation, Arizona has always been, and continues to be, a largely metropolitan area. Settlers lived almost exclusively in towns. Mining and irrigation tended to concentrate settlements, ranching kept prospective homesteaders out, and Indians made safety in numbers the common experience.

During the First World War Phoenix became a major producer of long-staple pima cotton. By the end of the war Phoenix was billing itself as the city "where winter never comes" and developed the tourist industry on which it still largely relies.

The introduction of air-conditioning following the Second World War made the subsequent population explosion possible. In 1890 the population of Arizona was eighty-eight thousand, not counting Indians, Chinese, and many Sonorians, as Hispanics were called. By 1940 it was five hundred thousand. By the late 1980's it was three and a half million, and it will exceed five million by the year 2000.

The Phoenix of the Second World War was a wide open city of seventy-five thousand. "Pleasure palaces" had always been tolerated, and there were more than forty of them. Gus Greenbaum operated the legal wire service for horse racing. The Democratic party machine ran the city, and everyone paid to stay in business.

In 1946 Eugene Pulliam purchased the *Arizona Republic* and the Phoenix *Gazette*. He supported the idea of reform. In 1948 the Charter Government Committee was organized to that end. It put together a slate of seven candidates, being careful to get the right mix. There was one woman, a labor candidate, two Episcopalians, a Catholic, a Mormon for mayor, and a Jew, Harry Rosenzweig.

When the labor candidate withdrew under pressure from his union, the committee was caught short. Rosenzweig recalls attending the strategy meeting to obtain a last-minute substitute. He suggested his lifelong friend Barry Goldwater. One present observed that they were not certain they wanted two Jews on the ticket but decided if Rosenzweig could persuade Goldwater, they would take him.

The Republicans won the governor's chair in 1950 on a fluke, but in 1952 they ran a statewide slate. With the support of Pulliam's *Republic* and *Gazette* Barry Goldwater was elected to the U.S. Senate and John Rhodes won one of two congressional seats. The Republican governor was reelected.

From this point until the mid-1970's these two men, Barry Goldwater and Harry Rosenzweig, dominated the state Republican party—Goldwater as a U.S. Senator and the philosophical leader and Rosenzweig as the party leader and fund raiser.

Three out of four Arizonans live in the Phoenix metropolitan area. The people who relocated to the state following the Second World War were moving from unemployment, snow, and the general restlessness of the times. They were largely Republicans. They added their numbers to the traditional conservatism of the state.

In a typical year in the mid-1980's more than 200,000 people moved to Arizona. Nearly 150,000 moved out. Because for every 4 who move to Arizona, 3 leave, the state has a transitory nature to its population. Public apathy in civic matters and politics is dominant. People move to Arizona to escape responsibility, not to embrace it anew.

Just over 11 percent of the state's population is retired. The senior population rose from 24,000 in 1940 to more than 300,000 in 1980. Retirees tend to live in retirement ghettos that are usually removed from the cities. Their attitude is that they have already done their part. They wish to be left alone. They vote in disproportionate numbers, and they vote conservative, antitax slates.

Phoenix has been the end of the funnel for white flight. Every year the percentage of its population that is white increases. The black population is just over 3 percent; the Hispanic is only 15 percent despite the city's proximity to Mexico.

The Phoenix of the 1986 gubernatorial campaign throve on growth and tourism despite the fact that every year the city grew hotter. The highs were not increasing, but the average low temperature was rising. This "heat island" was created by asphalt and cement, which covered the ground and retained heat far into the night.

Arizona is a state of entrancing beauty. It is nature with the covering scraped clean, the rugged essence of the earth exposed as it was before topsoil, before grass and trees. The dry mountain air is intoxicating, the desert horizon stretches so far you must turn to take it all in, and the colors of the sky and rock below are unlike any found elsewhere. The place is loved or hated; there is no in between.

Nevertheless, Phoenix is a major city with no downtown of consequence, no sense of identity. The average Arizonan is content, uninvolved, and profiting from the steady growth of the state. It is rare to meet a native. People talk about "back home" and subscribe to their former local newspapers. The communal memory is brief and never so brief as it applies to politics.

As new people moved to Arizona, party registration continued to switch in favor of Republicans. With the one man, one vote decision in the early

1960's the state legislature became Republican at the 1966 election. Burton Barr replaced Democrat Harold Giss as the "most powerful politician in Arizona."

Twenty years later Barr was persuaded by Ronald Reagan to run for governor.

*It's not socially acceptable in some circles to
admit you're voting for Evan Mecham.*
                    —SAM STEIGER *on why
                    Mecham scores low
                    in the polls*

*Our apathy put him in, and we should choke
on it, live with it. . . . Then, then maybe we'll
learn.*
                    —SENATOR JOHN HAYS

*I can't tolerate this type of activity [from Me-
cham], especially when it becomes a personal
vendetta.*
                    —BURTON KRUGLICK,
                    *Republican state
                    chairman,
                    May 28, 1986*

# 4

In practice it is personality that decides who runs the legislature regardless
of the official position. For nearly twenty years before Burton Barr it was
Harold Giss, sometimes president of the senate, a Democrat from Yuma
who ran not just the senate but the entire legislature. For the twenty-two
years after Giss, from 1966 until 1987, it was Burton Barr, a Republican,
making government work from his position as house majority leader.

Barr, craggy-faced, hyperactive, was the consummate deal maker and
was labeled "Joe pragmatic." If not universally liked—his intemperate social
manners were legendary—the energetic sixty-eight-year-old Barr was extraordinarily effective.

Bruce Babbitt was the only governor since George Hunt, Arizona's first
governor, to exercise real leadership. Barr, who was supposed to work against
the Democrat Babbitt, actually worked very well with him even when they
were trading barbs.

It was Barr who set the agenda for the legislature and for Arizona. If there was no crisis, Barr created the issue that would be the crisis that legislative session. A legislature must be seen by the public to accomplish something, and Barr saw to it the Arizona legislature solved a major problem every session.

It was not just his persuasive powers or his love of the deal that gave Barr such sway. Under the existing campaign finance laws Barr, who never faced significant opposition in his own north-central Phoenix district, could raise a large war chest, then distribute it to his troops. These funds often meant the difference between victory and defeat, and they were devastatingly effective in gathering legislators willing to work with him. Barr also had no reluctance to coerce and intimidate lawmakers to acquire their votes.

In 1978, the year the future speaker of the house, Joseph Lane, was first elected, he was regularly invited into the majority leader's office.

Joe Lane was a cattleman from southeastern Arizona, the former president of the state Cattlegrowers Association, and a solid, rural conservative Republican. He was a plainspoken, well-read, and educated rancher with a Rex Allen drawl.

By the second session Lane had been named assistant parliamentarian by the speaker. Within two years he was parliamentarian, a position that placed him in the leadership and made him an active participant in the conduct of the house on the floor. By 1984 Lane was majority whip.

During the summer of 1985 Burton Barr was flown to Washington, D.C., to meet with President Reagan at the behest of the congressman John McCain. He was told he should run for governor and returned to Phoenix "juiced up and committed." The party leadership under Burton Kruglick, Republican state chairman, actively supported him and all but extended its endorsement.

During January 1986 the *Republic* ran a two-part series that virtually anointed Barr as its selection for governor. On January 21, two days after the second *Republic* article, shortly after the legislative session began, Barr announced he was running for governor. Before the session ended, all but two legislative Republicans had publicly endorsed Barr. There was no opposition in sight.

With Barr running for governor and the speaker of the house moving up to the senate, there would be a wholesale change in house leadership. By now Joe Lane had established himself in the house. He had built a reputation for impeccable integrity and was known as a man who could get things done. He also enjoyed the support of the Democrats and moved to speaker with no difficulty.

In 1986 there was also a new majority leader, Jim Ratliff, and a new whip, Jane Dee Hull. Again, as it always does, the power followed the personality, and in 1986 it was Joe Lane who emerged as leader of the house.

There was a similar change in leadership at the senate as well. Longtime president, universally loved, Stan Turley, a devout Mormon, declined to seek reelection. Carl Kunasek replaced him.

Since both houses would continue to be run by the Republicans, and because Barr was considered a certain victor, the Republicans were facing the prospect of having the show all to themselves with the man labeled "the most powerful politician in Arizona," sitting in the governor's chair.

Evan Mecham did not accept that the two men, Giss and Barr, who ran the state legislature would each automatically be "the most powerful politician in Arizona." What Mecham saw was the "Phoenix Newspapers," meaning the *Arizona Republic* and the Phoenix *Gazette*, selling the public the same old line, while the secret power brokers pulled the strings behind the scenes. Mecham was amazed that the "Phoenix Newspapers" did not even bother to think up a new line.

Barr's election was, as Evan Mecham, would say, "all cut-and-dried." The situation to Mecham was much the same as it had been in 1964, when Richard Kleindienst was "anointed" to be the party's candidate.

Almost no Republican in the state legislature welcomed Mecham's entry into the 1986 gubernatorial election. When Max Hawkins called a press conference to be held at the downtown Phoenix Press Club on May 27, 1986, it was not big news. Hawkins had worked on Mecham's 1982 campaign, following a rancorous departure from the Department of Public Safety, and was known to be closely identified with him. He was also known as a vindictive, meanspirited man with a consummate belief in conspiracies.

Max Hawkins says he talked to Secretary of State Rose Mofford and tried to persuade her to switch parties and run as a Republican. Hawkins says he really wanted Attorney General Bob Corbin to run, but when Corbin made it clear he would not, Hawkins turned to Mecham. He recalls that Mecham suggested Hawkins run if he felt so strongly. Hawkins himself had been defeated in each of three attempts at public office as a Democrat. Mecham agreed to run if Hawkins could demonstrate there was enough support to make the effort worthwhile.

Despite his long history as a largely unsuccessful political candidate, Evan Mecham was best known in Arizona before the 1986 gubernatorial campaign as an automobile dealer. Because of the state's fast growth, high population turnover, and Mecham's lackluster performance in the 1982 primary, many Arizonans were unaware that he had ever run for public office.

Mecham says that he had genuinely meant it when he announced in 1982 he would never run again. Mecham called Bob Corbin and discussed the pending 1986 election. The attorney general said that he was unconcerned about running against Barr, according to Mecham, if that was what he (Corbin) decided to do, saying, "I've got enough to blow him out of the water." Corbin remembers talking to Mecham just after Barr had announced his candidacy. He told Evan Mecham that if Mecham survived the primary, Corbin would actively support him, as he had in the past.

At his press conference Hawkins announced he was initiating a one-man Draft Mecham movement. Hawkins launched into a furious attack on Burton Barr. Asked later that day to comment, Barr said, "Whatever Mr. Mecham wants to do, that's what America is all about."

When Mecham confirmed to the press that he just might enter the race, Burton Kruglick, the Republican state chairman, promptly endorsed Barr. Asked to respond, Mecham said that Kruglick "is part of the hierarchy that always supports who they want. What a bunch of malarkey. It's all cut and dried. That's a laugher."

His critics say that Mecham protests too much. This man who had run so many times in their view was like an old racehorse, too slow to win, too dense to understand he could not.

Hawkins found the necessary nominating signatures difficult to gather. He candidly admits that many of the signatures he ultimately submitted to the secretary of state were suspect. If there had been a challenge, they would not have stood up.

Though Mecham had not yet announced, his name was included in a poll, and on June 14 the *Republic* reported Barr with 42 percent, Mecham with 5 percent, the balance undecided.

Ten weeks to the day of the primary election Mecham announced his candidacy. He blasted the Phoenix 40, a coalition of city activists, and denounced "hidden and secret government control in Arizona." He attacked the two Democrats in the race but especially Barr.

Asked to reply, Barr's press aide said Barr had no response.

Joe Lane was pleased at the prospect of having Barr as governor. Here was a man who knew how to make the system work, and like most, he believed Barr would win.

Lane knew Mecham to be a loser. In politics once you acquire that reputation, you are finished, but Mecham had kept running until few took him seriously any longer. Lane viewed Mecham as no more than "token opposition."

Lane felt now that the legislative session was over it was important for Barr to tour the state. Barr was a Phoenix politician, who had to translate his legislative reputation into statewide support. Lane advised Barr to ignore Mecham, not to respond. The advice was, he later admitted, a mistake.

A large number of the Republicans in the legislature already united behind Barr were upset that Mecham had entered the race. Mecham was viewed as a spoiler even by legislators who would be perceived by the public as his loyal supporters in the dark days ahead.

In August Mecham publicly called on Attorney General Bob Corbin to investigate Barr for allegedly violating conflict of interest laws. This was reminiscent of 1964, when he had asked Governor Paul Fannin to check into possible conflicts of interest.

As he had in the past, Mecham decided to bank his campaign on a tabloid he would mail to every registered Republican in the state. He had little money and was supporting the campaign almost entirely from his own pocket. Mecham was largely responsible for writing and laying out the primary election tabloid. He was up most of the night, working on it some twenty hours straight before it was printed.

In late August, about two weeks before the primary election, Mecham distributed the tabloid with the headline BARR'S RECORD EXPOSED—CONCERNED REPUBLICANS DRAFT MECHAM. The six-page tabloid extolled Mecham's virtues and accused Barr of profiting from inside knowledge of freeway routes, lying about repealing a one-cent sales tax, and getting rich from public office. Much of the tabloid was a reprint of articles from other sources critical of Barr.

By mid-July the polls had shown Barr ahead of Mecham, 38 to 17 percent. In mid-August it was 44 to 18 percent. But in the last poll before the election, a week following the tabloid, Barr had dropped to 35 percent, and Mecham had moved up to 20 percent. Ominously those who were undecided had risen to 45 percent. Mecham had not profited directly at this point, but he had people thinking.

Joe Lane calls it that "poison tabloid." Mecham defends it as the truth, points out most of the attacks were penned by others, and adds that he did not call Barr names.

But Barr's supporters were enraged by two accusations they knew to be unfounded. Mecham attacked Barr for making permanent a sales tax that originally had been touted as temporary. Speaking earlier that year, Barr had joked when asked about it. "I lied," he said with a smile. Barr was known for his sense of humor, Mecham was known for not having one. To Barr's supporters Mecham had taken a harmless jest and turned it into an attack on Barr's morality and ethics.

Mecham also accused Barr of profiting from insider knowledge of state freeway routes. Joe Lane and others in the legislature knew this simply to be untrue. The mayor of Mecham's own city, Glendale, who had participated in the selection process, wrote an open letter denouncing Mecham's claim, stating he found it "repugnant." Barr had gone out of his way to have nothing to do with the selection of routes, and of all the attacks, this one offended Barr's supporters as the most spurious.

There is another reason why so many Barr supporters reacted so vehemently to the Mecham tabloid. Mecham's campaign tactics were common knowledge among them. He was known for these last-minute "hit pieces," as they were termed. The tabloid had been expected. At least some of the reaction was in response to the tabloids he had circulated in the past.

As the campaign progressed, Barr was listening to none of the voices that had guided him for years. The newspapers called Mecham the Harold Stassen of Arizona politics and rarely mentioned his name without also mentioning his four previous failed attempts to become governor.

Barr had his picture with Reagan ready to run, Kruglick was prepared to call out the Republican party in Arizona, but Barr, and most, saw no need to do any of it. That all would be saved for the general election.

At about the time of the tabloid the *Republic* formally endorsed Barr. There had been a time in Arizona when the paper's endorsement was the sweet kiss of victory. "Barr's opponent in the GOP primary, Glendale auto dealer Evan Mecham, does not offer a serious challenge," the paper wrote.

In an extraordinary event, on September 2, the three living Republican governors—Howard Pyle, Paul Fannin, and Jack Williams—all broke tradition and endorsed Barr.

Primary day featured a rare rain. Arizona treats rain, even a light one, much as the rest of the country treats a heavy snowfall. Rain is an excuse to stay home, to call in sick.

That primary day proved to have the lowest voter turnout in nearly forty years. It is an axiom in elections in Arizona that when there is a low turnout, the most committed voters go to the polls and the conservative candidate wins.

During the early evening, when Mecham jumped to a small lead that was to grow through the night, Barr remained in his downtown hotel room and out of sight.

Senator Carl Kunasek remembers the "pall of disbelief that evening" as it became apparent that Barr would fall. Kunasek kept thinking that this could not be happening.

Alan Stephens, the Democratic senate minority leader, was across the hall but could see that the Barr hotel room resembled a wake.

Mecham won 54 to 46 percent.

A few days later the *Republic* ran an analysis of the campaign entitled "Blind March to Judgment." It faulted the Barr campaign for failing to capitalize on Ronald Reagan's endorsement, for failing to take credit for Reagan's many achievements, for listening to incorrect polling data, for running a "closed shop" that would not admit volunteers and party activists, and, finally, for pervasive overconfidence.

In the analysis of Barr's loss there is more to consider. It is true that Barr, like almost everyone else, underestimated Evan Mecham. It is also true that Barr relied on a California consulting team that did not understand Arizona politics and overlooked the fact that Barr had never previously run a statewide campaign. The truth is he ran very hard and put in long hours but devoted himself to what he did best, raising money.

Politician after politician tells of offering help and being refused. Volunteers sat idle. Phone calls were not returned. One critic says that Arizona-newcomer soon-to-be U.S. Senator John McCain persuaded Barr that a television blitz in the general election was the key to victory, ignoring the traditional grass-roots effort that usually means success in Arizona.

Most of all, Barr, in the end, had too much political baggage. In concentrating on making the legislature work, he had presented an image to the public of a man with no issues in which he truly believed, only expedient positions required to get the necessary votes.

Finally, Evan Mecham proved the better campaigner. By entering the election late, he did not expose himself to public scrutiny for long. His long and checkered past was never exposed to public view. If his primary tabloid was largely off target, it did voice the suspicions most Arizonans felt toward Barr.

Mecham ran a smart campaign, if the measure of a campaign is victory. He generated the kind of support and marshaled the number of supporters he needed, and they voted when it counted. It is true that Barr ran an abominable campaign; it is also true that Mecham had correctly judged the public and ran a workmanlike, effective one.

Those who worked with Barr are reluctant to criticize him except anonymously. Almost all of them say the same thing. They cannot imagine where Barr managed to spend $1.27 million. They believe, almost unanimously, that Barr threw the election away. He had, as one said, "self-destructed." Mecham did not so much win as Barr lost.

Mecham reported that he spent $272,694: $130,000 from his own pocket, $40,000 from close relatives.

Party Chairman Burt Kruglick now reversed course in a dazzling display of political expediency and the morning following the election was in Glendale pledging the full support of the party.

Carl Kunasek had called Kruglick to express his concern at the Mecham victory. He and others in the leadership along with Mecham and Hawkins met later that day at the Barry Goldwater Center at the Republican state headquarters in east-central Phoenix to try to reach common ground. Kunasek expressed his concerns. Mecham backpedaled and was conciliatory. The party faithful, almost all Barr supporters, stood in line behind Mecham.

Evan Mecham says that Sam Steiger called him that day and offered to help. Steiger says that Mecham called him. Steiger relates that Mecham had contacted him earlier to work on the primary but that Steiger had refused because he did not believe Mecham had a prayer against Barr. He still did not give Mecham much of a chance in the general election, but he signed on because "it was the only war."

The fifty-eight-year-old Steiger was from New York City. Following his discharge from the army he took up ranching near Prescott. In 1960 he began the first of two terms in the state senate. In 1964 he ran for Congress and was defeated but in 1966 was elected. Ten years later he attempted the move to the U.S. Senate. Following a bitter primary with another Republican congressman he was defeated.

Steiger went into eclipse after that. He had financial difficulties. In 1982 he ran for governor as a Libertarian. Steiger is easily the most quotable Arizonan after Barry Goldwater. He is liked by almost everyone and in the years since his disastrous run for the U.S. Senate had become more of a showman than a serious politician. He was recognized to have political savvy, but his days in office were now behind him. It was not commonly known that he and Mecham had served together in the state senate in 1960, and when Steiger joined the campaign, it came as a surprise. The earthy Jewish Steiger just did not fit the image associated with the generally uptight, moralizing Mecham workers.

Almost at once Steiger contacted Donna Carlson and invited her out to Mecham's headquarters, where he had found the campaign in a shambles. Steiger says that Carlson was bright and tough and, with humor, that he "needed a right-wing loony" like her on the campaign.

In 1986 Donna Carlson was forty-eight years old. In person she easily passed for seven to ten years younger and photographed even younger than that. She was a handsome woman with a sultry voice and a penchant for feminine, even provocative dress. She was candid, clever and energetic. She had worked for the party and served five terms in the Arizona house. She had once been a member of the John Birch Society and had led the drive to defeat the ERA in Arizona.

She had run for Congress in 1982. After springing to an early lead, she finished last in an election John McCain won in his first try for public office not much more than a year after moving to Arizona. She took a job as the executive director for the Asphalt Rubber Producers Group. But politics is addictive, she says, and when Steiger called, she signed on with the Mecham campaign.

Carlson believed Mecham had a chance. Though she had a good job, this was the opportunity she wanted to get back into politics after her time in the political wasteland.

Mecham's espoused political agenda was the same as her own. In politics shifting alliances are the rule. Though Carlson would have preferred Barr and believed Mecham had defeated him unfairly, he was the Republican party's nominee. She had always been loyal to the party, and she truly believed that of the remaining choices, he would make the best governor.

Stan Turley, the retiring senate president, had been born in Snowflake, a small Mormon community in northeastern Arizona. Turley had attended Brigham Young University (BYU) for three years, served a two-year mission for the church, been active in a bishopric, served as a stake president and finally as a stake patriarch. His credentials as a faithful Latter-day Saint are impeccable. He had been a member of the Arizona legislature since 1964 and had served as speaker of the house before moving to the senate. He was elected senate president in 1982, only the third Arizonan ever to hold both positions. He was a unique, colorful, and beloved man, as plainspoken and kind as there is.

He had known Evan Mecham many years and generally was supportive of him, though in most elections Turley found himself supporting a Mecham opponent as they were usually good friends. When he saw the Mecham tabloid, he had been appalled. He had been elected speaker of the house the same year Burton Barr became house majority leader. He had worked with Barr for more than twenty years. In all those years he knew Barr had never profited from his office. When Mecham defeated Barr with a "dirty, vicious campaign," Turley was profoundly troubled.

He and his wife and another couple left the day of the primary for a State Department-sponsored trip to China. He learned of Barr's defeat in San Francisco, and all through the trip it weighed on him as he considered what he should do. It seemed so unfair to Turley that Barr should leave public service under a cloud. Because Mecham was a Mormon and had engaged in tactics Turley believed all good Latter-day Saints should disown, Turley felt a special obligation to make a statement.

If he said what he felt in his heart had to be said, he believed that would make it easier for others who were not LDS to speak up. Mecham would not be able to claim the attack was because of his religion. Turley was not a man to give press conferences or to give out releases, but when he returned from his trip, he wrote a simple statement and had his secretary type it. When he first saw it, she had changed his script and typed "unethical pygmy." He explained this was not an attack on Mecham's size and had her white out the *un*. He ran off a few copies, then carried them down to the press room and passed them out.

The portions of the release that appeared in the newspapers disappointed Turley because they focused on what he had to say about Mecham and disregarded his defense of Barr. The release begins, "I don't know whether anyone gives a 'ding' about my opinion on the primary election but for whatever it is worth. . . ." He defends Barr as one of the finest public servants in Arizona history and calls Mecham's campaign tactics "reprehensible." "Every public servant," he says, "must stand legitimate scrutiny for their actions, but to be branded as a crook by slanderous innuendos, libelous falsehoods, and irrelevant questions is despicable." He explained that it was not in Barr's nature to respond to such attacks. The release concludes with this damning judgment:

> For those of us who know him well, Ev's slander has no impact because we know what Burt is really like. As a self anointed savior of the State, Ev has failed the test of both common decency and fairness in this campaign. Both of these attributes are important in any chief executive. Ev will need to learn, sometime along the line, that you don't build yourself up by tearing someone else down. Burt is still tops while Ev has become an ethical pygmy.
>
> The worst part is that we no longer have the chance to elect the best candidate for Governor. The State will be the loser.

For this press release Turley was castigated by members of his church. One wrote that he hoped never to meet Turley in the Mormon temple again. Another wrote that he should not be allowed to serve the church as a patriarch. A relative wrote he was ashamed to be related to him.

As for Turley, he had no regrets and would do it again though Barr never said a word to Turley about this defense of him.

# 5

Whathat occurred in the 1986 general election in Arizona was as much a failure of the state's two major parties as it was any other factor. The truth of the matter was that both parties had managed to nominate candidates who were not widely supported by their own party.

The Democrats had selected the state superintendent of public instruction, Carolyn Warner. Warner was completing her third four-year term in that position and was fifty-five years old. Her husband, Ron, was a member of the Phoenix 40. Within the Arizona Democratic party she was nearly as unpopular as Mecham was among Republicans.

The only published poll pitting the two of them showed Mecham 40 percent, Warner 36 percent, undecided 24 percent.

In Barry Goldwater's last election in 1980 he had been challenged by Bill Schulz, a multimillionaire apartment developer. Schulz had run a brilliant campaign against a surprisingly unresponsive Goldwater. In fact, Schulz won the majority of the votes cast on election day. It was the absentee ballots, traditionally the most conservative, that put Goldwater back in the U.S. Senate for his final term.

Schulz, bright, combative, arrogant, with the scowl of a bulldog, had originally been a Republican. Angered by the Republican-controlled legislature's apartment-taxing policies, he had switched parties.

After losing to Goldwater, he immediately maneuvered to run for gov-

ernor, and it was generally conceded that he would be the likely winner.
Without explanation Schulz abruptly pulled out of the campaign, and it was
only then that Barr had decided to run.

Before the first week was out following the primary a Draft Schulz
movement began. The movement was sparked by Democrats unhappy with
Warner and moderate Republicans who could not countenance Mecham.
Schulz had to make a decision almost at once. To get on the ballot, he would
have to obtain the signatures of ten thousand registered voters who had not
voted in the primary and do it in about one week. That done, there would
be fifty days to the general election.

Glen Davis, executive director of the state Democratic party, characterized Schulz in the *Republic* as being emotionally unstable. When he and
others from the Democratic party first heard that Schulz was considering
entering the race, they met with him.

Schulz told them that there was "no way Evan Mecham could be
elected," that this would be a race between him and Warner. For an hour
and a half the men pleaded with him not to enter the race. Because he
would be running without party affiliation, they told him, he would almost
certainly finish dead last.

Contacted about the prospect of Schulz entering the race, Mecham
said, "I couldn't ask for anything better—a Republican running against two
Democrats." Later Mecham claimed that Schulz was really perceived as a
Republican and had taken more votes from him than from Warner.

A snap poll showed Mecham 28 percent, Warner 29 percent, Schulz
18 percent, the rest undecided.

It developed that the reason Schulz had originally withdrawn had been
the acute depression of his daughter. Under medical treatment she had
improved dramatically and now called for her father to run for governor. To
the displeasure of the Warner Democrats and the glee of the Mecham
Republicans Schulz entered the race.

On a Friday evening, shortly after the primary, the GOP made an
attempt at party unity by having Mecham address the Young Republicans.
When invited, Mecham agreed to compliment Barr at the awards ceremony.
He did not. The omission had immediate consequences.

The *Republic* reported that Burton Barr's wife, Louise, offered her
support to the Schulz campaign. Schulz hinted that there might be a spot
for Barr in his administration and Barr would not say if he would decline.

For the first time in any campaign for governor Evan Mecham shut up.
Warner was so upset at Schulz that most of her attacks were directed at
him. This time out Schulz was flustered, unprepared, and loose-lipped. He
was largely on the defensive, and when he did move on the attack, he lashed
out at Warner.

The Republican party was now the majority party in Arizona. The Mecham campaign made a decision to capitalize on his party affiliation. Steiger called an attorney he had worked with in Washington, D.C., Fred Craft, and asked for a letter of endorsement from Ronald Reagan. The next day Steiger received the letter by Federal Express.

In early October 1986 Steiger asked Craft to escort Mecham around Washington during a brief visit, arrange for the candidate to have his picture taken with the President and meet all the right people. Craft was happy to oblige.

Craft did not know Mecham and asked Steiger to describe him since Craft would be picking the candidate up at the airport. Steiger said, "He's a short little shit with a rug." Craft stammered, then said he did not believe he could spot Mecham with that description. Steiger said, "Take my word for it, you will."

Craft escorted Mecham around the Capitol and had him meet with Vice President George Bush, with Senator Bob Dole and then for two minutes in a photo opportunity with Ronald Reagan. Rather than rely on a White House photographer Craft arranged for one of his own and was impressed when everyone they contacted at the White House seemed to know the man. His name was Ron Hall, and Craft asked why everyone knew him. Hall explained that he did a lot of work like this and his wife worked for the National Security Agency. Later Craft learned his daughter, Fawn, worked for Oliver North.

In October the *Republic* ran an article by Keven Ann Willey calling attention to Mecham's longtime association with W. Cleon Skousen, "a fervent anti-communist" and director and founder of the National Center for Constitutional Studies. His organization had recently conducted seminars with CAUSA, a Reverend Sun Myung Moon support group.

Mecham defended CAUSA to the reporter, saying, "We happen to feel they're very fine people." The effect of the article was to lump Mecham, Skousen, Moon, and CAUSA all in the same package.

A few days later Mecham attacked the article, claiming it was factually inaccurate but neglecting to indicate where. Steiger had called the paper earlier and told it not to send Willey to a forthcoming news conference because she would not be allowed on the premises. Mecham said he did not think she could be fair.

Donna Carlson worked at campaign headquarters in Glendale at Mecham's car dealership. She learned immediately that Mecham would not take advice. She and the others with experience did their best to work around him. Their first step was to get Hawkins "the hell out of there." Hawkins acknowledges he played no part in the general election.

There was a constant hassle to raise money, and frequent meetings were held at James Colter's office to discuss that and other problems. Colter was the general election campaign manager. It was at one of these meetings that Carlson first saw Hugh Gregan and Barry Wolfson, though she did not know who they were at the time. At one point members of the campaign were asked to sign promissory notes Mecham would use to secure a loan. Carlson assumed it would be with a bank. She signed a note for five thousand dollars.

The *Republic* asked the three candidates to come down and meet with its editorial staff, which was trying to decide whom to endorse. Steiger was shocked that Mecham was even considering it, that he actually believed he had a chance to win the paper's endorsement. The day of the meeting Mecham called a press conference and announced that he would not be attending. "I don't need the support of the largest newspaper in the state. I won the primary with their total opposition," he announced. He went on to say, "Since I have no respect for the basic integrity of the *Republic*, it would be inappropriate for me to accept their endorsement." He announced, "I am the one who cannot be controlled. I am the man of the people."

By the end of October it was Schulz 38 percent, Warner 28 percent, Mecham 24 percent, undecided 10 percent.

Before the general election Steve Shadegg distributed an open letter to the state's Republicans. He recounted Mecham's long history of refusing to support the party or its candidates and of the elections with fellow Republicans he had jeopardized by his attacks.

He concluded by saying, "Mecham has been the perennial spoiler. . . . To vote for Mecham in the general election is to put party over principle. Mecham is a fanatical John Bircher who . . . has a hit list of Republican Party people he intends to destroy. He is a vengeful little man, a two-bit head with a $250 hairpiece. The party of honor and principle will be destroyed if Mecham is elected governor."

By rights Mecham should not have won the general election. During the campaign the Arizona Automobile Dealers Association placed his Pontiac dealership on probation for chronic tardiness in responding to complaints filed with its ethics committee. The association had voted to expel Mecham, but the executive board settled for placing him on probation.

In addition, about one week before the election the *Republic* reported that Mecham owed seven thousand dollars in back taxes on property he owned. He cautioned the reporter that she might be being set up by someone because the campaign was getting down to where people were desperate. A few days before the election, however, Mecham acknowledged that he had not paid six thousand dollars in taxes. Though this was not the first time Mecham had a problem with back taxes—in 1971 it had been reported that he owed sixty thousand dollars in back taxes—no mention was made of this.

But these setbacks did not affect the election's outcome. Warner stabilized in the polls. Schulz rose steadily until about ten days before the election, when a series of gaffes ended his hopes. First he said that school boards were largely ineffective because so many housewives served on them. Then, though he was running as an independent, he had defended his Democratic credentials, virtually eliminating the possibility of receiving serious numbers of Republican votes. Finally, he accused the public schools of engaging in kickbacks, an attack on Warner, and then, when confronted, had to retract.

The final poll published before the election, taken just before the last weekend, showed Mecham 28 percent, Warner 27 percent, Schulz 23 percent, the rest undecided. During the weekend voters made up their minds. Large numbers simply did not vote.

Mecham won 39.6 percent to Warner's 34.4 percent and Schulz's 25.8 percent.

For a man who had chased a dream as many years and as often as Evan Mecham, he was remarkably subdued in describing his reaction. As the microphones were thrust into his face that night, all he would say was he felt "pretty damned good." The morning paper ran a picture of him letting out a hoot with his arm raised in triumph.

He will only say now that it "felt good to win" especially since none of the nineteen daily papers in the state endorsed him. Crismon Lewis, a former Mecham employee and editor of the *Latter-day Sentinel*, an unofficial publication for Latter-day Saints in Arizona, later said, "When [Mecham] was elected the world called it luck, but thousands knelt in thanks. . . ."

Mecham offered nothing new during the 1986 campaign. He had supported the partial repeal of the state sales tax, a position similar to that he had taken in other elections when he had come out against various taxes. He had called for a reduction in the size of the Department of Public Safety, a position identical to one he had held previously even though he had called for the creation of such a department in 1964. Now he opposed it on "constitutional" grounds. It was an appeal that had no support with the electorate.

The Mecham tactics had been the same ones he had employed in the past. His use of tabloids at the last minute—there had been one in the general election as well—calling for an investigation of his opponent for conflicts of interest were standard Mecham ploys. But the turnover of population in Arizona allows such tactics to have a fresh appearance to large numbers of the electorate, and such was the case in 1986. Of those registered to vote in Arizona in the 1986 elections, barely half had lived in the state in 1980.

Mecham's constituency consisted almost entirely of the 15 percent of the state population that was LDS; most of the senior citizens retired in Arizona, who made up 11 percent of the population; and, finally, those remaining John Birchers for whom Mecham had always been their candidate, certainly no more than 5 percent of the total population. These were the groups that had maintained Mecham as a viable candidate all those years.

Previously, however, they were insufficient to raise him to victory in a general election.

In 1986 he was able to have the television campaign he wanted. By running the Goldwater endorsement repeatedly, he drew the mainstream Republican vote in the general election that was denied him in the past. This advertising blitz and two competitive candidates to split the vote made possible his election.

In all his campaigns Evan Mecham won a general election only twice. The first time was in 1960, when, by finishing second in the county, he was able to take a state senate seat. The second time was by a plurality of votes in a three-way race for governor. He never served in public office with the vote of the majority.

Alan Stephens had focused on some close legislative races during the evening though he was aware that Mecham was winning. After the outcomes were certain, he and other Democratic friends went to a Brookshires coffee shop on McDowell Road and talked until four in the morning, speculating what a Mecham administration would mean.

Stephens is a bright, politically astute observer. Perhaps his friends were as well. But none of them, absolutely none of them, could have imagined what Mecham's victory really meant for Arizona.

> *We see the smile that hides the hatred, the smooth and oily manner that masks the fury, the velvet glove that covers the fist. Because they are such experts at disguise, it is seldom possible to pinpoint the maliciousness of the evil.*
>
> —M. SCOTT PECK,
> People of the Lie, *read by* SENATOR TONY WEST *as he cast his vote for conviction*

> *Mecham would lie and lie and lie.*
> —JOE LANE

> *His total agenda is vengeance.*
> —SAM STEIGER

# 6

During the general election of 1986 Joe Lane stayed in his district in southeastern Arizona. On two or three occasions, once in Tucson, he met with candidate Evan Mecham. He escorted him around his district, made appearances with him, and never once suspected that Mecham had a temper.

If he was not the kind of man to joke around, be one of the guys, Mecham was at least always personable and pleasant. Lane found him to be an acceptable campaigner as long as he stayed vague and "did his grandfather thing."

Joe Lane had always considered that Evan Mecham was a pretty good guy and though he lacked the allure of a winner, Mecham and he agreed on the issues.

The problem, as Lane later worked it out, was that Mecham thought that he was trying to reform Arizona, that he was on a God-directed mission.

Mecham, it seemed to Lane, was more concerned with principles than with solutions, with being right than with building a coalition.

Election night, when Tom Brokaw of NBC News predicted that Evan Mecham would win the election for governor of Arizona, Lane was surprised but immediately saw this as good news for the party.

Lane had put in his time in the legislature. He recognized that with the explosive growth of urban Arizona he might well be the last rural Arizonan ever to serve as speaker. He had waited to have the influence that would make it possible for him to bring about the changes he believed were good not just for the state but also for the ranchers and farmers. He expected to work with Evan Mecham, and he expected to get along with him. No one could have been more shocked than Joe Lane at what occurred during the first few weeks of the Mecham administration.

In 1986 Lane arrived early and devoted himself to his new duties as speaker. He had some limited contact with the Mecham transition team. But it was his clear impression that the Mecham people had not expected to win and were not prepared to assume office.

During the transition period following Mecham's election and before his inauguration the governor-elect met with a joint Republican caucus. Representative Jim Ratliff, the house majority leader, was present and told Mecham that he should not put Hawkins in as his chief of staff or in any position where he would have dealings with the legislature. He said in essence: "Don't push Hawkins down our throats."

Ratliff was a retired military man with a pleasant southern accent and a charming, droll manner. He had the knack of stating harsh realities without giving offense. Some of the newcomers would not take Ratliff seriously, believing he was out of touch, when in fact, he was on top of the issues. It was they who were out of touch for misjudging him.

Mecham did not respond to Ratliff's admonishment. He said to some of the criticism that he had done nothing in the campaign that had not previously been done to him. Mecham said that it had been a rough campaign and that he had been poorly treated by the press.

Senator Gregory Lunn attended that meeting as well. He recalls Mecham's speaking "to rally the troops." He and the candidate shook hands, and Lunn, as it turned out, was the first of the group to have his picture taken with Mecham.

One day during the election Donna Carlson was on her way to the airport to meet Mecham when Horace Lee Watkins,* one of the campaign

_____

*Horace Lee Watkins, Ralph Watkins, Mecham's chief campaign fund-raiser, and the author are not related.

hangers-on, approached her to give Mecham a message. "Would you tell Ev not to worry about the money," he said. "We're going to transfer another hundred thousand dollars."

She had not given it much thought then. No one ever knows everything that is going on in a campaign. Only after the election did events start to connect. She recalled that at about that time the campaign had received a substantial amount of money. Television spots to run Goldwater's endorsement were already committed, but there had not been the money to pay for them. Then suddenly there was.

Driving with her to Barry Goldwater's at about the same time, Steiger told her about a large amount of borrowed money that was being processed through a bank to keep the donor's name out of it. She told Steiger that it sounded to her "like money laundering." He assured her it all was perfectly legal.

Carlson had been a friend for many years of Peggy Griffith, a later Mecham appointee. At her request Griffith had come up from southern Arizona, stayed with Carlson in Phoenix, and worked in the headquarters during the general election.

After most days' furious activities she and Griffith would sit around late at night and talk. One night Griffith mentioned the name Hugh Gregan. "That sounds familiar," Carlson said. She recalled the name in connection with suspect industrial development bonds.

After the election Carlson decided that it must be the same man. She, Griffith, and a friend who had done polling for Mecham during the campaign went to a Mexican restaurant in Tempe one evening. Carlson had been stewing about the potential for a major scandal because she knew that Mecham had taken a great deal of money from a single source. She knew there was a "fat cat." Griffith told her that she had gone to Colter and told him that this Hugh Gregan was the same one being investigated by the attorney general. "It's too late," Colter said. "He's already loaned two hundred fifty thousand dollars to the campaign."

Given the confusion that exists in any campaign, especially in this one, the dinner group decided that Mecham probably did not know about the Gregan loan and that if he did, he did not know that Gregan was under investigation. Donna Carlson was elected to talk to the governor.

She spoke to Mecham in the transition office at the state capitol. During the conversation she found it hard to hold his attention as if he did not want to hear what she had to say. "Governor, I've just learned that the Hugh Gregan who was an active member of the campaign finance committee is the same person who was involved in some controversial industrial bond projects. I'm worried about his involvement in the campaign."

The campaign theme had been integrity. She told him that this did not look good. Since the damage was already done, she said to Mecham, "For God's sake, report it." Taking the money had been bad enough; not reporting it would be disaster.

In the grandfatherly manner that Mecham often has he replied, "Don't worry. I'm aware of it, and it will be taken care of."

Carlson was satisfied that Mecham was on top of the situation.

For a campaign bathed in generalities, in at least one regard Mecham had been specific about his intentions. He had said repeatedly that he would rescind Babbitt's executive order creating a paid state holiday for Martin Luther King, Jr. The *Republic* editorialized against Mecham's rescinding the holiday.

In defending his decision, Mecham said in early November, "It doesn't have anything to do with race or with Martin Luther King," making it perfectly clear to most Arizona politicians that he did not understand the issue at all.

It is likely that had Mecham left the decision up to the courts or had he taken the step with perceived reluctance, he would have faced little difficulty over it in Arizona. The state legislature had not passed the holiday because most residents of the state were against it. Dr. King was not a popular figure in Arizona.

It is even possible that had Evan Mecham said he was going to rescind the holiday because he believed Martin Luther King was a womanizing Communist, he would have faced little anger within Arizona. Kenneth V. Smith, a future Mecham press aide, was of the opinion that this was his true reason, and it would have been refreshing for Mecham simply to come out and state it publicly.

After announcing that the holiday issue had nothing to do with race or Dr. King, Mecham went on to say that King was "perhaps no more worthy or more unworthy than a lot of other people in the country." During a meeting with black leaders at the Valley Christian Center it was reported he patronizingly commented that some of his best friends were black. He then added, "You folks don't need another holiday. What you folks need are jobs."

Senator Carolyn Walker was present. The man, she thought, "does not even realize he has just insulted the whole room." She recalls that when someone asked about rescinding the Martin Luther King holiday, Mecham responded by saying, "Well, I tell you what. It wouldn't be the first thing I'll do as governor. I'll do it later on in the day."

The Reverend Dr. Warren H. Stewart, Sr., pastor of the largest black church in Phoenix, said, "I have never had a white man, in front of my face, be so condescending. I have never been so infuriated."

Shortly before his inauguration Mecham said, "Do I think King, the man, deserves a holiday? No." So while he insisted that his reasons had to do with the legality of the issue, a position supported by an opinion of Attorney General Corbin, it was apparent that he had another motive as well.

The governor-elect went so far as to respond to eighty-one letters from a class of students at Carl Hayden High School in Phoenix: "It is not my intent or purpose in any way to denigrate the reputation or dishonor the slain civil rights leader who died before most of you were born. However, I can tell from the tone of your letters that your studies concerning his life and times have been somewhat less than objective."

Mecham's aide Mac Matheson, who wrote most of Mecham's correspondence, added in his cover letter, "Organized activities of this sort are not pleasing to our Governor-elect and I thought you should be made aware of that fact. . . ."

Senator Greg Lunn of Tucson has the good looks of an actor and was once a television reporter. He is taller than average, athletically fit, and gregarious.

Phoenix conservatives view Tucson as the hotbed of liberalism. Moderate Republicans such as Lunn are called worse by some of their counterparts.

Lunn had first been elected to the state senate in 1980. He had had more than his share of differences with Barr and did not look forward to his governorship. Mecham had impressed Lunn as "ultraconservative with a populist point of view." He had also found him to be "polite, low-keyed, and ideological."

Though Lunn had anticipated Warner's winning the general election, he ended up not dreading the prospect of a Mecham administration. The "rhetoric led me to buoyancy," he once said. There was, he added in a moment of reflection, no sense of disaster.

During the transition Lunn had been one of a group of legislators which included Senate Majority Leader Bob Usdane, Senate President Carl Kunasek, and House Majority Leader Jim Ratliff, who had gone to Washington, D.C. While Mecham was there, they met with him. He was being shown around by Fred Craft, whom no one knew.

As Lunn observed Craft's behavior, it struck the senator that he was someone looking for an opportunity. It seemed to Lunn that Craft was extravagantly obsequious.

Everyone on that trip commented on Fred Craft's conduct, as Lunn recalls. Back in Phoenix Lunn learned that Mecham was attending meetings about the swapping of some federally controlled land in central Phoenix.

During these meetings Mecham had worked hard to keep each side from involving a lawyer. Mecham wanted direct negotiations. One day Craft showed up. Mecham said, "This is the only attorney I can trust." Lunn heard that Craft had flown in overnight at Mecham's request to be there.

Lunn found it remarkable that Craft was one of the few men Mecham really trusted. An observer on the Ninth Floor recognized and later noted that Craft exercised great influence over the governor, especially after May 1987. It seemed to Lunn that Craft and Mecham had a "father-son" relationship, and when he learned how short a time they had known each other, he was amazed.

Lorenzo Dow "Pat" Murphy started out as a reporter for the Miami, Florida, *Herald* in 1952. He was editor and publisher for two of its suburban newspapers for a time and in 1972 joined the *Arizona Republic* as editor. In 1985 he stepped down and became the newspaper's political columnist. In March 1986 he was named publisher of the *Arizona Republic* and the Phoenix *Gazette*.

About three weeks before Mecham was sworn in as governor Pat Murphy received a telephone call from a Mecham aide, who suggested that the publisher and his staff meet with Evan Mecham and his. The meeting took place on December 23, 1987, in the executive dining room of the *Republic* and *Gazette* building in downtown Phoenix.

Mecham got right to the point. "Are we going to have war for four years?" he asked. "I just want to know."

Murphy explained that though there would be differences, he would see that his papers were fair. If Mecham had complaints, Murphy would look into them, and he gave Mecham three numbers where he could always be reached. Mecham never called. On three public occasions when Mecham attacked the *Republic* and the *Gazette*, Murphy asked Mecham to write and give details of his objections. Mecham never did.

Murphy assumes from this that Mecham wanted an adversarial relationship. The public has doubts about papers, and such tactics can be "smart politics." Mecham had accomplished much during the general election by rejecting either paper's endorsement.

On December 19, Ed Buck, an unknown gay businessman, stood alone at the Capitol mall and distributed bumper stickers he had paid to have printed that said, RECALL EV. Buck confirmed to *Republic* reporter Sam Stanton that he was serious. A staff photographer took his picture, and on Sunday it appeared with a small article on the sixth page of the second section. Evan Mecham and his new press secretary, Ron Bellus, were reported to be amused.

\* \* \*

The inauguration took place outside on January 6, 1987, a cool, wind-swept day. Seated with Mecham was Ezra Taft Benson, president of the Church of Jesus Christ of Latter-day Saints. Also there was W. Cleon Skousen. Art Hamilton, the house minority leader, was conspicuously absent. The most visible black spokesman in the state, he explained his absence by saying, "I had other business, other business."

Ed Buck and a dozen protesters calling themselves the Mecham Watch-dog Committee were present. At the First Institutional Baptist Church, the spiritual bedrock of the small Phoenix black community, the Reverend Dr. Stewart preached to an emotion-charged crowd that Mecham was the mod-ern-day "Pharaoh of Arizona."

Following the ceremony at the Capitol Mecham held a short press conference and announced still again that he would rescind the King holiday "in a few days."

At seven o'clock that night Mecham attended a private reception at the Phoenix Civic Plaza, where supporters paid $250 to shake his hand. Mecham was exuberant in the tuxedo he had proudly announced purchasing from Sears.

By eight o'clock Mecham had joined the inaugural ball, passing between two long lines of the Arizona National Guard. Legislative leaders were pulled aside and instructed to join the procession as well. Most found it acutely embarrassing.

Sue Lane with her husband, Joe, likened it to a coronation ball. Rex Allen, Jr., sang a song. After Mecham's speech all the dignitaries seated up front rose to applaud except Sue Lane, who, in spite of Lane's persuasion, refused because she was so offended by the event.

Different participants in the events of Mecham's administration began at different times to believe that Evan Mecham might not be able to survive four years in office. One of the earliest was Senator John Hays, a Republican and, like Joe Lane, a rancher.

Hays was troubled in part by Mecham's simplemindedness. Mecham had suggested that Arizona solve its water problems by running a pipeline up from the Sea of Cortez, ignoring the fact that desalinating seawater is prohibitively expensive and conveniently forgetting that the Sea of Cortez was located in Mexico.

Hays agreed with one senator who described Mecham's new team as a color-enhanced rerun of *The Night of the Living Dead*, referring to all the defeated politicians with whom the new governor had surrounded himself. Looking over the sea of brown suits and tuxedoes, he thought that if Mecham couldn't even get his act together for a simple event like this, he would never be able to get an administration up and running.

Hays's thoughts, he knew, were tainted by the fact that he had despised Evan Mecham for years.

*   *   *

Joe Lane was not entirely displeased with the Mecham team. In 1979, when he was sworn in, it was Donna Carlson, chairman of the house Committee for Counties and Municipalities, who had taken him under her wing as vice-chairman and taught him what was what. He developed a great deal of respect for her legislative ability and an appreciation of her competence.

Following the inauguration in 1987 Joe Lane was concerned about the new legislative session because the state was facing a budget deficit. The tax code had a structural deficit built in, and in recent years each new legislature had had to make adjustments to balance the previous year's budget. About 65 percent of the budget in Arizona is devoted to education. Lane knew that unlike most of the legislators, Mecham had never served on a school board and did not understand education funding. Mecham had campaigned in favor of rolling back one cent of the sales tax, a change that would cost the state $320 million in revenue.

The day after the inauguration Mecham held a meeting with the legislative leaders on the Ninth Floor in what is called the protocol room. Lane, House Majority Leader Jim Ratliff, House Whip Jane Dee Hull, Senate President Carl Kunasek, Senate Majority Leader Bob Usdane, and Senate Whip Hal Runyan all were in attendance, along with some of Mecham's staff. This was an important meeting to set priorities, and Lane wanted it to go well.

Mecham began with a fifteen-minute presentation of his goals and desires. Everyone listened respectfully. He went around the table and asked each of the legislators what the major issues would be as he or she saw them. Mecham appeared receptive as he was told. He always carried with him a five-by-seven-inch notepad in which he took prodigious notes. He asked whom he should contact and dutifully recorded the information.

Mecham told the legislators to start planning for repeal of one cent of the state sales tax. Lane told the governor that the votes were simply not there. At once Mecham became visibly agitated. After an awkward time Mecham asked if it would be possible to repeal the tax one quarter at a time. Lane explained how much money it raised and described the deficit with which they were already dealing. Mecham was taken aback by the figure, and it was apparent to Lane that he had campaigned on the simplistic theme of repealing the tax without ever considering its impact on government revenues.

Mecham told Lane that it was the speaker's job to get the votes. Lane tried to explain the difficulties and changed the subject, planning to come back to this another time. Instead, Mecham was "hostile as hell" about the tax. Lane no longer recalls if Mecham blew up at this meeting or if it was the next one, but when he did, the governor slammed the desk with his hand, shouted, and cursed at the legislators. Those present were stunned.

Though he seemed to calm down quickly, Lane realized that Mecham was no longer listening and that it was pointless to try to conduct business.

Lane learned very quickly that losing his temper was common behavior for Evan Mecham. These tantrums prevented certain discussions from occurring and often resulted in Mecham's getting his way. Meetings with Mecham were strained and generally unpleasant. The first one was as good as meetings with Mecham ever were.

Despite the inauspicious beginning, on subsequent days Joe Lane met with Mecham and suggested to the governor that he "stroke people." He recommended that Mecham spend the first year traveling the state, cutting ribbons. Mecham had been elected by a plurality and needed to build a supporting majority among the electorate. His suggestions were ignored.

By the third day of his administration Mecham had been interviewed by the Chicago *Tribune*, Cable News Network, *New York Times*, NBC, and the *Times* of London.

A day or two before the state of the state, delivered one week following the inauguration, Jesse Jackson was in Arizona. He and Mecham flew to Window Rock in the DPS Beechcraft King Air to witness the swearing in of the Navajo tribal chairman Peter MacDonald. Jackson made a moral appeal to Mecham in an attempt to get him to change his mind on the King holiday. Lieutenant C. R. "Beau" Johnson, head of the governor's security detail, rode along. He watched Jackson and Mecham speak just a foot from each other and "something didn't fit." He found the scene incongruous. In Window Rock, Sam Steiger asked Jackson, "Well, Reverend, how did you like the governor?"

According to Steiger, Jackson replied, "You know, he's fine. We got along real well. I was amazed. He really seemed anxious to learn."

"I don't think he was learning," Steiger said, "I think he was teaching, Reverend."

"You might be right," Jackson responded.

Mecham announced rescinding the Martin Luther King holiday that morning in his state of the state speech. He defended his action by saying, "I did not choose to make this any part of a political issue or an issue in my administration. My part has been simply to respond to the actions of others."

Joe Lane was astounded that Mecham had taken a simple matter that could just as easily have been a victory in Arizona and turned it into a defeat. Steve Benson, the *Republic* political cartoonist, had voted for Mecham but was now entertaining serious second thoughts. He ran a cartoon of Mecham saying, "I have a scheme!"

There was irony in what Mecham did. In addition to not believing Dr. King deserved a holiday, he probably really did believe it was illegally constituted. But there are those close to him who say the relish with which he repealed the holiday came from the fact that it let him rescind an act of Bruce Babbitt, who was running for President at the time.

Joe Lane says that anyone Babbitt ever smiled on was out of the administration. This went so far as the Department of Public Safety bodyguard detail assigned to the governor. Mecham made it clear that its head, Beau Johnson, was not trusted because Mecham took him to be a Babbitt man and a source of leaks to Barr.

The next day Mecham appeared at a news conference with a glum Jesse Jackson and said, "We don't have [race] problems in Arizona."

The following Saturday Mecham addressed a group of political leaders and said in reference to the possibility of white backlash, "When that day comes when the majority says, 'We won't take it anymore,' I fear for the blacks." He announced he was not a bigot and said, "Bruce Babbitt doesn't love the black people. He didn't do them any good in creating this controversy."

On January 19, the day that the Arizona holiday was to have been celebrated, ten thousand people in near-freezing weather marched on the Capitol, where they presented a petition to Joe Lane. Given their mood, Lane recalls walking out to meet them as one of his braver moments.

Mecham made an appearance on the *Today* show with Jesse Jackson and was observed by a national audience telling Jackson, "I really resent you talking about moral leadership. . . . You are the one that lacks moral leadership, Jesse, not I."

That night Mecham appeared on the *MacNeil-Lehrer News Hour* with Bruce Babbitt. Mecham said, "I myself have never practiced discrimination in my life." He declined to say whether or not he would sign a Martin Luther King holiday bill if the legislature passed one.

Conventions were promptly canceled. Stevie Wonder announced he would boycott Arizona. In Phoenix two days later the black National Newspaper Publishers Association canceled its scheduled four-day convention in progress and left the state. The president of the Phoenix and Valley of the Sun Convention and Visitors Bureau, wondered, "Is this a drizzle or a hailstorm?"

> *Whatever you do, don't end up like them.*
> —EVAN MECHAM *in
> reference to Sam
> Stanton and Mike
> Murphy*
>
> *No matter what he did, Mecham was
> snakebit.*
> —SAM STANTON

# 7

Sam Stanton was searching for another class to complete his junior-year schedule at the University of Arizona when his sister Billie directed him to a line.

When Stanton reached the front and learned it was a journalism class, in which he as an accounting major had no interest, it was too late to register for anything else, so he went ahead and took it. In light of future events it is apparent that his older sister, a very successful journalist and the pride of the family, knew something about Stanton that he did not know about himself.

The following year Stanton switched his major to journalism and took a minor in political science. He went to work on the *Wildcat*, the respected student newspaper of the university, and by his senior year had been selected to be its editor. He served an internship with the *Republic* in Phoenix, was offered a job, and did not ever return to serve as editor at the *Wildcat*.

He spent three years at the business desk and a year and a half working night rewrite and serving as night city editor on weekends. In the fall of 1986 the *Republic* made changes in its Capitol coverage. Laurie Roberts was promoted to assistant city editor in charge of political coverage. Stanton says that no one especially wanted the governor's office, and he, being the newest reporter, took it more or less by default. Others say Roberts wanted an aggressive reporter to cover the new administration. Stanton assumed the state government beat during the transition on December 1, 1986. He was twenty-seven years old.

It is one of the ironies of the Mecham administration that Stanton's counterpart on the *Republic*'s sister paper, the Phoenix *Gazette*, was Mike Murphy. Murphy had been his chief rival on the *Wildcat*, and Murphy had been offered the editor position when Stanton had gone to work for the *Republic*.

The two newspapers are jointly owned. The *Republic* with a circulation of more than three hundred thousand is the morning paper and the state's largest. It has traditionally been the strongest voice in Arizona. The *Gazette* is the afternoon paper, with a circulation about one third that of the *Republic*. The rivalry between the papers is fierce.

Mike Murphy, who has the misfortune of bearing the same last name as the two papers' publisher, had served a summer internship for the *Gazette*. Shortly after returning to school, he was offered a job as a reporter and went to work on general assignments for four years until 1986, when he asked to cover politics. The governor's race was expected to be low-level, and since he was still a rookie, he covered it during the summer campaign. Mike Murphy was twenty-six years old.

The two reporters are very different in many regards. Stanton is tall, over six feet, and slender, with sandy hair and deep-set eyes whose perpetual dark circles worsen with fatigue. He is charming when he is not trying to get a story, and he has a way with women. Murphy is of average height with brown hair and boyish good looks. Stanton is given to cottons, a Banana Republic look, and you can easily picture him in khakis by a campfire in the bush. Murphy is Ivy League, more the fireplace-and-pipe sort.

There are other differences as well. Stanton is aggressive when he works a story and is likely to seize a source by the collar and shake a story out of him, sometimes literally. He pushes and pounds until people surrender. Murphy is soft-spoken and has the habit of trailing off as he speaks. You end up leaning toward him if you want to hear what he has to say. He is persistent and clever.

But if the two men were standing in a room with fifty others, it would not take long to realize they share the same profession. They both have quick, catlike eyes. People leaving and arriving are always noted. People speaking together are observed. They are good listeners, cautious, precise speakers. They have remarkable memories and a depth of experience that causes you to question how they could be so young and know so much.

The rivalry between them is palpable. The differences in the papers made it an unequal contest between these two reporters. Stanton admits that the *Republic* reporters treat their rivals like "a second-class rag." Murphy points out that the *Gazette* is usually overwhelmed by the larger *Republic*'s resources. The morning paper gets preference when a new source volunteers to come forward, and it is the paper from which the morning news shows take their stories. Murphy reveled in beating out the *Republic* because he had to work harder for the victory.

But the *Gazette* had at least one advantage. Stanton had to file late the night before. Murphy could chase a story first thing in the morning and, if he worked hard and was lucky, could catch the 11:00 A.M. deadline for the last afternoon edition.

All of the state's major papers maintain reporters at the Capitol press room on the ground floor of the senate building. Everyone can see everyone else, and sometimes that seems to be the main occupation as the reporters look for signs that someone has a hot story. Neither Murphy nor Stanton would go home as long as the other was in the press room. Murphy, Stanton, Laurie Asseo with the Associated Press, and Dave Hampton with KFYI radio were as likely as not to drink together after work as well because they had to watch one another to be certain no one was filing a late story. If they were drinking with you, they were not scooping you. All the reporters, but especially Stanton and Murphy, lived in a perpetual state of nervous exhaustion.

For a reporter the ultimate goal is to own a story, for the story to be so closely identified with your name that it and you are one. As it was for the two papers, so it became with the reporters: Stanton was to own the Mecham story, while Murphy ran a game and able second.

Stanton compliments Murphy in backhanded ways, calling him a "weasel" even when he is there, reminding him of his mistakes. But when he is serious and speaking on the record, when Murphy is nowhere in sight, he makes his true feelings known. "Mike Murphy," he says, "is, if not the best, one of the best reporters I have ever seen. He is an excellent writer."

And when Murphy knows Stanton is out of earshot, he says of his rival, "Sam is three hundred percent a journalist, one of the best I have ever met."

Stanton was taking over for Don Harris, the dean of the Capitol reporters, and since Harris continued to work out of the Capitol press room, he was able to break Stanton in. One of the first things Stanton did was to drive out to Mecham's auto dealership and purchase a copy of *Come Back America*. Mecham's brother Willard sold it to him.

Within days Stanton had written a story saying that the Mecham campaign was more than eight hundred thousand dollars in debt. Mecham acknowledged that he had taken out notes with people for several thousand dollars but would not provide names.

On December 5 Ron Bellus, Mecham's press secretary, did not have enough copies of Mecham's financial disclosure statement and Stanton ended up contacting Willard Mecham, the campaign treasurer, to obtain one. Wil-

lard Mecham lectured Stanton on how unfair the *Republic* was and told him
to use Murphy's copy. Stanton laughed at that. Murphy let him use the
*Gazette*'s copy? Fat chance.

Mike Murphy was following Mecham closely those first days. He attended meetings of the Arizona Commission on the Bicentennial of the Constitution. It was established by statute and included Chief Justice Francis X.
Gordon and the governor. The National Center for Constitutional Studies
was seeking recognition for a book called *The Making of America*, which the
commission was considering endorsing. California Governor George Deuk-
mejian, also a Republican, had rejected the book after some controversy.
Murphy heard one of the Arizona commission members questioning the
propriety of adopting it.

On a slow day Murphy read the book and immediately wondered about
it himself, pointing out to Mecham the use of the word "pickaninny" in an
essay in the book. Mecham defended it, saying, "As I was a boy growing
up, blacks themselves referred to their children as pickaninnies. That was
never intended to be an ethnic slur with anybody." He then added that he
did not see why blacks would object to the word.

The book had been written by his mentor, W. Cleon Skousen, who was
director and founder of the center. Mecham himself had served as director
of the center for Arizona.

Murphy wrote a story about the commission, referring to the book and
Mecham's defense of the word. His editor removed the reference before
running the story.

Murphy thought his editor had missed an important point and decided
to run the quote defending the word again as a weekend piece. He examined
the controversy surrounding *The Making of America* in California and nationwide, then ran Mecham's quote again. This time it stayed in.

On Monday Art Hamilton rose to denounce Mecham on the house floor.
The most eloquent speaker in the legislature, he was reputed to strike fear
in the hearts of Republicans when he rose with microphone in hand.

Hamilton had been reared one of thirteen children in a Phoenix public
housing project. He had been the house minority leader since 1981. Hamilton serves as the conscience of many white Arizonans on race issues.

Hamilton condemned Mecham's defense of the word as an "out and out
lie" and said his comments were "an affront to every citizen in this state."

Until Hamilton's speech Mecham's comments were not news. Murphy
had already erased the interview. Mecham could have denied saying it or
claimed Murphy had misquoted him. Instead, Mecham launched into another defense of the use of the word in the book "in a historical sense."

Questioned by others, Mecham suggested the reporters investigate

Bruce Babbitt's "real racial feelings," forgetting apparently that Babbitt had worked one summer in the Deep South registering black voters.

Mecham said that he did not understand why blacks would object to the word "pickaninny." He angrily defended himself by saying, "I'm not a racist. I've got black friends. I employ black people. I don't employ them because they're black. I employ them because they are the best people who applied for the cotton-picking job." He then attacked Art Hamilton for giving his speech.

Murphy was astounded by the national response. "Pickaninny" became the call word of the Mecham administration. About ten months later Sam Stanton was sent a newspaper article that is written in Hebrew. It includes a photograph of Mecham leaving a court building with his attorney. There is only a single word in English in the entire article: "pickaninny."

# 8

On the morning of January 12, 1987, Philip J. MacDonnell, superintendent of the Arizona Department of Liquor Licenses and Control, was waiting
to see Governor Evan Mecham with his resignation in his pocket.

MacDonnell was very likely the most popular department head in state
government. Betsey Bayless, removed by Mecham on inauguration day the
previous week from the Department of Administration and replaced by Max
Hawkins, was a very close second.

MacDonnell, like Bayless a conservative Republican, had been appointed two years before to clean up the liquor department. It had been a
monumental task, one that many legislators did not believe was possible.
Yet within the first year he had the department operating efficiently and
honestly. By the end of his second year it was widely regarded as the best-
managed department in state government.

Shortly after the election MacDonnell, along with the other department
heads, met with Mecham on the second floor of the executive office building.
Since MacDonnell was a Republican, it was considered likely he would be
retained or at the least among the last to be replaced.

There had been little discussion during the meeting. Mecham assured them that there would be no wholesale replacements, that he was looking for the best. They were all encouraged to submit résumés if they were interested in retaining their positions.

The effect of this speech was to create hope. Department heads began to ask legislators with whom they worked well and who they believed had influence with Mecham to contact him and his people on their behalf. Legislators hearing of this expected that Mecham was a man of his word and that some, if not large numbers, of the existing heads would be retained, at least initially.

This was encouraging since one of Babbitt's strengths had been the generally high quality of his appointments. The legislators also knew that Mecham would have his hands full just filling his Ninth Floor positions and those in state government that had already fallen vacant.

Mecham reinforced expectations for an orderly transition when, in early November, he announced, "I have emphasized throughout the recent campaign that no one is marked for removal [as a department manager] in advance and everyone desiring to stay will be honestly considered."

MacDonnell was surprised and pleased that the positions would be filled on merit and left the meeting believing he would be reappointed. During December he met with two senior advisers to Mecham and was reassured. He arranged to have his friends contact the governor's office on his behalf. The department heads who were friendly with one another had begun exchanging calls to compare notes.

On December 18, to everyone's surprise, Mecham sent a letter to fifteen department heads—MacDonnell was not one—instructing them to resign. When asked about the apparent shift in direction after the earlier assurances, Mecham's press secretary, Ron Bellus, said, "[T]o be honest with you, we were a little surprised that more resignations weren't forthcoming."

Three days after the inauguration the *Republic* termed the handling of the department heads "cavalier, clumsy and classless."

When criticized for one firing of a department head, Mecham said, "She had a high paying job. . . . Not taking anything away from her, but she'll have a hard time getting one that pays her as well."

Mecham told the annual meeting of the Maricopa County Republican Committee, "I hope the people in my administration will have more class than the people we're replacing. . . . What I say is not a castigation of all these people . . . but a lack of decency and cultural refinement that should take place in the political atmosphere." Apparently chafing under the criticism, he went on to say, "Not one single person ever came and courteously gave me the tender of their resignation. When I'm termed classless, may I turn the arrow around. I hope you Republicans will know and think, and never act accordingly." He said the criticism of his handling of the replacements was coming from "rabid left-wingers who really want to give me a rash."

Legislators reacted with outrage. One department head, stung by the attack, said, "How did anyone know?" He had been asked to submit a résumé, not a resignation.

MacDonnell had contacted Ray Russell, one of Mecham's special assistants, and had once again been reassured. MacDonnell knew, however, that some of the fifteen told to resign had been receiving similar assurances. When he read of Mecham's comments on January 11, he had his resignation typed and went to the Ninth Floor the first thing the next day, the Monday of the state of the state.

Once again Russell assured him that he would probably be reappointed. MacDonnell told Russell that he had seen the article and patted his coat pocket. "I have my resignation," he said pointedly. He explained that he was a good Republican, that he had not known that his resignation was expected, and that he was prepared to resign at once. Despite Russell's assurances, MacDonnell asked to see the governor. Russell thought that could be arranged though this was a busy day and took MacDonnell to Jim Colter, the chief of staff. MacDonnell explained his intentions once again and was told to wait outside the governor's office.

When Mecham was introduced to MacDonnell at about 10:30 A.M., he appeared surprised that MacDonnell wished to speak directly to him but showed him into his large office. Mecham took a place across the room though there was better seating available. MacDonnell told Mecham that had he known his resignation was expected, he would have resigned earlier, but regardless, he had it with him this morning. He told Mecham, "That's fine if you decide you want to replace me. It's your right."

Mecham assured MacDonnell that his resignation was not necessary, that nine chances out of ten he would be reappointed, and that he would make a decision by the end of the week.

On the basis of what he had learned from other department heads, MacDonnell did not believe him. More than once MacDonnell explained the politically wise way to remove him. When he was asked, MacDonnell would say he had resigned on his own. Mecham did not seem to grasp what MacDonnell was relating. He left the meeting not reassured at all.

Phil MacDonnell was as unlikely a candidate for Arizona state liquor superintendent as one was likely to find. He had been born and reared in Boston and on the day of his last meeting with Evan Mecham was thirty-nine years old. With his patrician manner, vaguely Boston accent, Irish good looks, and charm he was not the usual Arizona state appointee.

MacDonnell attended Harvard, was Harvard Law Review, and graduated cum laude. He clerked for the Ninth Circuit before joining Attorney

General Bruce Babbitt in 1975. He rose quickly to become director of special prosecutions and later chief counsel. He was responsible for the prosecution of the head of Lincoln Thrift, whose criminal misconduct had cost the state depositors forty million dollars. He wrote Arizona's racketeers influenced and corrupt organizations statutes known as Little RICO, its computer fraud statutes, and numerous other antiracketeering acts.

He worked a short time for Bob Corbin before running afoul of Twist's consummate ambition and had joined the United States attorney's office in Phoenix when Governor Bruce Babbitt asked him to take over state liquor, a department with a long and unsavory past.

He weeded out the incompetents, and increased penalties ten times. He orchestrated a comprehensive undercover operation which cost the mob its most lucrative bars in the state. By the time of his meeting with Mecham he had almost single-handedly rid the state of its nest of unwholesome bars. Not without reason was he the most respected department head in state government.

One week after speaking with Mecham, MacDonnell stood with some of his staff and watched the Martin Luther King holiday protesters pass under his window on their way to the Capitol and their meeting with Joe Lane. At 8:30 A.M. he received a call from Mecham.

The governor told him that he had decided to replace him. MacDonnell asked if he wanted his resignation that day so he could name a replacement in a few days. Mecham said no, that his replacement was on his way over. "Fine, if that's the way you want it," he said, unable to comprehend why Mecham was handling this so ineptly. MacDonnell offered his assistance in the transition, then went to his supervisors' meeting and told a thunderstruck staff that he was out and a man named Alberto Rodriguez was in.

About an hour later Ray Russell showed up with Rodriguez. MacDonnell had talked to his replacement for about half an hour when Rodriguez suddenly asked for MacDonnell's badge. MacDonnell made a special trip to his home since he did not carry it. After he gave the badge to Rodriguez, the new superintendent went to his hometown of Douglas in southern Arizona and flashed the badge all around. Later it became common knowledge that Rodriguez had been offered this position a month earlier.

Two days later the *Republic* reported that Alberto Rodriguez was under investigation by the attorney general for murder.

At this point no single action by Evan Mecham harmed his relations with the legislature more than his removal of Phil MacDonnell. Some of its most influential members had been misled into believing he would be staying on. One legislator said that MacDonnell deserved "the Heisman Trophy of state agency heads."

Mecham had pledged to run state government like a business. In removing state department heads, he had followed the standard business practice for car dealerships. Employees who are given notice in dealerships are able to cause mischief. Salesmen can dummy sales to obtain bogus commissions. The practice is to give no advance notice, to fire on the spot and watch the employee out the door.

Mecham had failed to recognize that what worked in the automobile business was not accepted practice elsewhere, and he paid the price for that failure.

When Joe Lane heard that Phil MacDonnell had been fired as liquor superintendent, he simply could not believe it, and when he learned who Evan Mecham thought was a suitable replacement, he came unglued.

Ron Bellus later wrote, "One person that had all the right qualifications and came with proper recommendations was Phil MacDonald [*sic*]." MacDonnell, however, "had been appointed by Babbitt," and Mecham told Bellus, "I just don't trust him." Bellus relates that "Mecham did trust . . . Alberto Rodriguez."

Ever since that first unpleasant meeting with Mecham and the meetings that followed, Joe Lane had given the governor, and how he might work with him, a great deal of thought. He was both puzzled and surprised by the confrontation. It seemed to him that Mecham was not accustomed to being told no. Lane suspected that Mecham had always surrounded himself with those who would agree with him. It had been Lane's experience in life that the most competent aides were the ones who disagreed with him the most.

After a half dozen meetings those first two weeks Mecham accused the leadership of not being able to get him the votes. Lane and others suggested that perhaps the governor would like to try to obtain his own votes if he thought it was so easy. Mecham quit trying to bully them after that, but their weekly meetings were strained.

Mecham started hosting a weekly breakfast for six or eight legislators at a time on the Ninth Floor, but these showed little sign of succeeding. He would walk through the legislature, buttonhole members of the party, and ask for their vote. "Can I count on you?" he would ask, and usually receive an evasive response.

Any reductions in a program could hurt a legislator in his own district. The proposed one-cent sales tax cut represented a great deal of revenue to the state and translated into a cut in programs. Mecham would not identify which programs he wanted to cut, and until he did, only those who were already his supporters were going to stand with him.

Another reality Mecham did not seem to grasp was that these men and women owed him nothing. He had not campaigned for any of them. He had never worked for the party and had little other than reflexive loyalty to his office on which to call.

Joe Lane was hearing that they should give the governor time, that he would come around. In the meantime, Mecham was being stonewalled until he received an education on how to run a state government.

That education was not going well.

# 9

Attorney General Bob Corbin was born in Indiana. He says he moved out west because he liked the values typified there and to Arizona because he had always been intrigued by the story of the Lost Dutchman Mine and wanted to look for it. In 1978 he ran for state attorney general and was elected. He was reelected in 1982 and again in 1986, when he faced no opposition, either in the primary or the general election.

Corbin had the reputation of being a maverick. He was an archconservative, a lifelong member of the National Rifle Association and a member of its national board. He had once indicted Richard Kleindienst, the longtime associate of Barry Goldwater and former U.S. attorney general who had resigned in disgrace during Watergate. Michael Scott, a former rodeo cowboy and federal prosecutor, had defended Kleindienst and secured his acquittal in Arizona. Nevertheless, the prosecution had established Corbin's credentials as someone who was not part of the traditional Republican party power structure.

Corbin closely resembles Mecham in physical appearance. He wears dark suits with cowboy boots and a western belt buckle. His office is decorated like something out of a western movie. He is a professional politician who has made few public missteps. The lack of opposition in 1986 demonstrates his popularity.

When Corbin first ran for attorney general, Steve Twist, who was then working at the legislature, came over to assist and was credited by many with pulling off the victory. Twist joined the attorney general's office and quickly became chief assistant attorney general.

During Twist's time with the legislature he had worked on the mammoth rewriting of the state's criminal code. He is tall and smooth. He gives a good first impression but often does not wear well. As Corbin's key aide he moved quickly to consolidate his authority. He is perceived both in and outside the attorney general's office as being the real brains. Whenever the office makes a move with political ramifications, the speculation is whether or not it is from Corbin's or Twist's agenda. It is commonly held that Twist is waiting in the wings for the day when Corbin will move on and Twist can be appointed or elected attorney general.

Corbin demonstrated no reluctance to prosecute associates of an incumbent governor. He had, in fact, indicted two of Babbitt's appointees. The senior staff working closely with Corbin and Twist consisted for the most part of excellent attorneys.

Questions were raised about Corbin's and Twist's motives for instigating certain actions. Attorney general opinions, even before Evan Mecham was governor, were often perceived as being politically expedient. The assistant attorneys general assigned to the various state agencies as legal counsels were suspected of spying for the attorney general and providing legal advice that served Corbin's and Twist's political purposes.

Corbin and Twist were recognized as masters at using the media. Television and newspaper reporters had almost total access. Reporters called Corbin directly, and if he was unavailable, he always called back promptly. The attorney general's office was expert in using news leaks. As a consequence, Corbin and Twist had excellent press.

When he assumed office Mecham had a meeting with Corbin and Twist at which Mecham complained about one of their senior staff, Assistant Attorney General John Shadegg, Steve Shadegg's son.

During the period of the transition John Shadegg had answered questions at a Mecham inaugural committee meeting on the provisions of Proposition 200, which had just been passed into law. When the inaugural funds obtained were later impounded by Corbin pending an investigation into whether they had been legally solicited, Corbin was criticized for John Shadegg's presence.*

Mecham did not want John Shadegg involved with the administration. Corbin assured Mecham that John Shadegg was a fine assistant attorney general and that his father's political opposition to Mecham would present no problem.

---

*John Shadegg has served the office of the attorney general in Arizona for several years with distinction. His reputation is impeccable. The repetition of allegations in this text is not to be taken as accurate or as holding any substance at all. They are presented solely to demonstrate the perceptions of the various factions involved in the Mecham controversies.

* * *

Donna Carlson had observed the strain between Mecham and the legislators "from the very beginning." She repeatedly heard how upset many of the Republican lawmakers were that no consultation was occurring with the Ninth Floor over appointments and the resulting lack of quality of many of them.

She herself thought a number of Mecham's nominees for public office were "frightening." She had the persistent impression that the best people were not being selected, that personal loyalty was Mecham's first and most essential criterion.

The removal of Betsey Bayless was causing trouble along with the ruckus over MacDonnell's removal. Carlson believed that Mecham was of the opinion that "Betsey Bayless needs to go home, get married and have babies." Even during the transition Mecham's propensity for married employees made itself felt in her life.

Steiger told her, "I don't believe this. Ev just called me in and said he had learned that you and I have been going together and he thinks I ought to marry you." She was more than a little surprised especially since Steiger was dating someone else at the time.

Mecham had no plan when he assumed office, no understanding of government, no programs. Carlson helped prepare a list of fourteen areas in which she knew the legislature was already going to act. These were incorporated into Mecham's state of the state address. At the end of the session she reviewed more than three hundred legislative bills and selected the ones from those areas for Mecham to tout as a show of his success.

Bob Corbin was having the same difficulty as the legislative leadership. A cordial relationship between the two men lasted only the first month Mecham was in office. Shortly after the inauguration Corbin learned that Mecham had paid Fred Craft for the work he had been doing in Washington during the transition. This was an apparent violation of the state procurement code, which required competitive bids and a written contract for such activities. Corbin had opened an investigation into the matter.

Before it was complete, Corbin received a call that Joseph C. Haldiman III was being introduced as the new head of Risk Management, the state's self-insuring agency. Corbin called Mecham directly and told him that his office was conducting a criminal investigation of Haldiman.*

Shortly after getting off the telephone, Corbin heard over the radio that Alberto Rodriguez had been named head of state liquor. Corbin called Mecham back and told him about his murder investigation of Rodriguez.

---

*Haldiman had previously lost his insurance license. As a consequence of the attorney general's investigation, Haldiman was sent to prison.

Corbin asked Mecham what his administration was doing to check into the backgrounds of new appointees. Mecham told Corbin that the Department of Public Safety was running criminal background checks. Corbin suggested Mecham run the appointees by his office since it might have knowledge of ongoing investigations that had not yet resulted in arrests. Mecham never did.

Corbin says that Mecham did not take these two calls well. According to Corbin, Mecham acted as if the attorney general was interfering in his business.

It is Mecham's position that this so-called murder investigation of Rodriguez was a sham intended to embarrass him and deny public office to a good man. He also contends that the news reports that Max Hawkins was introducing Haldiman around Risk Management as the new director are false, that he never intended to appoint him, that he was just asking his opinion about the operation of Risk Management.

Within days of Corbin's calls to Mecham the *Republic* reported that Corbin had been investigating Rodriguez since the previous April. According to Corbin, his office had inherited the inquiry from the FBI, which had checked into Rodriguez's background on another matter.* The *Republic* reported that when Rodriguez had been the mayor of Douglas, a border community, he had been the target of a recall drive, had been sued for libel by two city department heads, and had been an unsuccessful candidate for the state senate in 1980.

Rodriguez said the murder probe was being pushed by his "political enemies."

It was especially unwise for Mecham to be making appointments without prior consultation since it was up to the state senate to confirm many of them. It was bad enough that the governor would not ask what the senators thought first, but in most cases he did not even bother to tell them who was being appointed. In case after case leadership learned the bad news from reporters.

In large part Mecham's appointees were unknown. That would have been tolerable if they had long associations with the governor or if they were people of sterling qualifications, but many of them appeared simply to be opportunists.

The issue of appointments most concerned the new senate president, Carl Kunasek, since it would be up to him to get them approved. Kunasek

---

*The alleged homicide occurred in 1954 when Rodriguez had been a police officer in Douglas, Arizona.

A superior court judge later concluded that the killing had taken place just across the international border and that Arizona lacked jurisdiction. Asked by Rodriguez's attorney to speak more directly to whether or not the killing was justified, the judge declined.

was a pharmacist by profession and had lived in Mesa since moving to Arizona in 1961. He had retired when he was elected president in order to devote himself to state service.

He had been a Barr supporter and had been very troubled by Mecham's victory. Kunasek was bothered both by Mecham's claim that his single term in the legislature nearly thirty years before gave him exceptional knowledge about its workings and by Mecham's outlandish proclamations of what he would do once he was in office.

The new senate president was not troubled by all of Mecham's appointees. Alberto Rodriguez bothered him, however, because of the attorney general's investigation and because he was an opportunist. Rodriguez's wife had worked for the Mecham campaign in southern Arizona. That was the extent of his qualifications.

As that first session proceeded, Kunasek was finding Mecham "tough to work with," but he believed it was his role to effect the governor's will and to help make the administration work.

But that did not stop the senate leadership from hiring its own investigator to research Mecham's appointees. That, it seemed to Kunasek, was just common sense.

It was not as if Kunasek had not tried. He and Bob Usdane, senate majority leader, met in private with Mecham and discussed the appointment difficulties. Mecham listened and then proceeded, as Usdane later said, to make those "rotten appointments."

Mecham named Horace Lee Watkins to head a statewide antidrug task force which existed in name only. Then Mecham appeared to have originated the idea for turning the proposed task force into a new state agency in the middle of a controversial speech in Mesa. While Sam Steiger was denying to reporters there were any plans for a separate state agency to counter drugs, Mecham was announcing he planned to create the Arizona Drug Control Service with two hundred officers. Even Watkins was reportedly "perplexed" when informed.

Nothing further happened toward creating either the antidrug task force or new agency. Only six weeks later Watkins resigned just as the Mesa *Tribune* was about to run an article disclosing that his California insurance firm had gone bankrupt fourteen years before and that he had been censured by the Republican Central Committee for unethical campaign practices in an unsuccessful 1978 assembly race.

Watkins did not leave the Mecham administration. Instead, Max Hawkins placed him at the Department of Commerce, where Watkins performed unspecified duties while on the state payroll. In 1978 Mecham had called for dismantling this office under another name because he said Babbitt had been using it to build "a personal political machine at the expense of tax-payers."

Though a supporter of the governor, Representative Leslie Whiting Johnson, a fellow Mormon, was also disturbed by Mecham's appointments. She not only had serious reservations about some of the senior staff on the Ninth Floor but also about the lower-level staff that dealt with the public. One secretary, she understood, was hired for having done nothing more than "lick envelopes for the campaign." Johnson had been surprised to hear that Mecham would not schedule appointments more than six weeks in advance. That seemed an odd practice for a state's chief executive.

Johnson also had experienced trouble obtaining routine information, the dispersal of which Mecham insisted on making personally. Once she made repeated attempts to schedule the governor for a speaking engagement. The secretary she dealt with would not return calls. When Johnson finally reached her, the secretary told Johnson, "If you don't like it, that's too bad," and hung up on her.

The Ninth Floor secretaries seemed to feel that anyone who had not worked on Mecham's campaign could be treated rudely. Johnson learned that the appointments secretary often did not call to cancel engagements the governor could not attend. She simply erased them from the calendar.

Once Representative Johnson was contacted by an acquaintance about obtaining a secretarial position on the Ninth Floor. It seemed routine enough, and she agreed to put the aspirant in touch with the right party. After a great deal of persistence she was given the name of someone she was told could be of assistance. The staffer asked Johnson in which GOP campaign the aspirant had worked, if she was a loyal Republican and a good Christian. Johnson was informed that the staff could not hire a Mormon because there were more than enough on the Ninth Floor already. Johnson had the odd feeling there was a quota at work. After the conversation it occurred to Johnson that the staffer had never once asked if the aspirant was qualified for the job.

Johnson also learned early that the governor viewed criticism as disloyalty. He expected blind allegiance. She found most staff members on the Ninth Floor, including Chief of Staff Jim Colter, so inept that after a time she just worked around them and him.

Democrat Representative Debbie McCune, the House Minority Whip, was very concerned about Mecham's election when she saw the kind of people with whom he surrounded himself. The senior staff on the Ninth Floor were, in her opinion, "all political misfits." How can you field a team to run government from people angry at the system? she asked herself.

Even though he was new, it seemed to McCune that Mecham had the upper hand during most of the first legislative session since all new Republican leadership was also in place. The Republicans had been accustomed to working as a team under Barr, and they struggled to maintain that appearance as the session proceeded. But it was clear to her that the leadership was having difficulty with Mecham.

It was, she said later, like a family with problems that no one wanted anyone else to see.

> *I fear for Steve's personal salvation.*
> —Evan Mecham

> *It's my personal opinion that Evan Mecham is an utter, unequivocal disaster and embarrassment, not only to the state but to the religion that we both happen to be members of.*
> —Steve Benson

# 10

Steve Benson's family was devoutly Mormon. He received his Duty to God Award and was an Eagle Scout. He was called to one of the LDS missions in Japan and served two years there as a missionary. When he returned at age twenty-one, he enrolled at BYU.

Benson had always been interested in politics, just as his father and grandfather before him. His mother had been a member of the John Birch Society, and his father had been a financier for the Freeman Institute, as Skousen's National Center for Constitutional Studies was first called.

After graduation Steve went to Washington, D.C. and worked on the *View from the Capitol Dome*, a political newsletter. He drew political cartoons that were mailed to Republican candidates nationwide for the 1980 elections.

Pat Murphy, who was the editorial page editor for the *Arizona Republic*, hired Benson as the paper's new political cartoonist. By the time of the Mecham administration Steve Benson was syndicated to 170 newspapers nationwide.

He had been living in Mesa, the center of the Salt River valley's largest concentration of Mormons, just a month. One night he received a telephone call from a stranger who said he was Evan Mecham and wanted to welcome Benson to the valley. He explained that he was a fellow Mormon and a friend of his grandfather's. The caller espoused political philosophies Benson held, and the pair chatted amicably for a few minutes. Then "out of the clear blue, he launched into an attack on Phoenix Newspapers," Benson later recounted.

Mecham explained that he had been treated unfairly in the past by the

*Republic* and the *Gazette* and that his own newspaper, the *Evening American*, had been run out of business by Eugene Pulliam and his two papers. Benson says, "The distinct feeling I got was that Ev Mecham had a personal distaste for the company for which I now work[ed]. I [also] got the distinct impression that he felt that I was really in a position now to be an influence for good on what otherwise was a basically corrupt organization."

Nevertheless, Benson was not unhappy when, in 1986, Evan Mecham emerged as the Republican nominee. He perceived Mecham as a man who would pursue conservative causes and as a fellow Mormon with a shared faith. He considered Mecham the best of three poor choices and decided to take a wait-and-see attitude. If he had second thoughts the day Mecham rescinded the Martin Luther King holiday, by the end of that month he had become completely disenchanted with the new governor.

Benson drew approximately fifty negative Mecham cartoons during the following year. He was Mecham's most scathing critic. Within his own church he became the target of vicious attacks. The short tenure of Evan Mecham was catastrophic for many people but none more so than Steve Benson.

Steve Benson, former missionary, BYU graduate, second counselor to the Stake (Diocese) missionary effort, was also the grandson of Ezra Taft Benson, president of the Mormon Church.

Two days before the inauguration the *Republic* reported that Mecham would appoint his southern Arizona campaign manager, private investigator Bill Heuisler, as a special investigator to ferret out waste and corruption in state government.

In mid-January, following up on another reporter's story, Sam Stanton wrote that Heuisler had failed to disclose a history of arrests and courts-martial on his private investigator's license renewal and original application. None of the charges had been felonies, but one of his courts-martial had involved his threatening a prisoner with a gun and had resulted in two months in the brig. The other court-martial had produced a thirty-day sentence.

The difficulties were compounded when Heuisler denied the courts-martial and misrepresented the type of discharge he had received. Though the military trouble had occurred more than twenty years before, he had last been arrested in 1980.

The day of Stanton's second article on Heuisler Mecham confirmed that he would have already appointed him if not for the reports of his past convictions. At a press conference on the Ninth Floor in the protocol room. Mecham made a few perfunctory statements, then, in response to the reporters' questions, brought Heuisler out. Heuisler was reserved at first but soon became highly agitated. Watching Heuisler in action, Mike Murphy, who was also covering the conference, thought it was as if Mecham had "picked some guy off a construction site."

Heuisler was most notably upset with the Associated Press reporter Larry Lopez, who had run the original story. He refused to answer the reporter's questions and instead called him "slime." Heuisler denied having been fired from the Tucson Police Department. Then he threatened to break a chair over Lopez's head.

The course of the conference raised broader questions in Mike Murphy's mind about the administration.

Stanton was stunned. He decided that hereafter he would check out the governor's appointees. It occurred to him for the first time that this administration was a real "operation."

After Heuisler left the room, Bellus, Mecham's press secretary, admitted that Heuisler's behavior had not been appropriate. Mecham conceded that it had been a mistake to hold the conference but defended Heuisler by saying his arrest record "uphold[s] the traditions of the Marines." Shortly thereafter Heuisler withdrew his name from consideration.

Ron Bellus had worked at placing spots for the Mecham campaign after the Phoenix Press Box Association let him go. Though he had absolutely no experience, he was hired as Mecham's first press secretary. Sam Stanton describes him as a kind man who adopted Korean children and was known as a "straight arrow." Bellus was a graduate of Brigham Young University and a Mormon.

It was readily apparent that he was totally unsuited for his job. Bellus did not return reporters' telephone calls and seemed never to know what was taking place on the Ninth Floor. The reporters explained to Bellus that he could not shut them out, that they had jobs to do. Bellus treated the press like adversaries to be kept at bay.

About once a week Bellus sent the reporters on a wild-goose chase, telling them Mecham was speaking at some remote valley location when he was not. He apologized for it later.

During staff meetings the reporters loitered in the public waiting area outside. Bellus was convinced they could eavesdrop, so he brought out a radio, as Stanton called it, "a high tech scrambling device," tuned it to a rock station, and set it on the floor. Not long after that the reporters noticed metal strips on the inside of the door.

Bellus was so inept at his job that others on the Ninth Floor talked to reporters, fearing they would take out their frustration against Bellus on the governor.

"They honestly believed the reporters didn't have sources" on the Ninth Floor, Stanton says, leading Mecham aides to believe their information came from eavesdropping or bugging. The idea of bugging came to dominate Ninth Floor thinking.

Bellus's press releases were poorly written, often with misspelled words, and could not be relied on for accuracy. Bellus was convinced the press was unfair to Mecham. At one point he took a pile of *Republic* and *Gazette* articles and "critiqued" them. Mecham was sufficiently persuaded to ask for a private meeting with publisher Pat Murphy to present his "proof."

Legislators were calling for Bellus's removal almost immediately.

In late January Bellus asked Mike Murphy if he had heard that recall instigator Ed Buck had been arrested for using a forged prescription, saying, "We just nailed Ed Buck." His leak of the information was so ham-handed that Bellus's conduct rather than the arrest became the story.

Bellus was to write a self-published book after the administration was over. At one point during Bellus's unsuccessful campaign for the 1988 legislature he offered it as an inducement for contributions. Amateurishly written, replete with misspelled names and unsubstantiated rumors, the book had a printing of only four thousand, and Bellus was still left with undistributed copies. *New Times* executive editor Michael Lacey termed the book "a joke."

Referring to the reporters, Bellus writes that a "great injustice" was done to the governor "in an underhanded manner, [by] a few arrogant, self-serving individuals [who] managed to create an atmosphere of hostility and rancor unprecedented in Arizona history."

Bellus blames "liberal/moderate Democrats, homosexual activists, the 'Establishment' (Burton Barr, etc.), and the *Republic* and *Gazette*" for the "depth of hate that those elements were able to inflame in a large number of Arizonans and even those outside the state. This, of course, could not have been accomplished without the aid of a handful of press representatives—most notably, *Republic* and *Gazette* publisher Pat Murphy, *Republic* reporter Sam Stanton, *Gazette* columnist John Kolbe, and to a lesser degree *Gazette* reporter Mike Murphy, and Associated Press reporter Laurie Asseo."

Bellus attacks Sam Stanton's skills and ethics. He says that publisher Pat Murphy did not need to involve his four hundred reporters in his "conspiracy," not when he had Sam Stanton to use.

As head of the governor's security detail it was DPS Lieutenant Beau Johnson's custom to pick Mecham up at his home every month or so and drive him to his office. Mecham also sat in the front seat. Usually he spent his time on the car telephone, but on these occasions Johnson found an opportunity to ask Mecham how it was going with the security detail.

In February Johnson had just reached the freeway and had turned west toward Phoenix when Mecham asked, "Does Wence have any black blood?"

Mecham was referring to Wence Camacho, an officer on the detail. Camacho had told Johnson a week or so earlier that Mecham had asked him his feelings on the Martin Luther King holiday issue. Members of the governor's security detail were instructed not to discuss politics. Apparently Mecham was unhappy with Camacho's lack of an answer.

Johnson hardly knew how to respond to Mecham. He said, "Governor, not that I know of. He's full-blooded Hispanic."

Mecham said, "I think he'd be happier somewhere else."

Johnson explained that Camacho was quiet by nature, but he thought if Mecham would give him a chance, he would be very happy with him. "Wence does excellent work." Mecham insisted, however, and Camacho was transferred.

Camacho was deeply hurt when he learned he was off the detail. He met with Director Ralph Milstead to express his hurt and anger. He even discussed leaving DPS over it.

This was the second transfer Mecham had requested Johnson make from the security detail. Lori Norris had been the only female officer. Mecham told Johnson that he had been married for thirty-five years and was not comfortable being alone with a female. He said he was concerned with appearances. Norris was transferred even though Johnson considered her one of his best officers.

John Kolbe, the columnist for the *Gazette*, had covered Mecham's assorted campaigns as long as anyone. Since 1974 his articles had been observant and scathing as concerned Mecham. In 1986 and early in 1987 he had been no less articulate and, in the eyes of Mecham, no less critical.

On February 25, 1987, Kolbe ran a column mocking Mecham's performance at the National Governors' Association, where he had managed to obtain the group's endorsement for repeal of the fifty-five-mile-per-hour federal speed limit.

In *Come Back America*, Mecham says that the first step in his "Third American Revolution" was for the states to regain some power from the federal government "behind a small issue." He writes: "It had to be a winnable issue that we could turn to rapid success and get the states starting to realize they did have some power and no longer needed to remain vassals of a federal bureaucracy. Once we had one success, the second would be easier."

At the conference Mecham had won that victory. Shortly thereafter Congress allowed the states to raise the speed limit to sixty-five miles per hour if they wished. Mecham billed himself as "Mr. 65" and took obvious delight in his accomplishment.

In Kolbe's column, Craft is identified as "Mecham's Washington operative." Kolbe mentions Mecham's "naiveté" and downplays what Mecham considered not only a remarkable accomplishment but fulfillment of the first important step in the states' reclaiming power from Washington.

Mecham took exception to the Kolbe column. He summoned the newspaper's general manager to his office and told him that he would not permit Kolbe to attend any of his press conferences. Mecham told Bellus what he had done. He added, "I'd like to have [the DPS] just throw him down the elevator. But we'll try to keep him out." Bellus suggested he try ignoring Kolbe. Mecham responded, "No. That guy can't see anything good I'm doing. Why should he even be around?"

On March 2 the *Gazette* printed the governor's response to Kolbe's article. Mecham announced that henceforth Kolbe would be physically banned from his press conferences. He went so far as to talk to his DPS security detail about it. When objections were raised and it was pointed out that Mecham could not legally bar Kolbe from attending a public meeting, the governor announced that he would no longer respond to the columnist's questions. Ron Bellus called Kolbe "that Jackass."

Bellus announced that Mecham was considering a journalist accreditation system. As he planned it, columnists such as Kolbe would not qualify.

Mecham said, "As far as I'm concerned, [Kolbe] is a non-person, and that's it."

Asked to respond, Kolbe replied, "Does that mean I don't have to do my taxes this weekend?"

Following a torrent of criticism, Mecham, calling himself "just an old softie," announced that Kolbe could attend press conferences. On March 19 Mecham held a conference that was covered by television. Kolbe asked a smiling Mecham the first question. Mecham ignored him and asked if anyone had a question. Associated Press reporter Larry Lopez repeated Kolbe's question. Mecham ignored him and asked again if there were any questions. Mike Murphy had begun to repeat the question when Mecham interrupted, said, "It's good of you to be here. Thank you." He then walked stiffly off. The scene played on television statewide that night.

Bellus observed that Mecham had realized he "was being set up" during the conference. When the "chorus" of reporters parroted Kolbe's question, "Mecham was not impressed," according to Bellus.

As Mecham walked out of the room, Bellus thought, "What's with these guys? Why would they pull a stunt like that? Why did Larry ask that question exactly like Kolbe?"

In Mecham's private office the governor told Bellus that the reporters "were acting like a bunch of children." Bellus agreed.

"Well," the governor said, "if that's the way they want to play, let 'em."

The reporters refused to leave the room after Mecham walked out. One of the television reporters was especially incensed. Lieutenant Beau Johnson went to Bellus's secretary to inform her. She told Johnson that Bellus wanted him to go out and tell the reporters they would be getting nothing more and to leave.

Johnson was angry. He told the secretary that this was not his job. This was not the first time Bellus had asked him to do something Bellus should take care of personally. He said he would do it, but he did not like it.

Johnson went in to speak to the hostile reporters. He said, "Ron doesn't wish to speak with you now. If you want to talk to him, you'll have to call."

One reporter snapped back, "That's not acceptable!" The reporters knew Bellus almost never returned a telephone call. But after a time they all reluctantly left the room so Johnson could lock it.

Asked later why he had not responded to the reporters, Mecham replied, "I guess I didn't hear any questions." Asked why he would not answer Kolbe's question, he said, "Who? Was he there?"

Kolbe termed the governor's behavior "childish." He was not alone in that observation.

Much later, at a time when Sam Steiger was evaluating the Mecham administration, he said, "The lesson that [Mecham] learned in November of '86 was that you didn't need the media to win. What he didn't understand is that he did need it to survive."

Pollster Bruce Merrill was retained by the administration to determine the public's perception of the governor. He found a 63 percent unfavorable image. People reported that they did not like the way Mecham acted without thinking. The poll showed the public viewed Mecham as "arrogant and overbearing, narrow minded and stubborn." Merrill reported the results of the poll at a staff meeting on the Ninth Floor at a time when the Kolbe situation was still up in the air.

Mecham slammed the table with his hand and said, "I am governor of this state and I will run this state. It's time Pat Murphy and his cohorts learned their lesson. I will not apologize to John Kolbe." The staff looked on in shock.

On April 24 Mecham told a group of reporters at a conference, "You want to see history made? John Kolbe is now going to become a person." He then responded to Kolbe's question.

Representative Mark Killian had a history not unlike that of Steve Benson. His father had been a law partner of longtime Congressman John Rhodes. Just out of high school Killian had served as a staff assistant and personal page to Rhodes. He had been raised in a model LDS home. He was an Eagle Scout and received his Duty to God Award. He served a Mormon mission in Washington, D.C., and was in partnership with his brother when he was elected to the Arizona house. During the period of the Mecham administration he was a high priest and second counselor on his ward bishopric.

When Mecham won the primary election, it had been Killian's assessment that they would lose to the Democrats, so he had been excited at Mecham's subsequent victory and "happy for Ev."

Killian was soon unhappy with the Mecham administration, however. Killian thought that Mecham approached the job of governor from weakness. He needed to broaden his constituency, not narrow it. It seemed to Killian that Mecham "wanted controversy."

Not far into the administration Joe Lane and others in the leadership came to Killian and asked about his church, seeking an understanding of Mecham.

Killian frequently spoke to junior high schools in his district, one that was very conservative, had voted heavily for Mecham, and had a large LDS population. Just after Mecham had declared Kolbe to be a "non-person," Killian was addressing such a group. Following his usual prepared remarks, he took questions from the students.

An eighth grader called Mecham "a baby" for walking out of the press conference after ignoring Kolbe. Another said Mecham was "a bigot" for rescinding the Martin Luther King holiday. A third said Mecham should be recalled, and the "place went bananas."

Killian was shocked by the reaction. He knew that most of the young students were likely influenced by their parents' feelings and opinions. He told Donna Carlson what had taken place and she arranged for Killian to immediately meet personally with the governor. This was the first time he had ever been on the Ninth Floor and the first time he had met with Mecham. Killian told Mecham what had taken place. Before he could complete his evaluation, Mecham cut him off and said, "They don't understand. They only know what they read in the papers." He then explained to Killian that the "Phoenix Newspapers," the Phoenix 40, and others were out to get him.

Killian had heard about these rote speeches Mecham would launch into, "like a tape recorder." For twenty minutes Mecham spoke. In all his life Killian had never before talked to anyone who behaved like this. The meeting ended, and Killian "left in a state of shock." He thought, How does he operate if he thinks all these people are after him? Whom could Mecham trust?

Though Mecham's steady conflict with members of his own party was kept largely quiet during those first months, his frequent attacks on the media, and in particular on the *Republic* and the *Gazette*, were widely disseminated. There were, however, as many who were amused by his attacks on the media as were appalled by his administration and conduct. By late February, only five weeks into his administration, he was hinting that he planned a new tabloid to get his message across.

The stream of incidents from the Ninth Floor was unrelenting. In late January Sam Stanton wrote an article that reported Mecham's portrait had been placed over the state seal in the lobby to the governor's offices. Bellus denied the story. The next day at the request of the reporters Bellus lifted the portrait and discovered the seal. This occurred two weeks before Arizona was to celebrate seventy-five years of statehood.

At the same time Mecham's appointee to the Governor's Office for Children hired his former campaign manager to be his executive assistant, admitted that he did not know her background on children's issues, and then refused to disclose her salary.

Within a week Jim Cooper, Mecham's appointee as lobbyist for education, testified before the house Education Committee, "If [a] student wants to say that the world is flat, the teacher doesn't have the right to try to prove otherwise." Mecham agreed.

A few days later, on statewide radio, Mecham said, "The church I belong to does not allow homosexuals to participate under any circumstances." He publicly condemned the homosexual life-style as unacceptable.

The next day Laurie Asseo reported that a Mecham segment taped for *Good Morning America* featuring him with local schoolchildren had been canceled because of an allegation that someone with him had instructed the film crew to move black children away from Mecham. Bellus denied it.

Three days later Mecham supporters, apparently unaware it was a holiday and most of the newspapers' employees were off, picketed the *Republic* and *Gazette* building in downtown Phoenix.

The next day Barbara Blewster, a supporter of Mecham and a member of the John Birch Society and of the Coordinating Council of Republican Women, flew in Eldridge Cleaver to testify against the proposed Martin Luther King Holiday bill. She made the arrangements with Skousen's National Center for Constitutional Studies and paid Cleaver, now a Mormon, a fee to appear. She said, "I wanted to get a Negro who had been active in the civil rights movement and had been turned around."

The following day Corbin froze Mecham's inaugural fund for investigation.

The next week the *Republic* reported that some Republican legislators were already considering a consensus candidate in the event of a recall election.

Four days after that Heuisler testified before a state grand jury, which later determined there were no grounds to indict him.

Two weeks later Horace Lee Watkins resigned as head of Mecham's antidrug program under a cloud.

Five days later the full details of the Rodriguez murder investigation were reported by Sam Stanton along with allegations that Rodriguez had raped a woman in his squad car when he was a policeman in 1955, broken a woman's back in 1959 pulling her out of her car, and in 1980 assaulted a man outside a golf club. Details of the killing had Rodriguez, who was a policeman at the time, running up to an unarmed man who was in custody and shooting him twice. Rodriguez had never been convicted of any wrong-doing, and the charges for the golf club assault were dropped. He denied the versions of events published in the *Republic*, and except for the ongoing murder investigation no action was taken on the other allegations.

A week later the state personnel directory put out by Max Hawkins's Department of Administration listed the governor's name as "Evan Me-chan" [*sic*].

The next day the Reverend Dr. Stewart called for a convention boycott of Arizona.

Two days later Mecham said that though he had nothing special in mind, he would like a list of all the gays employed in state government. At the same time Mecham agreed with one of his appointees that working women caused divorce, saying, "I believe that is a given fact." He told E. J. Montini, a columnist with the *Republic*, that when he was operating his dealership, he "always had a few hard working gals around."

A highly respected member of Mecham's staff commonly accepted to be gay immediately resigned following a loud meeting with the governor.

The next week U2, the popular singing group, gave money to the recall committee following a performance in Arizona.

In early April the black chairman of the state liquor board resigned to protest Alberto Rodriguez's allegedly issuing liquor licenses improperly in a return to "the good old days." Rodriguez admitted doing nothing to suppress gambling in Douglas when he was mayor. The state liquor department is responsible for enforcing gambling laws in Arizona.

The next week Steiger was taken off the state payroll while he worked out a settlement with his former wife, then was placed back on the day after the agreement was reached.

The following day Rodriguez was withdrawn from consideration. Mecham said the senate committee could not give him a fair hearing.

*Republic* columnist Montini reported that Corbin was having to delay criminal investigations because his staff was spending so much time investigating the backgrounds of Mecham's appointees.

Mecham attacked Art Hamilton saying the house minority leader made "a fool of himself" by delivering his speech critical of Mecham for defending his use of the word "pickaninny."

Mecham denied he had a hit list of legislators.

In late April Corbin announced that Mecham did not knowingly break the law in paying Craft though Craft was required to return the money.

A few days later Sam Stanton revealed Mecham's unsavory dealings as a businessman.

These relatively minor events filled in the time between the major gaffes of the Mecham administration during its first months.

> *"Certain people would vote for Evan Mecham even if he raped a nun on the courthouse steps."*
> —JOE LANE

> *You've had your day. It's a one-day event. It's over, folks. Your one day is over. Your one day is over. It's not an event. You made it an event, it's over. Your day is over. We're on positive things.*
> —EVAN MECHAM *to reporters*

> *This has gone from day-to-day shooting himself in the foot to blowing his brains out.*
> —Republican legislator, unattributed

# 11

Steve Benson knew that the LDS Church had not sanctioned the candidacy of Evan Mecham and that the governor did not serve with the church's imprimatur. Benson was troubled by those Mormons in Arizona who made support of Evan Mecham the test of religious fidelity.

His grandfather, LDS President Ezra Taft Benson, had been to the governor's inauguration, but Benson knew that was no more significant than a Catholic bishop's attending the inauguration of a new Catholic governor. W. Cleon Skousen, Mecham's mentor, author of *The Making of America* and of *The Naked Communist*, had also been present.

There is a portion of the LDS Church, 10 percent or so, that believes a good Mormon must be of the right political persuasion to be true to the church. Skousen is its spokesman; Mecham, his disciple.

In *Come Back America* Mecham acknowledges his debt to Skousen. Mecham regularly donates to Skousen's National Center for Constitutional Studies, which has been "likened to a spruced-up John Birch Society" and "prizes his autographed collection of Skousen's books. . . ."

In 1979 the Mormon Church banned Skousen's National Center for Constitutional Studies from holding its meetings on church property, reportedly out of concern that his extremist teachings were being too closely associated with the church in general and that such meetings in church buildings implied approval of his program.

During a fund raiser for Mecham Skousen had "solemnly affirmed to a largely Mormon audience . . . that God foretold the gubernatorial candidate that he would attain the governorship to help save America from going to hell in the handbasket of socialism," Mormon writer Eduardo Pagan later wrote. Pagan said that "Skousen referred to Mecham as 'a modern day Isaiah' who also was 'beaten, spat upon, and persecuted for being a prophet.' "

Crismon Lewis, the editor of the *Latter-day Sentinel*, remarked to Steve Benson after Mecham's election, "I'm sure if you were to visit with [the governor] personally, he would share with you his story of why he decided to run. To the world, it looked like vain ambition. To the many who try to follow [spiritual] promptings in their lives, they knew there was another dimension to the decision."

One Mormon once tried to convince Pagan that "everything that's taking place is a continuation of the War in Heaven—read Ether in the Book of Mormon."

In *Come Back America* Mecham outlines his plans for saving the United States, based in substantial part on Skousen's teachings, from which he liberally quotes. Mecham proposes a constitutional amendment called the States' Bill of Rights. This would establish a Constitutional Compliance Committee that would assume the role of the U.S. Supreme Court in deciding what laws are constitutional. Congress would be required to pass legislation enacting the committee's "recommendations." Any member of Congress refusing to support such legislation would "be removed from office within 30 days." The plan would eliminate the Federal Reserve Bank and repeal the federal income tax. Social Security would be voluntary. The United States currency would be placed on a gold/silver standard, and all government borrowing would be outlawed.

Mecham did not campaign in 1986 on these issues, and almost no one in Arizona was aware of them.

The effect of Mecham's incumbency was immediately apparent in subtle ways throughout state government. Fellow employees whose religions were previously unknown emerged as unthinking, dogmatic supporters of the governor and were learned to be LDS. Regardless of the chain of authority in departments, the Mormon state employees tended to act in unison and were the first to meet the new Mecham department heads. Very quickly people who had worked together in harmony for years stopped speaking in the presence of Mormon co-workers because they were suspected, not without reason, of serving as spies.

Shirley Whitlock, president of the Arizona Eagle Forum and a devout Mormon, said, "[H]ow sad it is to see a member of the church join the stone throwers of the media in their campaign to vilify and destroy Gov. Mecham." She charged that Mormon critics of Mecham were a threat to the church and associated them with "fault-finders, shirkers, commandment-breakers, and apostate cliques."

It was Whitlock who, within weeks of the inauguration of Evan Mecham, wrote the church in Salt Lake City to ask that action be taken against Steve Benson.

The effect of these attacks on fellow Mormons was to silence large numbers of the membership of the church as they became disenchanted with Mecham. His supporters were the most vocal Latter-day Saints and were so effective that no prominent Mormon in the last days of Mecham's administration spoke out in support of his removal.

Benson, because of his impeccable credentials, was in a position to publicly speak. Criticizing was also his job.

As Benson watched the Mecham administration in operation, he was both amused and aghast. Mecham had a large autographed portrait of himself behind his chair in his office. Beside the elevators on the Ninth Floor was a huge picture of Mecham with a misidentified black athlete. Benson thought the picture hung there so Mecham could see it and reassure himself that he was not a racist.

Benson's first scathing Mecham cartoon had been run in March 1987, two months after Mecham took office. Entitled "Cro-Mecham Man (A Handy Field Guide)," it depicted the governor as a Neanderthal with a club, small mind, and short sight.

Benson drew three nationally syndicated cartoons a week on national and international issues, so his Mecham cartoons were not the steady stream his detractors want to believe, but he acknowledges doing double duty on some days to run a local Mecham cartoon. There was compensation toward the end of the administration when he was able to distribute his Mecham cartoons nationally.

In the spring of 1987 Benson received a telephone call at his office at the *Republic.* "This is Grandpa," President Benson said. He asked about the political situation in Arizona.

Benson knew his grandfather had more important things to do than worry about Evan Mecham. This was the first indication he had seen that there was any interest in the governor on the part of the church.

"Evan Mecham is his own worst enemy," Steve Benson said.

"Well, tell me about it."

For half an hour Benson told his grandfather how, in his opinion, Mecham had dug his own hole. He received no reaction, just a friendly thank-you at the conclusion of the conversation.

Benson met with his grandfather at a family gathering later that spring at a time when many of the governor's supporters were attempting to draw parallels between what was taking place with Mecham and the difficulties Ezra Taft Benson had experienced when he had been secretary of agriculture under Dwight D. Eisenhower. Both were religious men under attack by the infidel press, they were saying. The future president of the Mormon Church had received his fair measure of criticism for speaking frankly. Benson asked him about that.

"Well, Steven," his grandfather said, "Evan Mecham has made more political enemies than is necessary." He added that though he had his own troubles, "I would never personally attack my enemies."

Benson concluded from this that his grandfather's view was that Mecham had unduly alienated the press.

Mecham asserts that "Pat Murphy has got [Steve Benson] under his Satanic influence." He calls Benson "mean" and "venomous."

Pat Murphy is visibly angry at such attacks. "Steve Benson is his own man," he states. He points out that Benson "is the most devout man I know."

Benson was troubled by the actions of so many members of his faith who were tying the church's lot to Mecham's. Though he received ugly telephone calls and letters, he also received letters from Mormons who spoke out against Mecham and found themselves verbally attacked by fellow church members as a consequence.

Nothing had prepared Benson for dealing with his current dilemma. It was growing-up time and a painful one at that.

> *If you were inundated on a day-to-day basis with the antics of this country bumpkin who has shown himself unequipped to be governor, I believe you could understand my feelings more accurately.*
> —STEVE BENSON *to his parents*

> *The governor has some institutionalized demons that he believes in; I think he does believe that the press is out to get him. And if the press can be made an issue, then the debate becomes "Is the press fair or unfair?" not whether Governor Mecham is doing his job or not. But after a while he's going to run out of demons.*
> —PAT MURPHY, *publisher of the* Republic *and the* Gazette

# 12

When Evan Mecham attacks the "Phoenix Newspapers" and their pervasive influence over the economic and political life of Phoenix and of the state, he is attacking the *Republic* and the *Gazette* of the 1950's and 1960's. By the time of the death of publisher Eugene Pulliam in 1975 the compelling influence of the two papers was in serious decline, a decline that continued under Darrow "Duke" Tully, who resigned in disgrace in December 1985.

In addition to the two largest papers in the Valley of the Sun, there is the Scottsdale *Progress* and the Mesa *Tribune* as well as two talk radio stations and local television stations. Dave Hampton with radio station KFYI was known as an energetic reporter. Lew Ruggiero with Channel 12 was feared by print journalists because of his tenacity and ability to find a story they had missed.

The *New Times*, distributed free each week in Phoenix, ran a steady stream of Mecham stories. In addition, the two Tucson papers, the *Arizona Daily Star* and the Tucson *Citizen*, maintained reporters at the Capitol.

The days when the *Republic* and the *Gazette* had the news all to themselves were long over by the time Evan Mecham was at last elected governor. They were still the dominant source of news, but they no longer had a monopoly. There were plenty of hungry reporters and aggressive publishers looking to scoop them.

Both Sam Stanton and Mike Murphy say that the single biggest lost opportunity in the conduct of the Mecham administration was its failure to play the media against itself through the systematic leaking of stories. Instead, Mecham lumped all the media together and treated them with equal contempt. Though he attacked the "Phoenix Newspapers" as being most unfair, he had not been supported by any of the state's nineteen dailies, and both the Tucson papers called for his resignation before either the *Republic* or the *Gazette*.

Neither of Pat Murphy's papers endorsed Evan Mecham, and Murphy candidly acknowledges that he feared for the worst under his administration; but on the night of his election victory the publisher personally typed a letter to Mecham and had it hand delivered. Because of Mecham's constant attacks on his papers, Murphy says he felt "a special responsibility" to write it.

It begins, "All thinking Arizonans will join in congratulating you on your victory, and in wishing you the best of luck in your new challenge." It concludes with "Differences aside [four former governors and I] were bound together in a common sense of responsibility to the state. My hope is that we will find that common ground as you embark on this new adventure."

The letter was not published in his papers, nor was it made a topic of discussion during the Mecham administration. It was instead a private communication that Pat Murphy presents as an indication that he did not set out to attack Evan Mecham.

An examination of the first few months' coverage of Mecham reveals the usual photographs of a governor meeting with members of the legislature and visitors, routine coverage of his speaking engagements, and the customary courtesy reporting that all governors receive.

The day after the election the *Republic* reported that during the campaign Mecham had "talked about managing the state in a spirit of 'cooperation rather than confrontation.'" The editorial that day said, "It is one thing to run a campaign and win. It is quite another to govern and lead. The choices are his."

In early December the *Republic* came out in favor of Babbitt's hiring Mecham's transition staff so they would not have to continue working without pay. The day of the inauguration the lead *Republic* editorial called for support of Evan Mecham. The editorial the next day commented that Mecham's speech had contained something for everybody and was a good beginning.

Several days later, though noting the ineptness of the firing of former department heads in state government, an editorial commented that Mecham's administration appeared to be shaping up. Later that month, when members of the black National Newspaper Publishers Association canceled its convention midstream and vowed to return home to write editorials condemning Mecham's conduct, Pat Murphy castigated them in his weekly column, referring to their leaving Phoenix "in a huff" and saying, "They should know better than to show political passions."

Reporters for the *Republic* and the *Gazette*, both on the record and in confidence, state categorically that they were not directed or manipulated in their Mecham coverage. Don Harris, Mecham's favorite reporter, states without equivocation that he and the other reporters acted independently.

Sam Stanton confesses with some reluctance that at one point, out of a sense of fairness, he treated the constant conspiracy allegations from Mecham supporters as a possibility and investigated it as a legitimate news story. He found nothing.

Pat Murphy states, and his staff at all levels confirm, that the publisher is not involved in the day-to-day conduct of either news reporting or the formation of individual editorial positions.

In mid-February *Republic* columnist E. J. Montini wrote a column saying that the paper's reporters and editors had been asked by Pat Murphy not to appear to be picking on the governor. Montini then wrote that three state employees had been in contact with the columnist because of alleged improper and irregular personal questions Mecham appointees had been asking them.

An examination of the uncensored personal notes of working reporters for the *Republic* and the *Gazette* disclose occasional personal notes from Pat Murphy with "For your information" articles from other papers but no instructions or directives. Sam Stanton's editor, Laurie Roberts, says that she never received directions, directly or by implication, on how to cover the administration. The Evan Mecham coverage by the *Republic* was generated almost entirely by her and the Capitol reporters she supervised.

Sam Stanton says that reporters from across the country would arrive in Phoenix convinced that he and the others were creating the controversy or slanting the news to make Mecham look bad, only to shake their heads in disbelief at the reality a few days later.

Because Mecham had attacked the *Republic* and the *Gazette* so vociferously, Pat Murphy soon found himself part of the story. He accounts for the large volume of coverage of the Mecham administration to the news it was generating and also to the fact that his own papers had to cover Mecham's accusations against them and him. Murphy was often interviewed by his own reporters. He found it unusual and disturbing.

In March 1987 Murphy delivered before the Arizona Chamber of Commerce a speech in which he publicly attacked Evan Mecham for his conduct as governor. This was at the time that columnist John Kolbe had been declared a "non-person" and Ron Bellus was talking about a credentials system for reporters. Mecham had also refused to allow Murphy's papers to send the reporters they wished with the governor on his trip to Honduras. He had tried to maneuver the *Republic* into sending Don Harris rather than Sam Stanton. By this time reporter Mike Murphy was routinely filing public disclosure requests with Bellus to obtain Mecham's itinerary.

Pat Murphy's speech was covered by Sam Stanton and Don Harris. Murphy said that "the next four years will involve a bruising collision between the brutish, ideological juggernaut being fueled by the governor and his advisers. . . ." Mecham's advisers were marked by "paranoia . . . ," ". . . isolation from reality . . . ," and "small-minded vindictiveness."

But Pat Murphy came out in opposition to Mecham's recall, stating, "He was elected for four years, we ought to let him have four years."

Asked to respond, Mecham said, "I don't think [Pat Murphy] has the ability to look at anything but what he himself deems as the answer, and he appoints himself as the arbiter and judge. The people of Arizona have spoken and elected a governor. I wasn't his choice. He would like to get me out of the office. He will never be happy or cease. I don't believe he has the ability to change. He must be an unhappy man having to look at me on the pages of his newspaper every day in one form or another. And I feel sorry for him, because he has to be very unhappy. If I could help him, I would. I wish I knew what to do for him."

Much later, in a very different forum, Mecham testified publicly that he believed Pat Murphy hated him.

On April 19, 1987, Pat Murphy went public with Mecham's tantrums. In his column he wrote that in a meeting the previous week Mecham "showed [behind closed doors] a temper he conceals in public," that he had repeatedly pounded his fist on the table in front of legislators, accused Republicans of disloyalty, and threatened to run candidates against them. One legislator, Murphy reported, "walked out in disgust and slammed the door" as he left.

Murphy has been criticized for his anti-Mecham speeches and columns. He acknowledges it was an unusual role for a publisher. He defends his actions by pointing out that Mecham's tactics effectively silenced the business community in Arizona. Almost until the end none spoke out even though the negative influence of the governor's conduct and policies on the state was readily apparent.

As Murphy sees it, at one point Ed Buck, leading the recall effort, was the most influential person in the state. "What does that say about leadership in Arizona?"

In almost the same breath with which Evan Mecham attacks the "Phoenix Newspapers" he attacks the Phoenix 40. Pat Murphy approached Eugene Pulliam in 1972 and suggested the formation of a group of local business leaders that would act in the best interests of Phoenix and the state. Heads of the largest banks and utilities and others formed the group. At one time four editors of the *Republic* and the *Gazette* were members.

Murphy denies having attended a meeting in years though he is still a member emeritus. The Phoenix 40 erred, in Murphy's opinion, by electing to keep its rolls secret and by conducting its meetings in secrecy. Such behavior has only fed suspicion about the group and its purposes. It has also erred in denying membership to women, blacks, and Hispanics.

Murphy believes the motives of the Phoenix 40 are worthy and points out that it supported the expansion of the attorney general's office in the early 1970's and the creation of the state grand jury, but he says that its methods have greatly reduced its effectiveness. Murphy ran articles critical of the Phoenix 40, and three years before Mecham was elected the *Republic* disclosed the membership of the group; by 1989 the Phoenix 40 had abandoned closed meetings and secret membership. Members of the Phoenix 40 are not the power brokers Mecham believes they are, according to Murphy.

The publisher of the *Republic* and the *Gazette* met a second time with Mecham in May 1987 to review Mecham's "proof" that the two papers were biased against him. They met in the basement of the Phoenix Sheraton for a ninety-minute lunch. Murphy was "uncomfortable about representations the governor might make," so he took the corporate attorney along with him.

At the meeting Mecham did most of the talking, "boasting" in large measure about his accomplishments as governor. He made accusations about the coverage of the two Phoenix papers and gave Murphy 376 articles with comments. "This is the proof of your unfairness and inaccuracies," he said.

The comments were found to be of no value, consisting as they did of Bellus's opinion that the story was unfair or slanted. Bellus had written comments such as "So what?," "This stinks," "Another Stanton story. Need I say more?" Murphy had all the articles checked and determined that none was inaccurate.

Mecham made a show of canceling his personal subscription to the *Republic* following an article critical of his wife's attire on a trip with him, though Bellus notes that Mecham demanded that all the papers be clipped and on Mecham's desk by nine every morning. Murphy reports that the papers experienced approximately five hundred cancellations protesting their coverage of the governor while the two papers as a whole had the second-highest growth in the *Republic*'s one-hundred-year history.

As the first legislative session came to an end and Arizona moved into the only summer of the Mecham administration, Murphy could not "recall when the newspaper[s] had ever been under such an attack."

Mecham is unabashed in asserting, "The Phoenix newspaper monopoly has had my political destruction as its goal for many years." He acknowledges meeting with Pat Murphy on two occasions following his election "to try to arrange a truce. At each meeting he said I need only show him where they were not fair and he would correct it. After each meeting the attacks were intensified. Even after giving [Murphy] a few hundred examples of their slanted coverage he [*sic*] maintains that they were fair."

Mecham claims that newspaper reporters routinely slant the news and look to the publisher for the angle they are to take. He often repeats a story that when he ran the *Evening American*, his reporters would solicit his instructions on how to slant the news. He says he responded with "Why don't you see if it will stand straight up on its own?"

Mecham blames the poor national and international opinion of him on the local newspaper coverage. As for Pat Murphy, Mecham holds that Murphy believes he is under no obligation to report the truth. Asked that very question, Pat Murphy responds by saying, "We have a responsibility [to report the truth]. . . . To this day Evan Mecham has been unable to document a campaign of lies or untruths."

Murphy adds, "Evan Mecham is the victim of his own hand."

The private contacts between Mecham and the reporters who covered him daily were, for the most part, not unpleasant. Sam Stanton recalls that even on the worst days Mecham would joke with the press. On April Fools' Day the *New Times* ran a spoof that listed the governor's office number and encouraged readers to call.

Stanton, Mike Murphy, and other reporters went to see the governor thinking he would be upset over the article. Instead, Mecham laughed and sang a cheery song from his childhood. His actions appeared to be entirely spontaneous. Instead of anger at the *New Times* spoof, Mecham had his staff simply refer callers to another number, which turned out to be at the *New Times*'s office.

At 2:00 P.M. Mecham held an impromptu press conference in which he declared "Press Corpse Appreciation Day," announced that he had just vetoed the bill repealing one cent of the sales tax, informed the reporters that he was now a sustaining member of the Mecham Watchdog Committee, announced he would be performing in concert with the Doobie Brothers, who had canceled their appearance in Arizona the previous week, and declared the day Round Earth Day, to be headed by Jim Cooper, his education lobbyist who had informed the house Education Committee that teachers did not have the right to correct parents if they taught at home that the earth was flat.

A few days later one of the Doobie Brothers called Stanton to learn what had happened because he was thinking about suing Mecham.

Mike Murphy tells how Mecham once spotted the reporter's dilapidated truck and said, "Mike, you and I have to have a talk." Mecham might have been governor, but in his heart he still had the moves of a car dealer. Murphy took it as a sincere gesture.

Not long after the Heuisler press conference Stanton went to Douglas to check into the background of Alberto Rodriguez, the new head of the state liquor department. Some supported their former mayor, but even more did not. People would ask Stanton if he was the Phoenix reporter and then pull him into an office and relate hair-raising stories, most of which he could not confirm.

Mecham was to withdraw the Rodriguez nomination only moments before the senate committee hearing was to commence. The woman who claimed Rodriguez had raped her years before was there to testify against him. Mecham says that is an example of just how far his enemies will go, to use a mentally unbalanced woman to get one of his nominees.

Sam Stanton recalls interviewing the woman, who calmly described the rape and said Rodriguez was not fit to hold office.

Mecham had always held out his skill as a private businessman and promised he would apply those abilities to his performance as governor. On May 1 Sam Stanton ran a story that provided Arizona with fresh insight into the kinds of business practices Mecham considered proper and sound.

In 1981 Mecham had purchased a building in Tacoma, Washington along with two local partners. His son Dennis ran a car dealership there for just over one year, but it was not a success and closed. The partnership then rented the building to a church and to a carpet outlet.

In 1984 one of the partners sued Mecham and claimed that Mecham had taken $8,500 of the partnership's money to purchase jewelry for himself. He also alleged that Mecham was mismanaging the partnership's money and had secretly borrowed $130,000 against the building, which he then gave to Mecham Pontiac in Glendale. Mecham denied the allegations.

The suit was dropped when Mecham agreed to buy out the partners. The partner to whom he owed the payments told Stanton that all twenty-six installments from Mecham were late and that the governor had not paid at all since taking office. The partner had filed for foreclosure.

Mecham had not listed the Tacoma property on his personal disclosure statement. Asked about that omission, Mecham responded, "I don't have to list [the property] separately." His position was that the property was owned by Mecham Pontiac and that he had listed the car dealership.

Asked about the late and missing payments, Mecham told Stanton it was an inadvertent error by his bookkeeper, the same story he had told the *Republic* reporter some months before when explaining his unpaid taxes.

# 13

As the session progressed, Joe Lane was hearing more and more that Mecham was perceived as devious and underhanded in his dealings. Legislators returning from meetings with the governor would check with one another to learn what had been said and promised. It was soon clear that Mecham was inclined to speak out of both sides of his mouth.

Mecham was also perceived as bizarre by some members of the legislature. Senator Hays and Senator Lunn went to see Mecham about an issue but were not able to bring it up. Mecham was ranting about John Kolbe, calling him that "son of a bitch" over and over. Hays did not know Mormons used that kind of language. He found Mecham's conduct so bizarre and irrational he was grateful he had brought along a witness.

At the same meeting Lunn observed that Mecham was in a fifteen-minute "rage." The governor "seemed almost possessed" on the subject of Kolbe and was incapable of hearing what they had come to discuss.

As Mecham's reputation for both deceit and strange behavior grew, few legislators would meet with him alone.

During a subsequent legislative leadership meeting with Mecham, Senator Lunn viewed the governor with fresh skepticism. When he heard Mecham announce that he wanted to abolish RUCO, Arizona's consumer watchdog agency, Lunn told Mecham that would be politically unwise. RUCO was very popular, and its strongest supporters were retirees who depended on it to keep utility costs down.

Mecham had said with a smile, "When I put Ted Humes in there it won't make any difference." Lunn had been taken aback and went public with Mecham's observation. Mecham accused him of having "a creative memory." Soon Lunn began hearing that Mecham was talking to people in his district, attacking him and telling them Mecham planned to recruit an opponent to run against him in the next primary.

Hays voted against Humes for confirmation. Later he was persuaded to vote for Max Hawkins, a move for which he never forgave himself. In voting for Hawkins, Hays delivered a speech in which he said that "mediocrity is not a disqualification under the law but ought to be."

There was a meeting in March of that first session between Mecham, Steve Twist, Al Heinz, the executive director of the Arizona Prosecuting Attorneys Association, Representative John Wettaw, and Donna Carlson to discuss the drug bill that the governor had adopted as his own. Hearings were about to occur.

Wettaw was a professor at Northern Arizona University in Flagstaff and chairman of the house Appropriations Committee. Mecham had previously complained to Joe Lane about Wettaw's serving in such a position since a significant percent of the state budget went to the universities. It seemed to Mecham to be a clear conflict of interest.

At this time Lane had very serious reservations about Mecham concerning the university budget. He thought that Mecham had an antiuniversity bias and that his desire to restrict its budget was not just related to fiscal responsibility. His attack on Wettaw was the same sort of thing.

Lane had to admit that Mecham had a point, however; there was an appearance of impropriety. It was something of which both the house leadership and Wettaw were aware. As a result, he bent over backward to be fair. Wettaw was simply the best budget man the house had and had proved his worth again and again. In Lane's opinion, Wettaw never let his position with the university affect his performance for the legislature.

At the March meeting Carlson heard Wettaw inform the governor that he was reluctant to schedule his committee's meeting on the drug bill because he did not believe he had the votes for passage. On hearing this, Mecham pointed his finger at Wettaw and said, "Perhaps some legislators don't want to pass the bill because they're trying to protect their drug-using friends." Twist was shocked, as was Carlson. They all looked at one another in stunned amazement.

Wettaw's hands started shaking, and Carlson recalls that he left at once.

Wettaw stormed over to the house and shouted at Lane's staff. Lane had to soothe everyone and calm Wettaw though he knew Wettaw's anger was justified.

"Donna," Lane said when he called her, "what the hell is going on up there on the Ninth Floor? . . . Don't you folks realize how hard it is to keep our caucus together when half of them are already mad at the governor, and he pulls this kind of a deal?"

She understood, and in fact, so did Lane. It was Mecham who did not seem to realize, or care about, the effect his conduct was having on the legislature.

When Donna Carlson joined the administration, there had been no organization and no basic understanding of how state government worked. In addition Mecham did not delegate authority and had no compunction about overriding a subordinate.

Mecham's reputation for cooperating with no one was well established before he became governor. It was, however, Carlson's job to create cooperation with the legislature or, that failing, to create its appearance.

She knew that it was widely believed by the Republicans in the legislature that Mecham was forcing them to vote on issues that could not pass for the sole purpose of building a record he could use against them when he ran his own brand of Republican in their next primaries.

She also knew it was true. More than once she had heard Mecham say, "We'll see that they'll have some opposition."

And these were the men and women who were supposed to be his allies, the people of his own party, and the people she was called on to deal with every day.

Shortly after the inauguration Carlson spotted an odd list of names proposed for appointment to a state regulatory commission for bonds. She knew the proposed nominees were connected to Hugh Gregan. This had the appearance of a payoff and was potentially dynamite. Both she and special assistant Edith Richardson violently objected and were told the names would not be submitted.

In February 1987, just a few weeks later, Sam Stanton called her and asked if she knew anything about a large loan to the campaign. Carlson took a deep breath, lied, and said she did not.

Stanton, in fact, wrote an article mentioning a large loan; but he could not pin it down, and he could not establish if anything illegal had occurred. When asked to be more specific after acknowledging he had taken out personal loans, Mecham had been quoted as saying, "I honestly can't tell you." And that was the end of it for a time.

But Carlson could not escape the feeling that this would not go away.

Despite her advice to Mecham, she suspected the loan had not been reported and was so certain she did not check the reports herself to confirm it. She just did not want to know.

When she looked back on the campaign, it was apparent to her that Horace Lee Watkins had been the bagman.

Donna Carlson enjoyed very little of that session. She found it difficult to learn Mecham's position on issues, and when she went to the legislature, the members expected her to explain the governor's latest gaffe. She made excuses and tried to smooth things over.

While she was trying to build goodwill, or at least a workable coalition, she watched Mecham tear it down at almost every opportunity. Not long into the session he assigned his various aides the task of lobbying individual members of the legislature to gain support for his budget and the repeal of one cent of the sales tax. Mecham said, "I want you to take notes on what they say so we can compile a report for their constituents."

Special assistant Edith Richardson did just that following a meeting with Senator Hal Runyan. When Mecham saw the notes, he picked up the telephone and called Bob Usdane. In no time Runyan knew what had happened, and word swept the legislature that Mecham's staff was spying on them.

On one occasion Carlson was in the position of being unable to justify Mecham's conduct or tell the truth about it to a group of lawmakers. She evaded their questions and was ashamed of herself for it. Her consternation was apparent. One of the legislators finally said to her, "Mrs. Carlson, why don't you just lie to us?"

Legislators tell of her breaking down in tears in their offices over what was going on.

Her situation on the Ninth Floor was unenviable. She was not trusted by many except Sam Steiger. Ron Bellus complained that she spent more time at the legislature than she did on the Ninth Floor. Since she was the legislative liaison, she was not troubled by that. But Bellus relates that he "bumped into her on several occasions in the capitol press corps office in the senate building just 'chatting away.' " Bellus's assistant reported back to him that she had spotted Carlson in the press room as well. Bellus saw no reason for her to be there.

It was important that loyal members of the governor's staff not be seen speaking to the "enemy," as the press and almost everyone not hired by Mecham came to be known.

> *To know Evan Mecham is to distrust him.*
>
> —SENATOR GREG LUNN
>
> *He's got a hit list.*
>
> —SENATOR ALAN
> STEPHENS,
> *senate minority leader*
>
> *He assembled every hanger-on and those
> whose only qualification was loyalty to Evan
> Mecham.*
>
> —SENATOR GREG LUNN

# 14

Toward the end of that first session the senate Republican caucus held a closed meeting with the governor in an attempt to discuss and, it was hoped, to resolve problems. Mecham had been soliciting pressure from his constituents on the senators and had recently done so in a mailing. In the caucus Mecham made a pitch for them all to work together. Senator Lunn confronted him on the mailing. The question was put to Mecham directly but politely.

Mecham exploded. "You've never helped me!" he shouted, directing his comment to the stunned group.

As Lunn's colleagues brought back with them a steady stream of disturbing stories about their meetings with the governor, Lunn was utterly shocked to hear, within a month of the inauguration, members of the legislature talking about Mecham's "psychosis" and what it involved.

During his first month in office Mecham had instructed his staff not to discuss the Martin Luther King holiday flap. He was called upon, however, to defend and to explain his actions over and over. Clearly he was exasperated by a phenomenon he considered a creature of the media and was frustrated that it would not disappear.

Initially Mecham had defended "pickaninny" for its use in "an historical sense," but on at least two occasions he said he found nothing wrong with the word. It was clear the ethnic slur was acceptable to him. The word continued to dog him.

By this time it was increasingly apparent to large numbers of those who dealt with the governor on a regular basis that Evan Mecham could not handle controversy. As each crisis occurred, Mecham responded to reporters' questions in a thin-lipped grimace with incomplete, frequently incoherent sentences. Ironically, he sought more exposure, apparently feeling he could turn events to his favor by getting his message out, as he put it.

Mecham did not handle stress well. There were more than hints that he could not cope. Each week, virtually each day, he lashed out at his enemies, seemingly convinced there was nothing improper in his utterances or conduct—that the fault lay with outside forces that sought to destroy him, the same forces that had for so long denied him his due.

In 1987 Representative Jim Skelly was chairman of the house Judiciary Committee, as he had been for a number of years. A self-styled "right-winger" best known for his dogged opposition to abortion, he had supported Mecham in every gubernatorial primary he had ever entered until 1986, when Skelly supported his longtime friend Burton Barr.

It did not take long for Skelly to become concerned about the new administration. Except for Donna Carlson, he viewed the Ninth Floor staff as "amateur night." He and two colleagues attended a meeting with Mecham during those first weeks. As they left to see the newly retired chief justice, his female companion said to them, "Now we're going to talk to a nice person."

Chief Assistant Attorney General Steve Twist, Senator Tony West, and Representative Jim Skelly had met during the previous summer. West wanted to strengthen the state's already tough drug laws. West drafted a bill that he and Skelly were to sponsor in their respective houses. West suggested that they give the drug bill to Barr for use in his campaign, and they all agreed; but Barr elected not to make it an issue.

Mecham had campaigned against drugs, but when he took office, he had no drug program. The three Republicans agreed to let Mecham latch on to West's bill and take it as his own, claiming it as one of his greatest accomplishments that session. Skelly recalls, however, that Mecham alienated so many of the legislators that the bill nearly failed to pass. The Democrats in particular peeled off in droves.

One of the key elements of the bill, from Mecham's point of view, empowered the governor to appoint special pro tem drug judges to the superior court. Mecham and the new chief justice, Democrat Frank Gordon, had verbally sparred over it. The two had previously experienced their share of difficulty on the Bicentennial Commission. Gordon opposed any circumventing of the state's merit selection of judges.

Skelly recognized that he could not get the drug bill out of his committee with that provision, and the attorney general's office and county prosecutors were suspicious of any effort by Mecham to acquire a measure of control over the judiciary. At a meeting with Mecham, Al Heinz, Donna Carlson, and several state legislators, including Joe Lane's chief of staff, Rick Collins, Skelly had outlined the trouble. Mecham had behaved "like a little kid" at learning the bill would not clear committee. Carlson recalls that the governor "threw a fit."

Mecham said petulantly, "We'll just have to let the bill drop." That made no sense at all to Skelly. Mecham became increasingly obnoxious. It seemed to Skelly that Mecham childishly wanted to take his ball and go home if they would not play the game by his rules.

A shouting match ensued during which Mecham attacked several legislators. He launched into a tirade against Joe Lane, shaking his finger and saying, "I know more about politics in my little finger than Joe Lane does." Then: "I'm going to get Joe Lane because he doesn't have any balls." Those present could not believe what they were witnessing.

One of Mecham's troubled appointments was Russell Ritchie, named to be director of the Department of Revenue. His first nominee for the position, Rex Waite, had withdrawn from the job the day he reported for work. Waite had previously headed a bank in southern Arizona that had declared bankruptcy. At the time of his appointment he was running a Swensen's ice cream parlor.

No sooner had Ritchie been named than Mike Murphy of the *Gazette* disclosed that he had not filed his federal or Arizona taxes on time. In addition, the company of which he said he was president had had its license first suspended for lacking insurance and then revoked for operating after the license was suspended. It also owed more than five thousand dollars in back taxes. A few days later the *Republic* revealed that Ritchie was really the treasurer of the company, not the president, as he claimed.

The incumbent acting director of the Department of Revenue was quoted over the weekend as saying that it could be a violation of the law not to file a state income tax return on time. He was fired by Mecham the following Monday.

Mecham's appointees had been under constant attack, and he appeared personally to testify before the senate committee that was considering Ritchie's nomination. Donna Carlson and others on his staff had urged Mecham to withdraw his name. Despite Mecham's intense personal pitch, the committee voted eight to one to refuse Ritchie the position.

Mecham was enraged. He returned to his office and a short time later called a press conference in which he said, "I think you can say that the Senate is, by this vote, trying to reject their governor." To a shocked gathering he then announced that the number two man at Revenue would be the acting director and that Mecham was appointing Ritchie in his place, a position that did not require senate confirmation.

Evan Mecham's own staff was stunned by the stupidity of it.

In March of that first session a sixteen-year-old high school student, Todd Sprague* founder and president of his school's Teen-age Republican Club and regular contributor to *Footprints*, a Christian-oriented political newsletter, announced he was organizing an Evan Mecham Fan Club. A few days later Sprague held his organizational meeting with fifty supporters of the governor in attendance. Sprague wore his "I love Ev" T-shirt. Mecham aide Mac Matheson and Mecham's son Dennis were there.

Asked what he thought of the new club, Mecham said, "[T]hat kid [Todd Sprague] is dynamite."

It was at 10:15 A.M. on Saturday, August 1, 1987, that Representative Chris Herstam knew Evan Mecham would never survive as governor.

Months before that momentous, personal revelation it had seemed to Herstam that he was cast in the role of opponent to Governor Evan Mecham. "We were destined by the issues to be at odds," he later said. As chairman of the house Ways and Means Committee, Herstam could not support Mecham's sales tax rollback on principle alone. Before the two had met, the gauntlet had been tossed. Herstam had been one of the few Republican legislators who did not sign the Mecham endorsement sheet.

Just a few weeks into the new term Herstam wrote a column for a community paper critical of Mecham's proposed tax cut and of some of his appointments. Jim Colter came down to speak with him on a Friday. Colter told Herstam that he was appalled by the column, that it was not something he would expect from him. Colter had become visibly agitated and pounded on Herstam's desk as he said, "This big-spending, high-tax Republican-controlled legislature has got to be brought under control!"

It was clear to Herstam that he was not going to be Mecham's kind of Republican.

Immediately after that Herstam called Burt Kruglick, chairman of the state Republican party, and told him what had just taken place. He told the chairman that the Republican party in Arizona was headed for disaster.

---

*The name has been changed since the individual identified here as Todd Sprague was a juvenile during the Mecham administration.

"[Mecham] is going over a cliff and is going to take this party with him unless we do something."

"What do you want me to do about it?" Kruglick asked.

Herstam told him that Mecham was going to be at war with the legislature, that they should start to distance themselves from the governor. Kruglick thanked him for the call.

As the legislative session progressed, Herstam had occasion to call Kruglick on two other similar occasions. On those occasions Kruglick did not thank him.

At about the time of the Colter visit Herstam attended a meeting on the Ninth Floor with the chairmen of the various house committees. Mecham told them what he wanted. One of the representatives disagreed with Mecham concerning his comments on education, and Mecham lost his temper. He shouted at the representative and slammed his hand on the table repeatedly.

Herstam recognized that he did not have much of a historical perspective since he had only been elected in 1982; but he still found Mecham's appointments absurd. Mecham, he concluded, gave no thought to what was good for Arizona. Everything, absolutely everything, was part of the grand conspiracy, from what Herstam could tell.

In February 1987 Herstam attended a semiprivate meeting with Mecham along with his senate counterpart, Jeff Hill. Mecham asked Herstam the status of a bill. Herstam indicated that he thought it might pass. Mecham replied, "Good," then turned to Hill and began a pointed conversation about the one-cent sales tax repeal, a bill Herstam had publicly opposed on many occasions. The conversation lasted for a time, and it seemed apparent to Herstam that Mecham was playing "a little game" to make a point by excluding him in an overtly rude manner.

The Democrats were "looking into a black hole" as that legislative session began since the Republicans controlled both houses and the Ninth Floor.

Other legislators who were to play prominent roles in subsequent events had their own experiences and observations of that first session. From Democratic Representative Debbie McCune's point of view as the session was well underway the Republicans behaved as if "they didn't need us." The Republicans were determined to make it work alone. She struggled not to take it all personally. The Democrats might have been the minority party, but heretofore they had always been a part of the process.

McCune was disappointed in what she observed in the new governor. It looked to her as if "he seemed to enjoy causing distress." She later said that Mecham "had a way of being confrontational that made people uncomfortable."

About a month into the session six or seven Democrats were asked to attend a luncheon with Mecham. McCune understood the occasion was arranged so the governor could say that he was including the Democrats in his administration. House Minority Leader Art Hamilton recalls that luncheon. It seemed to him that Mecham called it because he had heard that the Democrats were unhappy and he wanted to say they had met. Edith Richardson was there and passing out sandwiches when Mecham joined them. He announced to the gathering, "I have nothing to say but thought we should meet."

Mecham sat at the table, then turned to McCune and asked her aggressively, "Can you say the blessing?" as if she would not know how or might take exception.

Hamilton had nothing to say to Mecham, and the governor had nothing to say to him. Later Hamilton learned that Mecham had been offended because he did not eat. Hamilton responds, "I wasn't hungry."

It was apparent to McCune that her Republican colleagues recognized that their governor was not doing a competent job. She realized very quickly that the information she was receiving was valid only for the duration of the conversation when it applied to the governor's staff. "All sorts of stories" would come down from the Ninth Floor, and soon she was prepared to believe almost anything.

After a time she consulted with a psychologist to seek answers to the new governor's behavior.

Art Hamilton had first been elected house minority leader in 1981. When Mecham was elected governor, Hamilton realized that the state was "in for rough sledding." He knew Mecham to be rigid and an ideologue, but it did not occur to him that Mecham "would see himself as an imperial governor."

Hamilton acknowledges being angry when Mecham rescinded the Martin Luther King holiday. He had hoped that Mecham would grow into his new position. But Mecham had not been satisfied merely rescinding it. In Hamilton's opinion, he had gone out of his way to make this "a very personal issue."

Hamilton was nearly the only black member of the Arizona House of Representatives for many years and it was largely due to his efforts and the respect with which he was held that the house passed the Martin Luther King state holiday bill each year only to see it die in the senate.

Hamilton is critical of his Republican brethren. It seemed to him that "they erred by going along with Mecham." They tried to appease the man and with a "dictator-like mentality, the more you appease, the more he expects it." The Republicans "created the Mecham monster."

Carolyn Walker, the state's only black senator, was also a native of Arizona, had been a legislator since 1982, and was serving her first term in the senate that year. She viewed Mecham "as a buffoon." Not long into that first session she decided that he was also "meanspirited."

This is not an observation limited to political adversaries of either party. When assured that their comments will not be attributed, staunch legislative supporters of Mecham admit that he is "mean," "immature," subject to "temper tantrums," possessed of a certain "meanness," that "in the blink of an eye you were the enemy," that he was a "mean son of a gun."

Later fellow Mormon Representative Mark Killian delivered a speech regarding Mecham that spoke for more of those who voted with the governor than one would normally expect.

There is an aspect to the Mecham administration that even his most vocal critics are reluctant to discuss. The generally mediocre quality of Mecham's appointments was not the only problem with them. As one legislator put it in strictest confidence, "white trash" had come to the Capitol with Mecham.

Mecham's people lacked the common social graces and were usually attired in polyester. His appointees and staff were not known for intelligence. Explaining even routine matters required patience. Mispronounced and inappropriate English was as much the rule as not.

Many of those who dealt with Mecham and his staff on a daily basis found the experience socially demeaning. The absence of everyday politeness and common courtesy caused these contacts to become excruciating.

The vast majority of his personally selected cadre reflected the same qualities as their boss. They were known for their single-minded loyalty to their governor and their smug clannishness.

> *We usually back Republicans, but he's a different kind of Republican.*
> —WILLIAM L. RABY,
> *chairman, state*
> *Chamber of Commerce*
>
> *I'm different.*
> —EVAN MECHAM

# 15

Donna Carlson was responsible for preparing Mecham's veto messages and knew that he vetoed bills sponsored by fellow Republicans "as a way of punishing his legislative enemies."

Just before leaving the state at the end of that first session and without consulting the leadership in the legislature, Mecham vetoed five bills that "some legislators viewed as a kick in the teeth to loyal supporters. . . ." Mecham said he had been in a hurry to leave the state.

Mecham vetoed House Majority Leader Jim Ratliff's bill on utility liability even though Ratliff had been his most ardent supporter in the house and the only member of the house leadership to stand unswervingly by him. Asked to comment, a visibly angered Ratliff said, "My only message to the governor is, if he thinks that people advising him to veto [my bill] can help him run the state of Arizona better than I can, then let them."

Ratliff was not the only loyal Republican in leadership to suffer this fate. Mecham also vetoed Senate Majority Leader Bob Usdane's bill on city bonding authority. Usdane, who had been reported as very angry on receiving the news of the veto, put on a supportive face as he said, "I'd say that the cooperation was not great . . . but it's his prerogative" to veto bills.

Senator Greg Lunn had sponsored a superfund bill, one of the few meaningful environmental issues to reach any Arizona governor's desk, only to see Mecham veto it. Carlson wrote the governor's veto message, which talked about his opposition to new taxes. The real reason was Lunn's negative remarks concerning Mecham.

Lunn was summoned to see Mecham about that bill along with Representatives David Bartlett and Larry Hawke, who had also supported it. It was predicated on users' fees and would not have required a tax increase, in Lunn's view.

Lunn knew that he had not been sent for because Mecham was going to sign it, yet when their meeting started, the governor solicited their comments in support as if he were truly undecided.

But after the men spoke, Mecham said, "I want you to know there is nothing personal about this," as he vetoed the bill in their presence. Later Lunn heard that Mecham retold with glee the story of how he had stuck it to Lunn.

It was not just Mecham's adversaries or those he had offended, however, who found fault in his conduct. One staffer, a loyal supporter to the end and beyond, who worked on the Ninth Floor watched Mecham with regret. She observed that he valued loyalty above competence, and it troubled her.

Of the rank-and-file employees on the Ninth Floor, this staffer observed that just under half of them were LDS. The employees divided along religious lines in forming friendships. The Mormons saw themselves as more loyal to Mecham than the others.

Of the special assistants, Edith Richardson was "violently disliked" by many with whom she worked and was called the "Black Widow"; she was believed to make lists of enemies and used her friends to settle scores.

According to this loyal staffer, Colter was incompetent and had no business being chief of staff. Bellus was unable to do his job. Steiger's advice was not listened to often enough. Hawkins was a strange man with a vendetta and too much influence over the governor.

The employees were loyal and caring but incompetent and inept. Too many of the personalities were volatile, and that continually led to confrontation.

This Mecham supporter found the governor to be a good employer. He arrived each day with a smile and a kind word for everyone. He worked seven days a week, all day, with single-minded concentration and was a "dynamo of energy." He traveled throughout the state, and it was not unusual for him to give three speeches in a day. He jogged faithfully three times a week. His wife, Florence, usually packed him a very light lunch. The genuine affection between the pair was readily apparent.

This supporter was distressed, however, with Mecham's failure to return loyalty. She recalls one legislator who stood by the governor unswervingly. When he called for even routine considerations, Mecham would dismiss the request behind his back with "He's nobody."

In the end, it seemed to her, Mecham was not receptive to change or to suggestions. Mecham exhibited no concern for the chaos on the Ninth Floor, the difficulties of his administration, or the impending recall until October 1987, when the dam broke.

Senator Tony West, a Republican, was a native of Phoenix. A devout Catholic, West was a deacon and was known for his interest in religious matters.

As West watched Mecham in action, it was almost as if the governor "had a phobia against competency and credibility." Some of his appointments simply "defied logic."

Tony West split with Mecham over dealings that West considered matters of character and of honor. West is known as an ardent supporter of the Department of Public Safety and as a friend of its director, Ralph Milstead. Mecham had assured West that he would make no move to oust Milstead without telling West of it first. In West's opinion, Mecham violated that agreement within months.

In March of that first session West learned that Mecham's budget deleted all funding for the solar oasis project in downtown Phoenix that the Environmental Research Laboratory at the University of Arizona in Tucson was overseeing. Babbitt had earmarked three million dollars for it from a special fund paid the state by Exxon in a settlement that could be spent only on environmental matters.

West called Mecham and arranged for him to fly to Tucson to see the program for himself. Mecham, West, and West's two sons, flew down in the DPS airplane. The laboratory deals with the kinds of quality-of-life issues that are almost never addressed. It funded a biosphere to test ecology, solar cooling towers that promised inexpensive cooling for desert cities, genetic research, and more.

Mecham received the grand tour and West could "see the lights come on" in the governor's face. He told West, "I just didn't know." West felt very good about what had happened. He discussed the funding and its source. "I'll restore the funding," Mecham said without prompting, and the two men shook hands on it as West's teenage sons looked on.

West was elated at the success of the mission until a month later, when he learned that Mecham had budgeted the project for one and a half million instead of the full three.

In late May 1987 Mecham summoned West to his office. Three other senators—Pete Corpstein, Wayne Stump, and Jeff Hill—were there as well. These four men were the senate's most conservative, and if they banded together, in the caucus they could deny the senate leadership a budget bill.

Mecham harangued the men on the budget and the possibility of a tax increase. He wanted these four men to stand together so the leadership would be forced to deal with Mecham. He would work to reduce the budget even further.

The next day Carl Kunasek asked West to come to his office early in the evening. When West arrived, there was Mecham, along with Bob Usdane, Wayne Stump, and others. They were told that Governor Mecham "has acquiesced to our figures." Stump could not believe it and required that Mecham say the words himself before he would.

For West this was the last straw. This man had asked them to side with him, to stand against their own leadership. Then, once he had them in line, he had bailed out.

That was plenty for Senator Tony West.

In the end it all came down to mathematics. There are only ninety members of the Arizona legislature, sixty in the house, thirty in the senate. When the impeachment vote came, Mecham had little support from Democrats in the house and no support in the senate. Mecham did not require every Republican vote to be spared impeachment by the house, but he needed most of them just as he would need most in the senate to avoid conviction.

One by one Mecham gave nearly every member of both houses a very intimate reason to vote against him. Most believe they rose above such petty considerations, but they could not escape what their personal experiences told them of the character of Evan Mecham.

One observer who was close to Mecham later called what occurred an "impeachment of personality."

> *I've got a four year lease on the [governor's] office.*
>
> —EVAN MECHAM

> *[Mecham] doesn't intend to pass up this opportunity to leave his imprint on Arizona.*
>
> —ART HAMILTON, *house minority leader*

> *[Mecham] told [Todd Sprague] to go screw himself.*
>
> —ED BUCK, *recall founder*

# 16

When embattled Arizona Governor Evan Mecham summoned the state senate Democratic minority leader, Alan Stephens, to his office a few weeks after the end of the legislative session, no one could have been more surprised than the senator himself. This was their first and would prove to be their only meeting.

As soon as the senator was seated, Mecham launched into a speech lasting perhaps half an hour. There was no opportunity for interruption or for questions.

The thrust of his comments was that the special legislative session about to begin would take up the appointment of Max Hawkins. Mecham wanted him confirmed as director of the Department of Administration, the state's superagency. Hawkins had been "acting" director since January and was clearly rankled at not being the permanent director. Mecham wanted Democratic votes.

Stephens was intrigued. In normal times there would be no need for a Republican governor to solicit opposition votes. But these were not normal times, and the governor's party was balking at confirming the unpopular Hawkins.

"Governor," Stephens said, "if you are genuinely interested in cooperation from Democrats, then I would suggest you stop your attacks on us." Mecham had just returned from a trip to Yuma, on the Colorado River in southern Arizona, where he had strongly attacked Democratic legislators Stephens considered to be among the state's finest.

Mecham's manner changed instantaneously. He glowered at Stephens and said, "I've taken a few shots from you, Stephens. I just did that to let you know I can urinate on you anytime I want."

Senator Stephens rose from his chair and left the office without another word.

Mecham was writing a personal column several newspapers carried in order to bypass the "Phoenix Newspapers." In May the Green Valley *News* discontinued carrying him with the following announcement:

### NO MECHAM COLUMN

For the last six weeks, the *Green Valley News* has published Arizona Gov. Evan Mecham's column entitled, "Plain Talk", (his title).

. . . Our experience with the governor's press staff has convinced us that the governor could use a lot more help than he appears to be getting from that office.

Here's why. Of the six columns published by the *News* only two have been mailed to arrive at our offices in time for publication. . . .

The four columns were dictated to one of our editors over the telephone after they failed to arrive at our offices on time and after we called to ensure that the column could be published.

The reasons why the columns didn't reach us sound interesting, to say the least. One week, the press office "ran out of postage." Yes, that's what they told us.

Another week, the governor's press aide's secretary gave it to "someone" but he or she didn't mail it. Another week, the staff didn't offer any excuse at all! After we called to get that column dictated, we asked a member of the governor's staff if she would let us read it back to her to make sure we had taken it down accurately. She said she didn't have time.

Last Friday, we called to get the column dictated again because of the Memorial Day holiday. We reached a new staff member in the press office.

He said he would see if he could locate the column and call us back. He never did.

So the governor's column, which failed to arrive at all, will not appear today in the *Green Valley News* and will not in the future if the governor's staff can't get its act together.

We hope for Arizona's sake that the governor's press staff isn't typical of all the people who work for the Mecham administration. If it is, we're all in trouble. Big trouble.

In late June Governor Mecham called the legislature into special session. Even though Senator Stephens had not delivered his votes, as Mecham had requested, Max Hawkins was confirmed as director of the Department of Administration. Other legislation was also passed.

Mecham called an unusual second summer special session for July 20 to consider additional bills. As it worked out, the timing was auspicious for a number of Republican legislators as well, but for very different reasons.

In a sudden and completely unexpected move Mecham announced the creation of a Martin Luther King holiday—of sorts. On June 18, after having repeatedly said that King did not deserve special recognition, Mecham announced that he had signed a governor's proclamation declaring the third Sunday in January to be Martin Luther King, Jr., Civil Rights Day. This was not a state holiday and placated no one.

Asked to comment, Ed Buck said, "Mr. Mecham has just created the state's first nonholiday."

Mecham denied that this move was intended to "derail" the recall.

In early July Sam Stanton was the only Phoenix reporter to cover Mecham's attendance at the Western Governors' Association in Snowbird, Utah. Because Mecham had roots in Utah and because a recall movement was about to begin against him in Arizona, he was the media star of the conference though the governors shunned him. Donna Carlson was there and received the same treatment from the staffs of the other governors.

The conference center reminded Stanton of a minimum security prison. He was incredibly bored. One afternoon he stepped outside to watch the only pleasant view, the Uintah Mountains, and to smoke a cigarette.

As soon as he went back inside, the reporter from Salt Lake City was scribbling furiously and wanted to know if Mecham was always like that. Stanton asked what he meant with a sinking heart. He had picked a fine time for a smoke. The reporter told him that Mecham had just lectured the guest speaker, the president of Sony, about shoddy Japanese products and urged him to come to his car dealership in Glendale, where he would sell him a good American-built Pontiac.

Mecham had livened things up a bit the week before the conference, when he delivered a speech in Tucson to the National Guard Association of

Arizona in which he announced that "I'm not sure but what maybe we have became a little bit too much a democracy . . . ,"

In Utah Mecham appeared for an interview with a Salt Lake City television station. Asked about the National Basketball Association's cancellation of a convention in Phoenix, he said, "Well, the N.B.A., I guess they forget how many white people they get coming to watch them play."

Mecham was back in the national news.

During the first week of July Mecham's campaign committee established a special state account for ninety thousand dollars raised during the inaugural ball. It was decided in April that the money could not be used for its original purpose—to pay off Mecham campaign debts—because of a change in state law. The Maricopa County Attorney's Office had negotiated the settlement. The money would "be used for such things as gifts for dignitaries who visit Arizona."

Deputy Maricopa County Attorney Howard Schwartz said a 1978 law allowed the governor to use either private or public money to establish such a fund. He assumed the state would audit the account.

On June 28, 1987, Pat Murphy wrote in his *Republic* column, that with the pending recall drive, "Ugly days of political division lie ahead for the state, unnecessary days, in my view. For, in the absence of any stronger evidence of gross misconduct, I cannot find a reason to recall Mecham. . . . Mecham was elected to four years, and is entitled to serve out his term. . . ."

Thirty-three-year-old Ed Buck first realized that he could move people to action at the Republican National Convention in 1972, when as a teenager he had persuaded a crowd to tear down a fence. The experience had both frightened and enlightened him.

Buck had been raised in Phoenix. He is over six feet tall, a handsome man who worked as an international male model for five years before returning to Phoenix in 1981. In 1983 he purchased a small computer business that he operated for three years before selling it at a substantial profit that reportedly made him wealthy. It was in the fall of 1986 that he was free of his business and looking for another project in which to involve himself.

For the leader of the movement that was to set the stage for Mecham's removal Buck was surprisingly apolitical. He had been a registered Libertarian until May 1986, when he became a Republican. Because of AIDS, the usually quiescent gay community in Phoenix had become organized and softly vocal during 1985 and 1986. Buck's gay friends were generally aghast at Mecham's election, and the businessman started listening closely to Arizona's governor-elect.

He did not like what he heard. It seemed to him that Mecham would be "a boneheaded arrogant dictator." Buck had great faith in his ability to read people, and at once he believed he understood Evan Mecham. Almost for the fun of it Buck printed up some RECALL EV bumper stickers and went to the Capitol mall to distribute them even before Mecham had been inaugurated.

After the *Republic* and *Gazette* articles, Buck's telephone started ringing constantly. People were asking Buck what they could do. Many had stories about Mecham and the kind of dishonest car dealer he had been. He began to put the names and addresses into his computer. He gathered about a dozen of these and picketed the inauguration. The telephone continued to ring.

Though Mecham and Bellus were reported to be amused at Buck's efforts, Bellus had gone out of his way in late January to leak Buck's putative arrest for using a copy of a prescription in an attempt to obtain more drugs than had been prescribed by his dentist. Some weeks later Buck bargained to have prosecution deferred while he participated in a drug treatment program.

In early February Buck announced he had fourteen hundred names in his computer.

On February 24, 1987, Alberto Rodriguez ordered one of his liquor investigators, Elizabeth Keane, to conduct a record check on Buck. She did not know the name but knew that because Rodriguez had personally ordered her to do it, something was very wrong.

In his office she asked Rodriguez repeatedly if he was doing this because of a criminal investigation. Otherwise she knew that under Arizona law it was illegal. Rodriguez had averted his eyes, then become angry at her persistence and said yes, he was conducting a criminal investigation. There was a meeting with the governor that morning, and Rodriguez was eager to have the information before he attended it.

At the Phoenix Police Department Keane had the records clerk call Rodriguez directly, then document his request.* When she learned who Buck was, she felt used and for a time considered working on the recall drive.

Buck's original plan for what called itself the Mecham Watchdog Committee was simply to observe and document the governor's behavior. Under the Arizona constitution no recall effort could be filed with the secretary of state until an official had served at least six months in office.

Mecham and his staff made an early decision to attack Buck's sexual

---

*The attorney general conducted a criminal investigation into this, and other actions, of Alberto Rodriguez while he was acting superintendent. He eventually determined there was no basis for charging Rodriguez with criminal wrongdoing. A subsequent audit by the auditor general concluded there were a number of irregularities during the terms of both Mecham appointees to the state liquor department.

preference. Shortly after Mecham was sworn in, a member of his staff held a press conference and attacked Buck for his homosexuality.

Buck's background was not pristine. In addition to the forged prescription charge, he had been convicted of a misdemeanor violation of disturbing the peace for having touched the crotch of a companion in an adult bookstore. Buck responded to his conduct's being made public by simply saying that Ed Buck and what Ed Buck did were not the issue, that Evan Mecham was.

Within two months of the inauguration Ed Buck decided that the recall was "for real." The *New Times* reported that one poll ranked "Mecham as the state's biggest problem, second only to drugs but ahead of air pollution and traffic congestion."

Buck consulted with a behavioral psychologist he knew to discuss Mecham's personality. Buck was concerned that his attacks on Mecham would cause the governor to become more devious. He was assured that would not be the case. The psychologist told Buck that Mecham was not accustomed to having his authority questioned, that he was "authoritarian paranoid" and that attacks on his behavior would only exacerbate his conduct.

Buck initially ran the recall drive from his home. In May 1987 Buck organized the Watchdog Committee into the Mecham Recall Committee, Inc. That same month he opened an office in north-central Phoenix next to an American Opinion bookstore. "Never before," Buck announced, "has one man alienated so many people in such a short period of time."

Naomi Harward, age eighty, the former head of the Arizona branch of the Gray Panthers and a professor emeritus at Arizona State University, served as chairwoman of the recall committee. There was also a president. Both appointments were attempts to distance Buck from the recall, so it would not be successfully branded as a gay movement. Harward, the widowed mother of two daughters, responded to reporters' questions on the gay issue by saying, "I was very enthusiastic about my husband." Regardless of the formal organization, however, Buck was the primary force and remained the committee's spokesman and point man.

Buck appeared on talk shows to attack Mecham. Todd Sprague for the Evan Mecham Fan Club was his frequent debate opponent. Sprague would attack Buck's homosexuality in crass terms; Buck would gently chide him for it.

Sprague appeared with the encouragement of the Mecham staff. He was working on the Ninth Floor as a volunteer and was closely identified with the governor. Within two months Sprague was Mecham's most vocal supporter and was making frequent appearances on radio and television.

Buck estimated the committee would spend $250,000 in the recall drive. It received unspecified donations from the rock group U2 and from Peter, Paul and Mary. The committee would have four months from the day it took out petitions to gather 216,746 valid signatures to force a recall election.

On Monday, July 6, 1987, Ed Buck and his committee obtained petitions for the recall of Governor Evan Mecham. Buck was criticized for his timing by many who sympathized with him. The *New Times* ran an article in early June that said, "[Buck] will begin the drive in July, meaning that half the 120-day, signature-gathering period will fall during Arizona's hottest and most sparsely populated time of the year."

Buck believed, however, that the momentum was going his way and that he should strike "while the iron is hot."

The state GOP chairman, Burt Kruglick, released a statement attacking the tactics of the committee. "Buck and his fringe group of homosexual agitators are lying and deceiving the public." In Snowbird, Utah, Mecham was quoted as saying, "At least a recall election, I think, would shut 'em up." He then added, "If a band of homosexuals and a few dissident Democrats can do that, why, heavens, the state deserves what else they can get."

Buck announced he had five thousand volunteers ready to circulate petitions. He set their goal as 350,000 signatures to allow a margin for invalid signatures. That was 3,000 signatures a day. Sprague claimed his fan club had two thousand members who would work against the recall drive.

The Friday after taking out petitions the Mecham Recall Committee held a kickoff party. That week the committee was virtually broke. It spent what money it had on the do-or-die party. The affair was held in downtown Phoenix at the Hyatt Regency. Buck was uncertain how many would show up. The committee was charging fifteen dollars a couple. He ordered food for three hundred, then at the last second raised it to five hundred. More than five thousand people came.

Members of Mecham's staff had been circulating their own bumper sticker that said, QUEER ED BUCK'S RECALL. Buck's concern that Mecham could successfully attack the recall committee as an organization of Democrats unhappy with the outcome of the election and as one dominated by gay activists was well taken. Sprague had constantly attacked Buck's sexuality on the radio and in the press. Gay bashing was Mecham's chosen tactic, and unless Buck was willing to withdraw from his own movement, there was the fear among those who wanted Mecham recalled that his presence would divert the issue from Mecham and ruin the drive before it had a chance to succeed. As it turned out, Buck's sexual preferences ceased being an issue at the same time the recall drive officially began.

Todd Sprague was a convicted child molester.

Buck had received calls almost at once about Sprague's arrest record. He had known for months before it became public knowledge. He did not believe he could use the information, however. He had said all along that sex was not the issue, that Evan Mecham was. For him to attack Sprague as a child molester was to play Mecham's game.

Ed Buck shares the viewpoint of reporters who covered the events that Sprague was involved for the publicity and in order to feel important. Buck had hinted to Sprague that he knew about his record in an attempt to have the youngster stop his constant gay bashing during their debates. At one point Sprague called Buck to talk about it. Buck says that he told Sprague to go public because it would come out eventually anyway. He suggested Sprague say that his record was not the issue, that the administration was. Sprague had declined to do so.

# 17

The same day the committee took out its petitions, *Gazette* columnist Dennis Wagner divulged Sprague's record. Wagner wrote that he went to interview Sprague at his home and did not initially tell him what he had confirmed with a juvenile court official. Wagner knew that two years before, Sprague had been found to have molested an eight-year-old girl he had been baby-sitting. Sprague had been placed on probation, a term that ended three weeks after Mecham took office.

Sprague told the columnist that he no longer considered Buck's sexual preference to be the issue. He said that he and Buck had shaken hands over it.

While Wagner was there, Kurt Davis, a Republican party official, called to ask Sprague to attend a recall fund raiser with thirty others wearing "I love Mecham" buttons.

Sprague said in reference to Gary Hart, whose scandal was news at the time, "I think when somebody is in the public eye like that, they put themselves in that position. I mean, if somebody came over and did that to me, I'd expect it." Wagner then told Sprague what he knew.

Sprague's eyes moistened. "Please don't bring that out," he asked. "I know you're a reporter. I was an immature 14-year old. Emotional. Just learning about life." He said he had hoped that because he was under eighteen, the offense would not come out. "I'm just hoping the people will forgive me—the people of the state. This is just going to ruin me."

Wagner wrote, "There is something sickening about exposing a juvenile's criminal record. [Sprague] is, after all, just a kid. Today is his 17th birthday. If he were any other teenager in the state, this would not be a story. But, of his own doing, [Todd Sprague] has become more than any other teenager. He has become a key player in the political machinations of Arizona. He has called meetings, issued press releases, written articles. He has endeared himself to Mecham, the governor who ferrets homosexuals out of the statehouse for the sake of morality."

That same day Mariel Antonino of the governor's staff issued an internal memorandum to the Ninth Floor staff. It stated in part, "The formation of the Evan Mecham Fam [sic] Club was completely at [Todd Sprague's] own instigation. . . . His involvement with the Governor's office has been at [Todd's] own request. He has spent 5 days on a part time volunteer basis. . . . The Governor's office has no further involvement in this matter."

The day after Kruglick's attack on the committee the recall group released a statement saying, "The blue book of the John Birch Society details the use of character assassination as a useful tool in defusing the effectiveness of political enemies." Heterosexual members of the committee threatened to sue Kruglick and Mecham for slander. In response, Kruglick said his earlier release was the first time he had ever mentioned Buck's homosexuality and said that he would "probably never do it again."

According to Buck, when asked about Todd Sprague, Mecham said, "What are you asking me for? I never molested any children."

Though Mecham had called Sprague the night of the first *Gazette* article and suggested that the teenager disassociate himself, Mecham told reporters, "Nobody ran him off. We never put him on our staff, so we never did any background check on him." Kurt Davis said, "We don't have any contact with him."

Sprague's mother was so upset she called Dennis Wagner and said, "[Mecham] is a blatantly arrogant man." She said the administration had used her son, then, once he had become a liability, had dumped him. Later she signed the recall petition.

Despite, or perhaps because of, all the publicity, Todd Sprague remained active in the Evan Mecham Fan Club and continued to seek opportunities to appear in public.

Buck suggested that now the state could turn its attention to the real issue: Evan Mecham and whether or not he should remain Arizona's governor.

Until October 1987 the recall dominated the politics of and public discussions in Arizona.

Two weeks before leaving for Utah, on the last Friday in June, Mecham appeared spontaneously before a special committee that was evaluating bids to lead Arizona's attempt to acquire the supercollider that eventually went to Texas. Earlier that day Mecham heard from special assistant Ray Russell that the bid submitted by his friend Fred Craft had been dropped by the committee. An angry Mecham went over to the committee meeting and told it he wanted Craft for the job.

Mecham praised Craft for the work he had performed in Washington for the governor's office and pointed out the contacts Craft had that would assist him in obtaining the federal project for Arizona. He attacked unnamed "people who are bad-mouthing Fred Craft for political reasons."

The Arizona congressional delegation had written the committee recommending that one criterion they adopt was to hire someone only with the "highest integrity and professional reputation." That phrase, according to John Kolbe's *Gazette* article, had been directed at Fred Craft, who had been accused of unethical practices.

Mecham told the committee that he could not work with any other bidder and that if it did not give the contract to Craft, he would drop his support for the project.

Peter Carruthers, head of the University of Arizona's Physics Department and a member of the committee, asked Mecham as the governor prepared to leave, "Governor, I am confused. Are you telling us that if we don't involve Craft, we will lose your support for the project?"

Mecham responded, "Yes, that's what I mean."

Donna Carlson was on the Ninth Floor when Mecham returned from the committee meeting, acting "very pleased with himself" as he told her about it. He related to her that he had told the committee "he would withdraw his support of the project if Fred Craft and Dennis Revell [Ronald Reagan's son-in-law] were not involved."

When John Kolbe reported what had occurred, Mecham called a press conference and angrily denied making the threat. He accused Kolbe of misreporting what had occurred "in order to get me." He released an eleven-page statement "blasting" the *Republic* and the *Gazette* and reporting what he called the "real facts."

Four of the five members of the committee confirmed Kolbe's report and said that Mecham had tried to influence them. One said, "I was flabbergasted." Another said, "We can't cover up for [Mecham] when he says things that are not true."

The only member of the committee who did not confirm Mecham's conduct was his special assistant fellow Mormon Ray Russell, who had no comment.

Members of the committee privately said they were expecting an apology from Mecham. Instead, Max Hawkins announced he was investigating members of the committee for "collusion" and for involving "outside forces" during committee talks.

Shortly after this Craft pulled out of consideration for the job when Mecham hired him for eighty thousand dollars a year to represent the state in Washington. Craft was to be paid out of Mecham's discretionary funds.

Greg Lunn heard of this incident, and it was for him the last straw. In addition to everything else, he could see no reason for publicly defending the governor. Mecham was the one always talking about integrity, and here he was attempting to influence an independent committee into delivering a lucrative state contract to the pocket of a friend. Lunn also knew that the respected members of the select committee were deeply offended by what the governor had attempted.

The second special session of the summer was arriving soon, and Lunn decided it would be an opportunity for him to speak out. He considered what he wanted to say and was working on the speech, which he was to deliver the first day of the session, when he joined fellow legislator Representative Larry Hawke, also from Tucson, at the Veterans of Foreign Wars hall for a drink the Thursday before. Hawke asked, "Has Herstam called you?" Lunn said he had not.

Hawke told him that a group of Republicans in the house also wanted to do something about Mecham and were of the opinion they had to go public. They were looking for support in the senate. Lunn was noncommittal since he did not know what the representatives had in mind but said he would entertain a call.

No one contacted him. On Sunday Lunn was staying at the Sheraton in Phoenix working on his remarks. He learned that eleven Republicans were holding a press conference on Tuesday. Lunn was apprised of the joint statement, but he was "not in a mood to water down" his remarks and declined to participate.

No one admits to first suggesting the Dirty Dozen, as the group came to be known, but almost everyone says that Chris Herstam was the moving force.

In early July thirteen Republican members of the house met at the University Club in central Phoenix near the Heard Museum to discuss Evan Mecham. Herstam told the gathering that "this man has been a disaster" and that he believed they needed to send him the message that they would no longer put up with him. It was important that the public know that there

were many Republicans who disagreed with their governor. It was unfair of
them to expect the leaders to do it since they had to work personally with
the governor and make the system work, but rank-and-file representatives
such as themselves could speak out.

They decided to issue a joint statement on the second day of the special
session. They drafted a statement that all of them could support, but when
it came time, two of the thirteen declined. They were not yet ready. Both
of them did speak out later. So the Dirty Dozen consisted of eleven members
when it called its press conference.

Mark Killian recalls that he was coming to accept that Evan Mecham
just could not survive four years in office. When Killian read the statement
in private, he told Herstam that he wanted to be the one to read it for the
group. Like Stan Turley, he believed the statement coming from a brother
Mormon would have a greater impact among Mecham's supporters.

Herstam was surprised at the offer. He was also pleased Killian would
do it.

Herstam was technically not part of the house leadership, but as chairman of the Ways and Means Committee he was only a breath away. He
informed Joe Lane what they were up to. Lane said they all were independent lawmakers and were free to do as they saw fit. It was, Lane later said,
a way to send Mecham a message without involving the leadership.

That Monday Gregg Lunn rose to speak on the senate floor. "Party
loyalty," he said, "has propelled most of us to be circumspect in our remarks,
but I'm left to wonder what the greater danger is: the specter of Republicans
fighting among ourselves or the specter of maintaining our meek silence
while our fortunes swirl down the drain. Loyalty to this party may, in the
near term, require a distancing from this governor."

Lunn listed Mecham's failings, then said that the Republicans were
becoming the party known for having "a lock on the bigot vote, the anti-
intellectual vote and the homophobic vote."

When supporters of the governor said that Mecham's problems were
caused by his being one of the few honest politicians, Lunn said that "precisely the opposite is true," pointing to Mecham's improper attempt to
influence the selection of a lobbyist for the supercollider.

When the speech was over, four senators came up to Lunn and shook
his hand. By the end of the day other senators were distancing themselves
from Lunn.

"Thank God somebody said it," John Hays said afterward. Another
legislator said that he thought Lunn was going to switch parties right on the
senate floor.

* * *

The next day Killian read the statement of the Dirty Dozen. Herstam was standing there looking into more cameras than he had ever seen before. The representatives were "extremely disappointed with the governor's inappropriate interference" in the supercollider contract, and they were "dismayed" by Mecham's decision to hire Fred Craft as a lobbyist for his office out of the governor's funds after the house had rejected a proposal to do it. His action "goes against strong legislative sentiment and . . . further exacerbates the already strained relations between the governor and state legislature."

The group was soundly criticized by others in the party, especially the party chairman, Burt Kruglick, who insinuated they did not have the courage to tell Mecham to his face, and a secret meeting was scheduled for Saturday, August 1, when they could present their objections to the governor personally.

It is not likely that these eleven representatives or Senator Lunn were aware of the nearly identical actions of their precursors in 1964. On that occasion it had been one senator and twelve representatives, all Republicans, who published a condemnation of Evan Mecham. These legislators in 1987 would have agreed with the statement from twenty-three years before that said in part, "[Mecham's] conduct reflects unfavorably on our entire party . . ." and that "he seems poorly acquainted with the processes of state government. . . ." Those earlier legislators had charged Mecham with "sheer obstructionism . . ." and "a pattern of negativism. . . ." The twelve legislators in 1987 would have found nothing in the earlier statement with which to disagree, certainly not the following: "Through association with [Mecham] and close study of his tactics we doubt that he understands the basic elements of teamwork that are essential to successful leadership."

Herstam recalls that Saturday meeting with Governor Mecham very well. He had suggested they meet at Mecham's home, but the governor refused. The eleven representatives met out in the parking lot before proceeding to the Ninth Floor. They planned nothing but reminded one another to speak their minds and not hold back. Though she was not part of the group, House Whip Jane Dee Hull was present for the meeting.

They sat at the table in the governor's conference room. Herstam took a seat at the end, facing Mecham directly. Colter, Bellus, Donna Carlson, and others of the governor's staff were present, standing or sitting around by the walls.

Herstam led off. As he delivered his thoughts to the governor, he could not get the man to look him in the eye. Instead, Mecham was taking "voluminous notes" in his notepad.

Herstam began by saying, "Governor, we're here to tell you that your administration is in serious trouble. The recall is moving. You have a window period of a few weeks to save it." Herstam told Mecham that he needed a wholesale housecleaning on the Ninth Floor and specifically that most of his staff, including some of those present, needed to go. Herstam delivered a forceful and, he believed, accurate recitation of what Mecham had to do to save himself.

Herstam recalls that Mecham snickered as Herstam spoke. When the legislator was finished, Mecham said, "I don't believe it's time to take the razor blades out and cut the wrists yet."

In turn each of the Dirty Dozen spoke, addressing his or her concerns. Herstam thought Mecham received a complete picture of the problems as the group saw them. Because Mecham was constantly demanding that his critics "be specific," the legislators were precisely that. Herstam was never so proud of his colleagues as he was that day.

The meeting lasted ninety minutes. Mecham never acknowledged a single error on his part. There were thirty-six in the house Republican caucus. This group represented nearly one third of it. It included seven chairmen and four committee vice-chairmen. Herstam thought Hull was sobered by what she was witnessing.

It was apparent by the conclusion of the meeting at 10:15 A.M. that Mecham was very angry. The legislators rose out of respect as the governor prepared to leave. As Mecham passed Herstam, he said in a derisive tone, "You were awful quiet, Chris."

Herstam thought the comment was completely inappropriate considering the circumstances and realized that their message had not gone home. He knew at that precise moment that Mecham was "destined for failure."

# PART TWO

"And sex, heh-heh, unknown to me, the reason Donna [Carlson] was on my staff was over sex. Hadn't been for sex, ha-ha, I'd probably still be governor. . . . Her and Steiger, her and Milstead, her and Twist, and who else do you wanna name? . . . Listen, listen, if you want a zinger of a book, then there's a lotta questions you need to answer.

—EVAN MECHAM *to author*

> *I'm not sure the recall's going to be success-*
> *ful. . . . [I]t is the nature of people—partic-*
> *ularly of Arizonans—to give a guy . . . his*
> *four years. Unless he really does something*
> *even more bizarre than he's already done . . .*
> *we have to aim for four very long years.*
> —ART HAMILTON, *house*
> *minority leader*
>
> *Did [Ed Buck] get into his fag bag with you?*
> —MAX HAWKINS *to*
> *author*

# 18

Three weeks following the senate speech of Senator Lunn and the public statement of the Dirty Dozen, the Republican party chairman, Burton Kruglick, called a private meeting at his residence in an attempt to mediate the serious problems Mecham was having with his fellow Republicans in the legislature. Senator Lunn attended, as did most of the eleven representatives who had been present at the August 1 meeting with Mecham.

Also present were "elder statesmen" of the party, including former Governor and U.S. Senator Paul Fannin, former Governor Jack Williams, and former Congressman Eldon Rudd. Other less public senior statesmen of the party were present as well.

They sat in a circle in the living room. It seemed to Lunn that the representatives "were ready for war." Kruglick told the tense gathering that he hoped to "defuse" Mecham's problems. No one was present to criticize; they were here for solutions. They all were in agreement that the party would suffer if the administration continued as it had. Kruglick wanted the elder statesmen to mediate between the Dirty Dozen and Mecham. He suggested a breakfast meeting with the governor.

It was quickly agreed, however, that there would be no breakfast meeting. It would serve no useful purpose. Lunn told the group, "The interests of the party lies in not supporting Mecham." He told the gathering that in

141

his opinion, Evan Mecham was incapable of the kind of change that was required. It seemed to Lunn that the tension had now become "sadness" and "depression" at the prospects ahead as they all looked into the hole that Mecham had dug for them.

Kruglick was not prepared to give up. He met Lunn as the senator prepared to leave. "Well, what do you think about this breakfast with the governor?" he asked.

"It's too late for that," Lunn replied, "and furthermore, if some of the things I've heard are true, we're not going to be talking about getting along, we'll be talking impeachment."

Fannin overheard that and spontaneously remarked, "Things can't have gone that far."

Lunn shook his head sadly and quietly left. It was the first time he had ever uttered the word "impeachment" openly. For Lunn this was the last-ditch effort to save Mecham. He viewed it as "a defining event" from which thereafter there was no turning from the cataclysm ahead.

On August 15 the Green Bay Packers played the Denver Broncos at Sun Devil Stadium in Tempe in a nationally televised preseason game. Mecham's staff had worked frantically to arrange for Mecham to toss the coin. When he walked onto the field amid catcalls and shouts, he was booed loudly. Mecham's DPS security detail was pelted with ice and food.

The stadium rang as over seventy thousand spectators spontaneously chanted, "Recall! Recall! Recall!" It was the loudest noise of the night.

Mecham denied hearing anything. Informed of that, an aide said, "Are you kidding? It sounded like 50,000 Zulu warriors out there."

During this time Mecham had meetings arranged with various groups in an attempt to bolster his sagging ratings. One such meeting was with representatives of the black community. As the two of them left, Mecham said to Carlson, "That was a good meeting, wasn't it? They're almost like real people."

Near the last day of August or perhaps in very early September, Donna Carlson went to see Jim Colter at his office on the Ninth Floor. She found Mecham's longtime confidant and chief of staff upset and acutely depressed. She asked what was bothering him.

"I don't think the governor understands the magnitude of the debt."

Carlson knew that finances were dominating the discussions of the senior staff. Mecham was concerned with paying for the tabloid he had just mailed, and this clearly was weighing on Colter. Carlson herself had been asked to sign another promissory note to help finance it and had refused.

"We've got this loan facing us," Colter said. He told her that Hugh Gregan was not very happy. "It's due on November 1st. I don't know how we're going to raise the money to pay it off. I just don't think [Mecham] understands. I had to loan [Mecham] $80,000 from the Protocol Fund."

Carlson shot up out of her chair and cursed. "People go to jail for things like that," she said. She could not believe what she was hearing. She had served on the Ninth Floor's protocol committee, which was exploring ways to disperse the monies from that account. The committee believed it was now state money under the terms of the agreement the inaugural committee had reached and could be spent only to "promote the best interests of the state."

"What if somebody asks for an accounting of the funds?" she asked.

"I guess we'll have to give it to them."

"Did the money go to the tabloid?" she asked.

"No."

With a sinking heart she said, "For the governor's personal use?"

"Yes."

Carlson spoke to Sam Steiger the same day about the loan of state funds to the governor. He told her he did not know about it. Later she said his initial response was more "colorful" than hers.

Ed Buck's intuitive guess that it would be best to take out recall petitions the first day legally possible proved correct. By mid-September Buck announced the committee had gathered more than 216,000, technically enough to force an election. In reality, it had to collect more because a certain percentage always proved invalid.

The effect of this announcement on the state was electrifying. Various shopping malls had gone to court to keep the recall petitioners out. Nearly everyone had seen lone recall workers roasting in 115-degree afternoon heat next to card tables in asphalt parking lots. It did not seem possible that so many signatures could have been obtained under such conditions.

Buck says that ten thousand people worked on the recall drive in one form or another. Of those, more than six thousand actually circulated petitions, collecting signatures at the average rate of four thousand a day. In one ten-day period well into the drive the group garnered forty-six thousand signatures. In one single day they received over fifteen thousand.

But there was some truth to what the experts had predicted. Long after the events Buck acknowledged that the committee received almost no signatures the last week in August.

According to Buck, Mecham was the recall committee's secret weapon. Every time the signatures slowed down Mecham would make a public pronouncement that breathed fresh life into the movement. This happened time and again. Buck continued to consult with the psychologist to test with her ways that would cause Mecham to react to them. "All we could work on was Mecham's nerves," Buck says.

Initially Mecham demanded to know why Buck and his group wanted to recall him. Buck responded by saying the Arizona constitution did not require a reason for recalling a governor. In early July, just a few days before the committee took out its petitions with the secretary of state, Mecham had said, "I have always been waiting for a bill of particulars on what they see wrong with me."

Buck believed that Mecham was bothered that the committee would not say specifically why it wanted him removed from office. Mecham routinely required that his attackers "be specific." Once he heard the specific detail, he would say they did not have their facts correct or he would dismiss it as inconsequential. The technique often rattled his questioner and allowed Mecham to avoid confronting the cumulative effect of his conduct.

Buck could have been specific at any time but did not want to waste the opportunity especially since Mecham was so troubled by the lack of specifics. Shortly before taking out the petitions in early July, the committee prepared a statement it entitled "Call to Recall," listing why Evan Mecham should be removed from office. It could just as easily have handed it to the press. Instead, after checking with the psychologist to be certain of Mecham's reaction, Buck informed the media he would deliver the document to Mecham personally.

The reporters and television covered the event. Mecham refused to come out of his office and accept the document directly from Buck. Buck delivered a denunciation of the governor that played on statewide television that night and gave the "Call to Recall" far more attention than it would otherwise have received. It had the added effect of causing Mecham to appear petty.

Mecham's conduct in office galvanized public opposition. If embarrassment is not, strictly speaking, a legal reason to remove an elected official, the truth was that embarrassment over Mecham was the leading reason so many opposed him.

One former employee of the governor who had worked on one of Mecham's tabloids however signed a recall petition in retaliation for all the times he had heard Mecham say "nigger."

Buck personally received countless threats. There was a seemingly endless stream of calls to his home. Some callers lectured him on sin. One threatened to kill his dog. At one point a private investigator, reportedly used by Mecham supporters, sat in his car and watched Buck's home. Buck complained to the police, who told him there was nothing they could do.

It was during the intense heat of the summer that Steve Benson made his decision to sign the recall petition. His wife was driving their van when she spotted a recall worker at a card table with a small crowd of people waiting to sign. She asked if he wanted her to stop. Benson told her not to but within a few blocks had her go back.

The moment he signed the petition Benson says he "felt cleansed." Though the LDS Church does not have confession as a sacrament, Benson says he "felt like I had just come out of the confession box." It was like being "born again." After that he wanted everyone to sign and told his colleagues how good it felt actually to do it.

Also in August, *New Times* writer Deborah Laake published a revealing look into Mecham's background, drawing on her own upbringing as a Latter-day Saint. Watching the governor in action, she concluded that Mecham had learned his leadership skills not as a car salesman but as a Mormon bishop.

"Mecham began as a Mormon boy," she wrote, "and became a Mormon man. There is no other upbringing on earth so perfectly designed to transform someone with weak wits into a monster. . . . [Mormon boys] are told, in fact, that when they are older they will have the direct power to act for God on earth. That is how it is actually phrased."

She wrote that the male lay ministers of the LDS Church receive no training in psychology and no preparation for the power they wield once they assume offices of significance in the LDS Church. They are taught to rely on "divine inspiration" from God. "They believe they can and should handle anything. . . . It's exactly the tyrannical way Mecham has been behaving about a host of governmental issues."

She pointed out that Mecham's views on homosexuality were not those of others in leadership in the church, that she recently had met with two gay Mormon men, one of whom had told her that he had "worked with people who are high-up in the [Mormon] hierarchy" and toward whom he felt "very good and positive. . . ." She added that Mecham "doesn't represent mainstream Mormon thought about a lot of things, either. There are plenty of Mormons who aren't John Birch Society admirers.

"There are some swell Mormon men," she wrote. "They turn out fine when they take the teachings of their mystical heritage and stir them around with some liberal educations and a few brain cells. This wasn't Mecham's approach, however."

In early September 1987 Mecham appeared on Michael Grant's *Horizon* show on public television and said, "They can't do anything to me. I'm the governor of the state of Arizona . . . ," referring to the *Doonesbury* cartoon strips that had just started nationwide.

The strips ran for a week. One scene had Mecham patting the head of a black child while saying, "My! What a cute little pickaninny!" Another had him announcing a new appointment with the statement "Active in Fourth

Reich politics, Mr. Stone recently had all charges dropped. . . ." Still another had Mecham disclaiming any intolerance, saying, "It's ludicrous! I'm
a Mormon! Tolerance is a basic tenet of my faith!" The charges against
Mecham, however, were "Lies! Lies spread by queers and pickaninnies!"
according to one of the strips.

Mecham responded to the cartoons by saying they had "crossed the
point of decency." He said, "Garry Trudeau is trying to make money, he's
the bottom line making money, he couldn't care less. . . . I don't see any
mirth in them. They're not based on any facts, and they aren't funny."

Mecham was particularly incensed that the cartoons showed Mecham
saying "pickaninny." "I've never used the word pickaninny, never have. I
said the book was fine. They wanted me to disavow a book that used it in
a historical sense. You really have to reach to try to say I ever used the word
pickaninny." He added, "You know some time ago blacks . . . first it was
to call them coloreds, and then they wanted to be called Negroes, and now
they want to be called blacks, and I'll call them whatever they want to be
called."

On a national television show at this time Mecham made clearer his
true feelings in regard to the word "pickaninny." "I don't use the word, but
it isn't that bad."

Though he said, "I can't help what they do, and frankly, I don't care."
he confirmed that his private attorney was examining the *Doonesbury* strips
for a possible libel action.

Buck acknowledges mailing Trudeau the committee's standard packet,
a two-hour videocassette of local television newscasts on Mecham and forty
of Benson's cartoons as well as those by *Gazette* political cartoonist Len
Borozinski.

At this same time Mecham had mailed a tabloid, called *The Governor's
Report to the People of Arizona*, to the state's registered voters. He purchased television airtime and made two fifteen-minute presentations.

In Washington, D.C., a group of Arizonans living there held a fund
raiser to benefit the Mecham Recall Committee.

Three groups organized in support of the governor. One called itself
the East Valley Republican Club. The "East Valley" is generally a euphe-
mism for Mesa. Another was called the Committee to Rethink the Recall of
Ev. The third, Concerned Arizona Voters, was organized by a woman who
had moved to Arizona after Mecham had been elected. In Michigan she had
headed up an effort to recall the governor.

None of these groups was officially connected to the administration.
None had the numbers, money, or organization of the Mecham Recall Committee.

                                    *   *   *

Mecham, by his public statements and according to those working closely with him, did not take the recall drive seriously. He believed the average person supported his administration so the recall drive could not possibly legitimately obtain the necessary signatures to force an election.

Mecham also appeared offended by the recall drive. He took it as a personal affront and viewed it as an attack on him by gays and leftist Democrats who would not accept that he had been lawfully elected their governor. Because in his opinion the drive was led by gays, it was also immoral, and because the Democrats supported it rather than yield to the results of the last election, they were anticonstitutionalists.

Mecham's natural tendency, according to some of those who worked closely with him, was to accept whatever he heard that supported what he already believed. When Jim Colter and others brought him stories of massive recall fraud, he believed them.

Once it was apparent that the drive would file enough signatures, Mecham repeated again and again that there would never be a sufficient number of legitimate ones. In mid-September he told Mike Murphy that "when it gets to verification, that's a different ball game. . . . I think in that area they're in a world of hurt."

Mecham would not, could not, accept that more than 380,000 Arizonans wanted him out of office. He could not believe that the movement was funded from within the state or that it had local grass-roots support. Such a drive was being orchestrated by powerful forces out to destroy him. Stories of gays being bused in to sign petitions or visitors using false local addresses were often repeated by his staff.

It was an article of faith for Mecham that the Mecham Recall Committee was engaging in wholesale fraud.

> *We don't have discrimination. We haven't had a racial riot in my memory. . . .*
> —EVAN MECHAM
>
> *It's kind of like you keep expecting the other shoe to drop. We live in terror of what's going to happen next. . . .*
> —JANE DEE HULL,
> *house*
> *majority whip*
>
> *Golly, I don't know. I don't know whether he speaks English or not.*
> —EVAN MECHAM, *when asked how he would greet Pope John Paul II*

# 19

It was at this time, in early September 1987, that Donna Carlson drove to work from her condominium at Renaissance Park in central Phoenix not suspecting that this day would thereafter change her life and link it inexorably with that of Evan Mecham.

From her experience Mecham had almost single-handedly managed to alienate virtually everyone with whom he had to deal. Each crisis had created a new litmus test for his followers, and more often than not a smaller percentage passed muster. And loyalty was increasingly measured by whether or not you agreed with every utterance of the governor.

The precious months when the legislature was not in session were needed to regroup, make plans, soothe wounds, and forge coalitions. None of this had occurred. Mecham had shown time and again that he was incapable of planning more than a day, certainly no more than a week ahead.

Carlson had joined the administration looking for satisfaction, an opportunity to make a difference. She had also been looking ahead. One of the usual perks of serving as a governor's aide are the contacts acquired. Others in different administrations had parlayed positions such as hers into substantial ones in the private sector. Considering history and her abilities, there was no reason the same thing should not happen to her. But anyone important who could potentially help was now thoroughly alienated by Mecham, and it was apparent to her that having had a close association with the governor was going to be a liability, not an asset.

Donna Carlson had taken the Mesa *Tribune* articles on Horace Lee Watkins to Jim Colter at the time and pointed out the harm Watkins was causing the administration. She was disturbed that now, in early September, Mecham had appointed Watkins deputy director of the Department of Administration in charge of awarding lucrative prison construction contracts.

Sam Stanton, Mike Murphy and Rosemary Schabert Case with the Mesa *Tribune* all had been pestering Carlson about Watkins since his reappointment. Finally, exasperated by all the calls, she asked Stanton what this was all about.

Stanton told her that Watkins was an ex-convict.

Carlson was enraged. She knew the story would appear in the press any day. She went straight to Bob Usdane, Republican majority leader in the senate, and Carl Kunasek, senate president, with the news. "How did this get past the governor?" she wanted to know. The pair were as shocked as she had been.

Carlson was angered with the Department of Public Safety and called Director Milstead to complain about the poor job the Department of Public Safety had done in screening Watkins. "We sent that over in January, after the governor took office," Milstead told her.

"You mean the governor and Colter know this?" Carlson replied. She could not believe that Mecham and his chief of staff would appoint Watkins to anything, let alone two positions, knowing he had been to prison.

"Yes."

After the conversation Carlson wondered, What do we owe this turkey to hang the governor out to dry just to get him a job? Mecham might demand loyalty from those around him, but he was well known not to reciprocate.

The more she thought about it, the more she felt she knew.

Carlson had come to believe that she and nearly every special assistant on the Ninth Floor was engaged in a criminal cover-up. It seemed only a matter of time before the roof fell in. She had looked the other way, rationalized her conduct long enough.

All the senior staff on the Ninth Floor knew that Mecham had borrowed money from an unnamed "fat cat." The papers ran articles from time to time mentioning that the Mecham campaign still had about three hundred thousand dollars in unpaid debts. No reporter had put his finger on the real issue yet. By the end of August Carlson had been convinced that Mecham could not survive as governor.

On this day in September she went to see about a memo Carlson had written Mecham. It had been placed in the priority read pile on the governor's desk. Carlson went over the papers on his desk. Mecham had a knack for losing important papers, even legislation he was reviewing for signature. Once a bill had become law without his signature because it had been lost.

As Carlson went through the priority read pile, the name from a letter jumped at her: BARRY WOLFSON.

She picked up the letter. It was a demand for payment of $250,000 Wolfson had lent Mecham for the campaign. Mecham was to pay the money by November 1, 1987, or Wolfson would take legal action. She felt in that moment as if the entire state had been betrayed. As she read the letter, she became very frightened.

She did not know what she was going to do or when she would do it, but as she left the governor's office, she knew she was going to do something about this.

As it turned out, Donna Carlson was going to bring down the state government.

Several days after discovering the Wolfson demand letter, Carlson flew with Evan Mecham in the Department of Public Safety plane to Globe, Arizona, for the first of a string of gubernatorial appearances intended to neutralize the recall. They had been met at their first stop by a camera crew she did not recognize but soon learned was with *The MacNeil-Lehrer News Hour*. No one had said a word to her about it. The crew followed them the entire day.

Immediately behind the pilot seat was a work area with a small table the governor often used. On the way back to Phoenix Mecham told Carlson he was going to fire Department of Public Safety Director Ralph Milstead and replace him with his own person.

Carlson was absolutely shocked. Not that this was the first time she heard of Mecham's desire to be rid of Milstead. There had been talk even during the transition period before the inauguration. Just weeks earlier one of Mecham's appointees, Alberto Gutier, had submitted a report to Mecham. Carlson had understood Gutier's job was to get a case on Milstead, whose term was fixed by law. After the report was delivered to Mecham, Steiger told Carlson, "I can't believe it. Milstead's clean. We couldn't find any reason to fire him, but the governor told me to keep on looking until we find something." She had heard nothing since then.

"Governor," Carlson said, "you can't fire him without cause."

"I've got it," he replied.

Carlson told Mecham that this was a crazy thing to do. She told him this would only enflame the recall movement. Mecham was insistent and made it clear that this time he would not change his mind.

When they landed at the airport from Globe and returned to the Capitol, Carlson went straight to Sam Steiger's office. "Sam," she said, "he's going to fire Ralph Milstead."

Steiger was responsible for the Department of Public Safety. "I'm through with this deal," he said. "There's nothing we can do about it anymore. He'll sue the hell out of the state. By the way, have you met Milstead's replacement?"

"Who?"

"Carroll Pennington. He seems like a nice guy. He used to be with the highway patrol."

Carlson knew about Pennington. She knew he was not well regarded by DPS, the old highway patrol's successor. She did not share Steiger's feeling that he was a nice guy. She knew Pennington was a protégé of Max Hawkins, and felt if he took over DPS, Hawkins would have Pennington running it like the Gestapo.

She looked down the hallway and spotted, coming out of Ray Russell's office, Pennington and Thad Curtis, interim superintendent of the liquor department, both dressed in blue suits. Curtis had always seemed nice enough to her, just not very smart. Hell, she thought, this is pretty imminent.

She went immediately to her office and called Ralph Milstead. She told him that there was something she needed to talk to him about at once. They arranged to meet for dinner that night at Cafe de Perouges on Seventh Street.

Milstead had risen steadily through the ranks of the Phoenix Police Department and obtained a degree in public management and later a master's degree in police administration. He retired as a major—the youngest officer ever to achieve that rank—and was promptly recruited by Babbitt to take over the state Department of Public Safety. Milstead had been reappointed to a second five-year term in 1985.

Milstead had always prided himself in his ability to work for anyone. When Mecham was elected and Milstead first heard that his job might be in jeopardy, he had viewed Mecham as a challenge. He had never been seriously concerned that he would not be able to find a way to work with Mecham, not initially at least.

Milstead is a strappingly good-looking man. Though he was forty-nine years old at the time he looked many years younger. Each year he set physical-conditioning goals for himself. The outward result of this was a man of uncommon physical fitness. Inwardly it had helped produce an intensely competitive man of unusual toughness and discipline.

Carlson talked about a number of things, about the recall, about Ed Buck. Finally she told Milstead about Pennington and Curtis, that Mecham intended to fire Milstead and put them in charge of DPS. She was to arrange a meeting with key legislators so Mecham could tell them his intentions.

Some weeks before, Milstead had seen a copy of the paper Thad Curtis had written for Mecham that was later identified as the Curtis Report. Amateurishly written, it called for the dismantling of a large part of the DPS, talked about "constitutional agencies," about the "liberalism" that had crept into Arizona law enforcement, about making DPS back into the Arizona Highway Patrol again, about the compelling need for "a bright white Arizona Highway Patrol car, with nice markings." It concluded with the rousing call, gratuitously cribbed from Mecham's own work, "COME BACK ARIZONA!"

Milstead also knew something Carlson did not. He knew that Curtis had been forced out of the old Highway Patrol and believed that he was not suitable to be an officer with the department, let alone a senior member of staff.

"That's interesting," Milstead said. "I thought Curtis was going back to Tucson." Curtis was on loan to the administration from the Pima County sheriff's office in Tucson, and his six-month leave of absence was just about up.

They talked about the Curtis Report. "Even Jim Colter thinks Curtis is illiterate after reading the paper," she said.

Milstead's immediate reaction to the meeting with Carlson was to arrange for the leak of the Curtis Report. He did not do it himself. He just let it be known that he was about to be removed and it would be nice for people to know what Mecham had in mind for DPS. He also called his most influential supporters and arranged for them to start contacting Mecham on his behalf.

One week later he and Carlson met again. Since she had broken confidence with the governor, her intent to leave the administration was becoming critical. She had cut the string. "There's something more I need to tell you," she said.*

She told Milstead everything she knew. She told him about the secret loan, about Mecham's taking the Protocol Fund money for his car dealership,

---

*While Carlson and Milstead agree on the substance of these two meetings they have different recollections of what matters were discussed on which night. The order here relies heavily on Milstead's account since he retained notes from both meetings.

about the Wolfson demand letter. She told him that all of them on the Ninth Floor had kept this secret, and she wanted to know if she could be held criminally liable for having remained quiet all this time.

This was all so much Milstead hardly knew what to think. He did not know if anything could be done about the secret campaign loan. He was not knowledgeable about campaign finance law, and he assumed the paper trail would be carefully covered. He had no idea if the Protocol Fund borrowing was illegal or not.

At one point he excused himself to go to the rest room. Carlson thought that he was wiring himself but then decided it made no difference. She no longer cared. While Milstead was gone, Ronnie Lopez, Bruce Babbitt's former chief of staff, came over to speak to her. If word gets back to the Ninth Floor that I've been seen in a bar with Ralph Milstead, she thought, I'll be fired and won't have to bother resigning.

When Milstead returned, he acquired a stubby pencil from their waiter and started taking notes on a napkin. Carlson seemed very frightened now. Her voice had changed as she had told him about the secret campaign loan. "Why tell me?" he asked.

"I know you were the one person who would do something about it," she said.

"What do you want me to do with this information?" Milstead asked her. She wanted him to do whatever had to be done.

At one point—neither of them remembers when or who said it—one of them said, "Do you realize what we are talking about could bring the governor down?" The other agreed.

Despite her assurance to Milstead, Carlson was not certain he would do anything with the information. She wanted him to, she could not keep it a secret any longer, but she just did not know if he would do what he should. There was a great deal at stake here.

Carlson recalls that one time when she spoke to Milstead, she asked him what if Bob Corbin wouldn't do anything with this? Milstead replied, "Well, Corbin can do it. There's the state grand jury."

Carlson and Milstead spoke by telephone during the next two weeks. Milstead had his people check on the names with which she had provided him. He had been able to confirm that Hugh Gregan and Barry Wolfson were real people and potentially had access to the kind of money Carlson believed they had lent the campaign. He had left his meeting with her under the impression that the two men were out of California, and this had slowed checking them out. He asked her to get some documents for him.

Shortly after 7:00 P.M. on October 6 they met again at Cafe de Perouges. Carlson gave him copies of documents that showed Gregan's and Wolfson's names had been under consideration for appointment to a state board that approved bonding districts. This would be the payoff in Milstead's eye.

Neither, in fact, had been appointed, but the documents confirmed what Carlson had told him. This also matched what Horace Lee Watkins had been bragging about all along.

It was as if a dam had broken since Carlson had told Milstead about the loan. She did not feel good at having betrayed the governor's trust, but she felt even more intensely his betrayal of those who had supported him, especially the members of his own party who had stayed with him through every embarrassment. She attended a legislative conference in Hawaii where she decided to tell Carl Kunasek, the senate president. She felt he deserved better than to be blindsided like this. She asked Kunasek to join her for a cup of coffee at a coffee shop where they would not be observed.

"Here's what's happening," she told him. "You'd better distance yourself. The bottom's going to fall out." Kunasek was ashen. She told him about the loan and the consequences as she saw them. She told him what Mecham had done with the Protocol Fund after agreeing to use it only for the legitimate purposes of the state. She concluded by saying, "There's going to be a big scandal." She did not want Kunasek hurt by it.

Back in Phoenix she met with Senator Usdane and told him she was meeting with Milstead. She told him about the loan and the Protocol Fund. She told Usdane that she was leaving the administration.

Representative Lela Steffey, one of Evan Mecham's staunchest supporters, was serving as the national convention chairperson for the National Order of Women Legislators. The convention met in Phoenix from October 5 through 9 that year.

The morning after Milstead obtained the documents from Carlson he was to participate on a panel discussion at the convention for one hour. Attorney General Bob Corbin was the panel moderator.

When the men arrived, Milstead told Corbin that he had to speak with him before he left. After the panel discussion the two men located an unoccupied hearing room and met in private. Milstead told him that a source he would not name had reliably informed him of a secret campaign loan to Evan Mecham. He told Corbin what he knew and what he had been able to confirm.

Corbin was "astounded." The attorney general told Milstead that he simply could not believe that Mecham would do something like this. Milstead also told him about the Protocol Fund, and Corbin took that news just as seriously, to Milstead's surprise. Corbin told Milstead that he would be in touch.

That day, or early the next, an investigator for the attorney general, George Graham, contacted Milstead as the first step in opening an official investigation into the complaint. Milstead repeated what he knew. He did not have Carlson's permission to use her name and did not give it. The attorney general's office was very eager to know Milstead's source, and he would have liked to tell them because it was evident to him they thought the governor's DPS detail was the leak.

This was a matter of some concern to Milstead because Mecham had made it clear he did not trust his detail. He viewed it as a pipeline to Milstead and as a source for every leak off the Ninth Floor. Milstead was sensitive to anyone's believing his men were violating their promise of confidentiality and wanted to assure the attorney general that his men were not the leak.

After about a week Twist made it clear to Milstead that he needed the director's source. Milstead said he would check and see if the source would approve it.

On October 13 Donna Carlson resigned from the administration. Mecham was in the Orient, and she had hoped to wait until he returned; but she knew the lid would not stay on the scandal much longer, and she wanted to be out when it blew.

Before resigning, she went to Steiger and begged him to leave. More than once he had talked about "bailing off this crazy ship before it sinks." Following one meeting with Mecham, Steiger had told her, "I don't know how much longer we can hold this S.O.B. together. I really don't think he needs any of us anyway. He just told me he gets his advice from a higher authority, and I think he really believes it." Steiger stayed on, in what proved a tragic error in judgment.

It is difficult to overstate the impact Donna Carlson's resignation had on the governor's relations with the legislature. It had been Mecham's ability to hold Carlson's loyalty that had reassured the legislators even in the darkest times. "She has ethics," Jane Dee Hull said about her upon hearing word Carlson had finally left the administration. "Donna is a professional, and the only thing a legislative lobbyist has is her word."

The leaders in the legislature all knew of instances in which Carlson had informed them of the governor's opinion and marshaled the troops only to have Mecham switch directions within hours. "Many times she brought a message down here that was counteracted later," Joe Lane said. She had dealt honestly and fairly with them. They all knew her personal situation and that she would not lightly leave her job.

Hull, who had discussed the resignation with Carlson privately, said, "I don't know what triggered it now, but I knew she's been getting more and more upset with what's going on up there."

The weekend of October 17 and 18 Corbin went into the Superstition Mountains with a camera crew from *Good Morning America*. Corbin claims he moved to Arizona in part because he was so taken by the legend of the Lost Dutchman Mine. As he tells it, he spends every free moment in the mountains. In fact, this photo opportunity and one similar circumstance were the only times he went into the Superstitions during a two-year period.

Milstead reached Carlson a few days after her resignation. "I've talked to the attorney general," he said, "and he wants to know my source. Are you willing to talk to him?" She told Milstead that she did not want her name involved. He tried to persuade her, but she was insistent.

Milstead learned from his legislative liaison that Carlson had been talking to Kunasek and that word of the loan was getting out. His liaison had been asked by Kunasek to check into the loan. Though Milstead had many years' experience with sources, he could not believe that Carlson was talking. But his experience had taught him that once a source starts to talk, it usually keeps talking. That was proving true here.

Carlson left on a short trip to California uncertain what she should do. The Saturday she returned to Phoenix was October 17. She tried to reach Corbin at his home but could not. She left word with his wife that it was important she speak with him in confidence. Corbin's wife suggested Carlson drop by the house late Sunday, when her husband was expected back.

When Corbin returned from the Superstition Mountains, he called home and learned that Carlson was trying to reach him. He would be tied up with the film crew for some time yet and made a breakfast date with her for first thing the following morning. The two met at Humpty Dumpty's on Central and Camelback at eight o'clock.

When Carlson arrived, the first person she spotted was Lew Ruggiero, the television investigative reporter. He did not recognize her in casual dress. She sat with Corbin and ordered coffee. She told him that she was Milstead's source.

"Will you meet with our investigator?" Corbin asked. Carlson agreed.

Before Milstead could get back to the attorney general, Twist called Milstead and told him not to bother, that the source was now talking directly with them.

> May I say that if you are unhappy with my leadership, that [*sic*] perhaps it is you who should resign. As for this administration, we have just begun.
>
> —EVAN MECHAM, *responding to legislator's letter*
>
> *Kinda be careful, because you might get your tit in a wringer by saying something that isn't quite proper.*
>
> —EVAN MECHAM

# 20

In mid-September Mecham attended a fiesta in central Phoenix in celebration of Mexico's Independence Day. It was a predominantly Hispanic crowd, boisterous and mildly intoxicated by the time he mounted a stage to speak. The crowd was jeering the governor, and several times the master of ceremonies had to ask that it show him some respect.

It was one of Mecham's most unpleasant public appearances. Afterward the governor was driven home by a Hispanic DPS officer. Mecham talked to the officer about the teachings of the Mormon Church and about Lamanites, as the dark-skinned people of America are called in the Book of Mormon. He discussed the conflict that existed between the dark- and white-skinned peoples, an example of which he had just witnessed.

The officer informed Beau Johnson of the conversation. Johnson listened and wondered "why Mecham would bring this up, especially to a Hispanic officer."

On September 16 Mecham traveled to Utah to deliver a keynote address in Salt Lake City to a "gathering of self-proclaimed constitutional scholars assembled by W. Cleon Skousen's National Center for Constitutional Studies." Susan Carson with Tucson's *Arizona Daily Star* quoted Mecham as saying, "I want you to recognize tonight on this 200th anniversary [of the Constitution] that this is a great Christian nation that recognizes Jesus Christ as the God of the land. It is the best place in the world for Jews, Hindus and atheists . . . and everybody else because [the Constitution] is human rights and freedom to all." The speech received virtually no media coverage. The proclamation was very similar to one Mecham had made in 1964, when he said, "This nation was founded on Christian principles."

Ken Smith had worked for eight years as a reporter for the Los Angeles *Daily Journal*. For four years he was a spokesman for the County Supervisors Association in Sacramento. He had worked with Dennis Revell, Ronald Reagan's son-in-law, and it was through him that Fred Craft first suggested Smith might work for Evan Mecham of Arizona. Smith was reportedly a close friend of Maureen Reagan's.

Early that summer, following the first legislative session, Smith heard that Ron Bellus might be leaving the administration. Craft made calls on his behalf, and in August Smith flew over to meet with Evan Mecham.

When he met with the governor, Smith told him that he was "over-exposed" to the media. Mecham informed Smith that he did not understand Arizona politics, to which Smith replied, "Politics is politics." He told Mecham that at least half his problem was the media and that the media should be receiving half his resources. Smith told him that he needed a complete housecleaning of his staff, including the secretaries. Mecham hedged, but Smith thought the governor had agreed substantially on the direction Smith wanted to move him. The key ingredient, that Smith would announce all negative news and let Mecham announce the positives, was abrogated within days.

One of the serious problems Smith faced was the sincere but, in his view, misguided notion of the governor and his staff that Mecham needed only to get his message out. As far as Smith was concerned, Mecham should go into hiding for a long time.

It is unlikely that any press secretary could have been a success with Evan Mecham. After his administration was over, Mecham once remarked that Smith had the same problem as Bellus: He wanted to speak for Evan Mecham, and no one but Evan Mecham speaks for him.

That point had been made in the presence of the reporters the previous March when Bellus had been speaking to them. Mecham came out of his office and said, "Ron, your conference is over. Would you please go back to your office?" Bellus had complied.

Now Bellus was out and Smith was in. But Mecham was still Mecham.

On September 25 the Mesa *Tribune*, which had disclosed some unsavory aspects of Horace Lee Watkins's background the previous spring, ran a copyrighted story reporting that the governor's new appointee to head prison construction had been convicted of armed robbery and had served a prison sentence. The story was inaccurate because Watkins had plea-bargained and had actually been found guilty of mail robbery in 1960. There was no proof he had used a gun in committing the offense, and he had not been found guilty of armed robbery.

Since Watkins had committed the robbery when he was an adult but when he was nineteen years old, he qualified for sentencing under the Federal Youthful Offenders Act. He served time at Lompoc, then finished his prison term at a federal youth camp in Tucson. His conviction had been set aside in 1964.

Mecham had been incensed at this inaccurate reporting, and Ken Smith had to work hard to talk him out of holding a press conference denouncing the Mesa *Tribune*. Watkins threatened to sue the newspaper.

A reporter's worst nightmare came true for Sam Stanton on September 29, 1987. Sam Stanton became part of the story he was covering. He later said, "You don't know what it is like until someone shoves a microphone into your face."

In late September Mecham mailed twenty-five thousand copies of a letter nationwide in an attempt to raise $1.2 million within forty-five days. He had television spots and a tabloid for which to pay. The letter read in part:

> Dear Fellow Conservative:
>
> As Governor of the great state of Arizona, I want to extend to you an unprecedented invitation.
>
> I would like you to pick up and move to Arizona.
>
> That's right, I want you to sell your house, pack your belongings, quit your job and come to the most beautiful state in the Union. . . .
>
> You see, right now, I'm under attack from some of the most powerful and dangerous liberal groups of the nation.
>
> They're bringing the enormous resources of their national organizations into Arizona to fight against me. . . .
>
> In a day and age when militant gay leaders are feeding the nation a steady diet of their "alternative life-styles" and they stand before the nightly news cameras demanding that the taxpayers pay for their AIDS treatments, I feel it is important for conservatives to stand up for traditional American values. . . .
>
> As conservatives we must not let the left get away with these intimidation tactics. These left wing groups are seeking to scare us away from even disagreeing with them.

If I lose this historic battle it will make it even more dangerous for other conservatives to stand up for our traditional American family values.

Here in Arizona we are fighting a battle to see whether it is possible anymore for a conservative to speak his mind.

If we lose, it will have a terrible chilling effect on those who advocate our traditional values in the future. . . .

Without your contribution I will risk being crushed by the millions of dollars the militant liberals and the homosexual lobby plan to spend against me.

The governor had not announced his intention to solicit funds, so the letter came as a surprise. Its strident language and blatant appeal to arch conservatives and homophobics raised eyebrows.

A reporter contacted Ken Smith, and asked him about the letter. As with many major events, Smith had not heard of it before this and went to see Mecham, who was speaking to Jim Colter. Mecham told Smith that he knew nothing about the letter. Then he recalled that some of his people were preparing a letter to be mailed nationally.

Smith began receiving more calls from reporters. He asked one to provide him with a copy of the letter. Once he had it, he went back to see Mecham, who was now in Colter's office. Smith showed Mecham the letter, asked if it was legitimate and if it bore his signature.

Mecham was perturbed that Smith was asking him again about the letter. Though Smith had been on staff only two or three weeks, Mecham was already starting to treat him as if he were a pesty reporter rather than one of his own people.

"Yes, that's my letter. What's the problem?" He then turned on his heel and went to his office before Smith could explain the difficulty.

As Smith stood there wondering if he should follow Mecham, Colter left the office through another door. Since Colter was technically his boss, Smith went hunting for him.

There are different interpretations of Colter's behavior during his time with the Mecham administration. One observer who dealt almost daily with him believed he was in the early stages of Alzheimer's disease. Donna Carlson knew he took medication and thought that accounted for his sleepiness and lack of focus. Others thought he suffered some kind of mental collapse on the Ninth Floor.

Smith located Colter in the men's room. Colter "was standing in front of the mirror, sweating, folding and unfolding paper towels. He opened his mouth a couple of times as if he were going to speak but said nothing."

Smith asked if he was ill, and Colter shook his head, indicating that he was not. Smith left the men's room and never again asked Colter a difficult question. He went to the Ninth Floor lobby and met with the press.

During his meeting with the reporters Smith confirmed that Mecham had signed the letter. At this point Smith was trying to limit the letter to no more than a one-day story but could see that was not working. The conference lasted longer than he would have liked and ended with Smith promising to obtain more information.

Smith had been promised access to Mecham as a condition of his employment. As this day progressed, it became apparent that was not going to occur. He decided to force the issue. Mecham was in a meeting, so Smith gave his secretary a note to hand to the governor saying Smith must speak to Mecham at once regarding the fund-raising letter.

Instead of responding, Mecham "dodged" Smith for the next hour. Smith finally caught up with him in Colter's office. As Smith asked Mecham about the specifics of the letter, so he could relay them back to the press, the governor became evasive. He finally confirmed that he had approved the letter in concept, that he had seen an earlier draft but not this one, and that the office signature machine had been used to affix his signature. Mecham saw nothing wrong with the letter, then instructed Smith not to discuss it further with reporters.

Instead Smith met with the press, as he had said he would. He told them he had been mistaken earlier. He relayed what he now knew, including that the signature machine had been used and with Mecham's authorization. He conceded the letter was "a little rough" but defended it as "fairly standard in political fund raising." The reporters thought they were getting the runaround, and Mike Murphy recalls they were virtually "shrieking" at Smith to get the facts.

The reporters were testy by this time. Some of them had talked to Smith earlier, and now they had two different answers to what seemed to them a simple request. They had become accustomed to the incompetence of the Ninth Floor and had hoped that Smith would improve matters somewhat, if only in providing them with accurate information the first time it was requested or at least in telling them he did not know. Mike Murphy saw Smith being "extremely useless" in this situation and in what proved to be one of the turning points of the Mecham administration.

As the events unfolded, Smith became "disgusted" with the performance of the press. Smith concluded "that the reporters collectively were not very bright or sophisticated." His press relations went downhill from that point.

The reporters were fascinated by the signature machine. Until now none of them had really considered that the governor had one. Elected officials usually do, but in this case it sounded as if the machine had run amok, and that made it news.

A few minutes after Smith left Mecham called the press room. Now Mecham denied approving the letter. He said that he was trying to learn who had authorized the use of his signature machine. He said, "I don't know who approved the letter and I don't remember, as I read the letter, I don't remember having seen the content before. That's all the answers I've got for you."

Now Smith summoned the reporters to the governor's office for an additional explanation. Mecham confirmed that he had approved the project. Commenting on the contents of the letter, he said, "I read it, and it isn't like I'd say it." Mecham said that twenty thousand additional letters scheduled to be mailed would not go out.

Sam Stanton decided that was going to be the story and was ready to go with it. Other reporters had written their stories and also considered the story over when they learned that Mecham would be holding another hastily called press conference. This struck Mike Murphy as typical. Mecham just did not know when to stop.

The governor had a statement to make on another matter, but because of the letter, there were more television cameras than usual. Mecham made his scheduled statement, then read a clarifying prepared statement on the letter and fielded questions from the reporters concerning it and the signature machine.

By this time in the administration Sam Stanton was getting on Mecham's nerves. Murphy could see it, and so could Smith. Stanton always stood closest to the governor, and Murphy always positioned himself a half step behind his rival. Smith was standing about six feet behind the governor to his left, watching with horror what occurred.

Stanton, it seemed to Smith, was taunting the governor over the letter and signature. Stanton and Murphy thought they were trying to get a straight answer. Mecham permitted tough questions, and the reporters were accustomed to asking them.

Mecham concluded he had said enough and walked off to leave the room. Until this point in his administration, in Murphy's opinion, the average person tended to believe what Mecham said about the print media. As Mecham walked away, Stanton asked the question again. He simply did not have a straight answer and was concerned about getting one.

"Governor, we've gotten several different stories here. Can you tell us what the true version is?"

Mecham had reached the door. All he needed was to keep walking. He had given the reporters a "definite straight statement" about the issue, and they should have accepted it. Sam Stanton was calling him "a liar." Not until the administration was over would he concede that what he did next was a mistake. Others termed it a disaster.

In front of the television cameras Mecham, clearly out of control, marched up to Stanton. He stuck his finger up in Stanton's face. His left hand, held to his side, quivered in visible rage. To Stanton it looked as if the governor had just "snapped."

"Sam, when I make a statement, you hadn't better say what the truth is!" Mecham said in a loud voice.

"I'm not saying—"

"Listen! Don't you . . . you are questioning my integrity. I gave you the statement, I gave you the statement."

"I am most certainly not, Governor."

"Don't ever ask me for a true statement again!"

"I'm not alleging anything. That's not what I said."

"Don't ever—"

"That's not what I said."

"That's exactly what you said!"

The two were talking on top of each other. Mecham was angry; Stanton, respectful and apparently taken aback. The press had received at least three different versions of the events surrounding the letter. It seemed simple enough to Stanton. Instead, there was the governor having a tantrum on television. Stanton, and others, had seen this type of behavior in private but never in public and in front of cameras. Mecham turned on his heel and marched off.

The reporters shoved recorders in Stanton's face. *Republic* reporter Don Harris, Stanton's friend, the dean of the Capitol press room, immediately asked for his reaction.

Harris had worked as a reporter initially in Chicago and since 1973 for the *Arizona Republic*. He had first covered a Mecham campaign in 1978. He contacted his editor, Laurie Roberts, and said, "You're not going to believe what just happened." He suggested a story on the confrontation between Mecham and Stanton. After that he attended press conferences as a backup for Stanton and to cover anything that might happen involving him. Stanton had become part of the story. It was the first time in Harris's career that something like this had occurred.

Laurie Roberts first heard of what had taken place when Harris and Stanton called her. About once a month she had been cautioning Stanton not to do anything to provoke the governor. Mecham's temper was well known, to reporters if not the public and she did not want any of her reporters doing anything that would create a scene. When Stanton got on the telephone, he told her what had happened in the breathless manner he has when he is hot on a story and excited. He was concerned she would think he had done something wrong, and he assured Roberts more than once that he had done nothing to provoke the reaction.

Roberts went to the television, which was already running the scene, and watched it played over and over. For the first time, it seemed to her, the public was seeing the "portrait of a man out of control." Analyzing Stanton's conduct, she was "very relieved and proud at how he conducted himself, how he stood his ground." Roberts says that she was "never prouder" of a colleague than of Sam Stanton at that moment.

Roberts called him back and told him, "You did a damn good story." Then she chastised him for filing late. He had spent so much time being interviewed he had been slow in submitting his own story.

That night, and over and over, statewide and nationwide, the scene played on television.

Mecham apparently realized he had made a mistake. Though he had already gone home, he arranged to make the rounds of the local television stations. "Nobody calls me a liar, particularly a reporter from the *Arizona Republic*, as unaccustomed to the truth as they are," he said.

The significance of the scene with Stanton, it seemed to Joe Lane, was that now the public saw what the members of the legislature had been witnessing for most of a year. Until now Mecham had been careful to keep such behavior from the public.

Lane and a few of the others were amused at the quote that emerged. Mecham had unintentionally said the opposite of what he meant. "Don't ever ask me for a true statement again!" Or perhaps he had slipped and said exactly what he really felt.

The next day, when Sam Stanton saw Mecham, the governor looked "gray." Everyone was talking about Mecham's being crazy. As they were walking, Mecham suddenly said to Stanton, "Come on, Sam, smile."

Later that day House Majority Whip Jane Dee Hull called Stanton into her office and asked him if he thought the governor was losing his mind. She told him the legislature simply had to take control because it feared for Mecham's mental state.

Stanton was troubled by this. Who was he to comment on the governor's mental state? He was just a reporter, not a psychologist.

Republican legislators who had been edging away from the governor for some months found Mecham's public display of temper the last straw. It was one thing for Alan Stephens to criticize the governor. From a Democrat that was expected. The public statements of the Dirty Dozen had been highly unusual. What occurred over the next two days was unprecedented.

First, Chris Herstam publicly abandoned Mecham and called for Republicans to unite behind an unspecified Republican candidate in any recall election that might transpire. Republican Representative Jack Jewitt joined in his call.

Next, Senator Greg Lunn called for Mecham to resign. Jim Green, Jim Hartdegen, and Larry Hawke joined him. All four legislators were Republicans.

That Sunday Sam Stanton ran an article revealing that for the first time, more Arizonans favored Mecham's recall than opposed it.

On October 8 Barry Goldwater delivered a speech at Arizona State University. He said that it had likely been his endorsement of Mecham the previous fall that had made the governor's election possible. "I think until you understand the man better," Goldwater said, "you can't understand why he does these things. . . . I think he honestly feels he's got an eight hundred number straight up to God."

Goldwater predicted that the recall drive would succeed. To spare the state, Goldwater called on Mecham to resign.

# 21

One of the responsibilities of special assistants to Governor Mecham was state agency oversight. At 10:30 A.M. on October 1, 1987, Sam Steiger called Ronald D. Johnson, a former justice of the peace and a Mecham reappointee to the state Board of Pardon and Paroles.

The board was scheduled to vote on whether to fire its executive secretary. Steiger told Johnson that if he voted to remove her, he would no longer be a part-time justice of the peace and his resignation from the board would be requested.

Johnson called Bob Corbin, who told Johnson to "vote his conscience."

Johnson attended the noontime board meeting. He seconded the motion requesting the secretary's resignation, then voted with the majority in passing it, four to three.

The next day Johnson received a letter from Steiger saying, "[P]ermission granted you to act as a justice of the peace pro-tem is withdrawn effective immediately." Johnson took the letter to the attorney general's office. While there, with Mike Cudahy and an investigator looking on, Johnson called Steiger at his home and taped the conversation.

Steiger said, "I am doing exactly what I told you I am going to do and

I am not through with you yet. . . . I explained to you exactly how it was and you ignored me and that ain't the way we play the game. . . . Your vote yesterday was against the wishes of the people who hired you and that ain't the way it is played. . . . Now you give me all that jive shit about you want to be on a team. I told you what it took to be on a team and you couldn't come up with it."

Unaware that the conversation had been taped, Steiger categorically denied it had taken place when asked about it by reporters. He also stated, "There is no connection between the action I took and [Johnson's] vote, period."

Mecham responded to a reporter's question on the Steiger situation by saying, "No, I didn't put [Steiger] up to it. Bob Corbin trapped . . . tried to trap him."

Following a Superior Court hearing in which the tape recording of the conversation was played to a stunned courtroom, Steiger was charged with extortion.* Mecham immediately placed him on paid administrative leave.

Following Donna Carlson's resignation the previous week, it appeared that Mecham's administration was disintegrating. Lawmakers expressed shock and anger.

Steiger was a genuine Arizona folk hero who had made himself over into the embodiment of the western cowboy. He was one of two members of the governor's staff who brought Mecham any respect at all. The other had been Donna Carlson.

Steiger was a man who said exactly, and loquaciously, whatever was on his mind. He had served Mecham with flare and loyalty.

There is no question in Steiger's mind that Mecham believed he was called by God to be Arizona's governor. Steiger says that Mecham "really believes he is divinely inspired." His standard answer to problems was: "Don't worry, Sam. It looks bad, but I know it will be taken care of."

At this time the *Republic* ran an article reciting other reported incidents of impropriety by Mecham appointees in dealing with state agencies and boards.

The chairman of the state Transportation Board charged in the article that in August Steiger had pressured him and another member of the seven-member board on behalf of a paving and construction company in Tucson. A third board member reported Steiger's contacting him for the same reason.

Horace Lee Watkins was reported to have pressured the same board earlier in the summer over the hiring of bond underwriters to sell $275 million in highway construction bonds.

---

*Steiger was convicted and placed on probation. On September 21, 1989, the Arizona Court of Appeals set aside Steiger's conviction, deeming the statute unconstitutionally vague.

Watkins said that the chairman "is a liar." He admitted calling the board chairman but said he only wanted to know why the board was not awarding more of the bond business to Arizona companies. He acknowledged naming a dozen or so companies.

When informed by the reporter that most of them were not based in Arizona, Watkins reportedly said, "Aren't they? I don't know that much about the bond business." Asked by reporters to comment further, Watkins said he had simply been "gathering information at the governor's request."

At this time the business community began abandoning the governor. J. Fife Symington III, the former state Republican finance chairman, held a press conference and personally handed two thousand dollars to Ed Buck. This was the same amount of money he had donated to Mecham.

He said, "Senator Barry Goldwater has publicly stated that Governor Mecham should resign, and I whole-heartedly support that position. . . . [T]hree more years of [Mecham's] administration will have a severe and debilitating effect on Arizona." He called on other business leaders to join in the effort to oust Mecham, concluding with the comment that the state party leaders' stalwart defense of Mecham indicated that "they are prepared to take the Republican party over the cliff wrapped in a blanket of Mecham loyalty."

The state party chairman, Burton Kruglick, was not prepared to give up in attempts to mediate differences among the Republican party, the legislature, and Evan Mecham. On October 15, 1987, he held another meeting at his home. Attending were former Arizona Governors Jack Williams and Paul Fannin, former Congressman Eldon Rudd, Harry Rosenzweig, and House Majority Leader Jim Ratliff. None of the earlier lawmakers was there, but this time Evan Mecham attended.

Reporters nabbed the participants as they left. Ratliff said it had been agreed that the governor would "get some better staff." He also said Mecham believed he had the support of the public.

Kruglick thought that Goldwater's call for Mecham's resignation had influenced Mecham, who said that public perception is not the same as reality and that he recognized the need to change. "People perceive me as being a hard-liner. . . . Maybe I need to work hard at it. . . . Maybe I should change my style."

Though a "new" Mecham was supposed to have emerged from the meeting, within hours the governor appeared on his regular radio broadcast on KTAR and said of Goldwater, "I don't think that he knows very much about what's going on in state government."

The next day Mecham addressed a group of western newspaper executives and charged that publisher Pat Murphy had an "agenda." He repeated his unsubstantiated, often denied, story of Pat Murphy's publicly stating he would "get" Mecham.

He went on to say, "Pat Murphy has directed a campaign against me. . . . Pat now has his tail in a crack. His own career is on the line. . . . [A]fter I survive his assault, my hopes are that the Pulliam family . . . will put Mr. Murphy back on the copy desk."

Pat Murphy was present during the speech. He told his reporters and others that the accusations were "totally untrue." He pointed out that Mecham had made similar claims about Democrats and homosexuals. Their picture was taken with the governor stabbing his finger into the publisher's chest.

At almost the same hour the Mecham Recall Committee announced it had collected 302,287 signatures to date. Asked about the prospects of a recall election,. Mecham said, "Heavens, if they get the signatures, what does that say? It says we're going to have an election. I won the last one. If we have one, I'll win the next one."

> *You ask me if Bob Corbin is out to get me?*
> *You better believe he's out to get me.*
> *                              —EVAN MECHAM*
>
> *The governor thinks everybody's out to get*
> *him. . . .*
> *                              —BOB CORBIN*
>
> *When the horse is dead, dismount.*
> *                        —Old western proverb*

# 22

Jim Colter contacted attorney Murray Miller in early October to assist the governor in fighting the recall drive. Miller was a prominent local attorney and had won a number of headline-grabbing victories over the years.

Miller worked to prepare a legal challenge to the recall petitions for the governor. He interviewed witnesses to signatures and researched the law. Jim Colter served as the liaison with the Ninth Floor and brought Miller the latest stories of fraud. Before long Miller determined that the governor would not have much chance of success in the courts.

The two men organized a miniature "crisis team" that met frequently at Miller's east Phoenix home against Mummy Mountain. In mid-October Miller spoke directly to Mecham at such a meeting. He said to the governor, "It looks as if there is going to be a recall election whether we like it or not. All of the potential candidates are taking potshots at you. There is no way for you to answer if you are busy fighting the recall. My advice is to concede the recall and start running for governor again. You should tell the public that you are not concerned about winning. During such an election you can put your issues before the people."

Mecham would hear nothing of it. He told Miller, "There is no reason to do that when I don't think a recall is justified." According to Mecham, his sources were reporting massive signature fraud. Mecham was determined to fight any recall election.

170

\* \* \*

On October 18 *60 Minutes* ran a twenty-minute piece on the situation in Arizona. It was one of the most watched television broadcasts in Arizona history. Governor Mecham and his wife, Florence, saw the show at their home. Ken Smith joined them. Afterward Mecham commented that he thought he had done well.

The supporters of the governor considered the program a hatchet job that failed to portray the "positive" achievements of the Mecham administration.

For the rest, the spectacle that had become Arizona politics was there for the nation to see. Any thought that Arizona was struggling in the backwaters with its difficulty was at an end.

By this time Sam Stanton was exhausted. He lived each day sustained on nicotine, caffeine, and alcohol, and he was reaching the point where his nerve endings felt dead.

For ten months he had been working most waking hours seven days a week. He called his editor Laurie Roberts at all hours and on the weekends with stories. Both the *Republic* and the *Gazette* had taken to printing a table of contents on the front page listing the Mecham articles in the paper. The local television news shows now had their own "Mecham Report."

It had reached the point where if Stanton did not have an article on page A1, above the fold, he considered himself a failure. Before the Mecham administration just running an article anywhere in the paper two or three times a week was more than enough. Since the end of August there had been constant stories. The recall had taken off like a rocket. Trudeau's strip had focused national attention.

In addition to *60 Minutes*, Mecham made a second appearance on *The MacNeil-Lehrer News Hour*, had done the short-lived *Good Evening America*, and been on *Nightwatch*. *The New York Times*, Kansas City, Missouri, *Times*, the *News* of Mexico City, the *Economist* (London), *Business Week*, and many others had run articles. *Sports Illustrated* was now including Mecham in its "Scorecard" section since his pronouncement that "a lot of white people" go to National Basketball Association games.

During this period the thirty-third national organization canceled its Arizona convention, raising the cost to the state to fourteen million dollars.

The Tuesday after Donna Carlson met with Bob Corbin in the coffee shop Sam Stanton was tipped about the Gregan-Wolfson loan. Donna Carlson did not tell him. She did not give him the documents.

At almost the same time a source contacted Laurie Roberts and the *Republic*'s city editor. When Roberts called Stanton with the information, she learned he was already working on the story.

Stanton drove out to Tempe and interviewed Barry Wolfson. Wolfson was candid about the loan. He confirmed that he had extended a line of credit for $600,000 to Mecham during the general election and that he had wired two payments totaling $350,000 into a Mecham account.

Stanton obtained copies of the key documents. One of them was a letter from Mecham to Wolfson agreeing that the loan "will remain confidential." Stanton determined that Wolfson and Gregan were defendants in a civil fraud and racketeering suit filed by the attorney general.

Stanton filed the story. Roberts had him report to the *Republic* and *Gazette* building in downtown Phoenix so she and the city editor could review the documents for themselves. This was a first for him.

Laurie Roberts and the city editor worked on the story. They went through several drafts with Stanton. "We knew it was an important story," she said later. They were up until 10:00 P.M. on it. Stanton had gone out for a beer since his part was done and called her to have the final draft read. He was not happy with the lead and argued for a different, softer approach. When he was unable to persuade her, the story ran as was. Stanton had no sense that an avalanche was about to descend.

When Bob Corbin returned from his breakfast meeting with Donna Carlson, he had Barnett Lotstein, his most experienced trial prosecutor, Michael Cudahy, and an investigator from the public corruptions unit dispatched to her home to interview her.

On Tuesday Sam Stanton called Corbin for information on the investigation. Other than to confirm it Corbin had no comment. During their conversation Stanton told Corbin he had copies of the applicable documents. As soon as he got off the telephone, Corbin had a subpoena prepared for them. Twist went down to the *Republic*, where, he says, he received a "polite response." Pat Murphy refused to turn the documents over.

All four top men were meeting daily to coordinate this extraordinary investigation. Lotstein relates that though they were investigating a sitting governor, they labored to behave as they would in any other criminal case. The day the Stanton article broke Lotstein went personally to the secretary of state's office to obtain copies of the Mecham campaign disclosure statements. At this point he was curious if what was alleged had actually occurred and, if it had, whether it constituted a crime. It was remotely possible there was a plausible excuse for the omission since state law required omission to be a willful act for it to be a crime.

During the next few days the attorney general's office proceeded with interviews of those who had signed notes to guarantee the loan. Many of these were people still in the administration, and Lotstein recalls they were a very nervous lot.

Corbin says he was quickly unhappy with the level of cooperation the governor's office was extending, or rather in his opinion, not extending. In Arizona the attorney general cannot issue subpoenas. "We were getting stonewalled," he says. He claims he now directed the investigation be conducted under the auspices of the state grand jury, which could issue subpoenas.

In fact, almost from the first day of the investigation the attorney general was using the subpoena power of the grand jury.

These four men—Corbin, Twist, Lotstein, and Cudahy—all disavow that at this point they felt any sense of history in what they were doing. They say they were simply investigating allegations so they could make a determination.

But surely they knew they had embarked on a course from which it would be impossible to turn and from which there would emerge no winners.

Evan Mecham interprets the actions of the four men in a very different light. He holds, and has frequently stated, that Bob Corbin coveted the governorship and would do almost anything to achieve it. Corbin and Mecham had competed against each other in the Republican primary in 1974. Shortly after Barr had announced his candidacy in January 1986, Corbin publicly toyed with running against him, then withdrew after a day's vacillation. In mid-October 1987 Corbin said he had not ruled out the possibility of running for governor if there was a recall election.

Mecham took these to be clear signs that Corbin lusted for the office Mecham held. Mecham believes that Corbin went so far as to participate in the conspiracy against him to place the secretary of state in the governor's office and bring Corbin as attorney general "that much closer to his dream and just a heart beat away from the Governor's chair."

Evan Mecham believes he was removed from office by a wide-ranging, long-term criminal conspiracy in which Bob Corbin was "the willing tool of the Power Brokers." This portion of the conspiracy, Mecham says, was formulated during the period between his election and inauguration. Mecham believes that Pat Murphy told a companion in an elevator, "We're going to get Mecham, the snide little bastard."

Mecham says that when he told the "Power Brokers" of Arizona one week after his election that he was now in charge, "they" determined to have him removed from office at the earliest opportunity and by whatever means possible. Burton Barr, identified by Mecham as the former speaker of the house,* worked insidiously behind the scenes, pulling the strings and lining up the players to bring about Mecham's destruction. "This group was meeting regularly with Burton Barr, who said he would never forgive me, and would never stop trying to get even with me for defeating him. . . . It was a deliberately planned 'coup d'etat.' "

*Evan Mecham, *Impeachment: The Arizona Conspiracy* p. 10. Burton Barr never served as speaker of the Arizona house. He was for many years the house majority leader.

According to Mecham and his supporters, the Democratic party in Arizona was part of the conspiracy. It arranged for a Democratic activist, homosexual Ed Buck, to reregister as a Republican and to lead the recall movement against Mecham. Pat Murphy was then able to pass Buck off as a conservative businessman when in reality he had been trained in Yugoslavia "under Communist Party sponsorship" to be a political agitator. Buck also served as a front for the National Gay Rights Liberation Movement with the goal of turning Arizona into a homosexual sanctuary. During the recall drive homosexuals were bused in from California to register in Arizona and sign the recall petitions. Mecham says all the while the state Democratic party was raising money and turning these funds over to Buck and his band of homosexuals.

> *The Ninth Floor isn't under siege. There is some siege mentality, but it's with the press and perhaps some people in the Legislature, but certainly we aren't under siege.*
> —EVAN MECHAM
>
> WELCOME TO ARIZONA
> THE LAUGHS ARE ON US
> > *—Arizona state highway sign, according to Mark Russell*

# 23

On October 21, 1987, Joe Lane arose at his usual 5:00 A.M. As was his custom, he read the morning paper to see what Sam Stanton had written. The headline read: MECHAM KEPT $350,000 LOAN SECRET.

Lane read: "Gov. Evan Mecham received a $350,000 loan from an east Valley development attorney just before last fall's general election, according to documents obtained Tuesday by the *Arizona Republic*, but he failed to disclose the loan despite state law that requires such disclosure.

"The loan, which constituted about 30 percent of Mecham's $1.16 million campaign last year, was made by Barry Wolfson, who is a Tempe developer and attorney, after Mecham agreed to keep it confidential, according to the documents." Further in the article, Stanton wrote: "Wolfson, along with Chandler developer Hugh Gregan and several others, are defendants in a civil fraud and racketeering suit filed in August by the state attorney general's office. The suit alleges the misuse of $368 million in industrial-development bonds that were to be used to build low-income housing but which never were."

Lane was furious. It was one thing for Mecham to abuse members of the party and it was another for him to embarrass the state Lane loved, but by God, if on top of that and the indignities they had had to bear personally, Mecham was a crook as well, that was something else altogether.

Lane drove to the state house of representatives, where he met his chief of staff, Rick Collins, and Representative Jim Ratliff for breakfast and a discussion of business for that day. Lane had expected there would be a respite once the regular session was adjourned the previous May, but with the two special sessions and the recall movement starting its petition drive in July there had been a steady and devastating progression of damaging events. Now this.

When Sam Stanton entered the press room in the state senate building the morning his loan story broke, it was as if suddenly he were a superstar.

He was not yet thirty, but Stanton knew the power of the press, or thought he did until that morning. But suddenly people were behaving very strangely toward him, as though he had deposed the king.

It was common during this time to doubt a story once it was too late to do anything about it. More than once he had called sources in the middle of the night and asked, "Are you sure?" That was the great problem with Mecham stories. He had sewn government up so tight through intimidation and paranoia you could rarely obtain documents. Stanton wrote nearly all his stories based on sources. The fact that until now he had always been right did not lessen his anxiety.

What if the loan was listed after all? When he had reached Mecham about it, the governor had denied there was such a loan. Maybe in his rush to write the story he had missed an innocuous line in the forms that reported the loan in some acceptable manner. The need to double-check became overwhelming as did the need to get out of the press room and away from the acclaim.

He hurried the short distance across the Capitol mall from the senate to the secretary of state's office, where the campaign finance reports are filed. Lew Ruggiero was standing at the counter. "Lew, it's not in there, is it?" Stanton asked. "Relax, Sam," he said, "it's not there."

The effect of the article that day was mesmerizing. Everywhere Stanton went, even, perhaps especially, in the two legislative buildings, he was greeted as a conquering hero.

The state legislature was a madhouse. Jim Skelly, chairman of the house Judiciary Committee, delivered a letter to Speaker Joe Lane asking that he have house legal staff look into "possible courses of action" in light of "the serious allegations raised regarding the conduct of Governor Mecham."

Asked what he thought the house should do, Skelly replied it should wait for the attorney general to conclude his investigation. He said the house should not "go off half cocked." Asked about the possibility of impeachment, Skelly replied that the house should take whatever "preliminary action" was necessary should it come to that.

Skelly informed the reporters that grounds for impeachment in the

Arizona constitution were high crimes, misdemeanors, and malfeasance in office.

Asked what he thought, Lane said, "This is very serious business . . . [especially] . . . when you write a letter and say we'll keep this all secret. . . ." The reporters asked about the possibility of impeachment. "It's very premature to rush out and start making impeachment noises until we have some kind of an idea what we're talking about. This is a very serious charge, and I don't see any big rush to do anything. It's just an allegation. The attorney general has an ongoing investigation." Then he added, "[But] we've got to be prepared for anything."

Senate President Carl Kunasek said the senate would be prepared to act if it came to impeachment. Senate Majority Leader Bob Usdane said the senate was examining its responsibilities "if we come down to a problem like impeachment."

Joe Lane's chief of staff, Rick Collins, saw on the television news that Senator Tony West and other state senators had already met with Attorney General Corbin. If something was to be done, it was up to the house, not the senate, to act. He called Lane at home and arranged to join him for breakfast the next morning.

Throughout the day Mecham was uncharacteristically silent. His office issued a five-sentence statement in which the governor denied doing anything illegal. Mecham would not respond to questions posed about possible impeachment.

The day following the Wolfson loan disclosure the *Arizona Republic*, which had until now disapproved of the recall drive, ran an editorial in support: "[Mecham] should be recalled because . . . he either broke the law deliberately . . . or is so incompetent as to be a positive peril to the sensible and lawful operation of state government." The editorial went so far as to say that it was too late for Mecham to resign and that he should remain in office "until he can be recalled or impeached."

The *Republic* had now joined a number of other state dailies in its support of Mecham's removal from office. Three weeks earlier the Mesa *Tribune* had supported the recall, as did the *Arizona Daily Star* in Tucson and the Scottsdale *Progress*. Two papers from areas of strong gubernatorial support, the Green Valley *News* and the semiweekly Lake Havasu City *Today News*, withdrew their support of the governor.

Early that morning Joe Lane and Rick Collins breakfasted with Donald W. Jansen, the house legal counsel. What do we do? they asked one another. They all agreed that they had a constitutional duty to act.

Collins pointed out to Lane that no matter what he did, or did not do, there would be political consequences. It was a no-win situation. By 8:30

or 9:00 A.M. at the latest the reporters would be wanting a statement about the state senators who had already gone to see Corbin. The talk of impeachment was everywhere.

Lane said that if Mecham was cleared, that was fine; if he was not cleared, that was also fine.

Lane's district in southeastern Arizona contained a number of Mormon pioneer settlements. The district was nearly one-third LDS, and as many as 40 percent of the Republican primary voters were Mormons. Lane depended on the Mormon vote to stay in office. No one had to explain the risks to him.

"See if the attorney general will meet with us. Then see if Hamilton's in. Get his attorney and we'll go talk to the attorney general," he told Collins. Collins called Steve Twist and set up the meeting for 8:30 A.M.

Joe Lane, Rick Collins, Art Hamilton, minority counsel Eric Henderson, and Jane Hull all rode in the same car the short trip to the attorney general's office. They met in the attorney general's conference room with Bob Corbin, Steve Twist, Barnett Lotstein, Mike Cudahy, and John Shadegg. The meeting lasted about twenty minutes. Lane recalls it as being cordial and professional.

This was Thursday, only three days after Corbin had met Donna Carlson for breakfast and launched his investigation.

Lane thought that Corbin would brief them on the status of the investigation and thereafter keep them informed. Since the attorney general was already investigating, that made the most sense.

Almost at once Corbin explained that would not be possible. "Matters attending a grand jury are confidential" was all he would say on the subject. Corbin said they could go ahead on their own; indeed, if they wanted to know anything about the allegations, they would have to. Corbin was not going to give them anything.

Collins had known Corbin for several years and noticed that Corbin seemed confident and cocky. He was that way when he was sure of himself. Collins thought that Corbin was behaving like a man with enough to indict.

For Joe Lane this was a grim day. While it was the constitutional duty of the house to actually vote on impeachment, it fell to him as speaker of the house to determine if the first steps that would lead to a vote should be taken.

The idea of conducting his own investigation was a terrible waste of effort and of expense, Lane thought. They already had enough budget problems. But it was apparent to him that the house would need a special counsel to determine if there was any merit to the allegations and at the very least to clear the air. As the meeting broke up, he asked Corbin, Should the house proceed? Corbin answered, Yes, go ahead. We've got someone who's talking. Lane left the meeting with the opinion that indictments would be forthcoming.

The ride back to the Capitol was a somber affair. Lane knew now that there would be no easy way. Hamilton recalls that Lane was agitated. The speaker told all of them, "We're going to have to get into this thing." Hamilton did not disagree. No one in the car did.

During that day Joe Lane and Rick Collins met in the speaker's office and reviewed the options. The recall movement said it would be filing its signatures within a few weeks. Mecham had said repeatedly he intended to challenge every signature. Even if there were enough, an election would not come for six months. In Lane's view, this was something that could not wait. Evan Mecham could be a felon who might well have attained office illegally and had no right to it.

Some members of the house were publicly demanding hearings. Lane did not believe they would be effective in reaching the truth, and the possibility of members playing to the cameras was obvious. He did not want a circus.

Lane said he wanted an outstanding lawyer, preferably someone with judicial experience to serve as special counsel. He wanted to know the job had been done right. He did not care if the leaders picked a Democrat or a Republican. "We are all Arizonans," he said later. There was to be no litmus test beyond competence. After all, you don't investigate the possibility of impeaching a governor every day.

Collins began calling lawyers in whom he had confidence. By 4:00 P.M. he had assembled a list of twelve names. Four of them had served as superior court judges. Lane called a meeting of the house leaders for Friday, the next day, and they reviewed the list. Two of the attorneys were stricken at once. One was Warner Lee, who had worked for the Republicans during the last reapportionment, and the other was Paul Eckstein, who had performed a similar task for the Democrats. Both were seen as partisan.

They narrowed the list to the three best candidates. One was tied up in a trial that had just begun. Lane selected former Superior Court Judge William French to interview first. They arranged through the attorney who had given them French's name to contact him and see if there was preliminary interest and to set an appointment.

That night Lane told his wife, Sue, that they had to speak. He told her what he was planning to do and said, "You understand that if I hire special counsel, I will probably lose my seat?"

Sue asked how he would feel about himself if he didn't. "Not very damn good," he said.

"Then do what you have to do," she told him.

# 24

The day Jimmy Hoffa spit in the face of William P. French the federal prosecutor could have kicked himself for stupidity.

Oddly enough, of all the individuals involved in the impeachment of Evan Mecham, Bill French was nearly alone in being a native of Arizona. His father had been the chief of staff at St. Joseph's Hospital when French was born in Phoenix in 1931, but when his father died, the family had moved to Illinois. His mother did not remarry.

French attended Notre Dame on a football scholarship. He enlisted in the Marine Corps following graduation, then entered law school. When he was graduated in 1959, the U.S. attorney's office selected French as one of thirty lawyers for its honors program.

After Robert Kennedy took over, French was assigned to the Hoffa unit. For a year and a half French investigated the Teamsters' pension fund and Hoffa's own Local 299. Following his first trial, which ended in a hung jury, Hoffa was promptly indicted for jury tampering. The second trial, headed by James Neal, lasted six months, involved six prosecutors, eight or nine defendants, and a battery of defense lawyers.

It was at this time French entered an elevator occupied by Hoffa and his lawyers. Hoffa confronted French as soon as the elevator doors were closed. He spit into French's face and called him a son of a bitch. Afterward it occurred to French that Hoffa had been attempting to provoke a reaction. French was satisfied with a conviction.

Bobby Kennedy sent him to assist in heading off violence in the South in light of the new civil rights bill. First French went to Jackson, Mississippi, where Dr. Martin Luther King, Jr., had indicated his intent to march, then to Philadelphia, Mississippi, to work with the FBI in the investigation into the murder of three civil rights workers. French was standing there the day the FBI pulled the car out of the bog bank in what he described as a "grotesque scene."

French worked on Kennedy's New York senatorial race, then in 1964 accepted the offer of a law firm in Phoenix to take over its litigation division. Bill French had come home.

In 1978 he was appointed to the Maricopa County Superior Court. He stepped down in 1981, having served as the presiding criminal judge. Six years later, when Joe Lane, Rick Collins, and Jane Dee Hull met with him, he was head of the litigation department for Storey & Ross.

French had not enjoyed witnessing the 1986 election and by the fall of 1987 was embarrassed for the state. When he received the phone call, he had an idea of what was coming.

Bill French is over six feet three inches tall with a rugged build. He has a ruddy complexion and an elegant manner and wears his conservative suits as if he were a male model. On weekends he prefers cowboy boots and Levi's.

During that weekend Joe Lane was on the telephone informing key members of his caucus what was occurring. He did not bother to contact the ardent supporters of Governor Mecham because he did not want to tip his hand and he knew what they would say.

Joe Lane, Rick Collins, and Jane Dee Hull met with French in a corner conference room at his law office over the Monday lunch hour. Lane said, "I need somebody who can run an investigation." He told French that he needed to know if there was any merit to Corbin's investigation.

They told him what they were looking for. French told them what he had to offer and what he did not. All three of them asked questions. No one thought to ask if French had signed the recall petition, and French did not think to mention it.

The meeting lasted less than one hour. French recalls its tenor as "intense." The representatives went straight to business. Joe Lane was clearly in command, and French considered his leadership throughout to be marvelous.

Lane was impressed with French within the first five minutes. He found him calm and "very reasoned." He came across as a straight arrow.

Lane made it clear that impeachment was the last thing on his mind.

He was looking for the truth. He wanted to know if Evan Mecham was a crook.

Collins told everyone again and French for the first time that this would hurt all of them politically no matter what the outcome.

They discussed French's fee and obtained a break on the rate. Almost as an afterthought Lane asked about French's political affiliation. Following the discussion they took a five-minute break. When French returned, Lane offered him the job.

Back at the Capitol Collins began putting together a standard contract. He suggested setting aside fifty thousand dollars for the inquiry. Before it was all over, the house was to pay more than seven hundred thousand dollars.

By three that afternoon French was at the Capitol with Patricia Magrath, another Storey & Ross attorney. The press conference was conducted in the house chamber. Lane announced that he had hired a special counsel to conduct an investigation. He introduced French to answer questions. French appeared startled by the sudden exposure, and Lane concluded that he was probably not accustomed to events taking place so quickly or to the public glare. French admits that until this day the most he had ever said to the press before was "No comment." The conference went well.

French was low-keyed. Collins observed that he conducted himself like a surgeon preparing for an operation. French announced, "I enter this particular position with a completely open mind as to the accusations that have gone back and forth about the governor. I have no preconceived ideas."

When the conference was over, both Collins and Lane breathed more easily; they knew they had the right man. They received a flood of calls that reassured them further. French was widely viewed as a man of irreproachable character. If anyone could do the job, he could.

Asked to comment, Mecham told the Cable News Network, "I don't care what kind of counsel they get. I want to be sure that we've got proper counsel so that when they give this a clean bill of health, that everybody will know that the accusation was a terrible miscarriage of justice, of trying to do something, and really was bad, a bad thing to do."

By late afternoon French was back at his law office. He asked Patricia Magrath to serve as chief of staff. He knew her to be "bright and dedicated." If Rick Collins had thought they were hiring only Bill French, he was mistaken. Over the following months French drew on the resources of Storey & Ross as the circumstances required. At different times he had upwards of eight lawyers working the investigation or conducting legal research.

The first working day after the press conference French met with Corbin, Twist, Lotstein, Cudahy, John Shadegg, Joe Lane, and Jim Skelly, chairman of the house Judiciary Committee, the most likely forum for any impeachment hearings.

French understood that the attorney general could not share the ongoing state grand jury investigation with him. At this point Corbin was investigating allegations that favors or state appointments had been provided in exchange for the loan and the failure to report the loan itself. They discussed the level of cooperation that would be possible. The lawyers all understood that each branch of government would be going its own way.

Corbin was delighted when French told him that he would be conducting a broad investigation and would not be limiting its scope to just the Wolfson loan. He gave French a list of twenty-seven other allegations.

On November 5 French hired a retired DPS officer, Bill Woods, to serve as investigator. Woods had "lots of IOUs" that in the police fraternity would enhance his effectiveness.

By the first week in December French was persuaded that Evan Mecham was not fit for his office and was impeachable in no fewer than three articles.

# 25

In the last days before he left the Mecham administration, Sam Steiger went to see Evan Mecham in his office on the Ninth Floor. The recall petitions were about to be filed, and the rumblings of impeachment had to be taken seriously. Steiger told Mecham that in his judgment, there were going to be more than enough signatures to force an election.

Don't challenge the signatures, Steiger told Mecham. Call a snap recall election before your opposition has time to coalesce behind one candidate. It will stop the impeachment talk in its tracks, and you at least have a fighting chance of winning.

Steiger recalls that Mecham reacted as if Steiger had been sent by the enemy. That was their last meaningful contact. Thereafter Steiger, never again had an opportunity to advise the governor.

At that moment Steiger was almost certain that Mecham would not survive in office.

The day after Sam Stanton's disclosure of the Wolfson loan, Mecham's chief of staff, Jim Colter, resigned. It was unclear if he left on his own or was forced out.

Mecham canceled nearly all his appointments and remained largely silent. Two days after the Wolfson loan story broke, the *Republic* reported that Mecham, Colter, Edith Richardson, Ray Russell, Max Hawkins, and Horace Lee Watkins all were under subpoena to appear before the state grand jury when it next convened on November 3.

Of the original senior staff, only Richardson, who was to leave shortly to coordinate Mecham's recall campaign effort, and Russell remained on the Ninth Floor. Immediate replacements were recruited for Donna Carlson and Sam Steiger. Colter's position was open for a conspicuous period as Mecham shopped it around without success.

On October 23, 1987, Sam Stanton disclosed that two men recommended by Barry Wolfson to Mecham had been appointed to the state Housing Finance Review Board shortly after he took office. The board approved the issuing of bonds for low-income housing projects, such as the ones which had made millions for Wolfson and Gregan. One of the men claimed he was unaware he had been appointed, and there was doubt he had ever been notified. The other had served but denied any knowledge of the unreported campaign loan from Wolfson.

Stanton further disclosed that the loan had been arranged through a series of meetings with the Mecham campaign staff. To safeguard the loan, Mecham obtained promissory notes from fourteen individuals, none of whom said they knew the note would be assigned to Wolfson. The notes varied in size from twenty-five hundred to fifty thousand dollars and had been obtained from close relatives of the governor, members of the campaign, and party officials. They included Burton Kruglick, Ralph Watkins, and Donna Carlson.

Speaking sparingly now, Mecham was asked if he intended to resign. He replied, "That's not a pertinent question." He then refused to answer any questions, though a short time later he told Mike Murphy, "When people are concerned about me, whether I'm hanging in there or not, I tell you, I give ulcers, I don't get them."

Donna Carlson was visiting a friend in California. She called Peggy Griffith, who told her that the Wolfson loan was "all over the papers." Griffith was furious, even hostile when she learned that Carlson had been talking to the attorney general.

After the call Carlson was a "nervous wreck." She spoke to Steve Twist twice and then returned to Phoenix.

The attorney general's office was "floating subpoenas already." She asked Twist if there was a subpoena for her because if she testified without one, everyone was going to know who had blown the whistle. The attorney general had a subpoena issued for her. She spent more time with the attorney general's investigator now and testified twice before the state grand jury.

Carlson recalls those sessions. When she was a legislator, she had opposed creation of the state grand jury. She believed it to be a Star Chamber and had visions of wide-eyed prosecutors leading the sixteen grand jurors by their noses.

What she found was very different. It was more casual than she expected, but very serious. She recalls the "intensity with which they watched" her as she testified. One of the jurors she recognized as being from a prominent Mormon family in Mesa. The juror seemed openly hostile toward her.

At about this time Barry Wolfson called Jim Colter. During the conversation Wolfson said, "Well, how come you didn't disclose my loan?"

According to Wolfson, Colter replied, "Well, it's not a loan from you. It's a loan from Mecham."

Wolfson said, "Okay."

"Mecham lent the money to his campaign."

"Okay. You read the law. I haven't. And it's not my problem anyway. So whatever you say."

Wolfson was surprised and thought it illogical the way Colter described it to him. It seemed to Wolfson that the worst thing the Mecham campaign could have done was not report the loan. "It was eventually going to hit the papers, and if you didn't disclose it, it was just a stupid idea," he later said.

Wolfson assumed that Colter had done the legal research himself, but that did not give Wolfson much confidence. Colter struck Wolfson "as a real nice fellow but not . . . a real bright lawyer."

Toward the end of that October Senator Tony West, House Majority Whip Jane Dee Hull, and Representative George Weisz, all from District 18, called for Mecham's resignation at an emotional district meeting.

"I'm not going to be paying it back, no," Mecham told reporters the week following the Sam Stanton article on the Wolfson loan. "First of all, I don't owe any money. I didn't borrow any money. The campaign borrowed the money. I don't owe the loan. I won't be paying it back."

Barry Wolfson was at the Spanish-language television station for Phoenix, Channel 33, when he received word there was a call for him from someone who would not identify himself. It was Mecham. Wolfson thought that Mecham's publicly disowning the debt was "a rotten thing to say." He did not know if his feelings had been revealed to Mecham, but the governor ran him down and told Wolfson over the telephone that his "lawyers were forcing him to take certain positions and [Mecham] wanted [Wolfson] to know personally that he intended that [Wolfson] would be repaid somehow." Mecham told Wolfson that it was inaccurate to say the loan was to the campaign, that it had been to Mecham personally and he felt an obligation to repay it.

Wolfson told Mecham that he understood that was the governor's position and that it was no problem as long as Mecham in fact intended to repay him. Wolfson was just tired of getting the runaround.

The previous week Wolfson had told Dennis Wagner of the Phoenix *Gazette* that his reputation had been "ruined" by the scandal surrounding the arbitrage he and Gregan had engaged in. He said that no one in the bond business would deal with him. He told the paper that it was for this reason he had "bank-rolled the Mecham campaign." "I would have paid every penny I had to get different people into positions of power," he told Wagner.

A new law required state approval of municipal development bonds by the Housing Finance Review Board. According to its chairman, Wolfson and Gregan had appeared before the board the previous year seeking approval for another bond project in Cochise County but were turned down.

Wolfson said that it was "not entirely untrue" that he had influenced recent board appointments. Apparently having second thoughts, he asked Wagner to take that comment off the record. Wagner declined. His article was entitled "How a Developer Formed Ties to Mecham."

On October 26, 1987, the Mecham Recall Committee announced it had gathered more than 343,913 signatures, an amount now in excess of the votes Mecham had received to win office.

Jesse Jackson, speaking at a luncheon at the Sheraton Centre in New York City at this time, announced to an enthusiastic crowd that "Mr. Mecham" had resigned that day in Arizona. A reporter had given him the wrong information just as he prepared to give the speech. It was just one more sign that Arizona's spectacle had become a national issue.

On October 7 Mecham had departed on a trip to Japan and Taiwan, or, as he called it, Free China, to drum up business and divert attention from his crumbling administration. A sign of how profoundly events were now dictating his agenda was apparent on his return one week later, when eager to cite the accomplishments of his trade mission, he gave a press conference at the airport.

Reporters were uninterested and asked him about the calls for his resignation and Donna Carlson's departure from his staff. A clearly chagrined Mecham remarked, "Isn't it interesting that I come home, [and] all the press can think of is some minor items here relating to local politics?

October was a turning point; thereafter Evan Mecham concentrated on the state grand jury probe and his appearances under oath there and else-

where. To the extent his intemperate personality permitted, his public statements and the conduct of his administration were now directed to saving
his office and keeping him out of jail.

It was in October 1987 that most Arizonans realized that the Glendale
auto dealer, one way or another, would not remain governor for long.

# 26

On Sunday evening, November 3, Ed Buck received a telephone call unlike any he had received up until that time. As he listened, his companion saw Buck turn pale. The voice said, "Look, you son of a bitch, you aren't going to live to cross the street tomorrow." The next day the Mecham Recall Committee was scheduled to deliver its petitions to Secretary of State Rose Mofford and bring an end to the recall drive.

Buck also received a call from a state legislator who asked if he had been threatened and told him he was not alone. Mofford had received a threat that the Department of Public Safety was taking very seriously. There were reports that the neo-anarchist Posse Comitatus was planning to attack the armored car bearing the petitions. Sam Stanton called Buck that night to confirm death threats, and Buck asked him to keep it out of the news. Stanton found Buck to be primarily concerned about the safety of the petitions.

Buck contacted Garry Smith, president of the Mecham Recall Committee, and discussed the situation. The committee had originally retained the petitions in a safe-deposit box at Valley National Bank, but it soon had more than the box could handle. After some discussion the committee decided to put all its eggs in one basket, as Buck described it, and a safe house was selected. Only three people in the organization knew the password. Copies of original petitions were used for all committee work.

A rally had been scheduled for 2:00 P.M. the next day at the Capitol, after which the petitions were to be delivered en masse. Now they decided instead to have Smith use an unmarked van and deliver the petitions to Mofford in the Capitol parking garage at 11:30 that same morning.

Monday was one of those perfect Arizona days that bring so many newcomers to the state. The summer heat was at last gone. After Buck awoke, he spotted a plain brown Nova parked across from his house. He had become accustomed to surveillance by Mecham loyalists, but this day he was concerned in light of the previous night's death threat. He believed there were Mechamites who would stop at nothing to prevent delivery of the petitions.

He drove to recall headquarters and attempted to shake the car but could not. He arrived at headquarters with it still following him and spotted three identical cars. That was when he learned they held Phoenix Police Department plainclothes officers assigned to his protection.

Buck looked forward to the rally and to taking the symbolic boxes to Mofford's office. His mother would be attending. He had aimed for this day for eleven months, and he believed it would be one of the most satisfying moments of his life.

Sam Stanton thought there was a very good chance Buck was going to be killed. The emotion level in the state had built to a fever pitch. The Mecham Recall Committee rally was like a magnet for every homophobic wacko who supported the governor.

Concerned Arizona Voters and others gathered approximately 140 supporters of the governor and held a rally at the mall in front of the old Capitol building between the senate and house at about 1:00 P.M. They bore signs saying LET EV DO HIS JOB; EV MECHAM, THE BEST GOVERNOR ARIZONA HAS HAD; KEEP ARIZONA MORALLY CLEAN, and MECHAM'S AN HONEST MAN THAT SCARES THEM RATS.

Their leader told reporters, "We are concerned about the impact on all of us if our constitutional form of government can be overruled by a small, well-organized, well-funded group of zealots. This has been a calculated effort to remove Governor Mecham from office regardless of the consequences to the people of Arizona."

Recall supporters listened to music by Bruce Springsteen, Bob Dylan, and Stevie Wonder as they waited for the rally to begin. Dozens of local and national reporters and cameramen were covering the event. Sam Stanton spotted numerous security men in sunglasses in the crowd. In addition, Buck had hired a bodyguard.

The recall founder climbed on the edge of the water fountain with his bullhorn and addressed the crowd of about 250. Stanton thought Buck looked like a perfect target up there. From the reporter's perspective, Buck loved the limelight: "[Y]ou could see it in his eyes." Buck told the crowd that it was delivering duplicates, that the originals had already been taken to the secretary of state earlier.

After Buck, Naomi Harward, and Garry Smith had addressed the crowd, balloons inscribed with CELEBRATE DEMOCRACY were released. A Loomis armored truck arrived. Boxes with duplicate petitions were off-loaded and handed around. Buck and Harward picked up one each and, with "Born in the U.S.A." blasting in the background, marched across the street toward the east entrance to the old Capitol building to the very spot where, the year before, Buck had stood alone with his recall bumper stickers. The crowd followed, chanting, "Recall! Recall! Recall!"

Two middle-aged men wearing green rubber gloves carried signs that said, QUEER THE RECALL. They told Montini of the *Republic* the gloves were to protect against AIDS.

The Capitol mall complex is laid out awkwardly. Buck says he had obtained a permit from Department of Administration Director Max Hawkins to march into the old Capitol building, now almost entirely a museum, down the most direct route, a long connecting hallway, into the executive building housing the secretary of state's office as well as the governor's. The route is used by hundreds of visitors every day.

Unknown to Buck, Capitol security had locked the doors to prevent the Concerned Arizona Voters rally from moving into the building. There was concern for the state seal laid in the tile during territorial days and for the artifacts hanging on the walls. The security director, Lee Limbs, blocked the doorway and told Buck that he and his group could not pass. He had standing orders from the house speaker and the senate president to protect the museum. In the event of any disturbance the security people were to bar the doors. The crowd was told to march around the building and enter the executive building from its main entrance on the west side.

There were reports later that Buck knew this. Garry Smith told John Kolbe as the group marched to the east entrance, "We're going to get stopped up here. We're not supposed to be doing this."

There was pushing and shoving as the crowd crushed against the doors and chanted, "Hell, no, we won't go! Hell, no, we won't go!"

Buck shouted, "Nearly four hundred thousand people have an appointment with democracy!" Then he demanded to know why Limbs, who is black, would not let them through. "Why can't we go through the Capitol?" he shouted, face-to-face with Limbs. "We want answers!" With his blowhorn he turned and joined the chanting crowd. "Hell, no, we won't go!"

Limbs, along with other officers, persisted in blocking the way. Buck shouted, "Mr. Limbs, are you so stupid, you don't know who told you that?" Limbs told him those were Speaker Lane's orders. What Buck shouted next is in dispute, and Buck absolutely denies using the word "black" but it is most commonly reported to have been "This baboon won't let us in!" or, alternately, "This black baboon won't let us in!" or "This big baboon won't let us in!"

Rosemary Schabert Case, with the Mesa *Tribune*, described embarrassment rippling silently through the group closest to the door. One recall supporter holding a box of duplicate petitions murmured, "Watch it." Some supporters left.

Then Buck said into his blowhorn, "The speaker of the House, Mr. Joe Lane, has said these petitions are not to be coming through this building, a piece of public property! . . . Obviously, we have some people here who are trying to play dirty politics with us and they can be recalled too. It seems to me Mr. Joe Lane has said that he will not allow democracy in the very halls of the capitol of this state!" He shouted, "We are not going to allow some cheap politicians to interfere with democracy!"

Then he shouted at his followers, "We aren't moving until we see the man who gave you those instructions!"

The crowd began chanting, "Speaker of the house! Speaker of the house! Speaker of the house!"

To Mike Murphy in the crowd the situation was turning into "chaos." It was completely unnecessary since everyone knew the real petitions had already been delivered hours earlier.

Buck shouted, "We intend to walk through what is public property in exercising democracy!"

The crowd was now chanting, "Onward! Onward! Onward!" as it surged against the doors.

Suddenly Buck rushed from the Capitol doors to the house of representatives building on the north side of the mall. When Buck tried to enter an elevator without clearing with security—standard procedure—house officers stopped him.

Sam Stanton was more convinced than ever that something was going to happen to Buck. "I wanted to be there," he says. After all, he was not Buck's bodyguard. Just as Buck left the house of representatives, Stanton grabbed his coat so he would not be separated. Buck asked him what he was doing. Stanton says he told Buck that he wanted to be there to see it if Buck was killed.

Buck recalls the incident also. He says Stanton told him he wanted to see the blood when someone shot him.

Buck ran back into the mall. The Mecham supporters were chanting, "We want Ev! We want Ev!"

Buck shouted back at them with his blowhorn, "We want Ev, too, and we're going to get him before you do!"

Buck sprinted across the mall to the senate building with Stanton hanging on to him. Two dozen reporters and much of the crowd followed, scaring the daylights out of Capitol security. They were "running," according to Murphy, "like mad dogs." When he reached the senate building, Buck did not bother with elevators. He sprinted up the stairs for Senate President Carl Kunasek's office. A security officer tried to tackle him without success.

Fifteen or twenty reporters and cameramen were with him and a like number of the recall supporters. Sam Stanton, who usually hikes and runs up Squaw Peak in northeast Phoenix, was in horrible shape by this time, and the running was taking it all out of him.

Buck raced up the stairs, followed by fifty people, largely reporters. Buck did not know where the president's office was located and went to the third floor. A reporter, not Sam Stanton or Mike Murphy, shouted, "He's on the second floor!"

Buck ran down to the next floor and to the president's office where he was stopped by Kunasek's secretary. En route Mike Murphy ran full steam into a pillar and fell to the ground.

Kunasek's frightened secretary had her arm across the doorway. She told Kunasek later that Buck grabbed her on the shoulder and tried to force his way past her. Immediately afterward she was so distraught she left for the day.

"Is he trying to hide behind a woman?" Buck said, now virtually out of control. Buck located Senate majority leader Usdane's office. By this time the reporters and Buck were "all sweating like pigs," according to Stanton. Usdane asked Buck into his office. Buck told his followers to go back outside and wait for him.

Inside the office Usdane got a glass of water for Buck and spoke to him to calm him down. He had the reporters wait in the senate chambers. After fifteen minutes a composed Ed Buck emerged. He went out to join the crowd.

When the crowd started to "raise the roof," Rick Collins heard what was occurring. He knew Joe Lane was not responsible for locking the doors and gave instructions to let them through. Limbs had the doors unlocked. As the recall crowd marched triumphantly down the hallway to the lobby of the executive building, it chanted, "Recall Ev! Recall Ev! Recall Ev!"

In the lobby the crowd began cheering like a football pep rally. One reporter compared it with a 1960's antiwar rally. The shouts could be heard in Mofford's office on the seventh floor. State employees came out of their offices to watch from the mezzanine.

Overhead was an autographed picture of Evan Mecham smiling benignly.

Buck and nine others took the duplicate petitions up to the secretary of state's office. Some of the Concerned Arizona Voters had come to the lobby. When the recall crowd drew a corporate breath, the Mecham supporters shouted, "The good people speak!" The recall people responded, "No!"

And so it went as Buck delivered 32,401 petitions containing 388,988 signatures, nearly 40,000 more than Buck had targeted in July and far more than needed to schedule an election.

Later Buck apologized publicly and personally to Limbs. Much later Buck commented with regret that he had turned what should have been one of the greatest days of his life into a disaster. "It was taken from me," he said, taken by his own conduct.

Mike Murphy's article in the *Gazette* makes no mention of the baboon statement. Sam Stanton's article does not include it until the last paragraph and then only when Buck is reported as saying he regretted using the word.

Ken Smith points to this conspicuous nonreporting of a racial slur as a prime example of the treatment Mecham received from the press. He says, "[I]f one of Mecham's supporters had called Art Hamilton a [similar name] at a public rally covered by dozens of reporters and television cameras, it would have made national news." It seemed to Smith that the reporters had become part of the picture, especially when one had told Buck where the senate president's office was located. It was the local media's reporting of this event that persuaded Smith he was "fighting a losing battle in trying to get some evenhanded coverage."

Sam Stanton defends his article with mild embarrassment. He had not known that "baboon" was used as a racial slur. He thought Buck was referring to Limb's large size and obtuse manner.

After Mecham told Sam, "Don't ever ask me for a true statement again!" the reporter had taken the remark from his recorder and placed it on his answering machine. Now he replaced it with the recall crowd chanting, "The speaker of the house! The speaker of the house!"

Speaker Lane and President Kunasek were on a statewide tour to gauge public sentiment. Rick Collins called Joe Lane and told him what had taken place. Lane was enraged at the recall supporters' conduct. When Carl Kunasek learned what Buck had done to his secretary, he was beside himself with anger.

As a result of this near riot, although no one was arrested or injured, Joe Lane and Carl Kunasek had security procedures at the Capitol carefully reviewed. It was to prove a wise decision.

Unknown at the time and not reported for some months, Secretary of State Rose Mofford visited with Governor Mecham not long after receiving the recall petitions. She told him that on the basis of her decades of work with petitions of this type there was no question of there being sufficient numbers to force an election. She asked if he would waive the signature verification process, in which case she would call a recall election in late February.

Mecham told her that the Mecham Recall Committee had engaged in massive fraud and that there were not enough signatures to call an election. Mofford distributed the petitions to the state's fifteen county recorders for confirmation.

Ken Smith recalls Mofford's telling him that this had been one of the best petition drives she had ever seen in terms of complying with the law.

The Wolfson loan was due on the Sunday before the recall petitions were delivered. There was considerable speculation on whether or not Mecham intended to repay Wolfson. Certainly his public comments supported that conclusion.

The day the petitions were delivered Mecham confirmed that he had not been able to repay Wolfson. This further damaged his claim that he was a wealthy and successful businessman. He acknowledged publicly however that the debt was his own and said that he would sell assets if necessary to pay the loan off.

Sam Stanton reported that Mecham would repay Wolfson a hundred thousand dollars that week. This money came from Mecham's two brothers Willard and Wayne. Wolfson granted a thirty-day extension for the balance.

Toward the end of the story Stanton included the fact that Mecham had also borrowed "most of the $90,000 in the governor's Protocol Fund" and that now the money was repaid. The reporter had known for some time that Mecham had personally borrowed most of the money. He had talked to the attorney general about it and been told the loan was probably not improper because the funds did not belong to the state.

This was the first time that loan had been publicly disclosed. Both Ken Smith and Edith Richardson told Stanton they knew nothing of the loan to Mecham from the Protocol Fund.

What Stanton found so frustrating about the Protocol Fund story was that the original attorney general investigation which led to the impounding of the funds had been caused by his questions about the corporate donors on the inaugural program and by an article he had written. He had had this story from the beginning and had known about the loan for some time.

That Wednesday the *New Times* ran an article by Michael Lacey entitled "The Only Shocking Story Left." It consisted entirely of three columns without commentary. One listed victims, including Abraham Lincoln, John F. Kennedy, Martin Luther King, Jr., the last name of ten being Evan Mecham. The second column listed the names of the assassins: John Wilkes

Booth, Lee Harvey Oswald, James Earl Ray, and so forth. The last column listed the dates of the assassinations. Opposite Mecham's name under assassin and date were question marks.

Despite the quality of its writing and much of the fine reporting the weekly does, the *New Times* has difficulty being accepted as a serious newspaper in part because it is distributed free of charge, in part because its articles mix commentary with reporting, and in part because it behaves so irresponsibly at times. Lacey's article frightened the Department of Public Safety security detail members assigned to the governor.

Beau Johnson recalls thinking that "things were bad enough as they were" without this. He considered the article "reckless and uncalled for." It was like an invitation for some crazy to do something.

Mecham had been struck by boom mikes and recorders more than once as he walked in the midst of what the media termed a "cluster fuck." Now DPS asked the reporters to maintain some distance from him. Reporters were also asked to keep their eyes open. One reporter tackled a drunk lurching at the governor whom his security detail failed to spot. The reporters routinely began advising DPS of strange people hanging around or of unusual cars, and the officers came to rely on them.

Mecham loved crowds and waded into them with supreme indifference. Reporters were already concerned for his safety by the time of the *New Times* article. The fear of assassination escalated dramatically.

Death threats were now commonplace. They had reached a peak when Mecham had been booed at the football game in August and maintained that level thereafter. The *Republic* and the *Gazette* adopted an unofficial policy of not reporting threats, though a few went into print. At the time, the *Arizona Republic* reported a DPS source as saying that Mecham did not receive any more death threats than other Arizona governors.

The head of Mecham's security detail, Beau Johnson, later acknowledged this was disinformation. In fact, Mecham received four or five times as many threats as the last four most recent governors. Every day his answering machine was filled with threats against him. Johnson tells of having to deal with at least one death threat every day.

The energy level of the young reporters covering Mecham was nearly exhausted. Considering the pressure, barrage of stories, competition, and deadlines, veteran reporter Don Harris with the *Republic* was impressed with how often they got it right. Errors were exceedingly rare. The objections of the Mecham administration were primarily on the focus of the stories and their tenor, not on the facts, though accusations were made about those as well.

Sam Stanton was working nearly every waking hour. He had no time to do his laundry and bought new clothes every few days. Though his relationship with his girl friend was not the best, within the early months of the Mecham administration she broke up with him. Mike Murphy says his girl friend came to hate him as that year moved on. Another reporter in the thick of it was divorced.

Stanton lived in a small cottage in back of the home of one of the *Republic*'s editors. One day his landlord told him someone had been camped out up a eucalyptus tree in the alley for a week, keeping an eye on his place. Stanton was followed and had to shake a tail to meet sources.

There were doubts, plenty of them. The peaks were followed by valleys. Stanton talked to Don Harris to be certain he was not being excessive in his coverage and received assurances that it was just the nature of the story, not to be concerned.

Because of the kind of story they had, the hours and stress, the reporters created their own private world. They worked all day together and most nights drank together. Often while they drank, they responded to their pagers, made calls, and dictated stories over the telephone.

Everyone watched everyone else. They all had cellular telephones and soon learned which bars had metal in the ceiling. They would invent excuses to take the telephone outside if they were working on stories and did not want the others to know. They recognize it had the appearance of "pack journalism," but that was the way of the story.

At this time Sam Stanton and Mike Murphy were summoned to the *Republic* and *Gazette* building. They were taken into a conference room, where an officer from DPS explained to them that someone was researching their backgrounds to find information that would embarrass them and diminish their credibility. The reporters were presented with a half dozen photographs of private investigators believed to be following them. They were told to be careful. Stanton says he first really worried when a detective asked him if he owned a gun.

Murphy never spotted anyone in the photographs, but that very night Stanton went to the French Corner restaurant to meet someone and a man who looked very familiar sat next to him. Stanton took out the photographs, and there he was. Stanton called him by name, and he got up and left the bar. That was the only one he ever spotted.

Reporters were not the only ones receiving death threats. As speaker of the house Joe Lane exercised complete control over what would be done with the evidence Bill French and his investigator were gathering. Since the legislature was not in session Lane's single-handed responsibility was apparent to everyone. It was not a pleasant situation.

He and his staff were receiving "tremendous numbers of nasty phone calls." He accumulated a thick file of threatening letters. DPS cautioned him that the ones to fear were not legitimate Mecham supporters but rather the percentage of wackos that emotion-charged situations such as this attracted.

The telephone calls were clearly orchestrated. The same themes emerged on the same day, with almost identical wording. One secretary tells of jokingly asking a supposedly spontaneous caller to read the message back only to have him back up and do it, word for word.

On the radio talk shows the same pattern was evident. On both KTAR and KFYI the same callers supporting Mecham with almost the same lines could be heard day after day.

From the beginning, whenever Mecham spoke on the radio, his secretaries called supporters and asked that the governor receive nothing but positive calls. Mecham pointed to the flood of supportive calls he received as proof the press was slanting the news against him.

As the intensity increased, DPS showed Lane how to check his car for bombs, and patrols around his home were increased. The harassing calls at night were so numerous Sue Lane took to answering the telephone, "House of Representatives, speaker's office." She had visions of shotgun-wielding men driving by in pickup trucks and shooting up the house. These were ugly days.

# 27

Donna Carlson's longtime friend Peggy Griffith had been appointed to head the Governor's Office of Women's Services. During November 1987 construction was under way on the eighth floor of the executive building to build new offices for her.

On November 12, shortly before lunch, she left with her secretary, Terri Fields, to attend a meeting at the Department of Transportation just down the street. They ran into Horace Lee Watkins, who was on his way into the building.

Watkins said to Griffith, "Your friend, Donna Carlson, is a bad girl." Griffith responded with "So what else is new?" and went to her meeting.

At about 1:30 P.M. Griffith was on the eighth floor and spotted Watkins. His earlier comment about Carlson had made her curious, and she asked him if he had a minute. They went into a conference room. They sat side by side at a table, and she asked Watkins what he had meant.

Watkins said, "Donna is a W-H-O-R-E," spelling out the word. "She has a big mouth and there are some friends of the governor who are very angry. If she does not keep her mouth shut she will take a long boat ride and never come back."

Griffith said, "Wait, wait. You wouldn't want anything to harm Donna or the governor by that kind of action."

Watkins said, "We won't do it until spring or possibly summer."

"I spoke to Donna in California . . ." Griffith said when Watkins interrupted her.

"California is not far enough. She should go to Wisconsin and change her name." Griffith tried to interrupt, but Watkins continued. "Who the hell do they think they are, the God damn liars!"

"Who?"

Watkins named a prominent former Republican party official. "That God damn faggot . . ."

Griffith interrupted. "Wait a minute. That is strong stuff. I have known [him] for a number of years and he is not a faggot."

Watkins said, "Hell, everyone in [business] knows he is one and has known he is one for years. He, that God damn Burt Kruglick, and Donna are liars. They met Barry Wolfson and knew about the loan months ago. They better all keep their damn mouths shut."

"Lee, you have to do something to stop this," Griffith said.

"There is nothing that can stop it." Watkins rose from his chair and started out the door.

Griffith followed him, saying, "Lee, Lee . . ."

Watkins turned and grabbed her arm. "This conversation never happened."

Griffith went back to work for the rest of the day. That night she spoke to her husband, a former DPS officer for more than thirty years, and told him what Watkins had said. He told his wife that she had three options: She could speak to the governor directly, she could speak to Colonel Milstead, head of DPS, or she could talk to Carlson about the threats. He suggested she start with the governor.

That night Griffith attended a function in the East Valley, where she spoke to a longtime friend who knew Watkins better than she did. She told him generally what Watkins had said.

"Peg, go to the governor," he told her. "Yes, Lee is capable of doing what you stated. If he won't do it himself he has knowledge of people who will."

Horace Lee Watkins was born in Rockwell, Texas, in 1940. His family moved to Mesa when he was a child. He attended some high school there. In 1966 he moved to California and worked in part as a self-employed insurance broker in Anaheim. He was a partner in an insurance agency for a few years. In 1975 after one of his partners demanded an accounting of agency funds, the agency was burned by arson. Watkins was the primary suspect. Eventually he stopped cooperating with investigators and referred all questions to his attorney. Later the Anaheim fire marshal said, "We were convinced he was, in fact, responsible. This guy is a bad guy." Watkins denied his guilt.

In 1976 he filed bankruptcy. He was married and divorced at least three times.

His involvement in politics started early. In 1957 he was arrested for putting political posters on vehicles in Mesa. In 1974 he ran unsuccessfully for the California assembly. In 1977 he worked briefly as a political field representative for an assemblyman but was fired for his unsavory dealings and for claiming to be an assemblyman himself. He later acknowledged being fired but denied holding himself out as a legislator. The assemblyman said of Watkins, "He was a win-at-any-cost fellow, but he was incapable of winning."

Watkins ran unsuccessfully for the assembly again in 1978 and was soundly beaten when his own campaign consulting firm withdrew two weeks before the election.

He alienated the Orange County Republicans for "a reprehensible attempt at political extortion" in trying to force a woman candidate from the field by claiming the devout Mormon had once been a prostitute in Texas.

In 1980 he ran unsuccessfully for the Newport Beach City Council. This time he was censured by the Orange County Republican Party Ethics Committee "for failing to properly report campaign contributions," according to a news account.

His career in California was summed up by the Orange County clerk, Gary Granville, who said, "[Watkins] has a totally preposterous view of himself in connection with what was reality. He is just a born loser who pictures himself a born winner."

In 1982, when he moved back to Mesa, five outstanding judgments for business deals or loans were pending against him. One court file said, "Watkins has skipped to Arizona." Some high school friends put him in contact with a member of the legislature, saying Watkins was back in town and wanted to be involved in politics. He helped raise money for the Republican Legislative Campaign Committee and worked a few months for the senate as a special projects consultant, organizing a program for the homeless. When complaints were raised that this appeared to be a crass payoff for his help and that he was serving as an operative for one of the senators, the employment was discontinued.

In 1982 he also worked for a time raising money for Mecham's unsuccessful gubernatorial bid. He ran an insurance agency in Mesa after that, sold insurance for others, and worked as a consultant. It was while selling insurance Watkins had met Barry Wolfson and Hugh Gregan.

In 1985 he tried for public office still again, this time running for the Mesa City Council. He was defeated in March 1986. Just after the guber-

natorial primary that fall he joined Mecham as a fund raiser and served on
the Mecham finance committee.

Watkins's arrest in 1957 had not been his first. While in the Navy, he
was arrested in 1956 for petty theft and for being AWOL. In 1959 he was
arrested in Mesa on a warrant for petty theft. Six months later he was arrested
in El Centro, California, for armed robbery of a post office. Charges were
reduced, and he pleaded guilty to mail robbery. He was sentenced to prison
and served fourteen months.

One legislator who knew Watkins calls him "personable," though a
"little abrasive." Sam Stanton calls Watkins "a real piece of work." He says
Watkins "always had a smile" and describes it as a "barracuda grin." Mike
Murphy terms Watkins "pathetic."

Within weeks of the beginning of the Mecham administration Watkins
had arranged to meet Ralph Milstead for lunch at the Hungry Tiger near
Indian School Road and the freeway. Milstead found him to be reasonable
enough, but "it's what he says that makes him strange."

Watkins told Milstead that he was anxious to work with DPS and that
he was prepared to do anything he could for Milstead. He said that he would
be highly placed in the administration because he had raised so much money
for the campaign. Watkins told Milstead that he knew "where the skeletons
were buried."

Milstead says it is "pretty obvious when people come over to curry
favor," and that was what Watkins was up to. He asked Milstead if he could
have a police band radio installed in his car. It seemed to Milstead that
Watkins was one of those strange police buffs all career cops must endure.

The day following the threat, Friday, the thirteenth, Griffith was scheduled to see Mecham concerning her office activities. She waited for half an
hour only to be told by the governor's secretary about 9:00 A.M. that Mecham
would be unable to see her until the following week. Griffith said she could
not wait until the next week. She was told nothing could be done about it.

Griffith felt very strongly that she had to report the threat. Watkins
had not said anything would happen immediately, but Griffith believed
someone in authority should know about it. She went to the DPS security
office on the Ninth Floor and spoke to Officer Frank Martinez, who was
there alone.

Martinez could see that Griffith was "troubled and nervous." He asked
if he could help her.

"Frank, where's Beau?" she asked, referring to Beau Johnson, the commander of the executive security section of DPS.

Martinez told her Johnson would not be in until later and asked if he
could help her. Griffith told him about trying to meet with Mecham. She

said, "I need to talk to someone about a conversation I had with Lee Watkins the other day."

Griffith then told Martinez about her conversation with Watkins. Martinez recalls that Griffith told him that Watkins had said he knew the right people to accomplish what he was threatening.

Their conversation occurred just a few minutes before nine, and Griffith had a meeting scheduled for that hour. She told Martinez to have Johnson call her out of the meeting if need be.

Johnson arrived about twenty minutes later. Martinez explained what Griffith had told him. Johnson knew Griffith and that she could be excitable. He took that into account in deciding how to respond. Johnson called his immediate superior, Lieutenant Colonel James Chilcoat, and in a three-way conversation had him listen to Martinez directly.

It sounded to Johnson as if a crime might have occurred since it was a felony to tamper with a grand jury witness. Johnson said, "Colonel, I believe the governor should know about this right away." Chilcoat agreed.

Johnson found that Mecham was not in his office. He looked up the appropriate criminal statutes to be certain he was correct and that tampering with a grand jury witness was a felony. Johnson knew that Mecham and Watkins had "a special relationship," and he wanted to be prepared to make a good presentation so the governor would clearly understand the seriousness of the situation. Johnson wanted there to be no misunderstanding.

Griffith arrived around noon, after her meeting ended, and asked Johnson's help in getting in to see the governor. Johnson went to the office of Mecham's new chief of staff, Richard "Dick" Burke, carrying the criminal statutes with him. He told Burke what Griffith had told Johnson, informing him that he thought the governor should hear about it at once and specifically telling Burke it was a felony. Fred Craft was in Phoenix from his office in Washington, D.C., that day and walked into the office as they were speaking. Burke told Johnson he would rather Craft handled it.

Johnson and Craft went to Craft's temporary office, where Johnson described the situation as he understood it, informing him that he thought the governor should hear about it at once and specifically telling Burke it was a felony. Craft seemed shocked by what he heard and spontaneously said Watkins should be fired. Johnson and Craft had always got along, and Johnson considered the lawyer someone with whom he had a good working relationship. Craft asked Johnson to go with him to see the governor.

What precisely occurred in the governor's office next has been the subject of exhaustive investigation and different interpretation. Johnson was feeling good about the situation now that Burke, a former U.S. attorney in Arizona, and Craft, Mecham's Washington, D.C., attorney, had been apprised and appeared supportive.

Johnson recalls that he entered with Craft and Burke. The governor had just completed a telephone call and was standing behind his desk. Burke and Craft took positions in front of the desk. Johnson stood beside the desk. As he spoke, Mecham looked directly at Johnson and listened intently.

Johnson says he told Mecham of the conversation, including Watkins's threat against Carlson, and told Mecham this was possibly a crime and "may be a felony." Johnson saw the incident as tampering with a witness since the purpose of such a threat, if in fact Watkins had uttered it, was to influence Carlson's testimony. Describing the scene much later, Johnson said, "My whole point was to impress upon the governor the seriousness of the situation."

When Johnson was finished after a minute or so, Craft told Mecham that he should distance himself from these events and that this should be a matter that Max Hawkins, director of the Department of Administration and Watkins's boss, should handle. Mecham agreed. Johnson asked if he should set up the meeting. Mecham told him to.

Johnson said, "Fred, do you want to see Peggy?"

Craft indicated not. This surprised Johnson since Griffith was waiting and he thought the governor would be better informed to hear it from her personally.

Back at his office Johnson told Griffith she was to contact Hawkins and tell him what she knew. Griffith later said that Johnson told her the governor was very angry. Johnson does not recall that but does remember that Griffith was very upset that she was unable to meet with Mecham. He said he would arrange an interview for her with Hawkins and would call her. It was apparent that Griffith was uncomfortable with seeing Hawkins.

Griffith wanted to know if anyone else should be told. She was afraid for Donna Carlson and wondered if someone should inform her. Johnson told her she could tell anyone she saw fit to tell.

Johnson met with Hawkins and told him what he knew. Hawkins told Johnson that he doubted the sincerity of Watkins's threats against Donna Carlson but said he would meet with Griffith at 3:00 P.M.

At 3:50 P.M. Hawkins contacted Griffith, and they met in a Department of Commerce conference room. She told him about her conversation the previous day with Watkins and told him of her concerns over the threat. She said that at the least such remarks by a person working for the governor against someone else working for the governor were "inflammatory" and that she "had to accept them at face value." Because of Watkins's "past record," "facial expression," "body English," and "tone of voice," Griffith took the "threat to be real." She tried to express her "profound concern" over the situation. She said she would go the DPS if necessary and take a lie detector test.

Hawkins told her to be very careful because "DPS is not our friend. They are our enemy."

Griffith could not believe that. "I have never found DPS to be an enemy of the people," she said.

Someone opened the door and told Hawkins that the governor was looking for him. Hawkins left. Griffith went to the Ninth Floor and told Johnson that Hawkins had been summoned to the Ninth Floor and was with the governor. She told Johnson that she had told Hawkins about the threat. Johnson informed her that Watkins was also on the Ninth Floor and suggested she take the stairs.

Griffith told Johnson that she had advised Hawkins she was willing to take a polygraph and sign a statement if necessary. She wanted the statement prepared in case something happened to her.

That afternoon Johnson kept Chilcoat informed of events. Johnson considered the matter now to be in Chilcoat's hands. That evening Chilcoat called Johnson and told him to contact both Burke and Craft to urge that a law enforcement agency get involved. Johnson contacted Burke at his Prescott home and said, "This could be a felony. I'm really concerned this could come back and cause the governor problems." Burke seemed satisfied with how things were proceeding.

Johnson was unable to reach Craft until the next morning. When they did speak, he told Craft he did not think it was being handled properly and that this could really embarrass the governor. Craft was also satisfied.

Friday night at home, only a little more than two hours after Griffith last spoke to Johnson, she received a telephone call from a man she did not know. He said he was with the attorney general's office. He said he had information that Griffith had received a threat against Donna Carlson's life. He told her that he had obtained the information from Lieutenant Colonel Gary Phelps with DPS.

She was not willing to speak to the caller. She said she did know Phelps and would speak with him. The caller said Steve Twist had told him to contact her. She told him she had known Twist for a number of years, and he should give her a call first.

Concerned, she tried to reach both Burke and Craft since Johnson had mentioned they were present when he had spoken to the governor. She then called Mecham directly at his home.

Mecham had only one telephone number, was listed in the telephone book, and usually answered the telephone himself. Griffith told Mecham that someone who said he was from the attorney general's office had called and wanted to know about her conversation with Lee Watkins. She told the governor that the caller said Lieutenant Colonel Phelps had told him about the conversation with Watkins.

Mecham said, "Peg, it's okay. Don't be concerned, don't let this interrupt your weekend. It's okay. I want you to have a good weekend."

"Who the hell is messing with this investigation?" Griffith asked. "Excuse me, Evan, I am really angry."

"Peg, it's okay. I'll take care of it."

Later that night both Burke and Craft returned her calls, and she told them what she knew. They told her not to be concerned, that the situation was being taken care of. Burke told her that the DPS and the attorney general had open lines of communication and she should not be concerned.

At about the time Peggy Griffith was meeting for the last time on November 13 with Beau Johnson in his office, Ralph Milstead received a telephone call from Gary Phelps. Phelps told Milstead, who had been attending a sergeants' meeting for the Northern Division in Prescott, what he knew of the conversation between Watkins and Griffith.

By this time Milstead considered Watkins "kind of a crazy" and thought it "absolutely sounds like Lee Watkins." It was obvious to him that Donna Carlson had now been fingered as the informant.

Donna Carlson believes there is a connection between the death threat and the fact that just a few days earlier Murray Miller had motioned to obtain a copy of the first day's grand jury testimony, in which the attorney general's office outlined its case and witnesses. Judge O'Toole had ordered the transcript released with the proviso that only Miller and Evan Mecham be allowed to see it.

Milstead believed Watkins had been the bagman for the Wolfson loan, so this all fit for him. Watkins was "trying to scare Donna." Phelps told Milstead that he was giving the information to the attorney general. He was just keeping his superior informed. Milstead was in agreement.

Though no formal agreement existed, there was an informal arrangement that the DPS officers would not disclose information they learned while serving in the protection of the governor and his family. Mecham had been suspicious of this arrangement from the beginning. He did not trust Beau Johnson but had done nothing to have him removed.

Phelps's decision to relay the Griffith information to the attorney general was part of the system intended to keep the DPS security detail out of the investigation. The attorney general would deal directly with Watkins and Griffith. Milstead was pleased to have his men out of the chain.

The next morning at eight Phelps called Milstead and said, "We've got a big problem." Phelps told him that Griffith was refusing to talk to the attorney general's office. The attorney general now wanted Beau Johnson's and Frank Martinez's statements.

Milstead contacted Steve Twist and Mike Cudahy and asked, "What are you doing to me?" Milstead absolutely did not want his men giving statements to the attorney general. "Why get us involved?" he asked.

Evan Mecham was his boss. There was trouble enough as it was with all the talk that Mecham planned to remove him without adding this. Milstead wanted to be the good soldier and keep out of it.

During these conversations Milstead learned for the first time that no one had informed Donna Carlson about the threat.

Carlson was out of her apartment that day and arrived home from having her hair done and the grocery store at about 8:30 P.M. Milstead called within minutes. "Hello, Donna. We've been trying to get you," he said. "There has been a threat made on your life. I think you should contact the attorney general's office. They are aware of it." He told her the threat was from Watkins.

He asked her to call Peggy Griffith to see if she could be persuaded to cooperate. Carlson explained that she and Griffith were not speaking to each other at the time. He offered her protection, and she declined.

Carlson called Steve Twist at the attorney general's office. He put Cudahy on the telephone, and they told her what they knew. They tried to reassure her that everything was all right. Twist offered her protection, but with the security system at the complex where she lived she felt safe. She acknowledges becoming a little hysterical during this call.

She knew that Watkins "was a character" and that this had to be taken seriously. She knew this from talking to Milstead about Watkins's history of assault, one of which had involved a woman. The threat also brought back the years she had been a battered wife and made it doubly hard to deal with.

Not long after that Twist called Carlson back and wanted to know if she was really all right. She had been crying and said she was not. He suggested she come to the attorney general's office, which was only a few blocks away. At the office Carlson watched Twist on the telephone as he tried to put his investigation together. By midnight she was composed enough to go home.

Back at her condominium she checked the security lights then took a twelve-inch kitchen knife to bed with her. She awoke several times during the night to check the security panel. She ended up sleeping on the knife, and it left a deep welt on her leg for a long time afterward.

All day Saturday before reaching Carlson at her home, Milstead had tried to find a way out of this predicament. He made a series of calls to Twist, Cudahy, and Phelps. The attorney general wanted Martinez and Johnson down at their office to make a statement. For now Milstead instructed his people not to do anything while he tried to find a way around this dilemma.

Milstead spoke to Peggy Griffith early Saturday evening immediately following his call to Donna Carlson. Griffith said she was not at liberty to talk to him. "I will only talk to you," she said, "if the governor's lawyer,

Murray Miller, is sitting beside me." To Milstead, these sounded like instructions from the governor.

She continued: "If I don't get satisfaction [concerning Watkins], I'll be in your office with or without an appointment." She said, "Please give me some credit for intelligence. Donna has been my friend for seventeen years and will still be my friend when this is over. I won't let anything happen to her."

Taken with what Mecham was to tell Milstead the next day, this was confirmation for Milstead that Mecham had ordered Griffith not to cooperate with an outside investigation.

Milstead asked her if there was any immediate danger to Carlson's life. She told him she understood the threat was for the spring. He asked if Griffith would testify to the alleged threat, and she said she would come to his office on Monday and do whatever was necessary to complete a report. He told her that that was not necessary, that the attorney general was handling the investigation.

By 10:30 P.M. Milstead had made no progress, and it was agreed he and his staff would take the issue up the next day.

The next morning, Sunday, shortly after eight, Donna Carlson called Peggy Griffith. "Thank you," she said. "I know how difficult this is for you. I didn't sleep at all last night after I received the phone call from Ralph about the death threat. Thank you for caring about me. I love you."

Milstead was more concerned than most about the threat. He knew Watkins to be emotional, unpredictable, volatile, and not especially clever. Watkins had once used his finger to rob a post office, and Milstead figured he was just as likely to go ahead and kill Carlson as not. It's the "crazies" who do those kind of things, and Watkins fit the bill as far as Milstead was concerned.

Sunday morning Milstead was at his girl friend's house. He tried to call the governor but learned he was in church and would not be available until around noon. It was apparent to him that he would have to make his officers available to the attorney general. He called Twist and told him he would have his men down for statements later.

All his police training had been that an officer never lets a superior get blindsided by bad news. The night before, he had fallen asleep watching *Sleuth*, so now he finished it as he waited for Mecham to return from church.

On Saturday a process server had gone to Sam Stanton's home and pounded on the door. Stanton figured it was a subpoena from Murray Miller, so "naturally I grabbed a coat and left home." He hid out all that day.

The next morning at seven pounding started on the door again, but he still did not answer it. He did answer the telephone a bit later. It was Donna Carlson.

She told him about the death threat. She said she wanted him to know in case something happened. Stanton went to the office to escape the process server. He called the attorney general's office and talked to everyone he could find about the threat. He wrote the story, and it ran Monday.

Shortly after noon Milstead reached Mecham by telephone at his home. Milstead considered this a perfectly routine call. He "fully expected [Mecham] to say, 'Do whatever you have to do,' " because there was no other option.

Milstead was unaware of the extent of the distance between Mecham and Attorney General Bob Corbin. As a result, he was surprised at the "venom" in Mecham's voice when he spoke. From the way Mecham talked it was apparent to Milstead that he already knew about the death threat.

Milstead explained "the chain of events to date." He explained that Griffith had told Martinez, who had told Johnson. Johnson had then informed Chilcoat, who had told Gary Phelps, his superior. He reminded the governor of the policy that what took place on the Ninth Floor was "usually held in the strictest of confidence" but that now the attorney general was requesting their cooperation and wanted a statement from both Johnson and Martinez.

"Well, if you want my permission for them to talk to the attorney general, you can't have it. The answer's no," Mecham said.

Milstead explained that DPS usually cooperated with the attorney general. Sounding very angry, the governor interrupted Milstead and said, "What does your witness say, what does your witness say!"

Milstead started talking about Martinez, and again the governor interrupted. "No! Who's your witness?"

"Do you mean Peggy?" Milstead asked.

"Yes," Mecham said, "what's she saying?"

Milstead told the governor that she was not saying anything at this time, that he had talked to her the previous night and she would not say what Watkins had told her.

"Without her you don't have a case," Mecham asserted. Then, very angrily, he said, "I want Beau transferred. He should never have talked to anyone until he talked to me about this. There's nothing to this. I have looked into it, and it's nothing serious."

Then he said, "I don't want Frank or Beau giving any statements to the Attorney General. The Attorney General is out to hang me, and I'm not going to help him in any way." Sounding very emotional, Mecham said, "I don't want you to help him get me. Don't tell the Attorney General anything."

Milstead was taken aback. He explained that he would have to offer some explanation to the attorney general.

Mecham said, "Tell them the matter's been taken care of, that it was only a little spat between the governor's staff and that he isn't going to get any more information."

Milstead tried to persuade Mecham not to do this. But Mecham was emphatic. "Never! Don't give him any help."

Mecham told Milstead that Peggy Griffith was highly excitable and that he did not believe Donna Carlson was in any danger. Mecham told him that Watkins was not a violent man.

Milstead said, "O.K.," and hung up.

He immediately shot to his feet and shouted a profanity. He stomped around the room, muttering to himself, "I can't believe this, I can't believe he told me that." Milstead had never disobeyed an order from a superior before, but he knew he was going to disobey this one. His girlfriend later said Milstead got off the telephone with a very strange look on his face.

He had scribbled some notes as he was speaking to Mecham and fleshed them out now. Then he called Chilcoat and instructed him, Johnson, and Martinez to meet at the director's office. Phelps was also at that Sunday meeting. Milstead learned that Mecham had called Martinez and left a message telling him not to go down to the attorney general's office. After telling Johnson and Martinez they all were going down to give statements to the attorney general, he asked them to leave the room.

Once they were out, Milstead told Phelps and Chilcoat, "We have another problem. The governor told me not to do this."

They all went to the attorney general's office. Johnson and Martinez prepared statements. Milstead did not have a DPS report number assigned to them. The reports were given to the attorney general. In this way if Milstead were ever asked for the reports on the incident, he could truthfully reply that DPS did not have any. This was to be an attorney general's investigation.

Around three that afternoon, as they were finishing, Milstead casually mentioned to Barnett Lotstein that he had talked to Mecham that morning and Mecham had told him not to do this.

Lotstein's initial reaction was "God, I can't believe he would tell you that."

Milstead wanted everyone to know that he was paying a price for co-operating. Lotstein came over to him and told Milstead to write that up for him. Not thinking much of it, except that he had disobeyed the governor and there would be hell to pay for it, Milstead wrote the conversation from his hastily scribbled notes later that day.

\* \* \*

At five-thirty that Sunday afternoon, Sam Stanton called Peggy Griffith. She said, "Mr. Stanton, how did you get my unlisted phone number?"

"I have a multitude of sources," she recalls his saying. He asked her about the alleged threat on Donna Carlson's life.

"Mr. Stanton, sir. I have no comment. If you wish to speak to me on the functions of my office, sir, I will be glad to comment."

At ten-thirty that night George Graham, the dapper and scrupulously polite attorney general's investigator, served Griffith with a state grand jury subpoena for nine o'clock the next day.

> MECHAM: I haven't picked on the gays at all.
> They've come challenging me. I haven't done
> anything to the gays at all.
>
> KOPPEL: So you don't have problems with
> gays in government?
>
> MECHAM: I didn't say that.
> —EVAN MECHAM *on* Nightline

# 28

That Monday night, as part of Mecham's program to counter the press, he appeared with local anchorman Cameron Harper to answer questions. Harper went on the offensive from the beginning, and Mecham struggled through an uncomfortable interview. Toward the end Harper turned to the events of that weekend, some of which had appeared in Stanton's *Republic* article.

When first asked the question, Mecham replied, "Cameron, Cameron, Cameron. I think our agreement tonight was to keep our subjects to this other. Now you're violating the agreement, and I'm not going to comment on that. First of all, I haven't been involved."

After settling that there had been no agreement, Harper asked the question again, saying, "The allegation is that your former . . . that your former . . . Governor . . . Governor, are you listening?"

"I'm just asking, how long is this program to go? I understood we were to be through at 7 o'clock."

Harper repeated the question.

Mecham replied, "Oh . . . oh . . . oh . . . what . . . ah . . . well . . ."

"Did you know about that threat?" Harper asked for the fourth time.

"No, I didn't."

"Were you or anyone on your staff . . . ?"

"I haven't been involved in that, Cameron."

"Governor, why don't you listen to my question?"

"No. I told you that I know little or nothing about what you're talking about. Did you have another question I can respond to?"

"Yeah—" Harper began demonstrating once again that he was more than a pretty face—"I would like to, I'd like to know if you or anyone on your staff was informed that that threat had been made."

"Perhaps my chief of staff was."

"But you weren't?"

Mecham said, "I was not."

"And what happened when your chief of staff was told?"

"I don't know. I've hardly talked to him today. Is that a big part of this?"

"I'm curious about who told your chief of staff about that threat."

"Well, what's that . . . what's this all about? I thought we were here to talk about the Wolfson loan and things of that nature."

Lieutenant Beau Johnson went on vacation for several weeks after being removed as head of the governor's security detail as Mecham had ordered.* That night he was watching the interview at home on television. When Mecham denied knowing about the threat, he thought, How can you say that? He could not believe that Mecham would publicly deny being told. Johnson called Chilcoat at once to tell him what he had just heard. Johnson knew then this was going to get messy. He believed that at some point he would be put on the record and asked what had happened. It would come down to which of them was considered the liar.

As if *60 Minutes* had not been enough, the nation received further exposure to Arizona's governor on Friday, November 20, 1987, when Evan Mecham appeared on *Nightline.*

Ken Smith had tried for weeks to keep Mecham off the show. Finally Koppel himself called Mecham at his home and told him that his staff had been trying to arrange for his appearance. Mecham called Smith and chewed him out for not telling him about the request.

Under heavy security, Mecham appeared at the KTVK studio in Phoenix. The reporters watched the program live on a large-screen television from the waiting room. Much of the program focused on Mecham's position regarding gays in state service as the governor, according to Laurie Asseo in her Associated Press story, "bobbed and weaved like a fighter. . . ."

Mecham declined to acknowledge any shortcomings and returned to a theme that was to dominate his fight to remain in office. "The good people across this state, they see through all of this," he said. Mecham had repeatedly asserted that he would resign only when the "good people" asked

---

*Frank Martinez asked to be transferred from the governor's security detail that same Sunday.

him to. Increasingly the good people appeared to be anyone who would not ask him to step down.

The waiting room was packed. National correspondents were in residence by this time, and the local reporters were determined not to give up their story to them. As Mecham dodged Koppel and tried to direct the interview toward his "positive" accomplishments, many reporters called out to the television that Koppel was not being tough enough, that he let Mecham avoid questions.

Mecham had refused to answer their questions when he arrived, and he refused as he left. According to reporters, Laurie Asseo was shoved by one of the security guards. She told the AP bureau chief that "it was the hardest she'd ever been roughed up in her life." The reporters turned to Ken Smith, who was attempting to slip out with his fiancée and go to dinner. A shouting match ensued.

Smith denies that Asseo was pushed, and he denies shouting back at the reporters. He becomes visibly angry as he describes one reporter pulling his hand away from the car door so he could not open it. He says the same reporter shouted at his fiancée, "Shut up, you bitch. This is his job." Other reporters present decline specific comment about this.

It was a thoroughly unpleasant scene as Smith entered his car and refused comment.

The same day it was disclosed that Bill French had signed the recall petition. Judge Thomas O'Toole, who had been overseeing the state grand jury, had just removed himself from the process because he had signed a recall petition. French, who remembered that two or three months before, he had signed one as well, told Joe Lane.

Lane announced he saw no problem with it and said he would have hired French even had he known. "I don't like it a darn bit, but I'm not going to let him go because of that," he told reporters.

At this time Art Hamilton went public with his objections to what Lane was doing. He said that the house Democrats were being shut out of the investigation, and he asked for permission to hire minority counsel.

Lane denied the request but publicly assured Hamilton, "If we do anything, it will be bipartisan. I have no intention of cutting Art out."

On November 23 Max Hawkins had Horace Lee Watkins return to work. Watkins's attorney had his client take a lie detector test at Hawkins's suggestion. According to the attorney, the test established that Watkins "was truthful or not deceptive" in answering questions. Hawkins had not seen the test results. Watkins's lawyer would not identify the polygraph examiner or the questions that Watkins had been asked.

Senator Alan Stephens said, "The bozos are back on the bus."

* * *

Steve Benson and his wife attended Thanksgiving dinner every year with the same relatives in Mesa. Shortly before this Thanksgiving his wife called to ask what she should bring.

She was shocked to hear that while she and the children were welcome, her husband was not because of what he had done to Governor Mecham. The head of the family "said it would make him ill to have Steve Benson sitting across the table from him."

Benson's wife said she would not be coming because she would not eat Thanksgiving dinner without her husband.

When Deborah Laake of the *New Times* interviewed him, Benson mentioned the matter to her, and it became public knowledge. Benson told her, "They would not tell me to my face, but I would not be surprised if privately they are convinced I have abandoned the faith and have been responsible for the imminent destruction of a good and decent man."

The relative reversed himself and told Benson that he was sorry for what he had done, that it had not been very Christian. He invited the Bensons over.

By this time they had made other plans. Benson made it a point, however, to drop by because "families are forever" and politics should not drive a wedge between them.

At about this time Benson had a psychologist prepare a psychological profile for him on Evan Mecham. He found the four-page evaluation that described the narcissistic-paranoid personality disorder enlightening.

On November 26 it was disclosed that not only was Fred Craft receiving an annual salary of $80,000 for his part-time work in representing the governor in Washington, but he was also receiving another $60,000 for using his Washington law offices for the purpose. This $140,000 a year was $20,000 more than Mecham had requested from the legislature the previous summer, a request it had refused. When Mecham went ahead and hired Craft on his own, he had announced at the time, "We got him for a heck of a lot less than on a bid," and defended the lower price he was paying. Now it was apparent he was in fact paying more.

In late November Mecham's claim to integrity received another body blow. Less than a year before, the state supreme court had upheld a jury verdict against Mecham for fraudulent behavior with a young woman in the purchase of a car from him. Mecham had told her that her credit was approved when it had not been. He sold her trade-in, then repossessed the new car when her credit did not clear. A few months later Sam Stanton had published his account of the governor's business dealings in Tacoma. There had been Mecham's unseemly scramble to find money to repay Wolfson and then the disclosure that he had raided the Protocol Fund for his car dealership's use.

Now after a five-week trial a Maricopa County jury found that Mecham had been involved in cheating a veteran out of his invention. Frank Elliott, a Vietnam War veteran, had patented a "solar blanket" that could be retrofitted to mobile homes and reduce utility bills. He turned to an attorney, Dan M. Morris, for assistance and capital. Morris, who was active in the Mormon Church, told Elliott that fellow Mormons Evan, Willard, and Wayne Mecham were potential investors. What neither he nor the Mechams told Elliott was that Morris's law firm also represented the Mecham Investment Corporation, the company that planned to invest in his invention.

After Elliott had sold his patent rights along with 51 percent of his stock to Mecham Investment and agreed to what he believed was a five-year employment contract, he was fired. Only then did he learn of the conflict of interest.

His initial lawsuit against the Mechams and Morris was dismissed on a technicality when his lawyer failed to asked for a trial within the time limit. Elliott then sued his lawyer. To prove malpractice, he essentially had to establish the validity of his claim against the Mechams and Morris.

Mecham had not testified, but his deposition, in which he denied any wrongdoing, was read to the jury. Elliott was awarded $864,600. The losing attorney said he and the Mechams would appeal.

Elliott had listened to Mecham claim he had never before been accused of anything more serious than a traffic violation. He told E. J. Montini of the *Republic* when he wrote of it, "I knew different, but I had to let it all come out in the trial. The jury did the talking."

Only a few weeks later the *New Times* reported that a review of court records revealed that Mecham's integrity as a businessman had been questioned in thirty-six court cases since 1954. He was alleged to have failed to honor at least twenty-four promissory notes bearing his personal signature, totaling more than one hundred thousand dollars.

It was becoming increasingly difficult for Mecham to take the high moral ground.

Ever since the revelation of the Wolfson loan Mecham had scurried about the state, acting every bit the guilty man. In late October, on advice of his attorneys, he refused to answer questions about appointments that were allegedly related to Wolfson. In early November, after promising to "lay it out in its entirety" on television in Tucson, an appearance that was broadcast statewide, Mecham refused to answer questions about the Wolfson loan, again on advice of lawyers, he said. He did manage to blame his brother Willard Mecham. Schoolchildren quickly adopted the line "Willard did it!"

when questioned about anything and a bumper sticker suddenly appeared with the phrase.

Only a week later Mecham said again on television that he could not answer all questions on advice of counsel. He filed amended returns reporting the Wolfson loan. During the same interview he misspoke and said he had only promised Wolfson "better business," then corrected himself to have said, "better government."

In the final days of November Mecham was not talking to the press. Ken Smith threatened to have reporters who crowded too close to the governor arrested. Mecham canceled his bimonthly radio appearance and stopped writing a column that was published in two papers.

On the first day of December the Maricopa County recorder announced that a preliminary review of the recall petitions showed a validity rate of 70 percent. Pima County announced an 85 percent rate.

By this time Mecham had had several opportunities to explain the Wolfson loan and why it did not appear on his campaign finance reports. He had been on television and radio and was widely covered by the newspapers. His explanations were constantly shifting, and his clinging to technicalities was unseemly for a politician who had always bragged he owed nothing to any man, who said he told it like it was, and who had run on a theme of integrity.

Whether it was legal or not, whether intentional or not, Evan Mecham had concealed the Wolfson-Gregan loan from the voters, and that, at the very least, contradicted the spirit of the law, the will of the electorate, which had made it law, and his own long-standing public pronouncements.

Only Mecham and his decreasing band of fervent supporters missed the point.

> *An honest mistake was made, and it has been corrected.*
>
> > —EVAN MECHAM,
> > *November 16, 1987*
>
> *I didn't say it was a mistake. I've never said it was a mistake.*
>
> > —EVAN MECHAM,
> > *December 10, 1987*

# 29

Raising money had always been the Achilles' heel of any Mecham campaign. Mecham and his family usually contributed a substantial portion of his war chest. It was no different in 1986.

French soon discovered that when Evan Mecham won the Republican primary, he was virtually broke. For obvious reasons the usual Republican contributors shied away from giving him money even after he was the party's nominee.

Mecham obtained a three-hundred-thousand-dollar loan from Western Savings, run by the locally prominent Mormon Driggs family. John Driggs attended Mecham campaign meetings. As the important final weeks of the general campaign approached, however, that money had been spent. The situation was desperate. Western Savings was willing to lend another three hundred thousand dollars but required collateral, which Jim Colter later said Mecham either would not or could not provide.

Colter was devoting at least half his time as campaign manager to fund raising and was finding the job very difficult. To obtain the loan from Western Savings, he devised a plan whereby supporters need not actually give money. They needed only to sign a promissory note for fifty thousand dollars which Mecham could use to obtain the loan from Western Savings. Mecham would guarantee the loan and indemnify the supporters against any potential loss.

But even with this assurance Colter was having trouble finding sufficient signers.

Horace Lee Watkins had worked on the Mecham primary campaign in 1982 as a fund raiser and the day following Mecham's primary victory in 1986 told Mecham he wanted to help again. Thereafter he served on the campaign finance committee. In early October 1986 Watkins told Colter that he knew two men who had the ability to finance the entire campaign if they wished. He identified these men as Barry Wolfson and Hugh Gregan. Colter was delighted and urged Watkins to contact them.

It was Wolfson's recollection that he contacted Watkins to offer a contribution to the Mecham campaign and to arrange to meet the candidate. According to Wolfson, he was unhappy with how government was interfering in his line of work—bonds—and wanted to see a change in government.

On October 1 or 2 there was a finance committee meeting at campaign headquarters at Mecham Pontiac. Mecham, Jim Colter, Ralph Watkins, Vern Gasser, and others were there. Horace Lee Watkins brought Wolfson and Gregan along to meet the candidate. Before the general meeting started, Mecham, Watkins, Wolfson, and Gregan met in private.

Wolfson told Mecham that he and Gregan would be donating fifteen thousand dollars each to the campaign. He wished that their involvement be kept confidential. Charles Keating, a prominent developer, was making headlines at the time for his political contributions, and the men wanted no part of it.

Mecham had no problem with that. He left after about five minutes and the general meeting began. In addition to Wolfson and Gregan, three other potential contributors were present.

Colter presented the Western Savings' plan, though by this time Western had indicated it would not be acceptable. Wolfson listened to the presentation, then suggested to the group that it was needlessly complicated and might not work. He asked to be excused to speak to Gregan alone. After a few minutes Wolfson returned and said that under certain secure conditions he would be willing to provide a line of credit in the amount of six hundred thousand dollars, the campaign's projected needs. This was in addition to the fifteen-thousand-dollar contribution from both him and Gregan.

When the details were worked out it was suggested that Mecham obtain promissory notes that would collateralize any loans from Wolfson to the campaign. Wolfson would advance funds equal to the notes up to six hundred thousand dollars. Mecham assured him that their involvement would be confidential.

Within a day or so Wolfson had prepared a sample promissory note, a letter of assignment so Mecham could assign them to Wolfson, and a letter of agreement, which read:

Barry M. Wolfson
H. V. Gregan
1018 East Guadalupe Road
Tempe, AZ 85283
    Re. Campaign Funding
Dear Mr. Wolfson and Mr. Gregan:
    I anticipate my campaign needs through the election to be approximately $600,000, including $360,000 for television spots, $50,000 for radio time and $125,000 for a tabloid similar to the one used in the primary. You have agreed to advance up to $600,000 under the terms set below.
    Upon your receipt of a signed promissory note of at least $25,000 in the form attached and financial statements of the note's maker satisfactory to you, you will promptly deposit an amount equal to the principal amount of the note into a campaign account I designate (the "Campaign Account"). The Campaign Account may be drawn upon to pay for campaign expenses. I will give you a list of campaign expenditures each week.
    Once a week I will furnish you a list of contributions to my campaign. Whenever those contributions aggregate at least $100,000, I will promptly repay your advance to that extent. I will endorse each promissory note to you. If, after diligently pursuing repayment of the notes, you have not been fully repaid by November 1, 1987, I will repay you. You may designate one person to serve on my finance committee.
    I am relying upon your agreement to advance funds. Your agreement will remain confidential. Thank you for assistance.
                              Sincerely yours,
                              Evan Mecham
                              Barry Wolfson (signature)

    Colter was very pleased. The forms were ready within two days or so of the meeting, but it was not until October 15 and 16 that the promissory notes were signed. The signers gave them to Mecham for assignment. Because the name of Western Savings had been discussed extensively, because it had already lent three hundred thousand dollars, and because John Driggs, president of the company and a prominent Mormon, was participating in the meetings, most believed the notes were for use with Western Savings. Wolfson and Gregan were identified as contributors and men willing to assist the campaign, but not as the primary lenders.
    The campaign treasurer, Mecham's brother Willard, now opened a new campaign account at Valley National Bank with zero deposit. The campaign already had an account it had been using.

As soon as Colter had $250,000 in notes, Wolfson wired that amount into this new account from his own. This occurred on October 20, 1986. A check was then written to and deposited into the campaign's original account, from which the television ads were paid.

Within six days, however, Colter was desperate for money and was unable to secure more promissory notes.

Mecham had built his car dealership primarily on his skill as a television huckster. The campaign had targeted prime times for the Goldwater and Reagan slots in this final ten days of the campaign. Each slot had to be paid for before it ran. If the campaign missed a single payment, all slots were lost and were available to another candidate.

At ten o'clock in the morning on October 24, 1986, Colter called Watkins and told him he had to have a hundred thousand dollars by two that afternoon. He asked Watkins to contact Wolfson and see if he would advance the funds on Colter's promise that he would have the matching promissory notes by the next day.

Wolfson was not willing. Watkins suggested two fifty-thousand-dollar notes from Mecham himself instead. Wolfson was uncertain of this since in effect Mecham was guaranteeing the money twice but agreed anyway. Later it was Wolfson's recollection that Willard Mecham had called him with this request.

The money was wired into the new account that day.

Wolfson and Gregan jointly attended at least one finance committee meeting after reaching the agreement. Wolfson sat next to Colter, who said that a benefactor had solved the campaign's financial problems. He nodded toward Wolfson, who kicked him under the table. Thereafter Gregan attended meetings alone.

Though Wolfson, who served as Gregan's attorney in some matters, always insisted that the loans were solely from him and did not include Gregan in any way, the letter he prepared for Mecham to sign was addressed to both of them. Gregan was more often seen at meetings than Wolfson, and later Gregan called Willard Mecham about repayment. There was understandably some confusion about who had actually lent the money.

Shortly after Mecham's election as governor Peggy Griffith told Colter that she had finally recalled where she knew Gregan. She had some papers in Havasu City she wanted to show Colter.

On November 12, 1986, Colter received a letter from Wolfson that said in part: "Recent developments in the financial markets may be of some interest to us. As you may have noticed in the local papers, both Phoenix and Mesa are contemplating the issuance of taxable bonds for the purpose of funding economic development funds. . . ." Wolfson then described the workings of arbitrage. He went on: "On the negative side, you must consider some of the questions echoed by the City of Mesa and others as to whether the deals will be viewed simply as arbitrage gimmicks. . . . If you think there's an advantage to doing this, the Governor's office could recommend to the State financing people that they take a more active, aggressive role. . . . If you are interested, I can put you in touch with people. . . ."

By coincidence, the same day Griffith met with Colter and told him what she knew. She expressed doubts about Gregan's integrity. She had news accounts that alleged some irregularity in regard to his connection with industrial development bonds. When Griffith had served on an advisory council in southern Arizona, Gregan had tried to sell bonds to the city of Tombstone. Tombstone elected not to participate because the deal appeared unethical. She expressed her concern about Gregan's association with the campaign.

She said that it was a potentially embarrassing situation. In his notes of this conversation Colter wrote the word "corruption." Later Colter said that it never occurred to him that the association would not become public because too many people knew. In fact, only a handful knew for certain about the substantial campaign loan.

Colter said later that following his meeting with Griffith he realized for the first time that Wolfson and Gregan were not men with whom Evan Mecham should be connected. At subsequent finance committee meetings there were discussions of the need to distance the governor-elect from these men. Colter told Mecham about Griffith's information.

Donna Carlson, learning just who Hugh Gregan was from Griffith, met with the governor to alert him in case Colter had not. Mecham told her he was aware of the situation and was taking care of it.

Both Western Savings and Wolfson had been promised first rights to subsequent campaign contributions. Mecham took approximately three hundred thousand dollars from contributions that came in after his election and reported that he had repaid loans to himself with it. He sent Wolfson a check for a hundred thousand dollars. Actually his first check was made out to Gregan and Wolfson. Wolfson sent it back to have it made out to him alone.

Gregan attended the inauguration, the reception, and the inaugural ball. A few weeks after the administration began Gregan and Wolfson appeared before the state Housing Finance Review Board to argue for less regulation of their business. They found the board unreceptive.

Sam Udall, a trusting man, was named by Mecham to screen selections for appointments to unpaid positions in state government. He was told not to check recommendations from Wolfson for potential conflicts of interest. Altogether he received eight names from Wolfson or his firm. Three of them were named to the state Housing Finance Review Board.

One man had his name withdrawn after it had been submitted. This was at about the time Donna Carlson and Edith Richardson had vehemently objected to the nominations.

In March Wolfson and Gregan met with Mecham at his Pontiac dealership rather than at the governor's office. Under the terms of the agreement the loan was to have been repaid by March 15. The majority of the loan plus interest was still outstanding.

Mecham later recalled that the two men met with him to learn why Horace Lee Watkins did not have an office on the influential and prestigious Ninth Floor. They also told Mecham that they did not "think that the people in power, the so-called Phoenix 40, were in fact being swept out of power." They said they "were disappointed that there weren't any new faces. They were only a bunch of political hacks, [Mecham]'s cronies."

They discussed their concerns over Jim Colter's lack of ability, that he was really likable but "just not a heavyweight. . . ." They also talked to Mecham about Donna Carlson, who had opposed Wolfson's personnel recommendations, though Wolfson does not say he mentioned that.

Wolfson says he talked to Mecham about Watkins and told the governor he "ought to have some people with political savvy . . . on the Ninth Floor." Later Wolfson characterized this as "an extremely unfriendly conversation." He said he was treated like "a newspaper reporter with a microphone. . . . It was like he was at a press conference giving platitudes."

According to Wolfson, Gregan was the most tense over the situation. Gregan said that "despite Mecham claiming to be a businessman who wanted to make business better for Arizona . . . he was just another politician."

Mecham stood up and became red in the face, according to Wolfson, "just like he did with Stanton that day, and worse. . . ."

Mecham said, "Don't you ever call me a politician. Who the hell do you think you are? I'm a businessman, and I'm not just a politician, and don't you ever say that again." According to Wolfson, Mecham "went on like that for about five minutes, and then we pretty much left."

By summer Wolfson had arranged not to sue the promissory note holders because Mecham had not given him the campaign contributions as promised. The fail-safe date for the loan was November 1, 1987.

Wolfson was increasingly unhappy with the assurances Watkins kept giving him. He became concerned that he might not receive his money.

Mecham had two serious problems in repaying the loan. First, the level of contributions had been low. Second, Proposition 200 was retroactive. The new law had tied up nearly a hundred thousand dollars of the inaugural ball money and prevented Mecham from paying Wolfson off except from legitimate and reportable contributions.

Wolfson wrote a demand letter in July. This is likely the letter Donna Carlson found in Mecham's office.

> *I'm doing things that hasn't been done before.*
> —EVAN MECHAM
>
> *Evan Mecham was impeached for being incompetent.*
> —SENATOR CAROLYN WALKER

# 30

Joe Lane had thought he would have enough information with which to make a decision within two weeks to a month after hiring Bill French. Initially he had French and his people concentrating on the Wolfson loan. The Donna Carlson death threat occurred during that period, and the governor's loan from the Protocol Fund became public knowledge so the investigation was broadened to include those as well.

By the end of three weeks Lane was hearing enough to know that there was substance to the allegations against the governor. Lane was most personally offended by the Protocol Fund. All public officials understand that money with even a quasi-public appearance must be handled with great propriety. For Mecham to lend it to himself was appalling. "If I had done that with house funds," he said, "they would take me to that tree and hang me."

Joe Lane had hired Bill French as the speaker's investigator. He considered it his duty to act alone, a decision for which he was soundly criticized by the Mecham supporters in the caucus. The caucus could have stopped him any time it wanted but did not. The truth of the matter was most of his fellow Republicans in the house wanted this investigation as much as Joe Lane did.

Despite the traditional competition between the house and senate, the leaders in both bodies confer with one another. Usually in major events such as this neither house acted alone. This time was different. Joe Lane did not consult with his colleagues across the short mall. He was exercising a constitutional mandate. If anything came of it, the senate would have its duty as well. The investigation and any decision to impeach were a house function, not a function of the legislature.

Carl Kunasek acknowledges being angry over this. It seemed to him that the decision to proceed involved all of them. He was hurt that Lane did not talk to him and offended that most of what he learned came out of the newspapers.

Lane's chief of staff, Rick Collins, served as liaison with Bill French and his people. They spoke daily. Lane trusted Collins to keep him abreast of what French was uncovering without involving the speaker in the investigation or disclosing specifics.

Every week French briefed the leadership about what he had learned, again without going into details. The Democrats were always invited. They were uncertain of house security and not insensitive to the many friendships involved. Everyone knew that Jim Ratliff and Mecham spoke almost daily. No one questioned Ratliff's loyalty to Joe Lane, but the governor was, after all, the governor.

Joe Lane and Art Hamilton met on November 6 about the investigation. Hamilton wanted minority counsel for the Democrats. Even though French was a Democrat, he was seen as Joe Lane's man.

Hamilton was of the opinion from the beginning of the investigation that Lane had erred in going off on his own. He understands that Lane did it to shield the body of the house, but it was, nevertheless, a mistake. It seemed to Hamilton that the best model was Watergate. He favored extensive Judiciary Committee hearings, followed by a committee vote, then a full house vote.

Others closely involved in the process refute this approach and claim it is politically motivated. Under such a system the entire Mecham administration would have been open to scrutiny, the hearings would have lasted months, reputations would have been destroyed, representatives would have grandstanded for the cameras, and Mecham's supporters would have turned the process into a zoo.

Hamilton acknowledges that the house Democrats had their own motives for wanting hearings, but he believes the public would have been served well by full disclosure. He did not want a precedent established that could be used against a Democratic governor in the future. Hamilton believes the Republicans were acting in no small part because Mecham was "an embarrassment to the party." They wanted to deal with him as a political liability and limit the damage to themselves as much as possible.

On November 13 Joe Lane, Jane Dee Hull, and Rick Collins met with Pat Murphy to advise him of what they were attempting to accomplish. Lane asked that Murphy's two papers not mount a campaign to push him into hearings. He wanted to do this right and needed some time.

Rick Collins felt the meeting paid off only a week later, when Art Hamilton went public with his demand for separate counsel and the *Arizona Republic* and the Phoenix *Gazette* opposed the idea.

On November 18, following the first comprehensive French update that morning, Joe Lane and Art Hamilton met. Hamilton seemed to fear that the Republicans were up to something political in the investigation. He still wanted separate counsel for the Democrats, a request he made on three occasions. Some recall that the men disagreed. One recalls the pair, longtime colleagues and friends, blowing up at each other over it. Collins felt it necessary afterward to meet with Hamilton to keep open communications between the men.

Of all the major participants, French was best equipped to recognize the historic nature of his undertaking. He says that he did not see that aspect of it initially. In those first weeks he was conducting a sensitive investigation. Impeachment was not certain, only one option. His primary concern was that if he botched the job, he would be the one to take the fall. If he stumbled, there was no backing up. He felt as if it were all on his shoulders.

The Mecham administration was not cooperative with him. The governor refused ever to be interviewed. Mecham went on television, said he was aghast that the house was using subpoenas when all it had to do was ask, then returned to his office and stonewalled.

Joe Lane and Bill French were taken to court by Murray Miller over the investigation, but on November 11 the court cleared the path for them by declining jurisdiction. French's position was improved on December 2, when the court ruled that Corbin could turn over transcripts of the grand jury proceedings as long as French treated them as confidential.

The meeting that determined whether the house would proceed with the investigation and follow it to its logical conclusion occurred in Joe Lane's office also on December 2, 1987. It was attended by Joe Lane, Jane Dee Hull, Rick Collins, Bill French, and minority counsel Eric Henderson, appearing for Art Hamilton.

French told the gathering, "Yes, there is more than is in the papers." He told them that it was his evaluation of the evidence that Mecham had sought to conceal the Wolfson loan. In addition to this, French had a list of fifteen or twenty matters he had looked into.

Joe Lane knew they would have to focus on political and legal issues, to "concentrate things." He could not have French continuing to look under every rock. He was more than a little concerned about the cost. French thought there were five to seven issues with real substance.

French locked in on the Wolfson loan, the Protocol Fund, and the obstruction of the Donna Carlson death threat investigation.

There was no textbook on how to proceed now. Collins suggested an oral report by French before the entire house, accompanied by supporting written documentation. He suggested the presentation occur on a Friday so the house members would have a weekend to mull over the report and review the documents. A date in early January was tentatively selected.

\* \* \*

Debbie McCune had watched the Mecham administration attempts to discredit Donna Carlson once she left the Ninth Floor and found those attempts "very shocking." Things were "under a cloud" when the Democratic representative left the country in very early October. She and thirty-five others traveled to Israel on a trip sponsored by the Jewish Federation Community Council. Also with her were State Senator Carolyn Walker and local attorney Paul Eckstein and his wife. While they were out of the country, they were cut off from events in Arizona and were starved for news.

On Sunday, November 1—the same day *The New York Times Magazine* ran its article on Mecham—the group arrived in New York at 6:45 A.M. Debbie McCune called Phoenix and was able to speak to Art Hamilton, who told her of recent events.

She hung up and turned to her companions. "My God!" she said. "You won't believe this! Joe Lane's talking the big 'I' word!"

The group was stunned. Walker remembers thinking there was no way that Arizona would impeach anyone for a campaign financing violation. But Arizona had been turned on its head in the short time they had been absent.

# 31

$A$t least two statewide grand juries are impaneled in Arizona each year. The Twenty-third State Grand Jury had been organized in June 1987 and had met a few days each of the months thereafter. It is not unusual for such a grand jury to hear thirty cases in its six-month life. The last day of deliberations was scheduled to be December 3, 1987.

Sixteen jurors and four alternates are selected at random from throughout the state. No juror may vote for indictment unless he or she has sat for all the testimony on that particular case. Jurors fall by the wayside as the term progresses. By November 1987 the twenty-third State Grand Jury was down to eleven active members. Arizona statutes require a majority of the full panel, so it would take nine votes to indict Evan Mecham.

The state grand jury is an instrument of the attorney general's office, but its operation is supervised by the presiding judge of the county in which it is meeting. That is nearly always Maricopa County. By practice, the presiding judge delegates the responsibility to the presiding criminal judge. When Judge O'Toole recused himself because he had signed the recall petition, the presiding judge, Michael Dann, took over personally.

Americans in general and Arizonans in particular are sensitive to the potential abuses of a grand jury, and certain safeguards were built into the Arizona model that are progressive. A transcript is kept of the proceeding, and that record is provided to the indicted individual ten days after the true bill is handed up. The defense lawyer reviews the basis of the indictment and can challenge its sufficiency.

Other safeguards include informing a witness that he is a "target" of the investigation and allowing an attorney to be present during questioning. At any point the target may leave the room with his lawyer to seek advice, but the lawyer may not object, even for the record, and may not offer evidence on behalf of his client. It is an attorney general's show.

In its last weeks the Twenty-third State Grand Jury took up the inquiry into the Wolfson loan to Evan Mecham. Donna Carlson testified, as did Jim Colter, Horace Lee Watkins, Barry Wolfson, Ralph Watkins, Willard Mecham, and the attorney general's investigator George Graham.

With the disclosure of the Wolfson loan at the end of October, Murray Miller's role shifted from preparing a legal challenge to the recall to defending Evan Mecham, both from potential indictment by the attorney general and from impeachment by the house of representatives.

His approach with the attorney general was first to challenge whether or not Bob Corbin had a conflict of interest. Since the Office of the Attorney General provides legal advice to the Office of the Governor, it was Miller's position that same office could not now investigate a client in areas where legal advice had been given. The court ruled otherwise.

Miller's next tactic was to attempt to present a defense before the grand jury. Grand juries of the West are known for refusing to indict on occasion when they believe the target has been wrongly singled out. This approach was a long shot but worth a try considering the political climate.

Miller was representing Willard Mecham as well. Willard had served as Mecham's campaign treasurer and had prepared the documents Mecham signed and filed with the secretary of state. Miller asked for and received the right to have Willard Mecham make a statement to the grand jury.

Willard Mecham was sixty-seven years old and bore a resemblance to his better-known brother, though he did not wear a hairpiece and was conspicuously bald. He is mild-mannered and unassuming.

He told the grand jury of his childhood in Utah, and his testimony differed significantly from Evan Mecham's version of his upbringing. According to Willard Mecham, the family dairy farm had not been able to support the family during the Depression and his father had taken a job building roads for the Forest Service. Later the family sold the farm and purchased a small general store in Altamont. Willard Mecham had worked in that store until 1960, when he joined his younger brother in Glendale and began selling cars. In 1984 he had retired a millionaire, a fact the assistant attorneys general made several times.

Miller thought it went well. As a direct consequence of Willard Mecham's testimony Miller was able to put before the jurors two sworn documents that said essentially the way he had prepared the finance report forms was legal. Miller believed the jurors had been moved by Willard Mecham's testimony and was hoping to elicit a similar performance from the governor.

Grand jury matters are secret. Partly that is to allow the state to conduct its inquiry without public scrutiny, and partly it is to protect the target in the event no indictment is forthcoming.

A grand jury inquiry into a sitting governor is an open secret. These proceedings were conducted on a floor in the superior court where no other hearings were held. Sam Stanton, Mike Murphy, Laurie Asseo, and others simply camped out and watched who went in and who left. If a person had a lawyer, that meant he or she was a target.

To pass the time, the six or eight reporters covering the proceedings played penny-ante poker until one of the bailiffs informed them public gambling was against the law. Sam Stanton says that all of them were working their attorney general sources pretty well and getting nowhere.

Appearances were so widely reported in the press that Ken Smith started including Evan Mecham's in his governor's daily itinerary. Barnett Lotstein objected to that before Judge Dann, and Mecham agreed to discontinue the practice; but he pointed out the obvious fact that he was the governor and he could not keep something like this a secret.

That last day of the Twenty-third State Grand Jury Horace Lee Watkins testified, as did Willard Mecham and Barry Wolfson. There was speculation the next day on whether or not anyone had been indicted. Indictments were expected against Horace Lee Watkins and the governor at the least. In an unusual move Judge Dann gave the attorney general permission to disclose publicly certain information about the grand jury.

On December 7 Steve Twist released a statement saying that "neither the Mecham nor the Watkins investigation were [*sic*] concluded prior to the expiration of the term of the 23rd State Grand Jury, and the investigation into these matters is continuing." The term of the state grand jury had not been extended because the attorney general did not know how much more time was required.

The Twenty-fourth State Grand Jury had been requested routinely by Barnett Lotstein on October 22. It was to be impaneled on December 18 and first meet in early January.

Twist's announcement meant there would be no decision on indictments until after the New Year and at about the time the next session of the legislature was to commence.

The inquiry into the Mecham loan had begun when there were only eleven grand jurors remaining. It is standard attorney general practice not to begin an investigation unless there are at least twelve. In this case the attorney general made an exception. On the last night of the Twenty-third State Grand Jury there were only nine jurors present, one of whom was believed to be LDS. For there to be an indictment—that is if Barnett Lotstein and Mike Cudahy had intended to ask for one—all nine would have had to vote in favor. No vote was taken.

Shortly after the recall drive began, Richard Miller, an attorney in his late twenties, was drinking with friends at the Monastery in Phoenix. It was hot, even at night, and Miller had at least one beer more than prudent. He joined with others and signed a circulating recall petition.

When the flap broke over Bill French's having signed the petitions, Richard Miller, who was assisting Mecham's lawyer, his father, Murray Miller, pulled him aside and said, "You probably ought to know this." Murray Miller considered it for a moment and then told his son not to be concerned. There were nearly four hundred thousand signatures in the petitions. Who was going to check them all?

Murray Miller informed the governor. Mecham called Richard Miller to talk about it in what the young man describes as a thoroughly embarrassing moment. Then the governor told him not to worry about it.

A friend of the family, Paul Rubin with the *New Times*, called Richard Miller in early December. "I want you to be very careful because you are on the record," he said. Miller knew immediately what this call was going to be about. Rubin told him a group of students had been hired by the *New Times* to review the recall petitions. "We have six Richard Millers. Is one of them you?"

The product of legal training and working on his skills in understatement, Miller said, "Yes."

When pressed, he explained that what he did with his private life had nothing to do with his work.

The *New Times* broke the story in early December. The Mecham supporters had been having a field day with French's signing of the recall petition. House members were reported to be chuckling at this turn of events coming only two weeks later.

Ken Smith was quoted as saying that Mecham "is a forgiving man," who was "just looking for good legal counsel."

Joe Lane acknowledged the heat he had taken for hiring French. "The governor didn't seem to mind too much that his attorney signed the recall petition," he said. "So I'm not too upset that mine signed."

On Sunday morning, December 13, Evan Mecham attended a conservative Jewish men's club breakfast at the Ahavat Torah Congregation as part of his recent, unpublicized appearances with religious groups. It was an informal gathering from which the press had been excluded. Questions on any topic were entertained anyway, as was generally Mecham's practice.

Toward the end of the breakfast a member of the congregation asked Mecham, "Would you admit there are God-fearing people who signed a recall petition and not just gays and militants?"

Mecham said, "I never comment on the recall."

Another member brought up his remarks in Utah in September, when Mecham had called America a "great Christian nation." The member asked, "Did you say that?"

Mecham was being taped as he replied. "Yes, I said it and I will probably say it again. If it follows Christian principles, it will make a great land for everyone, allowing great freedom of religion for Jews, Mohammedans and everyone else." He added, "If that is a problem for anyone, then it is their problem."

Rabbi David Mayer said, "Jews get scared when they hear such statements. There have been many incidents in Jewish history when Jews living in a predominantly Christian society found themselves in a position known as dead."

Several members of the audience, some of whom were children of survivors of the Holocaust, walked out in anger.

The next day the Anti-Defamation League of B'nai B'rith denounced Mecham as "insensitive." Mecham responded by saying, "I'm not at all insensitive. . . . I have many good Jewish friends," and mentioned his attorney, Murray Miller, and Bob Usdane, senate majority leader.

Mecham called Murray Miller and said, "Murray, are you still talking to me?"

Miller replied, "Sure, Governor."

Mecham said, "I want you to know it isn't the way they portray it."

In Atlanta the *Constitution* ran an editorial that said in part, "One need not live in Arizona to understand why so many of that state's citizens have signed the recall petitions.

"It's not that Mecham is merely insensitive. His statements reveal him to be an astoundingly small-minded and foolish man.

"He lacks the intellectual bearing, the social insight and the grace to lead anything, much less serve as governor of a state. Too bad the recall voting is confined to Arizona. Mecham's notoriety has not been. He has become a *national* embarrassment."

A chorus of condemnation erupted from within the state as well. Burton Kruglick, the chairman of the state Republican party, who is also Jewish, suggested Mecham consider apologizing. Representative Cindy Resnick, a Tucson Democrat who is Jewish, also condemned the governor's remarks in an open letter to him in which she asked for a formal apology. Mecham responded with a letter that Ken Smith released publicly.

In the letter to Resnick, Mecham said, "It was the farthest thing from my mind to offend any person of any faith or background. . . . Therefore, knowing that I am believed to be insensitive or at least unaware of exactly how my comments would, or could be interpreted, I do sincerely apologize to those who have taken offense."

He continued, "It is obvious that this was a contrived situation. The leaders of the Anti-Defamation League put out a press release which was totally against the agreement of no press." The governor's appearance had been listed on his calendar distributed to the media.

Resnick said of Mecham's letter, "That's not an apology." She added, "It is classic Evan Mecham. Evan believes he is never wrong and other people have misinterpreted his position. He is apologizing for me for mis-interpreting his comment.

". . . Just 'I'm sorry.' Is that so hard? Is that so much to ask?"

Shortly before Christmas some of the reporters who covered Mecham daily thought it would be a nice idea to go to his home and sing Christmas carols. One of them called Ken Smith to see if it would be acceptable consid-ering the tenor of the times. It was agreed the appearance would be entirely off the record. Sam Stanton considered it for a moment but, to the relief of his editor, Laurie Roberts, decided it would not be appropriate. She had been concerned that Mecham might say something, and then what do you do, not cover it? Mike Murphy was invited and declined for similar reasons.

Mecham was meeting late with Miller that night at the lawyer's office when he called Florence at his home. Mecham told his wife that some of the reporters were going to drop by for caroling and he wanted to be certain that she had cookies for them.

Miller was shocked and asked the governor why he was going along with this.

Mecham said, "They have their job to do, and it's Christmas."

The reporters appeared and after carols were invited inside for punch and cookies with the governor and Mrs. Mecham. Stanton heard later that Mecham had enjoyed himself.

At about this time Mecham called the *Republic* to complain about an article on Horace Lee Watkins. He also complained about Steve Benson's cartoons, and he voiced his belief that Benson was under the control of Pat Murphy. Benson heard about the call. He left word at the governor's home that night for him to call back. Mecham returned the call at about 10:00 P.M. The governor was already in bed. The pair spoke for two hours.

They did not have much of a discussion. Mecham ran down a litany of objections against Benson. He told Benson that he was "disquieted" with his work. He was especially upset over Benson's recent cartoon that depicted the Mormon Angel Moroni atop the LDS temple in Salt Lake City with a banner hanging from its trumpet bearing the words "Resign Ev."

Benson had drawn the cartoon because of the persistent, and in his view reliable, reports that officials of the Mormon Church had asked Mecham to step down for the good of the church.

Benson was able to ask Mecham about his business dealings that had received press coverage and about the Wolfson loan. The answers were less than satisfactory.

At one point Mecham told Benson, "I was promised by President Benson that if I would obey the commandments, I would see this thing through." Blessings of comfort are common in the LDS Church, and Benson took it that Mecham had given such a blessing an inappropriate meaning. He was especially offended that Mecham would imply church sanctioning of his position as governor.

Mecham told Benson, "You have no right to judge me." Benson pointed out that this was politics, not religion. Mecham said to Benson during the conversation, "I don't break the commandments; *you* break the commandments." Mecham said, "Somewhere along the line you have fallen off the beam. You are under the control of Pat Murphy."

At about this point he told Florence to go to sleep. "I feel Steve Benson's spiritual salvation is at stake," he said.

Later, when Mecham mentioned the conversation on the CNN news program *Crossfire*, he told Pat Buchanan, "I told Steve I was concerned about him. I was a little worried about him personally, about his salvation, because I know his father and his grandfather, and they're good friends of mine."

Benson was becoming angry and bitter by this mix of politics and religion. He says that during the telephone call Mecham "was playing bishop again" and was absolutely "in no position to judge my worthiness." Benson believes that Mecham is "a dangerous man" who is "fundamentally unequipped to be governor."

Following impanelment, the Twenty-fourth State Grand Jury commenced its inquiry on January 4, 1988. Investigator George Graham testified, and through him the testimony of those who had appeared before the last grand jury was introduced. The affidavits received from Miller were not included. The Twenty-fourth State Grand Jury had what lawyers call a cold record to review, meaning they did not have the benefit of listening to the witnesses themselves. All they had were the bare words.

The state called a certified public accountant to testify and James Shumway from the secretary of state's office about the finance forms. An investigator read Willard Mecham's testimony out loud. Finally Evan Mecham himself appeared, first as a witness under questioning from Lotstein and later to read a prepared statement to the jury.

Under questioning Mecham had trouble explaining his conduct from the previous year. First Mecham swore he had not disclosed the debt he owed Wolfson because he had paid it off before the end of the year. When Lotstein read him the form that required reporting of all debts from any part of the year, Mecham said he had not listed it because all of the $350,000 had gone to the campaign and was not a personal debt to him. He testified the campaign did not have to disclose the money because it was his personal debt and he had lent it to the campaign. He explained that the loan from Wolfson did not have to be reported as a personal debt because there was no actual obligation to repay it until the following year, when the promissory notes fell due. The debt did not exist when he filed the reports.

The grand jury apparently found it difficult to follow.

In offering this explanation, Mecham was forgetting his own challenge to Richard Kleindienst in 1964 to join with him in disclosing their backers so the public could judge for themselves.

It is a tenet of Mecham and his supporters that the Twenty-fourth State Grand Jury was manipulated into indicting him. The practice of admitting testimony from an earlier grand jury is not uncommon, though in this case it was much criticized. Mecham's lawyers, both Miller and Michael Scott, who defended him at his criminal trial, took the view that the attorney general did not ask the Twenty-third State Grand Jury for an indictment because he knew he could not obtain one. The explanations of why the attorney general held the investigation over, they claim, are facile.

Lotstein and Cudahy respond by saying that the investigation initiated by the Twenty-third State Grand Jury was "unstructured." They had developed some testimony and gathered a great volume of documents that had to be reviewed.

They also point out that when the Twenty-third State Grand Jury was impaneled, they had no idea they would be investigating Evan Mecham. During the term a number of the jurors had signed recall petitions; others might well have made strong public statements on the performance of Governor Mecham. An Arizona court of appeals decision came down at this time allowing grand jurors to be examined after an indictment to determine if they had bias or prejudice against the accused.

They defend their conduct with the Twenty-fourth State Grand Jury as entirely proper. A grand jury proceeding is not a trial, and the target is not allowed to present a defense. It is intended to be an investigator's tool and is meant only to develop probable cause. The prosecutors present the evidence that tends to support the conclusion that a crime has occurred.

In this case both Evan and Willard Mecham were allowed to address the grand jury and give their side. Lotstein is of the opinion that if a target can persuade a grand jury not to indict, then he should not be indicted. Mecham was indicted, he says, because he had no defense.

In the end it was Lotstein's conclusion that Mecham was "his strongest witness against himself."

All sixteen grand jurors were present when Evan Mecham testified before the Twenty-fourth State Grand Jury. The majority of them asked questions of the governor. Clearly there was intense interest on their part. They did not hesitate to interrupt the assistant attorneys general.

Juror: "Do you normally sign a document without reading it beforehand?"

Mecham: "I sign lots of documents without reading them. . . ."

Another juror: "Why didn't Willard want everyone to know that Wolfson was a large contributor?"

Mecham: "Well, give me that again. . . ."

Another juror: "I would think with that much money involved in a campaign you would be a little bit more conscious of how that money is coming in and where it's going."

Mecham: "I was conscious that the money came in. It was a lot of money and it did finance the balance of the campaign that we needed. . . ."

Another juror: "And were you trying to keep those [other loans] secret?"

Mecham: "Oh no, no. They were actually loans from me. . . ."

Another juror: "You said earlier that you really were not aware that the people who made $50,000 promissory notes, those who signed them, whether they were aware of the arrangements with Wolfson or not. Since the investigation has begun have you made it a point to contact—to ask each of those individuals if they knew?"

Mecham: "I have not personally asked the people. I've been pretty busy and I haven't asked them. . . ."

Another juror: "If that's the case then they were aware of the arrangement with Wolfson. Was his name used in connection with that?"

Mecham: "I'll have to look at that and see if it was. I'm not sure."

Mecham's overall performance before the grand jury had been no better. He interrupted not just the assistant attorneys general but the jurors as well. He tried repeatedly to read into the record statements Judge Dann had ordered not read.

Mecham pointed the finger at everyone for his predicament. In his closing statement he failed to follow Judge Dann's instructions and tried to introduce expert testimony of an attorney he had retained to provide him with an opinion of state campaign finance law. Cudahy had taken him back before Dann, who had the governor now write out his remarks. The judge excised some of the statement for being beyond the scope of his instructions. The next day Mecham appeared before the state grand jury and resumed his remarks.

Though the grand jurors had been admonished not to read news accounts of what was occurring Mecham assumed they were disregarding those instructions. "I know many of you have read all types of newspaper accounts of me, and most of them have been disparaging and critical." He mentioned a political cartoon from the previous night.

He then accused the attorney general and the speaker of the house of a "concerted action" to remove him from office. He attacked Speaker Joe Lane and raised the specter of impeachment even though this jury had nothing to do with it.

He attacked Pat Murphy and said, ". . . I am told Mr. Murphy has offered or may have already paid Donna Carlson, the lady whose name was mentioned yesterday, $10,000 to write stories about me. One can only wonder what she would write for $50,000."

Following Mecham's attack on his enemies, the state concluded its presentation with the testimony of a certified public accountant who had reviewed the campaign finance disclosure filings. He testified there were 576 separate entries recording contributions and loans.

"Based [sic] on your examination of the 576 contributions and loans listed in Exhibit 5, how many of the 576 entries disclosed the name and amount of the actual contributor or lender to the campaign?"

"575."

"How many entries do not disclose the name of the actual contributor or lender?"

"Only one."

"Which is that?"

"That's the entry on page 26 of 2, the post-general report, Evan Mecham, Glendale, Arizona, $465,000."

"How did you determine that that particular entry did not reflect the name of the actual contributor or lender?"

"My independent examination of the deposit records, receipts and the checks and the wire transfers indicate that that amount of money was really four separate deposit items made up of a $250,000 wire transfer from Barry Wolfson, $100,000 wire transfer on a different date from Barry Wolfson, a $100,000 check from Western Savings and a $15,000 check from Mecham Pontiac."

". . . Were you able to determine how many [entries] involved the lumping together of contributions or loans from different sources?"

"Yes, I have."

"And how many were lumped together from different sources?"

"Only one."

"Which entry was that?"

"The same entry referred, the Evan Mecham $465,000."

All that remained was the voting. The sixteen grand jurors met without the assistant attorneys general. A short time later the foreman summoned them. "We have a unanimous vote for a draft and possible indictment."

He was handed a draft indictment, three counts against Evan and Willard Mecham and three counts against Evan Mecham alone. The grand jury returned to private deliberations.

A short time later the foreman summoned the assistant attorneys general again. "We have arrived at a vote and the way the Grand Jury proceeded was to consider each count separately. . . . Considering Count No. 1 a yes vote for Evan Mecham was cast by 14. A no vote by 1 and 1 abstention. . . . With regard to Willard Mecham, Count 1, yes vote, 13; no votes, 2; one abstention."

And so it proceeded. No vote was less than fourteen to indict Evan Mecham or less than thirteen to indict Willard Mecham. On one count both men received fifteen yes votes, one abstention.

At 3:18 P.M., Friday, January 8, 1988, the Twenty-fourth State Grand Jury returned a true bill to Judge Dann. Steve Twist, who had made an appearance for the occasion, recommended that summonses rather than warrants be issued.

Evan Mecham was now the first Arizona governor to be indicted, only the sixth United States governor to be indicted in the history of the country.

Just the day before Murray Miller had told Judge Dann in chambers, ". . . I think what the Court has done by foreclosing testimony of our experts to rebut the testimony of their non-authoritative witness . . . has successfully, I think, ensured the indictment of the Governor."

When no vote had been taken by the Twenty-third State Grand Jury and the attorney general had vigorously pursued the case with this one, there was no doubt in Miller's mind about the outcome.

Mike Cudahy called to ask Miller if he would accept service for his clients. At 4:30 P.M. Miller received the summonses. He interrupted Richard Miller, who was with a client, and asked if he would accompany him to the Capitol to inform the governor.

At almost exactly 5:00 P.M. they passed the attorney general's office and could see the television cameras set up for the news. Miller says it "frosted" him to see them so quick to announce the indictment when he had not even had time to inform the governor.

Despite Miller's certainty about what would happen, Evan Mecham seemed to have held out hope that he had persuaded the grand jury not to indict. As was so often the case, he believed his personal appearance had had a positive impact.

Murray and Richard Miller joined the governor in his corner working office. Also present were Ken Smith, Richard Burke, and Ray Russell. The men stood in a semicircle in front of his desk, where Evan Mecham was seated. Miller told him that both he and his brother had been indicted.

There was absolute silence as Mecham, staring down at his desk, took in the impact of the words. Then he said, "They want to put me in jail, don't they?"

The governor called his brother at once. He did not want him hearing about it from the media. He reached Willard's wife and told her the news, then tried to reassure her.

After the call the governor was obviously emotional. He wanted to go straight out and give an off-the-cuff statement. The group persuaded him otherwise.

There was some discussion on what the governor should say when he did speak. At 6:25 P.M. Mecham left the building without comment to the reporters. He had nothing to say when he reached his home. Some supporters were already there with pickets: GREAT JOB, EV; WE LOVE YOU.

Back in the office the men worked on a statement. Richard Miller left at about 8:00 P.M. in a futile attempt to obtain the grand jury transcripts. The law says ten days, and it was ten days before they saw them.

Down the street at the popular Capitol watering hole Oaxaca, tequila was on the house. The favorite toast was "Adios, Mecham." Just as the celebration cooled down, the television coverage of events began and charged the crowd anew.

Before six that night someone slipped into the law offices of Storey & Ross, where Bill French and his team were busy with the impeachment probe. Whoever it was hid as the building was shut down for the night.

To ensure security at the end of each day, French and his people locked their documents in a fireproof room on the floor where they worked. The building had a large measure of security, including guards and controlled access.

French had been alerted by reporters that something might be coming out of the attorney general's office that day. The lawyers had worked with a little transistor radio on, and it was over it that he had first heard of the indictments. French was anxious to see the indictments. They had been working in a corner office opposite the one where he had first met with Joe Lane.

Rick Collins had prepared two press releases for Joe Lane, one in the event of indictment, another if there was no indictment. When word came down, he went to the Capitol to release the appropriate statement.

When French finished at about 6:30 P.M., he made the unusual decision to rely entirely on the building's security and not lock up the documents because they would be working on them first thing the next day. All the papers they had were simply left spread over the table in the conference room.

Not long after they left, a secretary smelled smoke and complained to security, which did nothing. Shortly before, she had seen a man she did not know on the floor. Forty-five minutes after her complaining of smoke the fire alarm went off.

The arsonist had gained access to the litigation file room and destroyed it. Because the Mecham documents were on the other side of the floor in an area far from the fire, they were untouched by either the flames or the automatic sprinklers. No one was charged in the crime.

French received a telephone call from the secretary, who said that there "had been a terrible fire here." He went down that night to inspect the damage and was joined shortly by Joe Lane. They both were interviewed on live television, which had arrived ahead of them. The sprinklers had virtually gutted an entire quarter of the floor, and the fire had destroyed nearly everything in the file room.

In his statements at the time French downplayed why the fire would not affect the investigation, saying only that his papers were untouched. Long after the events he confided that had he and Patricia Magrath returned the papers to the presumably secure file room the fire would have stalled his inquiry for six weeks. That six-week delay could well have altered future events dramatically.

After the arson security was improved. French and his staff decided to continue simply leaving the documents out in the open. Only the accounting sheets were secured under lock and then in an area away from the file room.

Beau Johnson and Frank Martinez from DPS met with French the next day and arranged for permanent security for him. The Phoenix Police Department assumed responsibility for covering his house.

A week to ten days later the secretary spotted the same man on the floor. Security was unable to find him.

The day following the indictments, a Saturday, Mecham was ready to give his statement. He had been advised not to launch into an attack. The crowd attending was so large the conference had been moved from the Protocol Room to the lobby on the first floor.

The indictment had been front-page news nationwide. The *Washington Post*, the Dallas *Morning News*, *The New York Times*, and many other papers had carried it. Reporters had flown in just to cover the events. Not only was there today's conference, but on Monday Mecham was to deliver his second State of the State address to the legislature, and on Friday Bill French was scheduled to deliver his oral report to the house of representatives.

In the governor's office the same group of men from the previous night were working on Mecham's speech. As quickly as they prepared the document Mecham made changes. With only five minutes to go they still had untyped passages. The full impact of the indictment had come home and was a "horrible blow" to the governor. It seemed to Miller that Mecham could scarcely breathe.

As they were making changes, Willard Mecham's name came up. Evan Mecham was sitting down and suddenly started sobbing. He removed his glasses as the room lapsed into stony silence except for the governor's sobs. Mecham wiped his eyes with his handkerchief as he continued to sob.

As he kept crying, Miller was moved by the sight. He knew the kind of man Evan Mecham was publicly portrayed to be. He wondered what the public would think if they could see him as he was seeing him at this moment.

As he sobbed, Mecham said aloud, more to himself than to the others, "How can they do this to my family? To my brother? He is innocent. He didn't do anything. He just got caught up in a political campaign." Mecham continued wiping his eyes and spoke through his tears. "I can stand up to these charges. I can face it. I'm not guilty of any of it."

His tears finally stopped. He wiped his eyes a last time, then quickly composed himself. He was due in the lobby.

Clutching the latest revisions and his handwritten notes, Mecham stood up and walked toward the elevators. "Okay," he said, "let's go to work."

# PART THREE

§1. *Power of impeachment in the house of representatives; trial by senate*

*Section 1. The House of Representatives shall have the sole power of impeachment. The concurrence of a majority of all the members shall be necessary to an impeachment. All impeachments shall be tried by the Senate, and, when sitting for that purpose, the Senators shall be upon oath or affirmation to do justice according to law and evidence, and shall be presided over by the Chief Justice of the Supreme Court. . . .*

— *Arizona State Constitution*

> We'd like to wake up in the morning and re-
> alize it was just a bad dream and all went
> away.
>
> > —JACK LONDEN, *long-*
> > *time Mecham supporter,*
> > *Republican national*
> > *committeeman*
>
> *We may be talking impeachment.*
> > —REPRESENTATIVE JANE
> > DEE HULL, *house*
> > *majority whip*

# 32

The scene in the lobby was frantic. Sixty reporters and photographers were assembled in front of the elevators, facing a large portrait of the governor. There were eighteen television cameras in place. Boom mikes—signatures of the national networks—loomed toward the podium. The cameramen shouted at the reporters in front to sit down. Spectators watched from the mezzanine.

Outside, supporters picketed with signs that said, 8 MORE YEARS, EV, and MR. CORBIN, GOD IS WATCHING YOU.

Shortly after 2:00 P.M. the light on the elevator began to move from the ninth floor. One of the reporters called out, "Here he comes!" The cameramen shouted again for the reporters to sit down.

The elevator doors opened to a flurry of flashbulbs. Mecham emerged with a phalanx of security guards, who joined the uniformed Capitol police. A secretary had come down with a pitcher of water and a glass. Mecham, looking overcome with emotion, flashed a weak smile as he assumed the podium. There were so many microphones it took a few moments to make room for his text and notes.

"It was a sad and tragic day for the state of Arizona and the nation," he began, "to have to bear witness to a heinous travesty of justice committed by political opportunists in the Attorney General's office in an unbridled and flagrant abuse of the secret grand jury hearing."

Mecham, stumbling over words much more often than usual, said that he was "relieved" at the indictment. For those who had witnessed the scene just moments earlier Mecham was remarkably composed.

The most visible sign of what he had just experienced came when he read, "My great sorrow is over the depth of harassment, is for my family. . . . I'm extremely sorry that my brother Willard, who is the epitome of honesty and integrity and [has] never drawn a dis"—he stopped and swallowed, an aide moved to assist him, but he continued in a slightly different pitch— "honest breath in his life"—he stopped again to compose himself—"will be brought into this prosecution."

He recovered and proceeded with the rest of the speech, which consisted largely of an attack on Bob Corbin. "After one and a half years of constant investigation into everything I have done, this is all they have come up with. I am completely clean.

"I slept well last night," he said. "With a clear conscience, it is easy to sleep well."

Mecham continued that now it is "easy for all the world to see the depths that some will go in Arizona to remove me from office. . . . I now feel confident to be able to not only prove my innocence, but to also get to the bottom of those who would like to overthrow a constitutionally elected official."

In language to which Arizonans were now accustomed he said, "One of the good things that will come about is that hopefully this will bring everything out into public inspection where we can get a real clean up of these elements done."

In the most sobering denunciation of the twenty-minute speech he concluded forcefully, "I personally forgive all. . . . Vengeance is mine, saith the Lord. We need not try to get even with anyone in this life." Pause. "There is a just God in heaven who will mete out eternal justice to all in the hereafter. I thank you."

Without answering the questions shouted at him, he turned and returned to the elevator.

Back on the Ninth Floor he met with U.S. Senator John McCain and Burton Kruglick for forty-five minutes. No one needed to guess at the subject discussed.

That Monday Mecham delivered his second State of the State address to the legislature. A tense Joe Lane sat behind him and beside a stressed Carl Kunasek. Yellow spider mums were on each side of the podium as Mecham delivered an upbeat message that ignored the controversy engulfing his administration.

Dismissing the previous twelve months as "a year of noisy sensationalism," he listed the mundane concerns of state government. In conclusion he said, "There is inherent good in most difficulties. In life, whenever changes are being made, change alone can cause friction between people. Disagreement is always potentially present in the crafting of legislation and in the administration of government. A good rule to remember is: *we can disagree without being disagreeable*. Thank you, and God bless you all."

His references to mistakes in the speech were ignored. Events had moved beyond that.

The following day Mecham delivered a speech to the Phoenix Kiwanians and demonstrated once again the nature of his character. He began with a joke members of his security detail had heard many times:

"The most important question to be answered today at the Capitol was going to be to find the answer that if Pat Murphy, the distinguished publisher of the *Arizona Republic*, Cameron Harper, one of the self-appointed most distinguished reporters on television, and that great authority, another great authority on most everything that's great in the world, John Kolbe, who knows all the answers, that if those three all jumped off the top of the Valley Bank building, who would hit the pavement first. Well, she had me dumfounded. Finally, we asked several people through the hallway, collected quite a group. You know what the consensus was? Who cares?"

He talked about his *Nightline* appearance and criticized Sam Stanton's coverage of him. Then he said, "That same Sam Stanton that got a call on Sunday and wrote an article in yesterday's paper. It said someone called him that I was to a meeting in a hotel. That someone that called him was Ed Buck. Sam, I didn't know that Ed was such a close friend of yours. . . . Interesting things, I chuckle at 'em, I kinda get a kick outa them."

Sharing a moment of levity from his recent trip to the Far East, Mecham said, "I have to tell you I gave the president of the largest bank in the world a Ping putter from Karsten Manufacturers here, and the Japanese like to play golf. And their eyes really light up when you say we've got over 200 golf courses in Arizona. My goodness, golf course. Suddenly they got round eyes. I hope that wasn't anything out of line. Very courteous, very fine people."

One of the television crews ran Stanton down and interviewed him in the press room. They said Mecham had accused him of being homosexual. What was his response?

That night Sam Stanton was having dinner at Gregory's with a first date. While they were sitting at the bar his interview ran on television. Stanton explained to his date this kind of thing did not happen all the time, and no, he was not gay.

Later his editor, Laurie Roberts, jokingly asked him to straighten the matter up for her. Stanton said she should ask the women in the press room.

Senator Peter Rios condemned Mecham from the senate floor. "Today is another sad and embarrassing day in Arizona thanks to our governor," he said. "I've heard a couple of Mormon jokes, but I'm not that crude or insensitive" to repeat them. He said, "If the governor wants to know if he's out of line, yes, Mr. Governor, you were totally out of line."

A poll published that week showed that 65 percent of Arizonans wanted Evan Mecham to resign, and 56 percent supported his recall from office.

In early January half a dozen veteran Republican party leaders met with Barry Goldwater at his home in Paradise Valley. The focus of the meeting was to find some way to get Evan Mecham to step down. They asked Goldwater about his Watergate experiences with Nixon in an attempt to find some parallels that could serve as a guide. Carl Kunasek attended the meeting. He was interested in knowing what point in Watergate had been the point of no return.

Goldwater regaled them with stories of Mecham. They decided there was no point in putting together a team to approach the governor. Mecham would not listen to anyone. It was readily apparent that Mecham was not a Nixon.

If there was any doubt that Joe Lane meant business, that doubt had been dispelled on November 12, 1987, when he had the staffs of the Arizona Legislative Council and of the house of representatives distribute a "Report on Impeachment of Public Officers."

The eighty-odd page memorandum, which Mark Killian called a "driver's manual for impeachment," was intended to provide house members with an overview of the impeachment process. It contained a brief history and the role the house played in such a proceeding. The Arizona provisions of law were cited, as were excerpts from the state's two previous experiences, neither of which had involved a governor.

Though Joe Lane knew the impeachment effort must at some point become bipartisan if it was to succeed, he continued to resist Art Hamilton's efforts to obtain separate minority counsel. Lane had a large majority in his own caucus that supported what he was doing, but the Mecham supporters, almost entirely LDS or from districts with disproportionate Mormon populations, were publicly attacking him with even more vigor than the Democrats.

At this time Mecham was holding regular meetings with about a dozen sympathetic Republican members of the house. Killian, who had been critical of the governor but had not broken rank with him, said, "If I was in his position, I probably would be [rounding up support, too]."

There was a bizarre incident on December 16, when Department of Administration Director Max Hawkins, accompanied by a "nut," marched into the office of a representative and disassembled his telephone, looking for a bug. Rick Collins was both amused and irritated by the incident and reported it to DPS for investigation. Hawkins called Collins the next day to complain to him about his involving the state police.

The Democratic caucus was experiencing a division similar to the one Lane had, though for different reasons. There were members who had no interest in impeaching a Republican governor. They thought it best to let Mecham stay in office and do as much damage to Republicans as possible. Elections for all the legislative seats were less than a year away. With another year like the one they had just finished the Democrats stood a good chance of reclaiming at least one of the two houses, if not both.

Other Democrats did not want to turn this into a partisan issue. Being excluded from the process, however, made that very difficult. Democrats may have disagreed on whether or not to play politics with the impeachment probe, but they almost universally agreed with Hamilton's demand for public hearings.

By the first week in January things were coming to a head. Since the original grand jury had not indicted Mecham, there was doubt he ever would be. This placed the issue squarely in the house.

Joe Lane and the Republican leadership met with French for a full discussion of his findings on January 4. Art Hamilton had been asked to attend but sent his counsel instead and held a Democratic caucus. French said that he could not have his report ready until January 20. Lane said he was issuing a release saying it would be ready in ten days. They settled on Friday, January 15.

Art Hamilton emerged from the closed Democratic caucus and attacked Lane for freezing the Democrats out of the process. "The primary responsibility for the impeachment is ours, the House of Representatives," he said. "Only after public hearings, where witnesses can be called to testify," should a vote be taken by the full house.

Another Democratic representative spoke for others when he said, "There must be hearings. We must be able to weigh the evidence ourselves. We can't just take some lawyer's word for it, especially when it's a lawyer that we didn't hire."

Joe Lane responded that "all we're trying to do is essentially what a grand jury would do and that's determine probable cause. Does it look like somebody broke a law?" Asked specifically if there would be public hearings in addition to an oral report from French, he said, "We haven't figured that out yet."

Responding to the Democratic assertions, Majority Whip Jane Dee Hull said, "I think it's obvious the Democrats want to stall and keep this thing going on as long as possible. What is good for the state doesn't seem to be in their interests."

Hamilton said, "We believe impeachment is not the kind of decision that should be made in some kind of a Star Chamber setting where Bill French issues the report."

The danger that the impeachment probe could lapse into a partisan squabble was very real. Aware of this, Mecham had been courting Democrats in a patent attempt to maintain their division with the Republicans.

In late December Mecham had publicly demanded that Joe Lane bring the investigation to a conclusion and allow the house to decide if it should proceed further. He said he would be willing to testify voluntarily "before the appropriate legislative body" and answer all questions to "resolve this issue as quickly as possible."

On January 4 Mecham said, "I would like it to be public. . . . I would like everything to be in public. . . . I'd like to be under oath and answer every [question]. And I'd like to be able to ask them some questions too, and to have them under oath."

Jim Ratliff went to the speaker's office following a meeting with Mecham the previous night. He was extremely distressed. He told Rick Collins that during his discussion Mecham had kept a radio in the shape of a Coke can playing all the time. Mecham told Ratliff that he was being spied upon and he played the radio constantly to foil the effort. As Ratliff spoke, he shook his head in sadness and distress.

Collins had watched Ratliff's emotional roller coaster for months. Ratliff would return from discussions with the governor and take Mecham's side, but as events unfolded, he would switch. He was loyal to Mecham, but he was also loyal to Lane. He wanted to support his governor, but he could not countenance Mecham's conduct. The turmoil was killing him.

Rick Collins had continued to serve as liaison between French and the speaker. While Joe Lane knew the broad picture of the investigation, the details had been kept from him. Collins had cautioned the speaker that he could not reveal what he did not know.

By December 18 French had prepared portions of a preliminary report, which Collins reviewed. He saw at once that it was too legalistic. He told French the report would have to be written in simple English with the "bullets up front." He gave French standard auditor general reports to serve as models. These were reports in which the legislature had great faith and were in a format to which it was accustomed. They stated the findings on the first page and in plain language.

With Collins's input, French began to rework his written report. In the meantime, he was drafting the oral summary he would deliver to the full house. He and his staff had carefully reviewed the last Arizona impeachment in 1964, which involved two state corporation commissioners. William Rehnquist had served as the house prosecutor. He had lost the case in the senate but gone on to become chief justice of the United States. His staff joked that maybe French should work at losing.

Collins checked the equipment in the house chambers and the seating arrangements about two weeks ahead of the report. The last thing he wanted was for one of the representatives to have trouble seeing or hearing what was taking place.

One of the special problems Collins resolved had to do with French's height. He was so tall they had to place copies of the *Arizona Revised Statutes* under the speaker's podium to elevate it to an adequate height.

French was very concerned about his report leaking, and severe measures were taken to maintain its integrity. By January 8 he had a draft that was nearing final form. The press was besieging him to get information or hints of what he would report.

On the day of Mecham's State of the State, following the indictment and arson at French's law office the previous Friday, French went without fanfare to the house with his staff to check the equipment. That Wednesday he remained at home most of the day and worked with his team finalizing the oral presentation.

On January 12 Art Hamilton, Debbie McCune, and another Democratic representative met with Joe Lane. They told him that they expected at least one week following the oral presentation for deliberations. They also discussed obtaining minority counsel.

The next night Collins sealed the house chamber. Patricia Magrath and Bill Woods rehearsed the timing for the handing over of the transparencies and the operation of the overhead projector as well as other technical details that could have given the presentation an amateurish look. Miscues would affect its credibility. For that reason there was great concern with the minor details.

On Thursday French returned to the house and tested the dais for himself. Afterward he and his people rented a hotel room where they could work on the presentation in complete secrecy. They had taping equipment with them. French did two dry runs of his speech. They watched the tapes and critiqued his performance. He made a number of changes.

Mecham released a three-page letter of apology late Thursday which the *Arizona Republic* ran. Mecham said that he regretted not having hired an accountant to handle his campaign finance reports and that he had made mistakes in his handling of the Martin Luther King, Jr., holiday issue, in his selection of top staff, and in his failure to disclose the Wolfson loan.

"Like most Arizonans," he wrote, "I have tried to determine why our state is now so politically divided. I have come to the conclusion that some, but not all, of the blame rests with me. At times it seems as though I have become a lightning rod for sensational news.

"I apologize to the people of Arizona for any of my actions or mistakes which may have sparked embarrassing publicity for our state. I have been well-intentioned, but I now know that I may have been the cause of legitimate concerns."

At the same time his office was releasing this letter Mecham was delivering to legislators documents containing a letter claiming that Mecham had done nothing wrong. He requested that he be allowed to address house members following French's report.

Almost no one in the legislature believed he had written the first letter; few doubted that he had penned the second.

Asked by Mike Murphy about the letter of apology, Mecham said, "I don't know whether I'm seeking anyone's forgiveness." He concluded with "Draw your own conclusions—you will anyway, won't you?"

That morning Milstead had been jogging along the canal bank with a friend. When he arrived back at his car, there was a message for him to call Governor Mecham. He did at once. Sam Stanton had run an article in which he inadvertently reported that Milstead had been ordered by Mecham not to cooperate with the state grand jury. Stanton knew the details. He just wrote grand jury when he meant attorney general.

Mecham said he was concerned about the article. Milstead had not seen it. Mecham read some of it to him, then said, "What's that all about?"

"That is not correct," Milstead replied. "I called you, and it didn't have anything to do with cooperating with the grand jury. It had to do with cooperating with the attorney general. If you recall, you told me not to go to the attorney general."

Mecham said, "Well, did I give you permission to go?"

"No, you didn't."

"What did you do?" Mecham asked.

"I went."

Milstead recalls a pause at this point in the conversation. Mecham changed the subject for a few moments, then said, "Well, I didn't think we had to settle that on Sunday."

Milstead said, "Well, fine," and ended the conversation. Milstead took from this that until that moment it had not occurred to Mecham that Milstead had disobeyed him. Milstead thought that Mecham had expected his obedience just as he would have from a car lot boy at his dealership.

The same day French met with Ralph Milstead and read him the obstruction of justice charge to check for accuracy. Milstead confirmed the facts, and it was printed.

Collins had gone to extraordinary lengths to secure the printing of the

French Report, going so far as to say the printing was being done in the house. He instructed the supply clerk to purchase extra paper. He made a point of telling her that her staff would do the job at the last minute to avoid leaks and would have to work all night if necessary to get the job done. He was certain her staff would complain to the press about it.

The report was actually duplicated by Bill French's staff. Each report was numbered. Collins saw to it Joe Lane received number one. The copies were delivered to the house at 10:00 A.M. on January 15.

Larry Lopez, one of the Associated Press reporters, told Collins he had a lot of dirt on Joe Lane and if Collins would leak one of the reports to him, he would not have time to write stories on it. Collins threw him out of his office.

During this week U.S. Senator John McCain and U.S. Representative Jon Kyl, both Republicans, arranged with Mecham's attorney, Murray Miller, to speak with the governor at Miller's office. Others were present as well. The group saw a "storm gathering" and started working on Mecham. Kyl did most of the talking. He told Mecham that it would be best for the state if Mecham resigned. As Kyl spoke, McCain stared at the floor. Kyl urged that Mecham not put his family through the ordeal ahead.

Mecham became irritated and waved his finger in Kyl's face. The situation became so agitated that Miller stepped in and calmed them down. He suggested that the two lawmakers were out of line, that an indictment is nothing more than an accusation.

As the group prepared to leave, McCain stopped them and made a point of saying, "Let's agree to a no comment meeting." Everyone did.

Later that day Richard Miller was driving home when he heard McCain discussing the meeting on the radio. "Thank you, Mr. No Comment," he thought with disgust.

The Democrats had not forgotten Mecham's conduct that summer before the committee charged with selecting a supercollider lobbyist. It appeared to be an open-and-shut case of abuse of power.

This was one of the charges that French had looked into and the last he decided to reject. This fourth article lingered for weeks after the primary three had been selected. Even though it "stank," French did not like it because it smacked too much of political conduct the public tolerated and would have no "jury" appeal.

Rick Collins was uncomfortable with the fourth article because the entire supercollider effort had been botched by a number of people, not the least of whom was the governor. If Mecham's conduct was made an issue, it would allow him to open the entire process to scrutiny and put the state effort up for criticism. The only result would be to eliminate any chance of Arizona's receiving the project.

The supercollider effort had been a Republican proposal. That was one of its major appeals for the Democrats. They had nothing to lose if Republicans were made to look incompetent. From the beginning they had gathered affidavits and documents to build a case. Art Hamilton wanted this fourth article included, and French's unwillingness only fueled his suspicions.

Collins recalls that the fourth article was still viable up until the French Report, as Bill French's oral report came to be known, much to French's chagrin.

Murray Miller was concerned about the unsavory scene that would occur when Mecham showed up at the sheriff's office to have his mug shot and fingerprints taken. He made arrangements to have the formalities taken care of in his offices. On Thursday Mecham arrived along with Willard Mecham. They were fingerprinted and had their photographs taken. The day of the French Report the state's dailies carried the mug shots of a glum Willard and a grinning Evan Mecham.

As January 15 approached, Art Hamilton realized that the Democrats were going to be shut out of the process entirely. Withholding Democratic votes, if it came to that, had no appeal at all. He decided that he would no longer wait for Joe Lane to include them. It was time to take the initiative.

He contacted a law firm that did legal work for the Democratic party in Arizona, but it refused to be involved for fear of potential fallout. Another firm, Brown & Bain, had done a great deal for him and the party in the past, so it was with reluctance that he called Paul Eckstein of that firm to ask that he become minority special counsel.

Eckstein received the call at his office at noon, about an hour and a half before Bill French was set to go on statewide television from the floor of the house.

"You were hoping you wouldn't get this call," Hamilton said. "I have no right to ask this of you. I can't promise you will be paid. In fact, you won't get paid."

Eckstein knew why Hamilton had called. "How soon do you need me?" he asked.

"Right away. Bill French is about to give his report."

"You know I'm Carolyn Warner's campaign chairman." Warner had announced her intention to run in the recall election.

"Yeah," Hamilton said, "and I bet you signed a recall petition."

"Yes."

Hamilton said that would not be a problem. "Everyone will understand," he added.

Eckstein hurried over to the house to get a ticket to the gallery. As it was, he sat next to Jim Cooper, infamous for his flat earth crack. As French unfolded his findings, Cooper kept muttering, "Can you believe that?" over and over.

Paul Eckstein had always been fascinated by impeachment. Since law school he had gathered an extensive library on its history. At one point in the fall of 1987 he had thought he would have represented Evan Mecham to be a part of it.

Ironically Ken Smith had considered that very thing. It had seemed to him that the Jewish Democrat Paul Eckstein, who was Carolyn Warner's campaign manager, would have made perfect counsel for Evan Mecham. He had even suggested it to no avail. Eckstein was very well known in Democratic circles but was not a public figure. He was widely respected as an attorney but did not have the heavy-hitter reputation of Murray Miller.

He was born in 1940 and had lived in Phoenix since he was a child. He was a Harvard Law School graduate and had practiced with Brown & Bain for more than twenty years, primarily handling real estate, tax, labor, and corporate litigation. He had represented the Democrats in the last redistricting.

He was also the attorney for the Scottsdale *Progress*, *New Times*, and Phoenix Newspapers, Inc., the corporate parent of the *Arizona Republic* and the Phoenix *Gazette*. He served on the boards of numerous community service organizations. He had worked on Bruce Babbitt's 1982 gubernatorial campaign and Carolyn Warner's 1986 bid for governor. Since 1981 he and his wife had been the publishers of the *Greater Phoenix Jewish News*.

Eckstein is a handsome man, bright and full of wit. He looked forward to this challenge with relish. There was no slow realization of the significance of what was occurring for him. He knew beyond any doubt as he sat in the gallery and the house lights dimmed.

This was history.

# 33

The day of the French Report the *Arizona Republic* reported that Horace Lee Watkins had resigned his post as the state's prison construction chief late the previous day, "after it was revealed that he had failed to report an assault conviction on his application for a state insurance license."

Asked to comment, Mecham said, "He's gone, and that's the end of it. He was doing a good job."

Watkins had not listed his 1966 misdemeanor assault conviction on his 1984 application. "I had forgotten it. It happened 22 years ago. . . ."

Details of the arrest were made public for the first time. Watkins had met a woman at a gas station. He went with her to her apartment, "where Watkins attempted to force her to the floor and kiss her. She escaped from him and ran to a neighbor's yard, where Watkins tackled her, records show," the *Republic* reported. Charged initially with a felony, Watkins pleaded to simple assault and was placed on six months' probation.

Any lingering doubt about Watkins's potential for carrying out a threat against Donna Carlson was dispelled.

On January 15, 1988, Bill French was picked up at his home by Frank Martinez at six-thirty in the morning. DPS used a van for security reasons this day and drove to get Patricia Magrath and Bill Woods. They went to a private location and ran through the presentation again. At noon they were taken to the Arizona house of representatives. French went to the speaker's office, where lunch was served, but French was unable to eat. Senator John McCain's office sent someone by to obtain an advance copy of the report and was refused.

Outside, about thirty supporters of the governor were picketing. They carried signs saying, ED BUCK, YOU DIRTY SHMUCK, MECHAM 4 PRESIDENT, LET THE PEOPLE DECIDE. One sign which read, I SMELL A RAT! had the drawing of a large rodent on it. There was no one in a business suit present. An otherwise attractive woman had a clothespin stuck on her nose.

Since the day he had been hired Bill French and his staff had worked on the investigation every day for fourteen to sixteen hours. He was exhausted. His wife had not wanted him to take the job. As the inquiry increasingly became known by French's name, she was more and more concerned that he might take a public fall all by himself. There was so much beyond his control, and this was, after all, politics. It seemed a thankless task to her.

Joe Lane had not yet seen a draft of either the formal written report or the oral presentation. During the proceeding Lane was to leave the speaker's place at the dais and take his own desk toward the rear of the house. There was a line French was to use near the end of his speech, and when Lane heard the words, he was to leave his desk and walk in the dark to the dais. His cue began with, "justice is a much sterner virtue. . . ."

KAET television had arranged to provide the media feed. French was wired for sound, and he found the pack awkward. A camera was placed in the middle aisle two thirds of the way from the speaker's dais. Almost everyone in the state would watch.

French was very nervous as he waited in the speaker's office. Collins was coordinating the last-minute details and could see French looking pale. Just as they were about to begin, Collins turned to French, with whom he had worked nearly every day for over two and a half months. "Have a good time," he said.

Representative Mark Killian asked his father, a prominent attorney, to be in attendance so they could talk about it later. Murray Miller and his son obtained two of the half dozen seats assigned to Mecham and sat in the rear of the gallery with Ken Smith. It was oppressively hot there.

House members were milling around their chamber as 1:30 P.M. approached. Precisely on time Joe Lane called the house to order. In a demonstration of support by the house leadership, Jim Ratliff moved they sit as the committee of the whole for the purpose of receiving the report of Speaker of the House Special Counsel William French. Jane Dee Hull seconded the motion.

Lane cautioned the gallery that he would tolerate no outbursts and would clear it if necessary. As he spoke, copies of the documents that would be shown on the huge overhead projection screen were distributed. Members were to receive the complete written report following the presentation.

Lane then introduced Bill French. The secretaries and clerks in front of him filed out. Bill Woods and Patricia Magrath came out and took their places. Then Bill French emerged from the doorway, shook hands briefly with Lane, and assumed the dais. The house sat in absolute silence.

French was wearing a dark blue suit, black tie, and white shirt. The house lights dimmed. The remaining lights, which were focused on him, were so blinding that French had difficulty both with his script and in establishing eye contact with his audience. Jim Skelly was seated nearly in the middle of the chamber and French focused on him.

He began by explaining that his full report was in writing, that the speaker had asked him to present an oral synopsis of his findings. "I tell you this up front," he said. "We present facts, not flamboyance."

French was amazed at the "silence", which he later likened to a tomb. He had a rough beginning, then settled into the routine he had practiced.

He educated the body on the nature of "independent evidence," evidence he said that was created at a time when there was no controversy. He told the house that the purpose of an impeachment hearing is to determine "probable cause" for articles of impeachment. He emphasized the fairness of his investigation.

As Rick Collins had suggested, he now gave his "bullets": the Wolfson loan, borrowing the Protocol Fund, and obstructing the attorney general's investigation into the Watkins threat against Donna Carlson.

Two of these allegations had been the subject of a grand jury investigation. A great deal was publicly known about the Wolfson loan, but very little had been reported on the death threat. The third allegation involving the Protocol Fund had received so little public scrutiny it was virtually unknown.

As a consequence, French was presenting either new information or information already known but in a sequence not previously considered.

He began the Wolfson loan portion of his presentation with the conclusion that "Governor Mecham knowingly and intentionally failed to disclose" it in violation of a number of criminal statutes.

He based that conclusion in part on Mecham's letter of confidentiality to Wolfson, on the fact that he had "lumped" the Wolfson loan money with other money and reported it all as a personal loan from himself to the campaign, and on the creation of a separate bank account in which to process the money where it would not be revealed if the primary account were examined.

French said, "Coincidence? Unfortunately and disturbingly not."

He offered a motive by saying that newspaper accounts at the time mentioned the investigations into Wolfson and Gregan. Mecham had run a campaign opposed to influence peddling, and had it been known that one third of his campaign had come from a developer, the fact would have caused him difficulty.

During a finance committee meeting at the time of the Wolfson loan, Vern Gasser had taken notes. French had acquired these notes by subpoena.

These were not the notes of a secretary. Though legible, they consisted of phrases, words, and names at random. Some were underlined; others were circled. French flashed the Gasser notes on the overhead. Two phrases stuck out almost without his need to call attention to them.

French said, "This is what I referred to earlier as independent evidence and sometimes in the vernacular is called the smoking gun.

The first read, "don't show borrowed money." On the other side of the page and higher was another circled phrase: "show Evan Borrowed money."

French offered these statements as corroboration that the plan to conceal the loan was made at the very beginning. He termed it "clear and convincing evidence" that the "lump theory" had begun even then.

He reviewed the money flow from the accounts, how the money came in and out, and said, "In some circles it's called laundering."

His next bombshell was a simple receipt, signed by Willard Mecham, made out to Evan Mecham, for $350,000 and dated November 24, 1986. The significance was that Evan Mecham had never lent the campaign $350,000. According to French, the purpose of the receipt was to balance the books because the following day was the next campaign reporting period.

French called the receipt an "affirmative attempt" to disguise the loan and said it "had to be an intentional, willful act." He said the "conclusion seems to be clear, [that] with full knowledge of his obligation Evan Mecham violated the campaign disclosure law" and initiated a cover-up.

French now turned to the Protocol Fund. He referred to its "deceptive and unlawful use" for Mecham's "own personal and private" purposes. After expenses the Mecham inaugural committee had ninety-two thousand dollars remaining, which Bob Corbin had frozen. Because corporate contributions had been solicited and mixed with individual donations, the fund did not appear to be in compliance with the new campaign finance law. After some negotiation the chairman of the committee, William D. Long, wrote a letter to the Maricopa County attorney, which French now read in part:

> In order to avoid any risk of an unintentional violation of the law (or even an appearance thereof), or incurring the time and expense which would be necessary to obtain a judicial determination of the question, we have determined that the funds remaining in the Ticket Sales Account should not be applied to unpaid campaign expenses. Instead, we believe the entire balance re-

maining in the Ticket Sales Account should be held in a separately maintained account and expended, at the Governor's discretion, solely for purposes of promoting the interests of the state, or to promote and encourage citizen public service in the state, and comparable such purposes within the purview and pursuant to the provisions and the spirit, of A.R.S. Section 41-1105

The funds were then "turned over to the office of the Governor of Arizona, to be held and expended as stated above," the letter concluded. French noted that Evan Mecham received a copy of this agreement, which was dated June 26, 1987. Those who could sign on the account thereafter were Jim Colter and Edith Richardson.

Approximately two weeks later Mecham ordered Colter to give his dealership a check for eighty thousand dollars from the account. According to French, documents were prepared to show this to be a legitimate business transaction, but a deed of trust that would have made the loan public knowledge was never filed, the documents appeared to have been backdated one month, and the withdrawal was not recorded in the check register.

French then informed the house that Mecham had used twenty thousand dollars of the protocol money to make a payment toward his financially troubled Tacoma property.

The note matured on October 16 and was extended on the twenty-third of that month to December 16. Yet only two days later, on October 25, the loan was repaid. Why, French asked, when they had gone to the trouble of extending the due date? Because of the Wolfson loan disclosures and the start of the grand jury investigation, he concluded.

French said such use of money is "disquieting" and a felony.

Finally, French exposed to light the details of Horace Lee Watkins's threats against Donna Carlson, revealing for the first time that he had called her a "whore," and placed on the overhead the exact words used. He told of Mecham's being informed by Johnson and the governor's conversation with Milstead on Sunday. He placed Milstead's report for all to see and read with exquisite thoroughness what Mecham had ordered Milstead not to do.

Mecham's interview with television anchorman Cameron Harper was now flashed overhead for the house to read. This interview was technically not evidence. All it did was make Mecham out to be a liar.

French was nearing the completion of his report. He was talking steadily now and with commanding presence. He thanked the minority for allowing a bipartisan effort.

He said, "We respectfully request that you take the time to read and study the materials. None of the facts in the report are Republican or Democrat. They are just facts that we have gathered and obtained for your review and consideration. Your review and deliberation over this matter may lead you to the conclusion that no deceit, deception, perjury, or cover-up occurred.

"On the other hand, you may conclude that probable cause does exist and that articles of impeachment should be drawn up. That decision is yours."

French then told of a time when he had been a superior court judge and had been called upon to impose the death sentence on a young man. A more seasoned judge had counseled with him and said, "You're not here to have fun. Justice is a much sterner virtue than soft-spoken charity."

French now told the house in an even voice, "Likewise I respectfully say, you are not here to have fun. You're here to see that justice is done and remember that justice is a much sterner virtue than soft-spoken charity. Thank you."

Joe Lane had left his desk at hearing his cue and stood ready to assume the dais. There was no applause. As Bill French passed the speaker, Lane noted he was nearly ashen. Lane said quietly, "Good job." The chamber sat in absolute silence. The lights came up.

Art Hamilton announced a Democratic caucus starting immediately. Jim Ratliff moved that the house stand in recess until the next Monday. The motion carried, and at 2:18 P.M. the house adjourned.

French had entered the speaker's office. Frank Martinez met him and said, "Judge, this way." He smoothly escorted French to the basement. DPS had placed a dummy van in a conspicuous area near the house to attract the picketers. Martinez took French down the tunnel that connected with the senate across the mall to a second, discreet van. French was at his office within minutes.

Immediately after the report Murray Miller went to the Ninth Floor. Ken Smith, said as they went, "The word is everyone wants the governor impeached right now. Even the interns are crying." A group of high school interns were working on the Ninth Floor and until today had loyally stood behind the governor. The French Report had devastated their faith in him.

When Miller heard this, he realized the report had been more effective than he had thought. Mecham had sat in the Capitol cafeteria during the report but had heard enough to say he thought it unfair. He said French was trying to impeach him. He wanted to give an immediate speech but was dissuaded. Miller agreed, however, that some response was necessary to prevent events from taking over.

Before this day was complete, Sam Stanton knew that Evan Mecham was through as governor. Even Stanton had not known of Willard Mecham's receipt. He was "overwhelmed" by the fact that the Mechams had actually created a false document. He was impressed with the presentation. He was also troubled and moved by the experience.

When the French presentation was over, Stanton went across the mall to the press room to write his stories. He talked to Laurie Roberts, who instructed him to write three pieces. He did the shorter ones first. As he started the main story, the full impact of what was occurring came home, and he was suddenly overcome with nausea. He ran down the hall to the men's room and threw up.

Shortly before 7:00 P.M. Laurie Asseo reminded Stanton that the two of them were doing a live feed for *Horizon* in three minutes, which he had completely forgotten.

The Friday-night reporters' round table discussion is consistently *Horizon's* highest-rated night. This Friday was a blockbuster. Usually the reporters went out to Arizona State University and sat around a table with the host, Michael Grant. On occasion they took a feed directly from a senate hearing room. The reporters use earpieces and try to look at the camera intelligently. This is known in Arizona as the "vampire interview."

By this time Sam Stanton was gaunt with dark, sunken eyes. He was wearing no makeup and under the lights had an almost ghoulish appearance. At one point in the interview someone said something Stanton took to be especially stupid, and thinking they were off camera, he commented to Asseo, "What an asshole." He was relieved to learn later his mike was off; but he was on camera at the time, and it was not hard to gather what he had said.

People noticed his appearance and inquired about his health. Jane Dee Hull told him he had to start taking better care of himself.

Following the French Report, Paul Eckstein obtained the complete written report. He told Art Hamilton that he wanted time to read and consider it before commenting. Eckstein's first impressions were that the French Report had holes. During that weekend he turned several Brown & Bain attorneys loose to prepare an impeachment packet for the Democratic minority.

Gone unnoticed and not generally reported in Arizona was that this day had also been the fifty-ninth birthday of Dr. Martin Luther King, Jr.

# 34

Murray Miller spent the Friday night of the French Report working on
his response. The local television stations had agreed to give him equal time.
That Saturday he asked Ken Smith to locate one of those gag guns that shoots
out a flag with "bang." Smith found one but did not want Miller to use it,
and he tried to get it back just before Miller went on the air at 6:00 P.M.
Saturday from a conference room at the Capitol.

Miller was concerned with defusing the damage French had done by
his reference to a "smoking gun." Miller planned to treat this opportunity
as a dramatic presentation before a jury. He was not prepared for the attitude
of the reporters, who could not wait to start asking questions. Miller's pitch
clouded issues but did little to undermine the French Report. When he
pulled the toy gun out as a representation of French's smoking gun, the
photograph made national news but fell flat over statewide television.

The disclosure of Milstead's police report, with its quotation marks
around the governor's statements had raised the issue of whether or not
Milstead had taped Mecham. Milstead was not commenting, and French
had not said. Miller dodged questions by reporters on Mecham's response
to Milstead's account of the conversation. Mecham had refused to answer
questions, and it seemed obvious he would not until he knew if it was his
word against Milstead's or his word against a tape recorder.

Tom Fitzpatrick of the *New Times,* very likely the most seasoned reporter in the crowded room, asked Miller if Mecham had taped the con-

versation. Miller avoided the question. Miller recalls Laurie Asseo's yelling the same question at him. "Are you hiding something?" she demanded.

He thought they would take notes and ask for more detailed information. Instead, Fitzpatrick started up again on the tape as Miller left. One of the reporters followed him and his wife to La Posada on Lincoln Drive and badgered them as they entered. Miller's wife was petrified.

John Kolbe wrote about the response a few days later. "If it doesn't get any better than this, the governor had better start cleaning out his desk."

It had been apparent in the week prior to the French Report that hearings were going to take place. There were members who wanted to vote solely on the basis of the French Report and the supporting documents. Others were concerned that holding hearings, especially on the Wolfson loan, could violate Mecham's rights to a fair criminal trial in superior court. But the strongest and, in the end, most compelling argument was for fairness. How can we vote if Mecham has not had an opportunity to respond?

During that weekend delicate maneuvering transformed the speaker's investigation into a bipartisan house inquiry into possible impeachment.

Bill French had been approached with the name of more than one attorney to serve as minority counsel. When Paul Eckstein's name was mentioned, he agreed.

He knew Eckstein only by reputation, but he believed this was an attorney with whom he could work. The acceptance of Eckstein as cocounsel was a matter of great delicacy. He must be accepted and be perceived as playing a role of complete equality. This was agreed to over that weekend.

Hamilton could have hired whomever he wished, but selecting a man with whom French would cooperate made the best sense. There were political considerations, but above them was the need for the house to conduct this matter with absolute integrity. The eyes of the nation were on Arizona.

Rick Collins recalls Eckstein's joining the impeachment differently. Brown & Bain had been investigating the supercollider incident for some time and was assembling a report. Eckstein was rumored to be spearheading the effort, and his appearance as minority counsel had been expected even before the day of the French Report.

Joe Lane decided not to use the house Judiciary Committee for the hearings. Judiciary was a standing committee. Long after the impeachment hearings were complete it would be trying to conduct business. He wanted no lingering wounds.

Instead, he appointed its chairman, Jim Skelly, to head a Special House Select Committee on Impeachment. The select committee would last only for the duration of the hearings. There would be no baggage afterward. With a recommendation on the Democrats from Art Hamilton, Lane carefully selected members to balance it geographically and to house sentiment and to be certain its mix would survive any court challenge. He also decided the committee would ask questions and develop information independent of counsel. It would not take a vote or issue a report. Following the committee hearings the full house would vote.

Present on the select committee were Republican Mark Killian and Democrat Debbie McCune.

Joe Lane decided to have Skelly hold hearings whenever possible around the normal course of house business. Members of the house were encouraged, but not obligated, to attend. The select committee met on the Tuesday following the French Report to adopt rules, with the first witness testifying on Wednesday.

Mark Killian and his father stayed up until 1:00 A.M. reading the report. Killian spotted a number of holes, and he and his father worked on a series of questions the report raised. That Monday he asked Joe Lane if he could serve on the select committee. Once appointed, he expanded his list and prepared a hundred questions to ask. Forty to fifty of them were for Evan Mecham.

Debbie McCune was pleased there would be hearings. She believed very strongly that Mecham should have an opportunity to respond to the French Report. She also believed Democratic pressure had been instrumental in bringing the hearings about. After reviewing the documents, she had even more questions, and she was interested in making certain that the background material contained in the report received public disclosure. She felt it was "clear we needed guidance."

Under Paul Eckstein's direction the staff at Brown & Bain had discreetly assembled a brief memorandum entitled "Materials Submitted to Representative Hamilton by Brown & Bain, P.A. on Impeachment Procedures." It is a model of its kind and served as McCune's bible through the long days and nights immediately ahead.

Impeachment is a wholly political process. "Political" has come to mean smoke-filled rooms and underhanded dealings against the public interest. "Political" as it applies to impeachment means that the entire process is part of the established legislative governmental functions of the state.

Impeachment of a governor is intended to protect the people in the state, not the officeholder. Of the 2,096 American governors before Evan Mecham, only 15 had been impeached and just 7 were actually convicted and removed from office. One of those was later reelected governor of his state; another was elected to the U.S. Senate.

It is a common misconception to equate the house impeachment with actual conviction and removal. Impeachment is the rough political equivalent of indictment. Once the house voted to impeach, or accuse, the senate must then conduct a trial.

266       *Ronald J. Watkins*

Punishment in an impeachment is restricted to loss of office and, in some cases, loss of the right to hold public office in the state again. It is possible to be impeached for acts that are not crimes, though it is more likely the conduct will also be alleged to be criminal.

The Arizona constitution recognized this and clearly states that the impeachment of an official does not prevent his criminal indictment and separate court trial.

Because the legislative branch of government is given the authority to remove the chief executive, it is not a matter to be taken lightly. It is the practice of the accused to demand the same rights as a charged criminal. In fact, Arizona's constitution left the governor's rights up to each house of the legislature.

Because impeachment is a political process, it is generally not subject to the authority of courts. If the senate, for instance, had tried to remove Mecham without the house's first voting articles of impeachment, a court would have interfered and prevented it. But as long as the legislature stayed within the broad authority given it in the constitution, it was free to proceed as it wished.

The real control over potential abuse of impeachment is not so much judicial review as it is public pressure. Impeachment has a way of singling out individual lawmakers and makes it very difficult to hide in the pack. On election day each member of the legislature must face his or her voters.

Public perception and expectation of fairness cause the impeachment process to proceed very much like a judicial court. As tempting as it may have been for some members of the house to vote directly following the French Report, the fact was the governor had asked for an opportunity to respond, and most members of the house believed they owed him that, both to be fair and to be perceived as fair.

Just as Murray Miller had tried to present a defense before the state grand jury so it was his objective to put one before the select committee.

French, on the other hand, wished for the committee to proceed much as a grand jury would. In other words, he would call certain key witnesses, ask questions, and attempt to establish probable cause. Finally, the governor would have an opportunity, just as he had before the grand jury, to appear and make a statement.

Once French had presented his case, the house would vote on whether to impeach as a body. French did not want the house hearings to be a trial. The constitution called for that to occur in the senate following an affirmative vote of the house.

There are many differences between a criminal proceeding and an impeachment. No standard of proof was stated in the constitution. French had mentioned "probable cause", which is a legal standard, but in fact, the house did not have to adopt any standard. Or it could elect to adopt a higher standard such as "clear and convincing" or "beyond a reasonable doubt". In the end, no standard was set in the house, and each member was left to decide if he or she had heard enough.

It was the expectation of those who framed the Arizona constitution that the members of the legislature would be well informed as concerned the governor. Rather than have a jury who had never heard of the accused, the intent was to have a jury that knew him well.

There were sixty members of the house, many of whom had had personal experiences with Evan Mecham. Thirty-one votes were enough to impeach.

In the Senate were thirty members, nearly all with prior experiences with Mecham. It took twenty votes to convict.

If Democrats were to vote against the governor, this meant that Mecham required the support of the Republicans if he was to be spared impeachment and conviction.

Miller was concerned because so many members of the house and senate had broken publicly with the governor. Members were attacking him from the floor; some had called for his resignation; others wanted him removed by recall. Miller also believed that public sentiment had reached the point where the pressure on the house to impeach was virtually irresistible. His letters to Joe Lane and his public statements were intended to point that out.

Given the stated prejudice of so many lawmakers, Miller wanted those who would sit in judgment to be only those who were unbiased.

Unfortunately for Miller the state constitution selected the jury in this case. Even had he persuaded Joe Lane to exclude some house members from the process, Lane had no authority to do so. Impeachment was for the members of the house to decide, regardless of their perceived or real prejudices, and for the senators to try and judge.

Miller's critics would point out that there was not only bias against Mecham; he had a number of vocal supporters in the legislature. They would also say that the pressure being placed on the legislature was largely from "Mechamites," not from those who favored his ouster.

French was uncertain with whom to lead off. He met with Ralph Milstead the day before and the day of the hearings and decided to use him first. Milstead asked if French thought it would be appropriate to wear his uniform. French liked the mental image a uniform invoked and was impressed with the officer's appearance. He thought matters would be off to a good start with Milstead as first witness.

Mecham had been right during the 1986 campaign. Integrity was the issue, and Milstead reeked of it.

*   *   *

The Sunday before the hearings began, the *Arizona Republic* published Donna Carlson's story of her time in the administration. Entitled "Inside Mecham's Office," it revealed intimate details of Mecham's conduct.

For the first time the public read of Mecham's temper tantrums, of his "enemy" lists, of his crass abuse of the veto to punish Republican lawmakers, and of his single-minded rejection of the counsel of others. The public also learned how frightened Carlson had been when she had been threatened by Watkins.

The Monday following Carlson's article Max Hawkins gave a press conference on Mecham's orders in an attempt to refute allegations in the French Report. He claimed that he had already determined that the alleged death threat by Watkins was "frivolous" before the attorney general's office involved itself. Hawkins did not think Watkins, whom he had appointed his deputy director, had threatened Donna Carlson's life.

Hawkins said, "I think that [Watkins's] advice to Donna was good advice, and the best that I can remember it came something like, 'Tell your whore friend Donna to shut her mouth or she could suffer harm.' All right? I consider that a warning."

That day a letter from Mecham was delivered to the speaker's office for Representative Mark Killian. It contained questions for Killian to ask of witnesses. Rick Collins and others were troubled that Mecham was having direct contact with a member of the committee. Killian declined to use any of the questions and drew on those he and his father had prepared.

That same day six thousand marchers descended on the Capitol in wind and rain to demand a state holiday for Dr. Martin Luther King, Jr. "Give the state a holiday; give Mecham five to ten [years]," they chanted. One marcher carried a large sign that proclaimed, JAIL MECHAM.

Milstead was entirely comfortable as he began his testimony that Wednesday. He viewed testimony as a challenge, not an ordeal. He liked to make testimony a contest between himself and the adversary. He did extra research to know more than was in the police report, so that when he had a chance, he would drop the information on the adversary like a bombshell and gain the advantage. He had testified for thousands of hours on hundreds of previous occasions and routinely appeared before legislative committees. He recalls that the press was everywhere that day and the hearing room was packed.

Skelly read a letter to the governor from Joe Lane informing him of the hearings and inviting Mecham and his lawyer to attend. It concluded, "You will also be given an opportunity to appear and testify before the committee at a later committee hearing."

Mark Killian reminded everyone that in its current capacity the house was exercising judicial powers, and he wanted it clearly understood that the governor's rights as a witness under the constitution would not be violated.

Bill French then led Milstead through his carefully prepared questions about the obstruction of justice issue and his conversation with Mecham. He never asked, nor did Milstead volunteer, if the director had taped Mecham.

Paul Eckstein took over questioning and almost immediately asked, "Did you tape the telephone conversation that you had with Governor Mecham on November 15th?"

French had wanted Mecham to testify about that conversation without knowing if it had been recorded. Now he had to object to cocounsel's question. Eckstein backed off but said at some point they all would require an answer.

During a recess there was some discussion of the question. Mark Killian made it very clear that if no one else asked the question, he intended to. He did not believe that Mecham would testify unless he knew if Milstead had recorded him. Killian thought it essential that the governor answer their questions.

Representative George Weisz proceeded first for the committee members and immediately asked if Milstead had taped the conversation. Milstead replied that he had not but had relied on notes in preparing his report. Now Mecham knew. He was not expected to remain silent for long.

Killian questioned Milstead about whether or not he had informed the governor that what he was doing was a crime. Milstead said he had not.

That night Mecham went on television to denounce Milstead's version of their conversation calling it "the most far-fetched thing that I've ever heard of."

Public attention was already focused in another direction, however. Mecham claimed laser beams were being used to spy on him.

# 35

Mecham had attended the Phoenix Forum Breakfast Club on Tuesday the week of the house impeachment hearings. He remarked to a companion in a voice several in attendance heard, "Did you hear me on KTAR . . . ?" Mecham had been home and made three telephone calls to the talk station that day.

He said, "Do you want to know why I had the radio on at home? Whenever I'm in my house or my office, I always have a radio on. It keeps the lasers out."

"What lasers?" he was asked.

"The lasers for eavesdropping. They're eavesdropping on me. They're shooting lasers through the windows."

Mecham would not say who "they" were. One of those present did a double take, and several were reported to have been "aghast" at the remark.

One said, "I thought my hearing was failing. I couldn't believe it."

For months now it had been rumored that Mecham believed that either

270

the *Arizona Republic* and the Phoenix *Gazette* or the attorney general was using laser beams to monitor his private conversations. One story had Mecham saying the laser was located on top of the *Republic* and *Gazette* building.

Publisher Pat Murphy said, "For the governor to suggest such a preposterous plot casts a new light on the terrible and unthinking intellectual barrenness of the governor and those around him."

Asked to comment, Bob Corbin roared with amusement and said, "We don't have any ray gun pointed at him." That Christmas Corbin's staff had presented him with a toy ray gun, and he had his picture taken with it.

Steve Benson drew a cartoon of Mecham going to work dressed for laser tag. His wife was standing at the doorway, saying, "Bye, honey—may the force be with you!"

Concerns over eavesdropping in the Mecham administration were far more widespread than the public realized. One senior member of Mecham's staff had been crawling around above the false ceiling on the Ninth Floor trying to locate a bug when he fell through and broke his leg. Mecham had used funds out of the Protocol Fund to pay a private investigator to sweep his offices. Max Hawkins instructed his staff to talk in whispers.

Thad Curtis, Mecham's interim superintendent at the state liquor department, had abruptly started closing his blinds at work. Curtis once asked an employee to climb on a chair and check the false ceiling for a bug. Another time he stopped an important meeting in which assistant attorneys general were present because of his fears of bugging, then marched them outside and to the basement of the parking garage, where the stunned group completed the meeting standing around cars.

At the same time Mecham acknowledged that his difficulties were hurting his car dealership. He said there had been a drop of 35 percent in business. He also said that "master planning . . . by a combined set of forces" was behind the effort to remove him. "The whole scheme of things has been so well orchestrated, right down to the time things were done and everything. They did a masterful job of PR work."

Throughout state government and the Capitol employees as a gag began sporting tinfoil hats and tinfoil flags on their desks to ward off laser beams.

On Friday, January 22, Mecham appeared for his arraignment on the criminal indictment. The group, which included Murray Miller, Evan and Willard Mecham, Richard Miller, and Michael Scott, another attorney on the criminal case, were waiting near the elevators. The doors opened. Inside was a "chain gang" of county jail prisoners being taken to court appearances. They spotted Mecham. One called out, "It's the gov!" Another shouted, "You're going to be one of us now!"

A flustered governor was then called in for the arraignment. The court commissioner customarily enters a plea of not guilty and sets the trial date. The accused is never called upon to speak. Miller had told Mecham that he would not have to say anything.

With television cameras there Commissioner Patrick O'Neil asked, "As to the counts stated, how do you plead?"

Mecham seemed to be caught unprepared. He stammered, then finally said, "Not guilty."

As he was leaving the courthouse, the reporters asked if he was still confident. An apparently rattled Mecham said, "Hell, yes, I'm confident. I'm guilty." He quickly corrected himself. "I'm not guilty. Doesn't that give you some understanding that I'm confident?"

The driver of the governor's car then led the three-car caravan followed by reporters the wrong way down a one-way street.

During this period a woman who identified herself as Christina Johnston called Richard Miller at his law office. She told him that she had once had an affair with Ralph Milstead and was willing to give testimony against him. Miller considered her "just another nut," told her no thanks, and forgot about the call.

A few days later she called back and this time reached Murray Miller. She told him of the affair and said she knew a lot that could damage Milstead. Miller recalls that she sounded "like a vindictive lady, if not a kook". On the basis of what she had told him, all she could do was hurt the governor's case.

Miller thought, "She's going to be this Mormon governor's savior?" He dismissed the call.

During the next week the select committee heard testimony from Lieutenant Beau Johnson; Howard Schwartz, with the county attorney's office; Warner Lee, who was an attorney for the inaugural committee; Jim Shumway with the secretary of state's office; Richard Burke, Mecham's new chief of staff; Bill Woods, French's investigator; and William D. Long, head of Mecham's inaugural committee.

The decision to call Colter had been made at the last minute in response to requests from Mecham supporters on the committee who wanted to hear from the governor's people. Instead of appearing, Colter had flown to Australia. French was shocked when he heard of it. Colter did not return for the duration of the house hearings.

Johnson had never been so nervous in his life when he took his place to testify. He had served on the security detail for ten years and had not testified for some time. When he was called, he sat at the table for five minutes waiting for the questioning with two cameras pointed at him, in front of a packed hearing room, knowing that his every word would be analyzed.

Johnson testified to the sequence of events surrounding the death threat against Donna Carlson. If Ralph Milstead has the dark good looks of a Hollywood heavy, Johnson has the all-American looks of the hero.

He was known to everyone in the legislature. After Mecham had him removed as chief of his security detail the weekend of the death threat investigation, he had been named by Milstead head of house security during the impeachment hearings. When members had difficulty with a threat, it was to Johnson or one of his staff that they looked for assistance and protection.

He testified that he had first learned of Watkins's prison record shortly after Mecham took office since it was his responsibility to run record checks on all appointees. It was for this reason he had taken Peggy Griffith's story so seriously.

Asked by Debbie McCune if Johnson had handled similar situations involving gubernatorial appointees with criminal records differently, Johnson replied, "Representative McCune, I don't remember . . . that any candidate for appointment that had a felony conviction . . . was never, ever appointed that I can remember to any position. I don't remember any other similar incident like we have here occurring, no."

Mecham's Cameron Harper television appearance was played for the committee. In that interview Mecham had been asked if he knew about the death threat. "No. I didn't," Mecham replied.

Asked to respond, Johnson said, "That is not a true statement."

Johnson had been concerned about the incident not just as a policeman. "I didn't treat it as a personnel matter," he testified. "I thought if it came out, it would be embarrassing to the governor." He had attempted to handle the matter in a manner that would not hurt Mecham.

Johnson testified about the previous year's events when Mecham had declared John Kolbe be a nonperson. "I was told that during the next press conference, when [Mecham] gave a certain signal, . . . members of my detail were to remove Mr. Kolbe from the press conference. I told the governor it was against the law."

John Kolbe later spoke with Johnson, who said, "[Testifying] was the hardest thing I ever did."

Kolbe wrote:

Whether it's blaming Carlson for the failure of his non-existent legislative programs, or Pat Murphy for reporting his repeated racial slurs, or House speaker Joe Lane for carrying out an impeachment "vendetta," or his own brother for keeping shoddy campaign records, this callous discarding and disparagement of anyone no longer useful to him debases [sic] his office and the noble calling of politics. . . . Beau Johnson was willing to step into the line of fire for his boss . . . His absence [from the governor's security staff] is a continuing reminder, as if we needed more, of the ultimate ugliness of the Evan Mecham regime.

Howard Schwartz testified to the creation of the Protocol Fund. The agreement had been reached because otherwise the inaugural committee would have paid triple damages and suffered the loss of the money altogether.

Asked why he had allowed the money to remain under the control of the governor rather than be turned over to the state treasurer, Schwartz replied, "We're dealing with a brand-new governor, new administration, a brand-new law, and I'm talking to two honorable and credible attorneys who are saying that that's how the moneys are going to be disposed of. And basically, to be honest with you, I didn't feel it was incumbent on me to challenge their word."

As interesting as all this was to a state that was now following Mecham's travails like a soap opera, the real witness, the one everyone was waiting for, was Evan Mecham himself, who was now scheduled to appear on Monday, February 1.

The unanswered question was whether or not Mecham would even testify. Until now he had selected his own appearances and scrupulously avoided anyone with ability to cross-examine. He had not repeated his error in appearing before Cameron Harper. Mecham had told many stories about these events.

Bill French and Paul Eckstein grilling him promised to be enlightening as well as entertaining.

On Tuesday, January 26, 1988, Secretary of State Rose Mofford fulfilled her legal duty and called upon Evan Mecham to inform him that she had certified sufficient signatures—301,032—for a recall election. Mecham interrupted a long-distance telephone call at 2:00 P.M. to meet briefly with her, and Mofford said, "He was very gracious."

Under the recall statute Mecham now had five days in which to inform the secretary of state whether he would resign or face a recall election tentatively set for May 17.

That same day Jim Ratliff told Rick Collins and Joe Lane that it was all over for Evan Mecham. After listening to Jim Shumway's testimony the day before, Ratliff was convinced that Mecham should resign. He said he was meeting with Mecham to tell him so. He did not share the results of that meeting with Collins but the following day canceled a golf date. Since Ratliff never passed up a "golf course," especially Troon, one of the finest in the state, Collins took that to mean the meeting had not gone well.

The Democrats were undecided how to proceed with the fourth article, relating to the supercollider. Joe Lane told them they were certainly free to raise it at the hearings if that was their wish. In the end they decided against it, and the matter was dropped. The comprehensive report they had prepared was forwarded by Lane to the attorney general, unread.

Joe Lane had French first appear before the thirty-six-member Republican caucus on January 27, 1988. It was now the hope of the Mecham loyalists to break French. Some of the representatives had obviously been prepped, but the Mecham supporters in the caucus failed to ruffle the always courteous French. Joe Lane thought the caucus went well.

That week the nationally respected attorney James Neal was flown to Phoenix at the request of Fred Craft to have lunch with Mecham and review the situation. There was considerable speculation that he would take over Mecham's case from Murray Miller.

Craft said after the visit, "It's just a question of whether [Neal] has the time." When Neal left town, Craft was satisfied they had a deal. Instead, Neal declined the case for unspecified reasons.

Unknown at the time, Neal had called Bill French as soon as he arrived back in Nashville. In 1964 Neal had been head of the strike force on which French had served that had prosecuted Jimmy Hoffa. Hoffa had called Neal "the most vicious prosecutor who ever lived." Later Neal was one of the special prosecutors in Watergate.

French and Neal were good friends. Neal asked French how it looked for Mecham. French replied, "We're going to kick his ass."

In a stunning, nearly surrealistic move Mecham announced a tax hike.

Mecham's incomplete budget had been out of balance by over a hundred million dollars. Mecham, who had advocated tax cuts throughout his career, now advocated raising more than ninety million dollars by increasing various fees and taxes.

The proposal was lost in the swirl of events, and later Mecham denied he ever made such a proposal.

On Saturday, January 30, there was speculation that Mecham would resign. On Friday he used a private stairwell to hand-deliver a response to Mofford and asked that she open it at 6:00 P.M., Saturday.

The house Republicans caucused Saturday to suggest questions to French for Mecham's testimony on Monday. There was a vain hope that it would not come about.

That evening Mofford read the letter to the press. "I was legally elected by the people of Arizona to the office of governor, and I intend to fulfill my responsibilities. . . ." Mecham would not be stepping down.

Speaking now to a group of business leaders, Mecham said, "This is a little cleansing we have to go through. And I think it's good. I really think this recall election will be good. I think then, if we have a recall election— I presume it will be challenged—but if we have it, I think it will be good because then I believe that we can get out into a campaign mode . . . and present to the people that this is what we've done. . . . Then that will shut them up."

Most of that week Mecham demanded equal time before the house to counter the French Report. When that was not forthcoming, he said, "I'll have my day in court Monday [before the select committee]. On Monday, I'll cover the facts.

"I've been tried in the press for the last three and a half months, and . . . statements have been made, most of which are not true. But I'll have my opportunity and I hope you'll be tuned in so that you can get my side of the story.

"I think you'll be pleased with it. And I think you'll understand a lot of things you don't today."

On Monday most of the state turned to its radios and television sets as Mecham took his seat before the Special House Select Committee on Impeachment. Murray Miller sat to his right. Virtually the entire house was present.

Mecham had attacked the earlier secret grand jury. He had also attacked the "prosecutorial," one-sided presentation of the French Report and the select committee for refusing to allow his attorney to ask questions or interject himself in the house hearing process. Now was his turn to say his piece.

Witnesses were restricted to no more than ten minutes for opening statements. After much wrangling Mecham was allowed half an hour. Chairman Skelly asked Mecham if he planned to remain after reading his statement and answer questions.

"I intend to stay and answer questions from the members of the committee and the members of the House," Mecham replied.

"We do have counsel, Governor." Under the select committee rules French and Eckstein asked questions, followed by committee members. Mecham had omitted reference to them.

"I intend to stay and answer questions from the members of the committee and the members of the House," Mecham repeated. "That's what I said I would do, and that's what I have come to do."

Skelly placed the governor under oath and invited him to "please be frank and honest as you can be with us."

Mecham began with "I have always told the truth. Integrity is the number one issue. I expect the highest of integrity out of every member of the House, as they have every right to expect it of me. . . ." He then read a statement covering familiar territory with what had now become his standard answers.

There was no secret loan or secret bank account, according to Mecham. The records were there at the bank. Gasser's doodle sheet meant nothing. As for the Protocol Fund, Mecham had asked Colter how the funds were invested and been told at 5 percent interest. Mecham viewed this as a long-term fund and suggested to Colter that his son Dennis would pay more to use the money at Mecham Pontiac. When word of the loan became public, Mecham realized that borrowing it was "politically foolish," and paid it back.

As for the obstruction of justice charge, it had long been "a clear policy of security procedures on the Ninth Floor [that] all matters dealing with security are to be held in strictest confidence." He testified that Beau Johnson related to him that Horace Lee Watkins had "said some threatening words or made a threat about Donna Carlson to Peggy Griffith." Mecham saw this as a personnel matter and suggested that Max Hawkins look into it.

Refuting Johnson's testimony, Mecham said, "Nothing was ever said to me in the presence of Dr. Burke or Fred Craft that there was any kind of a death threat, a boat ride or a possible felony type of thing."

Hawkins reported that afternoon that it "was a lot of hot air and would go away." Mecham considered that the end of it. He then attacked the credibility of the various police reports the DPS officers had written. He acknowledged receiving a telephone call from Milstead but did not relate what was said.

Mecham concluded with "If the people do not want me to serve as your governor, they will tell me so in the polling booth. If they want me to continue to serve as your governor, they will likewise tell me so. I ask you to let the people, not the Legislature, decide. That is the American way. I always have and I always will abide by the free choice of a free people. Thank you and God bless you all."

Skelly now returned to the issue of house counsel. "Governor, I have a little problem. I think the members of the committee have a little problem. When we're on the Ninth Floor, we play by your rules. . . . We have committee rules that we have adopted, and in this particular case we had every member of the 10 member committee unanimously vote to adopt these rules."

Skelly read Rule No. 6, which provided for the order of questioning. Mecham's lawyer spoke up. Skelly said in his deep voice, "Mr. Miller, let's clear this up right now. You're here to give advice and counsel to Governor Mecham, but Governor Mecham is here to answer the questions, if you don't mind, please."

"I just don't want any of his rights violated, Mr. Chairman," Miller said, "and I think you're about to do that, because this requires a legal response—"

"Mr. Miller—"

"—and you're keeping me here as another potted plant, which I resent."

"No, that's the last thing you would ever be, Mr. Miller, is a potted plant." Laughter. "By the same token we're not filming *Perry Mason*. . . ."

Now Mecham said he did not want his constitutional rights violated either. He said that if he had had the right to cross-examine witnesses earlier, this "one-sided affair" would "already be decided" in his favor.

"Governor, is it because you feel that you might incriminate yourself?"

Mecham was worked up. ". . . I do not feel that Mr. French and Mr. Eckstein—in fact, if we were to talk about them, we would get into conflicts of interest, we would get into grave conflicts of interest, we would get into a lot of subjects, Mr. Chairman, and I'd rather not do that. I came in a friendly way today to answer the questions of the members of the House and shed light. . . . I think that the House is full of intelligent members that can ask all the questions they need to know, and I am inviting . . . any member of the House to ask any question they choose [*sic*]."

Skelly then stated, "Governor, you're familiar with Section 41-1155, which does say that 'each house of the Legislature may punish as a contempt, and by imprisonment, a breach of its privileges. . . , but only for one or more of the following offenses: refusing to attend or be examined as a witness, either before the House or a committee or before any person authorized by the House or by a committee to take such testimony in legislative proceedings. . . .' And this is not a threat, Governor, believe me. I'm just asking if you are familiar with it."

"I'm really not, Mr. Skelly, but it sure sounds threatening to me."

Skelly then recessed the hearing until after lunch.

Murray Miller had advised Mecham not to testify before the select committee. He believed the committee would "claw him to death."

One of the difficulties Miller faced in defending the governor from both impeachment and criminal indictment was Mecham's perceived need to make public statements on matters that were the subject of inquiry. It was one thing to make differing public statements, but his appearance before the select committee would create a sworn record that made his legal defense that much more difficult.

Mecham argued that he was the governor and he had to respond. Miller could not disagree with that. It was Mecham's position in their discussions that he had done nothing wrong and had nothing to hide.

Mecham had "a lot of things he wanted to say." Miller worked with him to shorten his answers and urged him to respond only to the questions. He found Mecham "difficult to control that way." Mecham in particular wanted to go after Skelly for what he believed was the chairman's improper influencing of a racing investigation.

Skelly was known to like the horses and was part owner of a horse. Mecham's accusation against Skelly was also well known. It had been investigated and was without merit, yet Mecham was convinced there was a cover-up. Miller strongly urged the governor to avoid a confrontation with Skelly. Miller cautioned Mecham that it would serve no useful purpose to resurrect the allegation. There was no proof, and it would come out sounding like slander. Later Miller said, "Here we're faced with impeachment, indictment, and recall, and he wants me to go find horses?"

Miller believed that "if skilled counsel asked the questions, it would be totally unfair." With the grand jury transcripts and Mecham's public statements they could make any public figure out to be a liar. He advised Mecham to answer only questions of the committee. That was the best he could do in terms of damage control.

"It was my judgment," Miller later said, "if it came to a stand-down, the house would opt to ask questions" rather than hold Mecham in contempt.

Evan Mecham suspected that Joe Lane would have him impeached once Bob Corbin had indicted him. Mecham believed that the speaker required an indictment to create adverse publicity so he could justify the impeachment. In normal times he believed the house would stay out of a grand jury matter. The fact that it did not convinced Mecham of what was really taking place.

Mecham believed that Burton Barr's fingerprints were all over this entire affair. In Mecham's opinion, Barr had never reconciled himself to his defeat at Mecham's hands and had set it as his goal to bring Mecham down. Mecham "felt pretty comfortable that he could weather the storm." He did not believe that Joe Lane "could pull it off."

During a recess in the proceedings Paul Eckstein went up to say hello to Mecham as a courtesy. They had never met. Eckstein was of the opinion that Mecham would not participate further once he had given his statement.

"Governor," he said, "I'm disappointed. I really wanted to ask you questions."

Mecham replied, "That wouldn't be fair. You've broken more laws than I ever have."

Neither of the men realized that the television camera was trained on them and the microphone was live. The whole state was listening in.

Eckstein laughed lightly, then said incredulously, "I've broken more laws than you have?" Miller, spotting the discussion, tried to pull Mecham away.

Mecham now made reference to Eckstein's appearance on a committee to raise funds for a Phoenix city councilman. The committee did not register with the secretary of state and was required to later. Eckstein walked away in disbelief.

When the committee reconvened, Skelly asked again, "Do you plàn to answer questions if Mr. French or Mr. Eckstein asks the questions?" Skelly was every bit as conservative as Mecham. They were clones on virtually every political issue. As if they were brothers who had been close in youth and were now grown into adulthood and bitter enmity, the tension between the men was palpable.

Mecham explained that he was different from the other witnesses. He was the accused and "I am the governor of this state." He said he was prepared to go to the mat over this issue if need be. "If we are to get to the bottom of [this], let's get on and get doing with it and do it . . . rather than you insisting that I submit to cross-examination of prosecutors."

In his deep, husky voice tainted with the cigarettes he chain-smoked Skelly said, "Governor, it's obvious that you feel that you should not comply with the rules as every other witness has. . . . In view of your refusal . . . this committee will adjourn until such time as you decide that you will comply with our rules. At such time we will be very happy to hear from you. Without objection, we will adjourn. Hearing none, so ordered."

Both supporters and opponents of the governor were demonstrating outside in the Capitol mall. As Mecham hurried to his car, one demonstrator launched into a tirade at point-blank range, shouting, "Recall, recall, you sneaky snake!," while another shouted, "What are you hiding?"

A Mecham supporter, an elderly woman, was threatened with a citation when she struck Ed Buck with her umbrella during a verbal exchange.

Democrats and Republicans were critical of Skelly for forcing the issue. Throughout the hearings he had publicly stated that the evidence was damaging to the governor. To explain his position, he said, "Impeachment is not based on whether you like or dislike the governor. It's based on the evidence. To me, thus far, the evidence is very damaging."

Following adjournment the house caucused. The votes were not there to support Joe Lane and Jim Skelly, who argued for a subpoena. Miller had been right. Mecham was rescheduled to appear on Wednesday at 9:00 A.M.

Since the members of the select committee would be asking the questions, two separate cram sessions took place all day Tuesday. The Democrats met at Brown & Bain; the Republicans at Storey & Ross.

French and Eckstein had established a sound working relationship by this time. All witnesses were interviewed in advance, and there had been no surprises. They divided the questions, and each side prepped its representatives for the questioning. Debbie McCune recalls a long day as they reviewed critical issues and questioning techniques. They did role playing, with one of the staff lawyers playing Mecham. Democrat Representative Jack Brown did not participate to any great extent. Brown was a Mormon from a small LDS community.

The primary technique they were taught was to ask the question, then continue asking it and rephrasing it until they obtained an answer—no matter how long it took.

That Monday night Mecham appeared before a crowd of two thousand in Mesa's Centennial Hall and was greeted as a conquering hero. The house's caving in was his first victory in memory. Mecham proclaimed, "Tonight in this hall, I see great hope for America. You and hundreds of thousands throughout Arizona are the hope. . . . God will give us the direction, but we are the ones that have to put the motive power to the drive wheels that push us along."

His words called to mind for the largely LDS crowd the words of a common Mormon song: "Put your shoulder to the wheel, push along. Do your duty with a heart full of song."

"If we listen to His direction," Mecham said, "He will tell us the course to steer. . . . Although there is not an establishment of religion, it is important to have God as a co-partner in all governmental acts.

On Tuesday the house leadership turned itself to considering the procedure to follow for delivering a bill of impeachment to the whole house. It was decided to utilize a strike-all motion, in which an existing bill that has already been through two readings could have everything in the text struck and a new bill substituted. Jane Dee Hull, who was monitoring the vote count and who was to be responsible for the procedure, needed twenty-four hours notice to have the proposed strike-everything amendment to the bill in place under house rules.

House Resolution 2002: *A Resolution urging the United States government to use its powers to precipitate a withdrawal of Soviet and Cuban military forces from Angola and to encourage peace and national reconciliation in Angola.*
—*Sixteenth day, Thirty-eighth Legislature, second reading*

*But Mecham will not go away. He is like one of those big pack rats who will move into your house and decide to stay forever. . . . The only way to get rid of a pack rat is to lure it out in the open . . . and blow its head off with a .22 Magnum or a .410 rat gun. But you don't want to miss or slightly wound the beast . . . because then he will slink back into the walls and die, leaving you with a pile of death and stinking black meat that will eventually poison the whole house. Welcome to Phoenix: This is Mecham country.*
—HUNTER THOMPSON

# 36

On Wednesday at 8:00 A.M. Joe Lane, Bill French, Art Hamilton, and others met to consider a tentative impeachment schedule and to review possible articles of impeachment. Hamilton had told Lane the day before that his people could not be ready for a floor vote before Friday.

When the hearing resumed at 9:00 A.M., Paul Eckstein and his staff were seated up with the Democrats, Bill French and his staff with the Republicans. Representative George Weisz, a former investigator for the attorney general, led off with questions relating to the obstruction of justice allegation.

Mecham denied that Beau Johnson had adequately reported Horace

Lee Watkins's arrest history to him. He recalled "around 20 some years before he had an assault charge on his record." Mecham did not remember any other arrests for Watkins. Pressed for details, he said Watkins had been arrested "when he was a boy of 17."

Mecham had known a young man named Ron Ludders for some years. When he applied for a state job, he had informed Mecham. He was hired by Max Hawkins and was responsible for Mecham's program of grounding agency vehicles as a cost-cutting measure. Weisz asked Mecham if he recalled Ludders calling him on July 21, 1987, to report that Watkins had assaulted him by grabbing and shaking him and ripping his shirt for no apparent reason.

"Ron called me one day and was quite disturbed that he and [Watkins] had had an altercation. I don't recall the extent of it." When Mecham was pressed for more, his memory did not improve.

Asked about his conversation with Milstead, Mecham said, "I made one statement, that I didn't want him taking Officer Martinez on Sunday afternoon to see the Attorney General. . . . It had been handled in the proper way, in an administrative way, and Colonel Milstead nor Beau Johnson ever gave me any information to the contrary."

Weisz asked Mecham about his Channel 10 interview in which he had denied hearing of any serious threat. Now under oath, Mecham was asked if that was true.

Mecham replied, "Let's go over this again. Any kind of a spat or an altercation needs to be looked into. You seem to be trying to work something on some relative degree that 'serious' means. Let's use the scale of one to ten, should we?"

"Governor—"

"Please, please. We've had a hard time on this, and I think maybe we're taking a lot of people's time, and I'd like to get to where you can understand what I'm saying because you seem to have quite a hard time and keep asking me the same question which is your right, and I'll keep answering, but you keep working this degree of serious.

"I was in the middle of a very busy day. I think when they came into my office, I was on the telephone. I turned around and listened and heard an altercation, an argument, a spat in the parking lot between two people. I said, 'This sounds like, you know, it's a personnel matter. Watkins works for Hawkins. Have the two of them get together and let's, you know, see if we can settle this,' and that dismisses it, quite frankly, and that's what was said, and nobody repeated anything, and they all left my office, and I went on with my affairs, so that's what it was.

"I can't tell you that I, in a scale of one to ten, assigned any particular seriousness to that. I can tell you that when Hawkins called me and said, 'This is a lot of hot air, and it will go away,' that I assessed it as zero as far as seriousness. Does that help?"

"Not really, Governor," Weisz said. Weisz had asked Mecham if he denied being told of a serious threat, not what Hawkins had told him.

"I'm sorry I'm not giving you the answer you seem to be conceived [*sic*] to want."

"No, I just want to get your impressions. It doesn't help understanding on your definitions, and I don't think you're answering the questions directly, but I will accept that at this point. If we can go to—"

"Mr. Weisz, I resent that. I resent that." Mecham was in a huff as he continued. "I have worked to answer every question, and you have questioned time and time again and tried to put meanings and insinuations and all that onto these, and I resent that highly.

"I have endeavored to answer every question completely and fairly and have answered the same question about 20 times, which I don't take any umbrage at.

"You have every right and if you want to ask every question 100 times, I will sit here as long as you want to, and we'll answer the questions. I resent when you say I haven't answered questions. That is not proper."

Weisz decided just to show the tape of the television interview and try again. Mecham heard himself tell Cameron Harper, "No, I didn't," in response to the question "Did you know about that threat?"

Weisz tried it again. "Is that a true statement?"

"Let's go back, Mr. Weisz, and let's see what he's talking about. Mr. Harper envisioned himself as a very clever interrogator, and he put words to try to elicit an answer that was other than it was. . . ." Finally Mecham testified, "I had heard nothing of any threat."

He accused Harper of working with French "to put this one together as the way this thing has been put together. . . ." Apparently forgetting that George Weisz would himself be voting on impeachment, he admonished the representative, "Please don't try to be tricky."

Weisz continued to bore in on what Mecham had heard. No matter how the governor attacked, misdirected, or accused, Weisz returned time and again to the same question. At last Mecham acknowledged he had heard "threat" but not "bodily harm," not "death threat."

"You heard threat, Governor?" Weisz asked tellingly.

"I heard that one thing, the one word, threat. Yes, I've mentioned before that there was in this altercation a threat to Donna. That's all I was told, there was a threat to Donna."

That single examination consumed the entire morning.

Just before the lunch break Mecham said, "Mr. Chairman, I have something to say first. A constituent has just reported that, although your hands are over the mike, there's another microphone that is picking up everything that you say. Also the radio station turns up the volume each time. I want this corrected so I can speak to my attorney before this hearing continues."

Mecham's concerns over eavesdropping had now spread to the hearing room. In fact, what was occurring was that the automatic gain for the television feed was adjusting when they whispered and tended to pick up Mecham's and Miller's voices. Dave Hampton of KFYI acknowledged he was turning the radio mike up manually but had been unable to hear anything. He said he would stop.

The afternoon *Gazette* contained a Kolbe article on Joe Lane. Kolbe pointed out that Lane's district was 62 percent Democrat to 29 percent Republican:

> . . . Governor Mecham is in deep trouble in a political body handily controlled by his own party. It is also a shining testament to the courage and sturdy integrity of a bald-headed, pink-cheeked rancher. . . . In addition to his title, Joe Lane has a political distinction he'd rather do without—as measured by those lopsided registration figures, he is *the most vulnerable Republican* in the Arizona House. In other words, he is the GOP lawmaker with the *most* reason to avoid the divisive Mecham swamp.
>
> But it is Lane who [*sic*] the governor has accused of lying and who has been made a key target of the phone-calling brigade organized by Edith Richardson, a former Mecham aide who's now assigned to keeping the governor's vaunted "good people" in a state of perpetual frenzy.
>
> Why Lane? Because he is doing his duty. . . . Lane, who already has resigned himself to the reality that he might not return next year, and impeachment panel chairman Jim Skelly . . . are providing daily object lessons in grace under extreme pressure.
>
> Some call it courage. There's another word for it. *Statesmanship.* . . .

Max Hawkins heard Tom Leykis on KFYI and called the talk show. Over the air he called Peggy Griffith "a naughty girl" and said, "Peggy is not emotionally stable." Informed of the remarks, Skelly said, "These people are superb at character assassination."

That afternoon Debbie McCune began questioning. She is a slight woman, a single mother in her early thirties, with a full head of dark hair and doelike, striking eyes. She is insightful, bright, and methodical.

Later she remarked that only a politician could really understand what this process meant to her and the others. They knew that this would be the "most serious political act we'll ever do . . . We all [also] knew we were dealing with another person's life."

She returned to when Mecham had learned of Watkins's arrest history. Mecham acknowledged receiving an arrest history from Beau Johnson on a slip of paper. In addition to the robbery charge, Mecham now recalled another charge: "There was just this little notation relative to being a—oh, an assault charge 20 some years before, that I believe the—the level of it was a misdemeanor, and that's really all that was there that I was aware of. . . . I didn't know it was a woman, but I knew he had been arrested on an assault charge."

Now McCune led Mecham through his knowledge of Watkins's conduct from the robbery charge to the assault charge to the altercation with Ludders, then to this question: "So then on November 13th, 1987, when the allegations were made about Watkins making a threat against Donna Carlson, you had some knowledge of his violent past?"

"Oh, I—I think I'd object to terminology that of his violent past. Here is a man who, oh, I don't know, his late 40s, I got a report on him, said when he was 17 years old, he didn't have a gun, but he had participated in some kind of robbery, and then over 20 years before he had been arrested on a simple assault charge. I rather doubt that you can categorize that as a violent past, you know, over 40 some years. I believe you're doing him a disservice to suggest that . . . I mean, these things just get blown all out of proportion because somebody wants to make Watkins this vicious felon when in reality he isn't vicious and he isn't a felon."

As McCune listened to the governor's answers and watched him during the hearings, it seemed to her that he was defensive, argumentative, and uncooperative. He was creating needless problems for himself.

She noticed something else. She was the only woman on the committee. When she questioned Mecham, his entire manner changed. The level of conflict between them was readily apparent even though she remained throughout scrupulously mild-mannered and even-tempered. Patricia Magrath took McCune aside later and told her that she had never seen such a change in manner in a witness before.

Mark Killian now asked Mecham, "Governor, I'm a little concerned about your undying devotion here to Mr. Watkins. Did you ever reprimand [Watkins] at any time during this? Did anybody suggest to [Watkins] that these type of statements were totally unproductive and possibly illegal or inappropriate for a government official to be involved in. Anything like that?"

"Sure did. I told Max Hawkins to tell him and I told him myself. I said Lee, keep your head down and your mouth shut or you're not gonna be here."

Killian was not unaware of what many of his colleagues thought. He had posed a number of questions that allowed the governor to respond in a sympathetic light. He also believed he had asked telling questions. He wanted to "expose Ev's proclivity for paranoia" to the public. He believed that would help the public understand his reaction to Milstead. Killian was trying to show that Mecham was a man with problems.

It seemed to Killian that Mecham was having his opportunity to answer the concerns of the house. He had his forum. Instead of resolving the problems, he was taking the attitude that he should be taken at his word.

Now David Bartlett, an attorney and a Tucson Democrat, began questioning. Mecham described his Friday-night conversation with Peggy Griffith, concluding, "I knew of nothing else that she was talking about, except someone was trying to talk to her from the Attorney General's office."

"Governor, please. Mr. Burke was in here and said he knew it was a serious threat, and it was communicated that way to you at the time he testified.

"Secondly, we have had police officers both sworn in here that when you were talking to Cameron Harper, you weren't exactly being candid, not only were you not being candid, you weren't telling the truth. We have their word, we have Colonel Milstead's word and the officer—Lieutenant Johnson's word, so we have different versions we are trying to deal with here and sort out.

"Our issue isn't a legal one. It's not a question of a violation of the statute. It's essentially whether you fundamentally violated your oath of office, whether or not you abused your power by either trying to obstruct justice or by trying to cover up what was pretty bad behavior. Your chief of staff assumed there would be a dual track investigation, but the head of the Department of Administration had a different view. I'll give you an example: When Max Hawkins gave you a report—First, let me go back to where we were."

"You're making a speech instead of a question, Mr. Bartlett, so you're going to have to go back and pick me up."

"I'm trying to get even with you. I don't have mine all prepared like you do so mine might not be as clean. Governor—"

Miller interjected. "You don't have any answers prepared, do you?"

Mecham responded. "I don't have no answers prepared, Mr. Bartlett."

"Oh, it's just the sheets of paper [in front of you]."

"Mr. Bartlett, please. Would you like to see my files?" Mecham suddenly shot to his feet. "Would you like me—" He was folding folders and preparing to carry them to Bartlett.

"No, governor, I don't want to see your files."

"Would you like to? I think that's kind of a direct insult, and I don't appreciate it. I don't know what questions are going to be asked here. I think that one is just a little bit—"

"Governor, we have contradictory testimony here. We're trying to weigh the credibility of your testimony against that of other people who said different things. . . ."

Mecham was sitting down now. His temper had subsided as quickly as it flared. At 4:00 P.M., as Bartlett continued his methodical inquiry, Mecham suddenly announced, "I'd kind of like to call a halt."

Skelly asked if he could come back that night. Mecham declined. Skelly asked if Mecham objected to giving Bartlett just five more minutes since he was finishing a point.

"Yes, I have objection," Mecham said. The hearing recessed until the following morning.

Thursday morning the house leadership met again for final review of the draft articles of impeachment. During the noon hour Jane Dee Hull signed the strike-everything resolution, allowing an impeachment vote as early as the next day.

Representative Jim Hartdegen, a Republican, was quoted in the *Republic* as saying, "Any legislator who's been here any length of time will probably side with Milstead and Johnson. In my dealings with Milstead, he's always been forthright. . . . I haven't had the same experience with the governor."

Mecham's loyal supporter Representative Lela Steffey was quoted as saying bitterly, "They've got the votes."

Representative John King, an attorney and a moderate Republican, began the questioning that morning. He suggested that 1986 had not been Mecham's first campaign for public office.

Mecham replied, "No. I think that's well-known that I had run before."

"Would you briefly relate to the committee and for the record the different political races that you have entered over the years?"

Omitting his 1952 defeat for the Arizona house of representatives, Mecham replied, "I ran for the state Senate in 1960 and the U.S. Senate in '62 and governor in '64 and governor in '74, '78, '82 and '86."

King asked, "Did part of your theme [in the 1986] election relate to your allegation that Burton Barr and Governor Babbitt were too close to special interest groups?"

"Well, if you would like to really be specific, let's go ahead and ask me to bring the tabloid we put out so that we could be very specific, Mr. King."

"We have the tabloid, Governor, if you would like to refer to it."

"Okay."

"I'm just asking you: As part of your campaign, was there a theme relating to allegations that Burton Barr and Governor Babbitt were too close to special interest groups?"

"Let's—Is there some—I don't really mind answering that, but can you give me an idea of your line of questioning?

"I understand that prosecutorial-type questions have been prepared for

you, Mr. King, and I have no objections to those. I don't know whether it
was Mr. French prepared them or who it was. I have no objection to those.
I'll answer all the questions, but can you give me an idea of what you're
driving at? That's just all I—"

"Governor, regardless of who prepared what questions—and so far I
don't think any of these questions have presented any problem to you—
we're just trying to find out what the facts are. There are no trick questions.
We're just trying to find out what the theme is. I can just read the first
paragraph of your tabloid, if you want me to."

Miller now conferred with his client.

"Mr. Chairman," King said, "apparently the governor is edgy about
these questions."

"Oh no, I'm not the least bit edgy, Mr. King."

King asked, "Governor, could you just read the first paragraph of the
tabloid, please."

"I really would still like to ask back, Mr. King. I have understood that
we were here in a hearing to bring light and truth, I believe was [sic] words
that was [sic] used, and relating to three specific issues.

"Yesterday we had an issue relating to my obstruction for justice. I don't
know why Mr. Bartlett and I didn't finish our conversation from yesterday.
I was rather prepared for Mr. Bartlett today, and I think we left some things
up in the air. He wanted to make the—to wind that one up, for example,
with the fact that Mr.—"

Skelly interjected, "Governor, excuse me."

"No. I'm answering, Mr. Skelly. I am answering and I am making a
little statement here, as I have a right to do for light and truth, Mr. Skelly."

"Governor, just a moment, please, if you don't mind." Skelly explained
that Mecham had discontinued the questioning by Bartlett the day before.
Now King was asking questions. "Now, if you want to put that statement in
the record, we have no problem with that, Governor, whatsoever. We will
all see copies of that."

Mecham said, "No."

"But we would appreciate it if you would be kind enough to answer
Mr. King's question."

Miller conferred again with Mecham. King restated his request.

"Mr. King, I'll humor you by reading it. I would still like to know: Are
we here to see whether or not campaign disclosure laws were not adhered
to, or are we here to talk politics? Which is it? . . ."

Mecham now read his campaign accusation against the "few insiders"
who had improper influence over state government. King then asked,
"Would it be fair to say that you wanted the voters to believe that you were
anti-special-interest-groups?"

Mecham presented the face of innocence. "I don't think I said anti anything. Let's read it again," and he did. "Does that make me anti anything? . . ."

It was apparent that Mecham wanted no one reminded of what he had promised as a candidate and compare it with what he had been doing in secret.

Mecham was increasingly angry with King. Then the representative asked, "Now, Governor, let me ask you a question. . . . Do you think it would be proper for me to have Al Capone, Jimmy Hoffa and Lucky Luciano each loan my campaign committee $10,000, and I could then show an aggregate of a $30,000 contribution from them since I would be eventually responsible for repayment of the loan?"

Mecham's anger boiled over. "Mr. King, the inference in using notorious criminals in talking to me is totally objectionable. I would ask you to withdraw that question and strike it from the record. That's an insult to the Governor of the State of Arizona plus to Evan Mecham personally. . . ."

"Governor, all I was doing was referring to—"

"No, no. You were insinuating as has been done so much that I'm some kind of a criminal, which I am not."

"I assure you there's no—"

"Find some other names, please, and rephrase your question."

King explained his reason for asking the question in this way. Mecham insisted he use Smith and Jones. King argued he was making a point. By Mecham's logic such people would have been concealed from public knowledge. Mecham continued to argue.

Mecham said, "As a person in my life, I have been in business for 35 to 38 years. I have dealt with tens of thousands of people. I have never been once accused in life of anything but maybe going too fast and getting a speeding ticket. . . ."

Suddenly Mecham switched subjects. "Mr. Chairman, I have been handed a note again that apparently something is happening to our switches. We thought they were fail-safe, and it says, 'I just got a call from Green Valley, 10:10, saying they can hear every word you're saying to the governor on the air.' "

Skelly assured him the kill switch was working. It was the members' voices the listener was hearing. No one was eavesdropping on the governor.

As the questioning came to an end, Skelly asked "one other question," as he had so often. He was like an experienced detective, waiting until the suspect believed the questions were over before asking the telling question.

"Oh, Governor," Skelly began, "let me ask you one other question, if I may. I'm sorry to prolong this. But I recall one night, and correct me if I'm mistaken on the statement I make, I recall one night hearing . . . one of the questions asked . . . that Wolfson had . . .

"Everyone knows the people who contribute to campaigns obviously have input into appointments and want to make recommendations on appointments. . . . I think that your statement was that Wolfson had made five recommendations to you, and you had appointed two of those people to positions in state government, neither of whom were [sic] in position to be helpful to Wolfson. Is that correct?"

"That's [sic] probably be pretty much correct. I don't recall the exact statement. . . ."

They bantered about dodging questions, then: "And my question is, both of them, however, were appointed to the Housing Finance Review Board, and that is the board that . . . approves the issuance of the IDA bonds or reviews the issuance of the IDA bonds, and that's the business Wolfson is in."

Mecham replied that IDA bonds were "passé" by then and said he had an interesting story to relate as concerned that question.

Skelly adjourned until the following morning.

Mark Killian met with the house leadership after the day's hearings and asked for a delay in the vote to allow him enough time to meet with Governor Mecham and ask for his resignation.

On the day Evan Mecham was to be impeached the house hearings resumed at 9:00 A.M. It was Friday, February 5, 1988. Joe Lane had been quoted in the previous night's paper as saying he did not think a vote would come until after the weekend. Mecham had a speaking engagement and had asked the committee to finish testimony by noon.

The committee now focused on Mecham's campaign reporting "lumpings" that concealed the Wolfson loan and on the Protocol Fund. The questioning was anticlimactic. Toward the end of the session Debbie McCune mentioned that unfortunately Colter was unavailable for questions.

Mecham said, "I didn't know when he went. I didn't know he was going, and somebody told me he went to Australia and sometimes I wish I were with him."

Toward the end of the hearings Mecham loyalist Gary Giordano led Mecham through a series of questions designed to allow the governor to state unequivocal denials to some of the allegations. Then it was time for the clearly strained and exhausted Mecham to give his concluding statement.

Despite his intemperate outbursts, Mecham had, for the most part, conducted himself no worse than he had the previous months as he dodged questions while at the same time insisting he was telling all there was to tell. Now the slow burn of rage boiled over. It is estimated that in the next few minutes Mecham cost himself up to ten votes in the House.

"Proceed, Governor."

"First of all, thank you for coming, irrespective of any condition, Mr. Skelly, and the committee, for giving me this time before you. Whether or not the bottom line of what happens, at least I have had an opportunity to tell the people of Arizona many things they haven't heard before, and I appreciate that. And I do appreciate the facilities of the public media . . . for broadcasting these to the people.

"I have a great concern relating to this, not as much for Evan Mecham as I do for Arizona and what has happened under this and is likely to happen according to the circumstances.

"I myself am going to get along all right. If you vote to impeach me there, pass a bill of impeachment, that's not the end of the world. I go over to the Senate, and at that place, then we really do have an opportunity for a fair trial. We are able to call our witnesses; we are able to cross-examine the other witnesses. And, quite frankly, I don't fear that in the least. It's very time-consuming, very expensive, very non-productive, but that will vindicate me and will take care of that.

"I am concerned, however, the atmosphere in which things are done when people talk about a sense of fairness. When I find a few things—and I have some questions just to throw out, not looking for answers. I have, I think, my answers. But I would say, for example, why did the House allow Joe Lane to pick you, Mr. Skelly, as the hand-picked chairman of this, when in reality you have been a very vocal critic of mine throughout and have wanted me to—to resign and have been very caustic and critical?"

Skelly interrupted. "Excuse me, Governor. I have never in my life asked for your resignation, so you really should get your facts straight."

"Mr. Skelly, you made statements like this: 'He's kind of like a jewel thief getting nailed with the goods and then telling the cop, "Let's forget about it." ' "

"That's a correct statement, and, Governor—"

"He hasn't finished the statement," Miller said.

Ignoring him Skelly concluded. "—I have never asked for your resignation."

"I will take that one back, then, if you haven't."

"Thank you, Governor."

"I apologize to you on that."

"Accepted."

"And, of course, 'nailed with the goods' and then telling the cop, 'Let's forget about it. I'll give the stuff back.' "Also, Mr. Skelly, other things, and I won't go into them, but relating to some investigations on the Attorney General's part that you had a hand in stopping that I was trying to get done. I've been chagrined."

"Governor, do you want to go into any details? I'm more than happy to hear about them." A few days earlier Jim Ratliff had told Skelly, "Jim, he's going to make a blast at some people." It seemed to Skelly that a "guy like Mecham feels he wins by discrediting the opposition," and that would be his tactic now.

Mecham looked as if he could not believe Skelly had just invited his attack. "Well, yes," he said. "Yes, I am. The racing commission. You own half a horse."

"That's correct. . . . I think it's the rear half, but . . ." Laughter.

"There was an investigation—"

"That figures," Miller said in an attempt to diffuse the situation. He and Skelly, one from Brooklyn, the other from the Bronx, had sparred good-naturedly more than once during the hearings. Mecham would have none of that.

"No," he said, "let's get this through. There was an investigation into it; if it was important we would bring in Judge McDonald to say how you got the people out to Turf Paradise and give them the story and then went down and got the Attorney General to stop the investigation, change the investigator and a number of things that really smacks of not being really concerned about it."

"Governor, you're a superb character assassin, but you don't have your facts right. . . . After this is over, I'll be most happy to talk with any member of the media. In fact, I just have expected this, Governor, knowing the way you operate, so I just have a little printed report on the actual facts of the case, which I will be most happy to distribute to every member of the media when we're finished."

"And after that, Mr. Skelly," Mecham said, "I'll see that they are furnished a *true* account of what happened."

A groan went up from the packed hearing room. There were gasps of shock.

"Representative Weisz said it would be the best idea for the state and for the governor that I resign. I don't think his question where he has—Of course, Mrs. Hull, she's on the committee, but she stated she's deeply concerned about the ugliness and divisiveness to the state. 'I personally must say our governor should resign.' And Representative Herstam, words like that, different ones.

"So what I really am concerned about is—for the group here is how many can make a decision based on facts in an area where you don't have the opportunity to have both sides presented. I'm grateful that I had a chance to come and present, under somewhat adverse conditions, my own side here, but it really disturbs me that a judgment will be made. Now, I don't know how that judgment will be. I read that already the votes—and that has to be everybody to make their own choice.

"For my part, I am not personally going to be hurt because I am going to be able to go on and acquit myself. I would only say one thing, that I will do that and I will be all right.

"I hope that everybody else recognizes that when they vote here, that they're going to have to live with their vote the rest of their life. Thank you."

Skelly said, ". . . Governor, we appreciate on behalf of this committee and the House your spending 13 hours down here with Mr. Miller, my landsman from New York.

"On behalf of myself, I want to thank the committee for its diligence, and without objection . . . we will adjourn. Hearing none, so ordered."

For Debbie McCune the significance of Mecham's attack on Skelly had been to demonstrate graphically to the state Mecham's vindictive nature. From that point on Mecham was "no longer a sympathetic character," and the effect of his attack was to "move people forward" toward a vote in favor of impeachment.

During her time of public exposure on the select committee McCune had received many more telephone calls and letters than usual. One man wrote, "I think you and your fellow committee men on the select committee acted like complete wimps when you did not throw Mecham in jail for failing to answer questions at today's hearing. I want this man out of office. *NOW.*"

Another wrote, "After 29, 28, 32, 43 years here—When can we Arizonans again be proud of our state? Even our son in the U.S. Army in West Germany has to defend Arizona! You were great today on T.V. IMPEACH MECHAM!"

And another: "In this letter I wish to strongly urge you to do what is best for the state of Arizona, my blood pressure and your political career: IMPEACH MECHAM."

Members of the public were mailing her suggested questions. There were also many opposing letters. "As one of the members of the Governor Mecham impeachment commeite [*sic*] as a Judge, your comments on T.V. yesterday were REPREHENSIBLE. I am in your district and to make up your mind before the hearings were over, convences [*sic*] me, you have already cooked your goose, no matter which way the impeachment comes out. In your mind, you have already convicted the Governor. Such conduct will not be tolirated [*sic*] by the people."

And then there were the telephone calls written down by her secretary as they were received. "Don't impeach governor. Is afraid of bloodshed." "Do not vote to impeach Governor Mecham. Let the people decide with a recall." "Vote no. Let it go to recall, makes her stomach sick. Wicked and they are evil people." "No impeachment."

She wrote to Art Hamilton. "Art, I have spoken to D.P.S. and house security, and requested that they begin to tape phone calls coming in on

#5161 and #4835. The calls are getting very volatile, and are clearly threat-
ening in nature. I am concerned that as we get closer to an actual vote, that
the threats will become more like the call that Mr. Raymond received this
morning. 'If you vote for impeachment you will be *dead* before the weekend
is over.' Any problem?"

And there was this telephone message for her: "Against impeachment.
Very beautiful— Satanism shows out your eyes every time you speak to
Mecham."

Joe Lane had watched Mecham's performance before the select committee, and it seemed to him that the governor had killed himself. Mecham
behaved as if he could just bulldoze his way over the committee and through
the house. That was a terrible miscalculation.

Because Mecham had to go alone with only a modest assist from his
lawyer, Lane thought the house members were getting a better and truer
picture of him. On average, 70 percent of the house members attended the
hearings on any given day, and Lane was pleased with how the members
were rising to their responsibility.

Most of the local radio stations had refused to carry ads by a group
calling itself Citizens Fighting Organized Crime, headed by Mecham supporter Barbara Blewster. The ads that did run accused organized crime,
"sexual sodomites," the media, and the Communist party of leading a "hate
campaign" against Evan Mecham.

As Mecham hurried to deliver still another luncheon speech, his supporters chanted in the mall, "We'll remember, in November, what you do
to Ev!"

Julian Sanders, who had first publicly announced that Ed Buck was gay,
was now heading something called Arizonans for Traditional Values. He
circulated a petition declaring the house hearings unconstitutional.

At 1:30 P.M. the house caucused. Paul Eckstein met with the Democrats
while French attended the Republican caucus. The mood of the Republicans
was "somber," and the atmosphere was so thick you could "cut it with a
knife." The overwhelming majority wanted to proceed at once. It did not
look forward to a weekend of badgering telephone calls. There were no
forceful arguments for delay until after the weekend.

Jim Skelly for one wanted to get it done. He had received three death
threats that week and wanted this over with. It was apparent to Skelly as
well that "if your mind wasn't made up by then, the weekend wouldn't
matter."

There was one volatile point at about 3:00 P.M., when Representative

Gary Giordano, "dancing around" in his comments, suggested that French was lying. French turned "beet red" and shot to his feet.

"Listen, buster," one lawmaker recalls him saying, "if you have a problem, just say it." Another remembers with relish that he said, "Listen, mister. Just say it." Another recalls the incident with equal delight and has French saying to Giordano, "You got something to say, mister, say it!"

Urbane, even-tempered Bill French recalls exactly what he said. "You better stand up because I'm not going to take that shit anymore!"

Patricia Magrath took French's arm. A profoundly intimidated Giordano, generally viewed as obtuse and unreliable, sat down and for once shut up. The effect of French's outburst was to persuade the members that he was committed to what he had presented to them. This was not politics. French believed in what he said. The caucus vote was nearly unanimous to proceed. Joe Lane decided to take the vote.

Throughout the state news reports had indicated the vote would not come until Monday. Now shows were interrupted, then preempted as the state turned its eyes to the chamber of the house of representatives.

At 4:00 P.M. a grim and determined Speaker Lane gaveled the house to order.

# 37

Following the caucus, Mark Killian, the returned Mormon missionary from Mesa, sat in his office alone to ponder his decision concerning the impeachment of Evan Mecham, high priest and former Mormon bishop.

At conflict were almost more emotions and demands than he could handle. As an individual and as a lawmaker he was deeply offended by Evan Mecham. The governor's conduct in office had been disgraceful.

The governor's unwarranted, slanderous attack on Jim Skelly, a man Killian respected and admired, angered him deeply. During this process the solid Mecham supporters in the house had regularly met. Killian watched some of them peel off after that.

He had spent hours talking to his father. John Rhodes, former Congressman and House minority leader, and the senior Killian had been law partners for years. It now looked as though Rhodes would be entering the recall election. Killian could not support Mecham for election.

It seemed to Killian that the house was in error not to have adopted some legal standard by which to judge the case. French was arguing probable cause, but Killian believed a higher standard should be used. One of the differences of the Arizona constitution from the U.S. Constitution was that the governor became "disabled" upon impeachment and lost all power until the senate trial was over. Secretary of State Rose Mofford would serve as acting governor until the senate trial was over. It seemed to Killian a higher standard was necessary to strip Mecham of his power as governor even if only for a month or two.

In addition, impeachment was an awesome act, and even if Mecham were acquitted, merely having been impeached would be a terrible burden for the man to carry.

Killian's heavily Mormon district had made its position known. Any vote other than no would almost certainly end his legislative career. Plenty of his colleagues believed he was incapable of voting any other way.

His religion also served to move him against voting for impeachment. He had a church to attend on Sunday, and if he voted to impeach Mecham, there would be consequences with many members. Mormons tend to stand together, Killian later acknowledged. "When one of us is attacked, we become defensive." Mecham had always used that to his advantage. Mormons instinctively wanted "to believe he was a good, righteous man." Killian had to work to see Mecham the man clearly.

He had little time in which to decide. He darkened the office and took out his Scriptures. He began to pray. "Heavenly Father . . ." He mouthed the words but felt no inspiration. "Lord," he prayed, "help me make the right decision." He was shaking and on the verge of tears as he sought guidance.

Chris Herstam knew that some members of the house did not believe that Mark Killian could vote for impeachment. He also knew they were wrong. He dropped by Killian's office en route to the house floor. He opened the door and saw a very distraught Killian holding his Scriptures. He did not want to interrupt, but he also wanted to help.

"Mark," he said, "do what you believe is right, and everything will work out." He left him there and took his place.

A few minutes later a stricken Mark Killian found his way to his desk. He had taken a bundle of paper work with him, thinking perhaps that in all that detail were the answers he sought. Skelly patted him on the back and said, "You'll be just fine."

Following his luncheon speech Evan Mecham had returned to a somber Ninth Floor. Mecham was considered a good boss. Everyone had seen his robust humor over little things. He was easily moved by small showings of affection. They all knew how disturbed he was that Willard Mecham had been indicted.

One secretary, who had watched him month after month, commented later that they were all "amazed that he didn't break under the pressure." As the afternoon wore on and it became apparent that the house would vote no one wanted to leave. It was like a wake.

Television sets were tuned to the live coverage. Ken Smith, Richard

Burke, and others had been watching developments. Before the voting started, Mecham began to leave for a speaking engagement in Lake Havasu City, one of his staunchest areas of support. The staff lined up outside his office. They were saying more than farewell for a weekend. If Mecham was impeached, no one knew if he or she would even be back to work on Monday. This could be good-bye.

The staff was in tears as Mecham moved slowly down the line from his corner office toward the elevators. One secretary watching him thought how small and frail he looked. This was a very hard walk for him. His head was up, however, and she was very proud of him.

It was as though the staff members wanted him to acknowledge each of them, and he did, one by one, touching hands, patting a shoulder, reassuring them it would be all right.

"Thank you," he said softly in that even monotone of his. "It's just beginning," he said. "We'll tell our story in the senate." Clearly he was touched by the spontaneous display.

There were procedural votes as House Resolution 2002 made its way to final passage. Ratliff's strike-all amendment, seconded by Hull, passed. The bill was then read for the third and final time by a red-jacketed page. Giordano placed a protest in the record.

Joe Lane called for the final vote. In the house there is a tote board, and at once the lights flashed. Experienced observers knew the outcome in an instant, but viewers at home were not certain what had happened.

Members began rising and asking the speaker's permission to explain their votes. One representative protested the action. "We come across like a bunch of politicos out to get the governor," he said. Another solemnly announced that he was voting for impeachment so the governor could have a chance to clear his name in the senate.

Bill English explained his vote against impeachment thus: "This [vote] should not be construed whatsoever as an endorsement of the questionable ethics, impropriety, naiveté, and downright stupidity surrounding many actions of the governor and of the governor's staff, which have created this unconscionable situation."

Leslie Whiting Johnson had been shocked when the board lit up with so many ayes. She rose and said, "What I understand . . . is what my heart tells me, and for that reason, I vote no."

Art Hamilton did not explain his vote. When he saw the margin, he was "surprised and pleased." He knew how much thought, energy, and pain had gone into the decision to impeach. He had seen members agonize over this vote.

Then Mark Killian rose. "Mr. Speaker, I rise to explain my vote." Lane recognized him. "I may have made some mistakes," Killian began, "and I'll admit that here; but I did try to be fair and to be open-minded." His voice now rose in pitch. "I resent Evan Mecham and everything he stands for. The way I was raised is nothing at all the way I see Mr. Mecham conduct his affairs.

"But yet I do understand, as some have suggested, that even the common criminal is allowed a fair hearing, more due process, and I have set, as my standard, clear and convincing evidence. . . ."

He said he objected to the house's not having followed precedent from the earlier impeachments. "I only ask, What is the rush?" He saw no reason why a vote could not be delayed. "This is the most important decision I'll ever make, and I don't feel I've had the time to really study the facts.

"I'm not so sure that Governor Mecham is worthy of the support of any Republican in the state. He has continually skated along life following the lowest common denominator of social behavior, and that's barely eking by the law.

"He can best be described by a man I admire greatly, . . . Stan Turley, as being an ethical pygmy. And his outlandish, rude, classless, John Birch accusations that he made against Mr. Skelly today turn my stomach, and Mr. Skelly, I am sorry"—Killian now broke into tears—"that anyone in the high office of governor of this state would conduct himself in such a manner, and from the bottom of my heart, Mr. Skelly"—now his voice dropped to a hoarse whisper—"I am sorry."

Killian could not continue. He lowered the microphone and rubbed his nose with the back of his hand several times. He massaged the microphone, and he tried to compose himself. He attempted to resume, then removed a handkerchief and began wiping his eyes under his glasses.

After a solid minute of silence he raised the microphone, and when he spoke, his voice was an octave higher. "Mr. Skelly is a man I respect—and love. He has helped me in my legislative career beyond belief. And I can't understand why the governor did what he did."

Now he removed his glasses and began wiping his eyes with his handkerchief as he continued in a strained voice. "I cannot condone his actions. Whatever happens, I hope, that when the senate does conduct [hearings] . . . they can get to the bottom of the truth.

"But again, as I have said, in my own mind clear and convincing evidence is not there on the three issues, so I have to oppose this vote." He replaced his microphone and sat down.

During his speech the unflappable Jim Skelly was turned partially away. Later he said had he made eye contact with Killian, he would have broken into tears. Now he cupped his hands across his eyes and leaned on the desk as others explained their votes.

Bill French had watched Mecham "talk himself into corners" before the select committee. He had watched Mecham "outright lie." Now he sat in the gallery and watched this historical event. He knew that if Mecham were impeached, he would be stripped of his power. That was his secret weapon. Once he was powerless, French believed the "senate would not put him back in office." As he listened to the speeches, he said to himself, "If we can get this vote, he's gone."

Steve Benson had attended some of the hearings with reporters from the *Republic*. At that moment he was watching the vote on television at the paper. He was standing with a group and thinking about the next day's cartoon. When the vote was finished, he felt a sense of "relief and cleansing" just as he had when he signed the recall petition.

The tote board was at last full. There was a long pause as Joe Lane spoke to one of his clerks. Whenever a bill passes, there are certain routines that occur, and it was these he was performing. But the routines ended. He stood erect and paused as if to reflect.

Since October, when he had announced the hiring of Bill French, Joe Lane had been the recipient of more abuse than any public official in state history. Because he was a rancher from a rural county and because this was his first term as speaker, he had not been well known. Now he was one of the best-known figures in the state. His simple statements and forthright manner had served to keep the eyes of the state on the ball. Mecham had squirmed and attacked. He had just that week called Joe Lane a liar.

With dignity and common decency Lane had weathered the abuse, and now in his southwestern drawl he spoke the most momentous words of his life and of the political life of Arizona: "By your vote of 46 ayes, 14 nays, you have passed House Resolution 2002. Signed in open session the clerk is instructed to record the action of the House and convey the Resolution to the Secretary of State."

With those words, Evan Mecham, governor of the state of Arizona, was impeached for high crimes, misdemeanors, or malfeasance in office.

# PART FOUR

§1. *Power of impeachment in house of representatives; trial by senate*
   *Section 1. The House of Representatives shall have the sole power of impeachment. The concurrence of a majority of all the members shall be necessary to an impeachment. All impeachments shall be tried by the Senate, and, when sitting for that purpose, the Senators shall be upon oath or affirmation to do justice according to law and evidence, and shall be presided over by the Chief Justice of the Supreme Court. . . .*

§2. *Conviction; grounds for impeachment; judgment; liability to trial*
   *Section 2. No person shall be convicted without a concurrence of two-thirds of the Senators elected. The Governor and other State and judicial officers, except justices of courts not of record, shall be liable to impeachment for high crimes, misdemeanors, or malfeasance in office, but judgment in such cases shall extend only to removal from office and disqualification to hold any office of honor, trust, or profit in the State. The party, whether convicted or acquitted, shall, nevertheless, be liable to trial and punishment according to law.*
   —Arizona State Constitution

> *Evan Mecham is not an ogre or a monster.*
> *Be sure you say that.*
> —SAM STANTON *to author*
>
> *I've never seen anyone crucified so. I admire*
> *you.*
> —*Mecham supporter to*
>    *governor following*
>    *house impeachment vote*
>
> *Some of them are having plastic surgery, I*
> *don't mean here, but in Japan.*
> —EVAN MECHAM *in defense*
>    *of his "round eyes"*
>    *remark*

# 38

It was apparent the members were too emotionally drained to proceed further. The leadership put the technical matters relating to the impeachment over until Monday. As the representatives filed out, the house was silent. There was no crowing or posturing. The lawmakers interviewed were glum and unhappy. People just wanted to go home.

When at last Joe Lane could think about what had happened that night, he felt an immense sense of release. It was "finally done" as if he had "ended a journey." He arrived home where Sue Lane had purchased a bottle of champagne in celebration. Lane sat there and relived the day for her, feeling "drained and exhausted." Afterward he sat in silence without a smile. They never opened the bottle.

Joe Lane described it as "a night of complete sadness." Sue Lane watched her husband, and it seemed to her that he had just come from a funeral.

Across the mall in the senate building members had been watching the house vote. Each district has two representatives as well as one senator, and there is often a close relationship among them. Districts tend to be heavily Republican or heavily Democratic, so more often than not all three legislators are of the same party.

The size of the house vote came as an absolute shock. Few senators will acknowledge they watched the voting. They had been advised by senate counsel some weeks before not to attend the house hearings. As the house had consumed itself with the impeachment inquiry and vote, a wall had descended between it and the senate. Contact between members was reduced dramatically and depended almost entirely on personal friendship.

Immediately after the house vote Evan Mecham called Senate President Carl Kunasek and informed him that he had been impeached. Joe Lane had been Mecham's adversary for a very long time, but Kunasek was close to the governor. He had been soundly criticized in the press and by members of his caucus for that loyalty.

Mecham told Kunasek he wanted an immediate trial in the senate. It was essential that he be cleared so he could get back to governing the state. Kunasek felt that honoring his request was the least he could do.

Mecham had learned of the news in Lake Havasu City, where he was delivering a speech to the Mohave County Republican party. Interrupted by several standing ovations, he proclaimed, "I now have the path open to clear myself of any of the charges. We can go from the grand jury and the one-sided hearing in the legislature in the house to a place where finally we'll choose up sides and it will be an even fight!"

Then, with fire in his eyes, thinking no doubt of the vote to come in the senate, he said, "It would be wise for anyone in office to be intimidated by the voters enough to listen to them, because they have a habit, when you're not intimidated enough to listen, they will replace you with someone who is."

Joe Lane had already tried to call Secretary of State Rose Mofford. Art Hamilton came in to see the speaker. He was in a very aggressive mood. He wanted to know who was going to prosecute the case in the senate. Rick Collins said that of course, Bill French and Paul Eckstein would; they had worked well together in the house. Lane agreed, and Hamilton was satisfied.

At about 8:00 P.M. Collins went looking for Jim Ratliff to have him join the meeting in the speaker's office. He found Ratliff on the telephone in the security office on the first floor, talking to Mecham in Lake Havasu City.

Governor Mecham asked Ratliff, "What's the ruling now on stepping down?"

Ratliff explained what he knew. Mecham said, "Fine." It seemed to Ratliff that Mecham was taking it very well. "We'll go from here," the governor said.

Sam Stanton was appalled at what the state was going through. He had counted thirty-eight votes for impeachment until Mecham launched into his attack on Skelly. The reporters had a pool on the vote, and Stanton had won with forty-six. He could not believe that the governor had just been impeached.

The next day Stanton called the Mecham supporters "who were still talking" to him and gathered comments. He wrote a piece for Monday with the headline ARIZONA WEPT, NATION WATCHED. He told Laurie Roberts that he just did not have it. There was not another story in him. He gave it up and went home.

Bill French and Paul Eckstein drew up the final thirteen-page draft of the articles of impeachment that weekend. They labored over them because it was important they be right. They took seventeen accusations and broke them into three articles.

The articles began:

The duly elected Board of Managers of the House of Representatives of the Thirty-Eighth Legislature of the State of Arizona, by the authority of the Arizona Constitution and House Resolution 2002, presents these Articles of Impeachment to the Senate of the State of Arizona.

Evan Mecham has served as Governor of the State of Arizona since January 5, 1987. To qualify as Governor, he took and subscribed to the oath of office required by Arizona Revised Statutes ("A.R.S.") Section 38-231, and thereby swore to support the Constitution of the United States and laws of the State of Arizona, and to faithfully and impartially discharge the duties of the Office of Governor.

Evan Mecham, while acting in his official capacity, has violated the high duties imposed upon him by the Office of Governor and by his solemn oath, and has committed high crimes, misdemeanors, or malfeasance in office in the State of Arizona, as set forth in the following Articles:

### ARTICLE 1
#### (Obstruction of Justice)

A. On or about November 15, 1987, Evan Mecham, while acting in his official capacity as Governor of the State of Arizona, knowingly attempted, by means of misrepresentation or intimidation, to obstruct, delay or prevent the communication of information or testimony relating to a violation of a criminal statute to the Arizona Attorney General by ordering the Director of the Arizona Department of Public Safety, Colonel Ralph Milstead, not to cooperate with the Attorney General's investigation into allegations concerning a threat by Lee Watkins directed against Donna

Carlson and/or by transferring Lieutenant Beau Johnson from the
Governor's security force, all in violation of A.R.S. Section 13-
2409. . . .

It concluded:

> "As set forth in the foregoing Articles, Evan Mecham has
> committed high crimes, misdemeanors, or malfeasance in office,
> and thus has acted in a manner contrary to public trust and his
> oath as Governor, and in violation of and contrary to the Consti-
> tution and laws of the State of Arizona, all to the great prejudice
> of the cause of law and justice, and to the manifest injury to the
> people of the State of Arizona. . . ."

Paul Eckstein believed French had taken the wrong path from the
beginning. He attributed it to French's background as a federal prosecutor
and as a judge. Had Eckstein been in on the investigation from the first, he
would not have emphasized criminal wrongdoing. He would have focused
on malfeasance and argued that it was not necessary to demonstrate that
Mecham had broken any law. Once you proceed down the road of alleging
that the governor has committed crimes, you lay the groundwork for the
opponents to argue the matter must be settled by a criminal court.

Though it was the Democrats' desire that Eckstein have equal footing
with French, Eckstein acknowledges that simply was not possible initially.
French had lived and breathed this case for months. Eckstein was playing
catch-up. In the three weeks before the start of the senate impeachment
trial Eckstein and his attorneys at Brown & Bain reviewed the material to
get on top of it. If French and he were not equal cocounsel, by the start of
the trial no one could tell.

The Saturday following the house vote Mecham continued his election-
style sweep of rural Arizona. In quick succession he flew to Willcox, Benson,
and Sunsite. In Joe Lane's backyard he said he had been impeached because
"they were afraid the people would keep me in office [in the recall election]."
He said he was being removed by "a few people in downtown Phoenix."
That night he appeared on the same stage with Joe Lane and watched his
nemesis receive the local Republican party's Man of the Year Award.

On Monday, February 8, 1988, the Board of Managers reviewed the
draft articles and made some changes in them. Shortly thereafter the house
of representatives formally adopted the three articles of impeachment. Representative Heinze Hink, a World War II veteran of the Wehrmacht and
member of the Board of Managers, officially carried them over to President

Carl Kunasek. A clearly distressed Kunasek told Hink and the gaggle of reporters and cameramen following him to wait in the lobby.

Kunasek considered the impeachment ill advised. He had been overwhelmed by the size of the vote and thought it spelled doom for the governor in the senate.

He had sent word to Joe Lane that he wanted to talk to him before there was a house vote, and had been refused. It seemed to Kunasek that impeachment could have waited until after the recall election and the governor's criminal trial. Mecham was virtually ineffective by this time, and the state could have tolerated a few months of embarrassment while those two events took place. If there was still a need for impeachment, the summer was soon enough.

Both critics and allies of Kunasek disdain such logic and say it simply reflects his lack of will to carry out his constitutional duty. The recall election had nothing to do with whether or not Mecham had committed impeachable acts, and his Superior Court trial concerned itself with only one of the articles. The state could not have an accused criminal as chief executive.

Kunasek's logic ignores the reality that if Mecham had won a recall election—not out of the question considering the crowded field—there would have been no political will to hold him accountable for what appeared to be impeachable acts. In addition, Mecham would have believed himself vindicated, and there would have been hell to pay.

The Monday following the house impeachment vote, the same day the house voted the articles of impeachment and transmitted them to the senate, Murray Miller called Kunasek and asked, "What can we do to slow this thing down?"

It was apparent to Kunasek that Miller did not know about Mecham's call to him on Friday. He told Miller there was nothing he could do. Over the weekend he had established dates, lined up support in the caucus, made public announcements. It was too late suddenly to back off and drag his heels.

That same Monday the Republican party chairman, Burton Kruglick, and the Democratic party chairman, Sam Goddard, jointly issued a public call for calm. A pastor appearing on KTAR talk radio had voiced support of the impeachment vote, and his church had been vandalized. Over that weekend Mecham Pontiac had also been vandalized, and someone had discharged a shotgun into Mecham's home while he and his wife slept.

An *Arizona Republic* editorial pointed out that Mecham's home had been the target of vandals throughout his administration and that he had suffered two break-ins by apparent burglars. The paper called for round-the-clock protection of Mecham and his residence.

*  *  *

The senate convened as a court of impeachment. The chief justice of the Arizona Supreme Court, who was to preside over the trial, was sworn, as were all of the senators. Senate Majority Leader Hal Runyan, who had suffered a stroke in November, was wheeled in for the first time since then and received a standing ovation as he joined the body to be sworn.

Mecham had been right when he charged there were senators too biased to be fair. Two of the senators were so prejudiced they initially expressed reservations about taking the oath.

Wayne Stump was a loyal Mecham supporter with views even more extreme in many regards than Mecham's, though with a congenial manner and reputation for integrity. Jeff Hill opposed impeachment of any Republican governor for any reason and made it clear he would not vote in favor of impeachment no matter what he heard during the trial. During a closed caucus he had declared, "I don't care if Evan Mecham is guilty of having sex with a yellow dog in the intersection of McDowell and Central"; he would not vote for conviction because the governor was prolife and antitax.

The men met with the leadership, and the nature of the oath was explained. Hill was adamant. A Catholic, he said he could no more vote for impeachment than he could switch religions. Finally, he was asked if God had descended from heaven and told him to switch, would he do it? He said if it came to that, certainly he would switch. With that, and his belief that God would have to appear personally to instruct him to vote aye, Hill took the oath, as did Stump.

# 39

The senate had quietly begun preparation for a trial shortly before the house vote. In early February the senate retained attorney John Lundin to serve as special impeachment counsel. Lundin worked quietly behind the scenes. As the senate's lawyer he was available to explain the law to the senate or to any senator and during the trial to advise on how to frame questions.

The state supreme court had also begun discreet preparations. While the house was conducting its public hearings, Chief Justice Francis X. Gordon, a Democrat appointed from the rural community of Kingman in northwestern Arizona, consulted with the vice chief justice. Two law clerks were then assigned to prepare memorandums on impeachment. The clerks attended part of the house hearings to develop a feeling for what was taking place. Gordon read the prepared material for two weeks.

Prior to the articles of impeachment Gordon advised Kunasek that he was ready to proceed if it came to that. The senate president invited the chief justice and his two clerks over for a talk. Lundin was also present, and they discussed the nature of the rules that would be necessary during any senate trial. The chief justice's clerks and Lundin then coordinated the preparation of the rules of procedure that governed the senate trial.

The Arizona constitution required that the senate convene as a court

311

of impeachment within ten days of receiving articles of impeachment. There would be little enough time to prepare once the articles were voted out of the house. Because no one wanted to give an impression that impeachment was a foregone conclusion, this preparation was done with extreme discretion.

Senator Greg Lunn had watched the first tentative conversations concerning impeachment in the Senate Republican caucus and wondered where it would go. When serious preparations had begun, he feared that Kunasek would attempt to delay matters, but that did not occur. As the events unfolded, it became clear to Lunn that Kunasek had enormous integrity.

Immediately after the senate had been convened as a court of impeachment, it met behind closed doors to discuss the proposed rules. The senate then met in public and adopted the rules without debate. The counsel for the house Board of Managers—French and Eckstein—and the counsel for the governor—Murray Miller—were given no opportunity to challenge the rules.*

At this time Gordon delivered a message, directed more to the people of Arizona than to the senators. It was believed to be in response to Mecham's call for to his supporters to "work on intimidating your representatives. . . ."

Gordon said, "You citizens of Arizona placed these people in office because you trusted their judgment and their integrity. Now you must let them do their jobs. . . . Pressuring your senator to vote based on anything other than his evaluation of the law and evidence is in effect pressuring your senator to violate the oath to uphold the Constitution."

Mecham supporters immediately attacked Gordon for attempting to deny them their First Amendment right to free speech.

---

*The rules of procedure were only occasionally the source of argument during the senate impeachment trial. They were carefully crafted from the 1964 Arizona senate impeachment trial and from recent impeachments in Alaska and Oklahoma. They were a mixture of rules of procedure and traditions that governed judicial courts, thus directing the trial along judicial lines. Governor Mecham had the right to be present, the right to summon witnesses, the right to testify in his behalf or not to testify. The chief justice served as the presiding officer and made all preliminary rulings. The court of impeachment sat as judge and jury. It had the right to reverse the presiding officer by majority vote. Free daily transcripts were provided to the senators, the governor, and the house Board of Managers. An individual senator could have any issue submitted to the entire senate for vote. A standard of proof of clear and convincing was established. This is a middle standard between preponderance and beyond a reasonable doubt. The rules did not allow any senator to be challenged on his right to sit, nor could any senator, member of the Board of Managers, or counsel for either side be called as a witness. Any senator could request a closed meeting of the court of impeachment. After a great deal of controversy concerning the possibility of secret agreements, closed meetings were quickly abandoned. The court of impeachment met in camera only twice, once to debate the rules and the second time to amend the rules to the governor's advantage. The rules could be waived or amended by a two thirds vote of the senators. Finally, after traditional examination, cross-examination, redirect, and recross, the senators could ask any question they wished. Only a vote of the majority of the court of impeachment could prevent a question by an individual senator. This did not occur.

* * *

In the house Joe Lane had made a conscious decision to transform the speaker's investigation into a bipartisan effort that was essential for an impeachment vote. In the senate the same transformation occurred, not in response to political reality but rather because of the state constitution and the necessities surrounding an impeachment trial.

When the senate organized itself as a court of impeachment, most of the old senate practices no longer applied. Gordon had indicated at once that he did not believe it was appropriate for the court of impeachment to begin each day with prayer. Kunasek settled that by calling a session of the senate, opening with prayer and the pledge of allegiance, as was customary, and then having the senate stand as the court of impeachment. Kunasek took his place with the other senators.

Exercising this senate perk did not alter the fundamental change that occurred when the senate sat as a court. The traditional senate leadership was no longer in place. Instead, the leaders sat and dealt with the trial among a body of thirty. Party differences were reduced dramatically, though not eliminated.

Gordon served as the presiding officer and brought a judicial presence that served as a constant reminder to the senators that this was a matter of profound significance. The effect of these changes was genuinely to transform the senate into a responsible body concerned with carrying out its constitutional mandate. It was definitely not business as usual.

Francis X. Gordon had been a member of the state supreme court since 1975 and had been sworn in as chief justice the same day he administered the oath of office to Evan Mecham. Gordon had been at odds with Mecham from the time the new governor took office. Shortly after becoming chief justice, Gordon joined the unanimous court in awarding judgment to the young woman customer who had sued Mecham Pontiac. Mecham had accused the "cotton-picking" court of a "total miscarriage of justice" in finding against him.

Within weeks of taking office Mecham had refused to appoint a new supreme court justice from the list of three names submitted to him by the Commission on Appellate Court Appointments. Gordon had chaired the commission and publicly accused Mecham of trying to politicize the process. Mecham had relented when he learned he could not pack the commission with his own appointees, and he had selected the only Republican of the three candidates.

Gordon had a private meeting with Mecham to discuss the judicial selection process, but for ten minutes Mecham lambasted the court's recent decision against him. The chief justice found himself defending the opinion instead of resolving the selection issue.

For the first six months of the Mecham administration Gordon and the new governor clashed on a variety of issues. In November Gordon had refused to remove the attorney general's staff from its investigation of Mecham. Gordon wrote the court's opinion that no conflict of interest existed. This led to Mecham's indictment.

It was not expected that these differences would affect Gordon's conduct as the presiding officer. His reputation for judicial integrity was impeccable. In the most recent state bar survey of lawyers Gordon had received a perfect 100 percent for integrity.

It is fair to say that newspaper and, to a lesser extent, television coverage had influenced the events of the past year leading up to the senate impeachment trial. Supporters of the governor tried to paint the print coverage as uniformly anti-Mecham. They focused on the *Arizona Republic* and the Phoenix *Gazette*. In fact, the coverage of the state's other dailies did not differ significantly from that of the two leading papers.

Contrary to the oft-repeated accusations, both papers routinely covered customary state government news. If they failed to give the kind of attention to Mecham's "positive" accomplishments, it was because there were so few. Most of what Mecham touted as his accomplishments were little more than ham-handed public relations moves. Mecham was big on tokenism, not just in occasional appointments but in announcing programs that never went beyond organizational meetings.

And Mecham used the press to great effect. He wanted to get his message out, and that he did. He seemed unable to accept the fact that the public generally rejected that message. He wrote articles for at least two newspapers in the state to bypass what he perceived as the bias of reporting.

Besides running his own column, Mecham's numerous pronouncements received wide dissemination, but the fact that his daily conduct as governor could not stand scrutiny was also something Mecham failed to understand. He was so certain in his belief that Pat Murphy and the "Phoenix Newspapers" were out to get him he could not accept his own shortcomings.

Mecham tried to counter what he took to be bad press by turning to television. However, his version of events shifted often, and his testy, ill-tempered responses to even routine questions required an act of faith to accept what he said.

With the beginning of house hearings and now with the start of the senate impeachment trial, television played an increasingly important role in his dying administration. The proceedings were covered live statewide. No longer could Mecham blame the press. He was there for the state to watch.

Mecham was not only the first governor in fifty-nine years to be impeached but also the first governor to be impeached on live television.

The people of Arizona could not get enough of the spectacle. The house impeachment vote had been seen by 96 percent of those watching television. People hurried to take care of business during the recesses from the proceedings. Nothing in Arizona history was watched with more devotion, amusement, and horror than the impeachment of Evan Mecham.

Television itself affected the events. When legislators spoke, they were as likely to address the camera as the person to whom they were ostensibly speaking. During each recess legislators checked their offices for messages, and some instructed their secretaries to stack those into for and against Mecham piles.

One chain-smoking senator was shocked to learn her habit was catching the attention of so many constituents. Senators customarily wander around during proceedings, engaging in quiet discussions, stretching and kicking their shoes off under their desks. This came to an end in response to viewer protests. The senate was very aware of the cameras.

For the first time most Arizonans knew their respective state lawmakers and watched the processes of government. There are those who rose in public esteem because of their conduct during the impeachment, others whose careers ended as a consequence.

On February 15 the much loved and admired House majority leader Jim Ratliff was hospitalized following a stroke. Joe Lane was informed within days that he was not expected to leave the hospital.

Ratliff had been tortured by the impeachment process, divided as he was between his loyalty to Governor Mecham and his loyalty to Speaker Lane. A measure of this conflict was that Ratliff made the motion to impeach Evan Mecham, then voted against it.

The senate court of impeachment granted Murray Miller a one-week delay in the start of the trial and set as a firm date Monday, February 29. Exactly one week earlier Miller learned that a Washington, D.C., attorney, Jerris Leonard, had been hired and was in Phoenix asking questions. Miller was told that Leonard and Fred Craft had spent five hours the day before with another attorney.

The next day Miller called Michael Scott, the lawyer who was handling Willard Mecham's criminal defense. Scott had attended law school with Craft. Miller asked Scott what he knew about Jerris Leonard. Scott told Miller that Leonard was with him at that very moment, and within two hours Leonard and Scott were at Miller's office.

Leonard informed Miller that he was taking charge of Mecham's defenses. He asked Scott to leave the room and then told Miller that Mecham could not afford him any longer. If Miller was interested in doing any work on the criminal trial, they would need to know his rate.

Leonard told Miller that Michael Scott was taking over the criminal defense of both Willard and Evan Mecham. If a second lawyer was needed, they would hire an inexpensive "briefcase attorney" to handle it.

Miller agreed to introduce Leonard as new counsel. When they met the next day, Miller told Leonard that Scott had told him Scott was *not* representing the governor. In addition, since Leonard knew absolutely nothing about either case, Leonard said it would verge on malpractice for Leonard to represent Mecham. The impeachment trial was to begin in just a few days, and there were boxes of material that required review. Leonard suggested that maybe he just ought to pack his bags and return to Washington.

When Miller called Scott and established that Scott was not representing Mecham in the criminal trial, Leonard told Miller, "Okay, you'll represent the governor on the criminal trial."

Miller asked, "What about the impeachment trial set for Monday, the twenty-ninth?"

Leonard said he would get that continued. Miller had just been through this fight with the senate and knew that was out of the question.

Miller called Gordon and told him there was a new attorney on the case who wanted to argue for another continuance. The senate voted to allow Leonard as counsel and denied the request for a continuance even though Gordon said the request was not unwarranted. The senate clearly believed that Leonard's late appearance was a ploy to stall the impeachment trial. That same day it was disclosed that Fred Craft had also been hired to assist in the governor's defense despite the fact that he was scheduled to appear as a witness on the obstruction of justice article.

Early Thursday afternoon Evan Mecham called Miller and asked to meet him at Miller's office. Mecham was "sheepish" as he spoke to Miller. He said, "Murray, they want you off the team. They don't think you'll cooperate with them."*

---

*Murray Miller relates that Evan Mecham came to see him in February 1989, one year after these events. He asked Miller's advice concerning his filing an action against Craft and Leonard for malpractice. Mecham allowed Miller to tape their conversation. He then told Miller that Craft had approached him and said he had a "hotshot lawyer who could really do a job" for him. Craft told Mecham he would put together a team of professionals and made a number of assurances. Mecham said he had been shocked that Craft had abruptly resigned his position as special assistant for the governor's office in Washington, D.C. Mecham had raised a significant war chest by this time to pay for his defense. Mecham told Miller that Craft resigned so he could represent the governor without a conflict and bill the war chest. Mecham told Miller that Craft had informed him that Miller planned to walk out on him after telling the senate he was not prepared. Mecham told Miller he had had no idea that Craft planned to defend him on the obstruction of justice article. He had been shocked since he knew Craft was a witness in the incident. Mecham told Miller that he believed he had been deceived by Craft, a man he had come to rely on very heavily. Miller knew from his many conversations with Mecham that the former governor had great faith in Craft. Mecham later filed an action with the Arizona Supreme Court alleging, among other things, inadequate counsel by Craft and Leonard.

Miller believed he had been extraordinarily cooperative given the high-handed treatment to which he had been subjected. He withdrew and was granted permission by the court of impeachment to address the body to let it know this was not a delaying ploy on his part.

The Monday following the impeachment vote, Mecham met with Rose Mofford and agreed to vacate his office. All security was oriented toward the Ninth Floor, and her new demands as acting governor required more space than she had as secretary of state. She offered him offices where he had worked during the transition, but he declined, preferring instead to work out of his Glendale office. This building had been his former residence, moved and converted into a sort of office building next to a Mormon church and across the street from a farm.

When Mofford's staff occupied the Ninth Floor, they discovered it nearly stripped. Even the telephone books and dictionaries had been taken. The governor's private telephone number had been transferred to Mecham's Glendale office. Mecham had also taken a new computer with him and left behind a bill for twelve thousand dollars from a service that provided copies of nationwide news articles.

Mofford immediately placed Max Hawkins on administrative leave, then at Mecham's request transferred him to work with the governor in Glendale. Mecham was provided with state-paid secretaries, but some feared that since he now had no duties, he would be using state employees to work on his recall election campaign.

Within the week Mecham was upset that Mofford had countermanded his order that all mail sent to the governor go first to him. He said he "cannot accept" that she would screen the mail first, then send it to him in Glendale the same day. Mecham supporters deluged the U.S. Postal Service with complaints that Mofford was breaking the law. Within days Mecham was accusing Mofford of dismantling his administration.

In Tucson an "emotionally distraught" Mecham aide gutted the governor's satellite office, even hauling away the flags and prying the state seal off the wall. He informed a state employee "that he was told by the governor to leave the walls bare."

When the senate declined to delay his impeachment trial, Mecham appeared on KTAR radio and said, "If we give in to these kind of powers that really are working to perform a coup in Arizona to replace a constitutionally elected governor . . . this country is going down the tubes."

Shortly before the start of the trial two thousand people showed up at a Bash for Mecham picnic to raise funds for his defense. Mecham delivered a speech to the enthusiastic crowd in which he said he did not hate anyone for what was taking place, "the ones we ought to hate aren't worth hating." He said, "God will do all the getting even we need."

On February 19 former Congressman John Rhodes announced that he was a candidate for governor in the scheduled recall election. "I just don't want to see the state go down the drain," he said. Barry Goldwater announced he would serve as honorary campaign manager. By this time 106 individuals had taken out petitions to run for governor, including a death row inmate and the rock star Alice Cooper, who had attended high school in Phoenix.

The Friday before the start of the impeachment trial the Arizona Supreme Court, without Gordon's participation, refused to intervene and order a delay. Mecham had argued the impeachment trial violated his constitutional rights to a fair criminal trial.

Mecham was calling senators to speak about issues other than the impeachment trial, prompting Kunasek to write a letter to Mecham asking that he refrain from such calls for the duration of the senate trial.

> *[Mecham]'s a political drunk driver. He was
> intoxicated with power and operating without
> good judgment or a conscience.*
> —E. J. MONTINI,
> Arizona Republic
> *columnist*

> *I saw fear on faces today.*
> —*Unidentified Democratic
> senator at beginning
> of impeachment trial*

# 40

According to Fred Craft, he never intended to assist in the defense of Evan Mecham. He had counseled Mecham that the governor needed the best attorney possible. Mecham had given him the go-ahead to recruit one. He approached several lawyers, including Griffin Bell and James Neal. He knew Jerris Leonard, who had been a good friend of former U.S. Attorney General John Mitchell and suggested he represent Mecham. Leonard met with Mecham in a Phoenix hotel room and agreed to take over the case.

Craft considered Miller a "self-promoter" and was concerned about the quality of representation Mecham was receiving especially since Miller ran a "one-man shop." Craft believed French was using twelve to fifteen people. The governor simply had to have a larger team.

According to Craft, the Thursday before the start of the impeachment trial Leonard called him and said that Miller was off the team. They talked options, but the bottom line was that if Craft did not assist, Leonard was off the case. Craft knew that Mecham was upset with him for resigning as the governor's representative in Washington, D.C. when Rose Mofford took over as acting governor. He flew out that Friday and learned that there had been no delay in the trial. It would start Monday.

Craft was concerned because no one remaining on board knew the players. Over that weekend they took a crash course. Their strategy consisted of Craft's taking the first article, stalling for time, while Leonard boned up on the next one. Christina Johnston contacted them, and Sunday night Craft took a sworn statement from her.

At 8:57 A.M. on February 29, 1988, the fiftieth day of the thirty-eighth Arizona Legislature, Chief Justice Francis X. Gordon called the impeachment trial to order. DPS security, which had been braced for large crowds, was surprised at the small turnout.

Mecham had elected not to be present that first day and except for the final session did not appear unless called upon to testify. Gordon had been a judge for so many years he was uncertain about his new role. The court of impeachment rules provided that all of Gordon's rulings were provisional and could be overturned by a majority vote. Gordon was not accustomed to being overruled and for the first two or three days of the trial felt his way gingerly.

The trial began much as court proceedings do. The only unusual occurrence was that as the senators took their places, they noticed the ninety-page Christina Johnston statement at each desk. Senator Greg Lunn thought it "seemed to preview a trial that would be in the gutter." It was quickly retrieved and had purportedly been circulated in error.

A sign of things to come took place when Jerris Leonard, the presumably suave Washington, D.C., attorney, turned to French and Eckstein and said, "You're running the show. Toot—toot!," suggesting the impeachment was a railroad job.

Craft was struggling with the flu during his opening statement. He claimed that Mecham was the victim of a "mutiny" by Milstead and Corbin. Craft's voice is high-pitched, and when he gets excited, as he often did during the trial, it rises in intensity. During opening statements Senator Alan Stephens, seated in the front row, remarked that he needed "cotton balls" for his ears. More than one present found Craft's voice to be nauseating.

In French's opening remarks he cautioned the senators to expect attacks on the character of the witnesses because "there is no defense . . . You've got to keep your eyes on the ball," he said, invoking an image from his days of varsity football with Notre Dame. "Look the ball into your hands. Don't be distracted."

That day certain senators complained that all of them had received a flyer from Evan Mecham they considered improper. It quoted Mecham's weekend statement in which he said the state was in a "constitutional crisis."

The same day Mofford fired Max Hawkins for publicly attacking Jim Skelly. Hawkins wanted Skelly brought up before the house Ethics Committee to answer Mecham's racing charges. Mecham attacked Mofford and said she was "totally out of line" for firing Hawkins.

French and Eckstein led off with Officer Frank Martinez, one of the DPS security detail assigned to the governor, for the purpose of testifying on what had taken place the day he learned from Peggy Griffith of her conversation with Horace Lee Watkins and of the events of that weekend.

As was true of all the officers on the governor's security detail, Martinez was of above average intelligence. Shortly after lunch, following his morning testimony, Paul Eckstein asked Martinez about a Sunday-morning telephone call Mecham had made to his home on November 28, 1987. Martinez had already stepped off the governor's detail at that point.

Martinez said, "They suspected bugs that were planted. [Mecham] even said that he had had his own people, a different firm . . . come in and do a sweep. He also said that they believed there were lasers up at his office"— Martinez was smiling now—"and he could—the communication level was up to two miles and things could be monitored up to a two mile radius. . ."

"Was that the last time you spoke with Governor Mecham?" Eckstein asked.

"No sir, it was not." To an incredulous senate Martinez said he had just received a telephone call from Mecham over the noon recess. Once Martinez was on the line, the caller told him to hold for the governor. Martinez considered the implication for a few moments and then hung up. Mecham later said the call had been inadvertent.

The senate sat in stunned silence as Eckstein returned to his place.

On March 3, 1988, Lieutenant Colonel James Chilcoat took the stand. By now Craft's style of cross-examination was established. In his attempt to stall this first article as long as possible, he asked the same questions repeatedly. Senators were complaining from the first day. One senator passing French in the hallway during a break asked under his breath if it would be possible to bring back Murray Miller. Another wanted to impeach Craft.

As Craft questioned Chilcoat, Gordon asked him to keep his voice down. The gallery clapped, and Gordon admonished the spectators.

As the questioning continued in much the same excruciating tenor, a middle-aged man in the gallery suddenly screamed out, "You make me sick! I gotta get out of here!" DPS quickly surrounded him and escorted him out. Later it was reported he had a long history of mental illness.

Gordon called an immediate recess. When they returned, Senator Usdane objected to Craft's tedious, repetitive questioning, saying he should not be allowed to "harass a witness." Gordon sustained the objection but pointed out it was up to French and Eckstein to object.

In fact, the two counsels for the house believed if they allowed Craft to continue as he was without objecting, in time the senators would have had enough. The total effect would be to strengthen their hand and move the entire process along more speedily. French noticed Gordon's inquiring looks from the bench but languidly ignored them.

Chilcoat, who served as legislative liaison for DPS and was well known to the senators, had been contacted by Horace Lee Watkins on Friday night, November 13, 1987. This was at the time the attorney general was investigating Watkins's conversation with Peggy Griffith.

An excited Watkins called Chilcoat at his home after dinner. He said that Governor Mecham had called him, and Watkins wanted to know what was going on with this investigation DPS was doing. Chilcoat did not want to give Watkins any information, so he suggested he call the attorney general. He told Watkins that there was a statewide grand jury in session, and he did not feel comfortable talking to him about it. He suggested again he contact the attorney general.

Asked how long the conversation lasted, Chilcoat replied, "It lasted as short as I could make it."

Chilcoat testified that he had first met Watkins at the Elephant Bar in northwest Phoenix in December 1986, shortly before Mecham took office. Watkins had told Chilcoat that he was slated to receive "a high powered job . . . one of the three top jobs" in the governor's office. He said, "Me and my people have raised a great deal of money and they're going to give me a job on the Ninth Floor."

That night Mecham appeared at a fund raiser at the Arizona State University Activity Center before a supportive crowd of four thousand, far fewer than the capacity of more than fourteen thousand. It was reported that many tickets were given away at the last minute to fill even those seats.

Mecham told an enthusiastic crowd, "You might tell your senator tonight to let the whole world in on what they're reading tonight," referring apparently to the Christina Johnston statement.

The next day Samuel A. Lewis, the director of the Department of Corrections (DOC), testified. Because Watkins worked for Hawkins as Mecham's director of prison construction, Lewis had dealt with him. Lewis and Milstead had worked together at DPS and were known to be friends.

Lewis testified that he first met Watkins when Watkins called him in early 1987 and identified himself as being in the governor's office. Watkins explained that he had been Mecham's biggest fund raiser.

Watkins asked Lewis to reduce the custody status of a state prison inmate because the inmate's father had been a major contributor to the Mecham campaign. Lewis refused, but Watkins persisted, though without success.

Watkins contacted Lewis later and said he was preparing a study on inmate rehabilitation. Lewis did not think Watkins was qualified for such an undertaking and told him so.

On June 9, 1987, Watkins and Lewis met again for lunch at the downtown Phoenix Sheraton. Watkins said he was looking into a job at Corrections.

Lewis had received calls to that effect from others despite his having told Steiger and Hawkins he did not want Watkins as an employee.

Watkins told Lewis again that he had been Mecham's biggest fund raiser and had been responsible for bringing in more than six hundred thousand dollars. He said he had arranged a loan that was still outstanding. According to Lewis, Watkins said, "The more money you raised for the campaign, the higher-level job you received in state government." Watkins bragged to Lewis that he "could bring the entire Mecham administration down."

Watkins also reportedly told Lewis that he was upset that he had not received a satisfactory position with the administration. Lewis was shocked by the conversation, especially when Watkins implied that if something worthy of him were not forthcoming, he would have no reason to keep quiet.

Lewis met with Bob Corbin and Steve Twist on a regular basis as director of DOC and informed them of this conversation. In October 1987 he met personally with Mecham and told the governor that Watkins was incompetent to serve as head of prison construction. He also told Mecham that Watkins was harming the governor and should be fired. According to Lewis, Mecham replied that Watkins "has a lot of energy and he will do us a fine job."

Following Craft's unsuccessful attempts to introduce Lewis's knowledge of a relationship between Christina Johnston and Milstead, the senators asked questions. Senator Peter Kay asked a series of rambling questions concerning prison construction that had nothing to do with the issues at hand. His would not be the last such question. It was as though the senators, having these officials on the stand under oath, could not resist asking whatever interested them.

Watkins told reporters that Lewis was "a lying S.O.B." who was "trying to cover his backside." He bragged that when he took the stand, he would call Lewis "a damn liar." Watkins said that Griffith had "a great imagination." He denied ever intending to harm Donna Carlson. Watkins's testimony was eagerly awaited.

Following Peggy Griffith, Bill French called "adverse witness" Horace Lee Watkins to the stand. With his insinuating grin Watkins took the oath. French went to the podium with a heavy folder.

"Mr. Presiding Officer, members of the Senate. Please state your full name."

"Horace Lee Watkins."

"What is your occupation, Mr. Watkins?"

"I am unemployed, sir." Watkins's barracuda grin blossomed.

"Were you formerly employed in the Mecham administration?"

Watkins paused, then reached into his right coat pocket, took out a piece of paper, unfolded it, and read, "Mr. French, on the advice of counsel

I respectfully refuse to answer any questions, asserting my Fifth Amendment rights."

"Mr. Watkins, you might want to leave that out," French said. The senate laughed.

Watkins leaned into the microphone, said, "I might," then smiled as if he were part of the humor instead of the brunt of it.

"Did you have a conversation with Peggy Griffith on November 12, 1987?"

"On the advice of counsel, Mr. French, I'm asserting my Fifth Amendment rights."

"On that same date did you threaten bodily injury to Donna Carlson?"

"Mr. French, asserting my Fifth Amendment rights, I refuse to answer." Watkins smiled again and held his eyes closed.

"Subsequent to the threats of November 12th did you have occasion to take polygraph examinations in connection with the threats?"

"Mr. French, asserting my Fifth Amendment rights, I refuse to answer."

"Isn't it a fact, sir, that you took six polygraph examinations before you passed . . . one?"

"Mr. French, asserting my Fifth Amendment rights, I refuse to answer on advice of counsel."

"Did you not, Mr. Watkins, spend two full days in a polygraph room where you took six polygraph examinations before you passed the first one?"

Now Dale Anderson, Watkins's lawyer, rose in objection. He asked that his client's Fifth Amendment rights be "vindicated." He told the court that this matter had been before the grand jury for months and Watkins did not know his "fate." Following an exchange among Gordon, French, and Anderson, Watkins said he would answer no questions at all. He was dismissed.

The court of impeachment considered granting Watkins immunity. French argued, saying, "We would be against granting immunity or giving the likes of Mr. Watkins a 'bath,' if you will, for all of the sins he may have committed, many of which we may not know about." Immunity was not granted.*

On March 7 DPS Director Ralph Milstead was called to the stand.

---

*Horace Lee Watkins was never charged for any offense arising from his employment in the Mecham administration. *Footprints* published Watkins's version of his conversation with Peggy Griffith: " 'Peggy and I were just talking in the parking lot after work. I said I couldn't believe that the publisher of the *New Times* could get away with the statement he made on television the other night, that Mecham should be taken in a back alley and pistol whipped,' asserted Watson [sic]. Watkins said he further remarked that, like the *New Times* publisher, 'There are a bunch of nuts out there.' Donna should be careful, [He] said he cautioned her friend Griffith with genuine concern. She was a traitor to the governor and didn't honor her commitments. Watkins said he pointed out. 'She could have problems. There are alot [sic] of crazies running around.' Watkins stressed that his remarks were of a concerned and advisory nature. They did not resemble in any way, nor were they intended to be, a threat, he said. Watkins' attorney, Dale Anderson, also says the allegations are absurd.' "

Mecham's attorneys had made it clear that they intended to attack Milstead's character. There could have been no other reason for trying to introduce Christina Johnston's statement. Gordon had earlier ruled that he would allow her to testify on what she knew of possible motive but that she could not testify on her purported sexual liaisons with the single Milstead since it had no relevance.

The day of his testimony before the Senate, Milstead took security precautions at the insistence of his staff. He drove to the house, waited there, and then used the connecting tunnel to the senate.

Milstead took the stand in a pearl gray pin-striped suit with a dark red striped tie.

The Department of Public Safety retained a psychologist for its use. Milstead consulted with him on several occasions in an attempt to understand Evan Mecham. On the basis of what the psychologist told Milstead it was apparent to him that Mecham was seriously mentally ill. From that point on Milstead considered Mecham "insane" and dealt with him accordingly.

Milstead recalls the direct examination under French went smoothly. Then Craft began his cross. Milstead had concluded that Craft was "a pretty poor attorney" and did not feel intimidated at all. To show his contempt, he turned away from Craft so that he was speaking directly to the senators, men and women with whom he had worked closely for nearly nine years. He had also served on committees with Gordon and knew him well.

As Craft proceeded with the cross, Milstead continued looking elsewhere. Milstead found Craft "unpleasant" and "did not like him." Milstead was enjoying the challenge, though he did not consider Craft a worthy opponent.

Craft's voice rose even for the mundane questions. It often had a screechy edge to it. Throughout, Milstead's voice remained calm and polite. The only sign of real involvement was the occasional bunching of Milstead's jaw muscles.

Despite Milstead's house testimony, the Mecham team still expressed doubts about whether or not the conversation with Mecham had been taped. Craft apparently found confirmation for its suspicions in Milstead's report when he had placed quotation marks around the governor's remarks and not his own.

"Aren't your words as important as the words of the person that you were speaking to?" Craft asked.

"When you write a departmental report . . ."

Craft interrupted. "Would you just answer me whether or not your questions and what you said are of equal importance to what the person you talked to are?"

"No, sir."

"Why?" Craft's propensity for asking questions to which he did not know the answers was no more exposed than here. Milstead had started to explain this was the way he was taught to write reports, but Craft had refused to accept that answer. So now Milstead turned in his chair, looked Craft directly in the eye, and in a steady, dignified voice said, "Because I'm not committing a crime."

In case the senators had missed the point, Craft said, "Because you're not committing a crime?"

"No, sir, I'm not. My words don't constitute a crime."

Milstead had testified to it twice, Craft had repeated it once, but not satisfied, Craft asked, "I see, and when did you draw this conclusion that your words did not constitute a crime but the governor's words did constitute a crime?"

"I'm not obstructing justice."

Leonard had a look of extreme distaste on his face. Craft proceeded with more questions that served to drive home Milstead's point.

French objected to Craft's shouting. Gordon said, "Mr. Craft, our amplification is adequate here. You don't need to raise your voice."

Craft led Milstead through the director's firing of Hawkins some years before for making sexist and racist remarks and causing bad morale at the Department of Public Safety.*

Later Craft asked about Mecham's request that Max Hawkins investigate the Watkins incident. Milstead replied, "Max Hawkins is not a law enforcement officer. He's not competent to investigate it. Watkins works for him, and Max Hawkins wouldn't be taken seriously anywhere on earth that I know of."

Milstead was on the stand for two days. Senator Carolyn Walker rose and pointed out that for the past several hours Craft's questions had had nothing to do with the conversation that was at issue. Craft offered an explanation. Senator Tony West rose to say he did not understand the explanation. West said that the trial was costing twenty thousand dollars a day, and he was receiving calls from the public objecting to Craft's redundant, irrelevant questions.

Leonard exploded and attacked the senators, in particular West. "Governor Mecham didn't bring this action. The house of representatives did. . . . Senator West, I'm sorry I'm not an Arizona taxpayer, and I'm sorry it's costing you twenty thousand dollars a day. The price of liberty and freedom is not cheap. . . ."

This was not the first, nor would it be the last, time when the governor's lawyers apparently forgot just who the jurors were in the trial.

\* \* \*

* Following an administrative appeal, Max Hawkins had been allowed to resign.

French and Eckstein called Watkins's lawyer, Dale Anderson, to testify that Watkins had taken a number of polygraph examinations. Anderson testified that Hawkins was of the opinion that Watkins was being "railroaded." Watkins had failed two tests outright and had inconclusive results on the others. Finally Anderson had called Max Hawkins to discuss the testing. He had recorded the conversation, and the Board of Managers' lawyers had a transcript.

Hawkins had told Anderson, "I love Lee, and I want to save his ass. . . . Screw what [Peggy Griffith] says she said. Just do a quick polygraph on the damn thing and we'll put him back [to work]. And that way, whatever comes down the line, I've got him insulated."

This was Mecham's independent investigation of the Griffith allegations against Watkins.

> *A lot of the rats have come out of their holes*
> *. . . and now we know who they are.*
> — EVAN MECHAM
>
> *We'll never have another leader like Joe Lane.*
> — *State senator,*
> *not for attribution*

# 41

Clandestine meetings were held at different locations in central and north Phoenix to discuss ways in which to persuade Evan Mecham to resign. Present at these meetings were Congressman Bob Stump, Dick Burke, Burt Kruglick, Carl Kunasek, and Tom Sullivan, one of the stalwarts of the Republican party who worked behind the scenes.

Fred Craft was exploring ways out of the situation as well. He believed Mecham would win the recall election and was trying to find a way for him to step down and still run in it. He acknowledges that he met with people to consider options but that nothing came of it. Asked directly if he attended the clandestine meetings, he says only he was willing to talk to find another way out of the disaster.

On March 9 Donna Carlson was called to testify. Following her testimony before the grand jury she had left the state to work on the Bob Dole presidential campaign. She learned Mecham had been impeached while watching the Cable News Network. By the day of her testimony she was "very drained."

She felt sorry for the senators, many of whom she knew well. She and they had worked to put Mecham in office, and now they were conducting an impeachment trial that would very likely remove him.

She knew that Mecham's lawyers were going to attempt to put her private life on trial. She and Milstead had no personal relationship, but she believed there was going to be an effort to suggest one. As a result, she had been mildly apprehensive, but when Craft and Leonard neglected to interview her before her testimony, she lost all respect for them. As she said much later, "The defense lawyers were inept."

She wore a burgundy suit and a high-collar silk blouse, and swept-back hair. For those who knew her the strain was there to see. Testifying in a husky whisper, Carlson established once and for all that she had taken the Watkins threat seriously. She knew that the Mesa Police Department had been summoned to Watkins's home for domestic violence. Her voice choked with emotion as she testified to the events of that weekend.

During his examination of Milstead, Craft had made it clear that he believed the Watkins threat and the attorney general's investigation had been leaked by those officially involved. He had questioned Milstead about possible contacts with Sam Stanton. Mecham routinely complained that he learned of allegations against members of his administration from the *Arizona Republic*.

Now asked what she had done upon learning of the threat, Carlson testified she informed her lawyer and told him he was free to report what she had said should anything happen to her. Next she spoke to a friend, who "told me that sometimes the best action was to make the threat very public. And he felt that was what I should do."

"Did you follow his advice?" Eckstein asked.

"Yes, I did. I called Sam Stanton of the *Arizona Republic*." Stanton's article had appeared in the following day's *Republic*.

Under questioning from Craft she described working on the Ninth Floor as "a three ring circus." She clearly established that Mecham knew of Watkins's background but constantly sought to protect him. At one point she quoted Jim Colter as saying to her, "I don't know why you keep complaining about Watkins, because we have to take care of him. He raised a lot of money for the campaign."

Most damaging of all, Carlson established who was the boss on the Ninth Floor; Evan Mecham.

Now the Cameron Harper interview was shown to the senate. By this point Craft's face was red and motley; Leonard had deep creases around his mouth and bags under his eyes.

French and Eckstein rested the house case on Article I. Craft and Leonard moved to dismiss it. Following argument the senate voted 25 to 4, one not voting,* to deny the motion.

The senate then dismissed Section F of the article, in which the governor was charged with unlawfully transferring Beau Johnson. The argument that the governor had the absolute right to remove anyone on his security detail was persuasive, and the motion passed, 17 to 12, one not voting.

Now the governor began his defense. Richard Burke and Ken Smith

---

*Senator Hal Runyan was intermittently in and out of the hospital during the impeachment trial. Videotapes of the proceedings and copies of all exhibits were taken to him each day. He was not present for this and other votes, with the exception of the final vote on conviction.

testified to the events of that Friday. Then Terri Fields, Peggy Griffith's secretary, was called. She had little to offer except her tough manner, tattoos, and a casual regard for the truth. Under questioning by senators, she acknowledged that her mother worked for Ray Russell, that she herself had been on welfare for a time, and that this, in her view, made her better qualified to perform Griffith's job than Griffith was. One senator pointed out that a statement she had typed was full of errors.

Antonio Corio, a facilities manager with the Department of Administration, was called by the governor's lawyers. Craft attempted to elicit information from him concerning the Watkins-Griffith conversation in the Capitol executive office building with no success. Then he asked if Corio had conducted a sweep of the Ninth Floor looking for electronic surveillance.

Asked what he found, Corio replied, "Not very much."

A clearly angry Craft asked that his own witness be declared hostile, to the amusement of the senate. Gordon declined. Corio testified that Max Hawkins, Lee Limbs, and another man went to the state purchasing office, in an attempt to learn what surveillance equipment the state had, apparently in search of lasers.

A few days later French and Eckstein released an affidavit from Corio in which the timid man said that just before he testified, Craft had told him, "I don't have time to fuck with you! They are going to send the governor to [prison]. Do you know that?" Craft then recited allegations against Milstead.

"I don't want you to tear me up like you have other witnesses," Corio said.

"If you answer my questions, I won't. If you don't, I will."

Fred Craft denied the conversation as reported in the affidavit.

Sam Steiger was called by the governor's team and did him no good either. Steiger testified that Mecham considered himself "divinely inspired" and was reluctant to take advice. Steiger's quick wit and ready disdain for lawyers served primarily as comic relief.

Max Hawkins took the stand in a tortured, restless, rambling recitation of his prejudices and limited vision. At fifty-five, with a wreath of white hair, he looked much older. His evaluation of the threat: Watkins "was blowing off hot air." No matter what questionable act of Watkins was brought to his attention, Hawkins could see nothing wrong with it.

In response to a senator's question Hawkins said he was fearful that Griffith had been bugging their conversation that Friday. Hawkins was suspicious because Griffith's husband worked at DPS and she was being formal as she talked to him.

On Saturday, March 12, Fred Craft conducted a press conference at the Capitol mall with Terri Fields and her ten-year-old son. Following her senate testimony, Fields had been arrested by DPS on an outstanding warrant.* Craft accused Milstead and his "henchmen" of tampering with a witness. "None of us is safe," Craft charged, "and we'd all better think about it."

Gordon was upset at Craft's conduct and called the counsels into his chamber, where he informed them that the rules of professional conduct did apply in this proceeding. He told them they were not to try the case in the press, and he did not want them making statements. Though there were no flagrant abuses thereafter, Gordon was still not entirely happy.

Christina Johnston's fifteen minutes of fame arrived on March 15. The day before, she had been observed in the building dressed in a highly provocative short skirt and transparent blouse. Senator Tony West thought if they put her on like that, it would have been clear what the governor's lawyers were really up to. When Sam Stanton spotted her, he thought, "This is the woman that's supposed to save the governor? No way!"

Ralph Milstead had given a general denial to Johnston's allegations of impropriety against him. He had prepared a press release to offer some explanation of his association with her but decided not to issue it. The problem was that they had been lovers. He could not deny the allegations in any detail without also going into their relationship.

He first met her in 1979, when she was dating a friend of his. He found her "stunning" and was "enthralled by her looks." At that time she was in her mid-thirties. He dated her for about six weeks in 1985, when they both were unattached. They met for lunch two or three times, and they had sex.

Milstead quickly learned that Johnston was incapable of talking about anything other than her nails, makeup, and hair. When she began showing up at his office and making scenes, he realized he had made "a real mistake in judgment." He introduced her to another DPS employee, who started seeing her, and soon they were married. The employee left the department, and Milstead refused to reinstate him because he had failed a psychological test. Shortly after that Johnston started contacting people about testifying against him.

According to Milstead, none of the allegations she made against him was true. He had never been in a hot tub, he had not misused his state vehicle, he had paid for her meals himself, and he had never romanced the wives of fellow officers. Milstead did, however, underestimate Johnston's ability for vindictiveness and tenacity.

Besides the damage Johnston's titillating allegations were doing his professional career, Milstead was especially troubled because he was involved with a woman he loved very much and felt he had to explain to her his relationship with Johnston.

On March 9, when Craft had listed Johnston as a witness, Gordon had

*It later developed the warrant was an error on the part of the court.

ruled that she could not testify to sexual activities or her allegations that
Milstead had intimidated people. She was permitted to offer testimony that
might indicate Milstead's possible motives, but since he had already ruled
that there would be no more cumulative testimony on that issue, it did not
appear she would have much to add.

Craft objected to Gordon's order restricting his examination to narrow
issues when the senators were allowed to ask any question they wished.
Told to proceed, Craft established that Johnston worked as a private investigator, then shortly asked, "And have you had a professional relationship
with [Ralph Milstead] based upon your employment?"

"None at all."

"Have you had a personal relationship with him?"

In her best daytime television voice Johnston said, "Personal and intimate." The gallery murmured.

Eckstein made a series of objections while Craft continued asking
questions that allowed Johnston to employ theatrics. Finally Gordon said to
Craft, "You're allowing her quite a free rein," and suggested more specific
questions.

As Craft solicited questions beyond the scope of Gordon's ruling, Eckstein continued objecting, and the presiding officer repeatedly sustained.
Finally, Craft exclaimed, "Your Honor, I don't understand what's going on
here. I guess maybe I don't know the rules."

Gordon replied, "I think that is a fair statement, Counsel."

By his statements and questions, clearly Craft was soliciting a motion
from the senate to allow him a free hand in questioning Johnston. None was
forthcoming.

Following lunch, Craft pointedly asked the senators to overrule Gordon,
saying, "This is a court of impeachment, not a court of law."

Not a single senator made the motion. Allowed to ask Johnston her
opinion of Milstead's reputation, Craft said, "And now would you tell us
what that opinion is?"

"My opinion is, his attitude towards people that he supposedly likes
and works with and the way he talks about them, huh, he's a liar, he's
corrupt, he's a egomaniac, and he's power-hungry. I'm sorry, but that's the
truth."

Craft said, "I have, obviously, no more questions."

French took the podium. "Mrs. Johnston, I get the impression you
don't like Colonel Milstead, is that correct?"

"Well, you know . . ."

"Do you or do you not?"

"At this time I'm very disgusted with him."

"No more questions."

Within days Christina Johnston had held two informal press conferences in the mall, where she released portions of her statement and preened for the cameras. She appeared on KTAR and vented her allegations against Milstead. She also surrendered herself on a misdemeanor warrant for her arrest for having allegedly claimed to be a state officer while repossessing a car.

The day following her testimony the *New Times* ran a front-page photograph of Milstead in jogging shorts and little else, kissing his girl friend. Posing for the photograph, Milstead later said, was "one of the dumbest things I've ever done." He expressed his regret and stated he was "embarrassed" by it. Coming as it did in the midst of the allegations by Johnston, the appearance was damaging to his image and affected public perception of him as director of the state police. Mofford reportedly instructed him to maintain a low profile, and thereafter he did.

In one instance the senators did overrule Gordon and allowed Craft and Leonard to call a DPS officer who, it turned out, had been on limited duty for some time; he suffered memory lapses, had been suicidal, and was in therapy. He was forced to disclose his medical condition publicly and expressed his pain at doing so. He had nothing to offer the senate except to demonstrate the compassion Milstead exercised toward his officers.

When he was finished, Senator John Mawhinney remarked, "This process is going to destroy a lot of lives. We just worked at destroying one because we didn't listen to [the presiding officer]." The court of impeachment did not overrule Gordon again.

On Wednesday, March 16, 1988, Evan Mecham took the stand in his own defense. Eckstein later acknowledged that he and French had a gentlemen's bet on which of them could get the governor out of his chair first.

They are admittedly sensitive on the subject of how they selected which one would first question Mecham. Eckstein confirms what was rumored: that he took the lead because he was Jewish and they thought it would get under Mecham's skin.

It was apparent by now, two weeks into the trial, that French had been correct: There was no defense. It was up to Mecham to counter the allegation of obstruction of justice against him. He was to testify for three days.

Mecham quickly put to rest any doubts of his intentions toward Ralph Milstead. Asked if he would have fired Milstead if he had known about the director's meeting with Donna Carlson, he replied, "I would have probably relieved her and gone ahead and dismissed him for cause right then if I'd known, you bet."

Mecham acknowledged calling Frank Martinez that Sunday but said it had nothing to do with obstructing justice. "I was disgusted that they'd want to goof up [Martinez]'s Sunday." Mecham denied to Eckstein that he'd ever heard the word "threat" from Beau Johnson when informed of the Griffith allegations against Watkins. Confronted with his contradictory testimony before the house impeachment committee, he admitted having heard the word "threat" but denied having heard "death threat," words Johnson never mentioned using.

Asked about the *Arizona Republic* and the Phoenix *Gazette*, Mecham made his feelings clear. "Pat [Murphy] hates me, and loves and protects [Bob Corbin]."

There was no question of Eckstein's getting under Mecham's skin. In response to Mecham's repeated assertion that he had never been accused of anything more serious than a traffic violation, Eckstein called the governor's attention to three civil suits that accused Mecham of impropriety. Mecham corrected himself and said no one had found him guilty. Eckstein showed him various settlements or judgments against Mecham. As Eckstein moved on to another subject, a visibly angry Mecham shook his finger at Eckstein and said, "You must listen to me, you must listen to me, you must listen to me, you are not going to impugn my integrity!"

During the senators' questioning period, Senator Chuy Higuera, best known until now for brandishing a dead cockroach in the senate chamber while demanding to know why the legislators were so underpaid that he had to live in a cockroach-infested hotel, focused on Mecham's testimony surrounding the transfer of Wence Camacho.

"Did you not ask Officer Johnson if Officer Camacho was part black?"

"No, I did not."

"Isn't it the real reason that you had Camacho transferred because he was too dark?"

"Heavens no, not at all, Senator, not in the least. He wasn't as dark as Frank Martinez. . . ."

"Isn't it the real reason that you transferred Mr. Camacho because he had kinky hair? I know Frank Martinez doesn't."

"Senator, I believe we should talk about that a little bit. I have noticed that you have wondered if there were ethnic slurs on the Ninth Floor with a number of people. . . . I don't look at the quality relative to the color of the skin or the facial figures or anything else. . . . I abhor anything that would be relative to discrimination. . . . I think if you'd look and see the color, the kinkiness of hair and the color, you'd look at a case of Mr. Lee Limbs, Chief Limbs. . . ."

In response to a question by Senator Carolyn Walker, Mecham said, ". . . Organized crime, Senator, is at the basis of the whole system." Senator Tony West wanted to know what Mecham had ever done about organized crime, then, if that was such a pervasive problem, or pornography for that matter. Mecham rambled on and on, but it was apparent he had no programs.

Senator Jaime Gutierrez asked Mecham for a specific example of why he had lost confidence in Beau Johnson. Mecham said, ". . . We later found, and it was verified, that Beau Johnson had handed [the Curtis Report] to the head people at DPS which he had no business getting into Jim [Colter]'s desk or there and taking it." He said, ". . . I have since [Johnson] left had complete confirmation that he was the one that did it. . . ."

On another day of testimony Senator Gutierrez returned to Johnson and the Curtis Report. Mecham said confirmation that Johnson took it was "by one of the officers, high officers in the DPS."

Asked about Horace Lee Watkins's prison background, which included his prison term, Mecham replied, "I think 'criminal background' is a little rough, Senator. I've heard him called a criminal . . . but the background that I knew of in this whole total span of time was that he had had an assault that was a misdemeanor. . . . I really hate to hear the word 'criminal' because that's a pretty serious word."

Explaining his administration's attitude on hiring those with criminal records, Mecham said, ". . . We seldom used anybody who had any charges. . . . We did make some exceptions. . . ."

Asked by Senator Alan Stephens why all these conservative Republicans would launch a campaign to oust him—Mecham had in fact supported Corbin for governor—Mecham said, "Senator, if we really knew that, I suspect some things, but if we really knew that that would be the sixty-four-dollar answer to the sixty-four-dollar question. . . . I wish I knew. . . ."

Senator John Hays returned to Johnson and the Curtis Report, asking how Mecham had confirmed that Johnson took it. "The verification that I got was come from DPS, Senator, that it was him that brought it in."

Senator John Mawhinney also wanted to know exactly how Mecham knew Johnson took the report. Mecham replied, "It was a person in the Department of DPS [sic]." Then again Mecham said, "It was verified by a person at DPS headquarters, Senator."

Here was the governor who had already publicly accused Beau Johnson of perjury in regard to his testimony on his conversation with Mecham repeatedly accusing Johnson of theft without saying on what information he based it. Mecham persisted in the allegation, but he would not name his source.

Senator Tony West now rose to speak. He pointed out they all were individuals of strong feelings and Mecham had such feelings toward Beau Johnson. "[But] in those strong feelings there seems to be some hostility to Lieutenant Johnson . . . and I'd like to know who . . . gave you the information that led you to believe that Lieutenant Johnson took [the Curtis Report] from . . . the Ninth Floor to the Department of Public Safety?"

"Senator, may I correct one thing? I don't have any hostility for Lieutenant Johnson, disappointment, not hostility, there's a great difference there. The other . . . the person that told that—if you would like to call an inquiry into that, I would be glad to furnish you the information—short of that I would rather not do that."

"Governor, I am asking for that name."

"Senator, I'd rather not give you that name."

"Governor, you have brought serious charges against Lieutenant Johnson, some, I think, that could impede his career, certainly some that could throw a light on these proceedings. You talk yourself about shreds of real evidence. I'm asking you for that shred of real evidence in this case and the charges you brought against Lieutenant Johnson to inform this body who that individual was."

"Senator, if there was any part of this case—the decision or necessity to have that information—it would be very simple to do so, and then I think we should go ahead and call in those people who are involved in that. If there was any—if that was really it—and if you desire to do so, certainly we'll cooperate with you, to do so, but, uh, I don't think that it is, under those circumstances, proper for me to do so, under these circumstances, because I see nothing that would assist me. . . . I'll certainly be glad, in any other occasion or at any other time, if we want to look into this—if any of you want to call for an inquiry into that—be most happy to give you all the information I know, and have you call in all the people and be involved."

"Governor, each of us are, [*sic*] unfortunately, forced to make a decision on this particular article . . . based on the veracity of Colonel Milstead or yourself. We have heard Colonel Milstead, we have heard those allegations to discredit him, we have heard you, we have heard those allegations to discredit you and to support you. You have brought charges against Lieutenant Johnson. In my judgment, your veracity is at stake on those charges, and I think that you should tell us who it was that gave you that information."

"Senator, I beg to differ with you. I brought no charges against Lieutenant Johnson. I have not brought charges against him. If I brought charges against him, it would be formally to say he stole something as it was mentioned here off of Jim Colter's office. I have not done that. I included that in a number of things as a pattern of things why I was uncomfortable with him and did not think that he should remain there. Had I really wanted to bring charges I would have done so, and done it while I was up on the Ninth Floor. . . ."

"Governor . . ."

". . . if I, if it should come to that, then it would be a formal hearing."

"Governor, that was my mistake. Perhaps it wasn't charges; certainly it was a serious allegation against Lieutenant Johnson, against his integrity, against his faithfulness to you and to the state of Arizona, if in fact he did the things that are alleged. And for once and the last time, I . . . would like to know who it was that gave you that information."

Mecham was clearly nervous by now. "Senator, I respectfully, uh, uh, will not answer that question under these circumstances."

"Okay, Governor . . . I'm not sure of your prerogatives, but I certainly want our staff to look and see if you have the prerogative not to answer the question when you know the answer."

West now asked how many different people Mecham believed hated him. He asked if Mecham had read the report clearing Jim Skelly of any wrongdoing as concerned the racehorse.

Then: "Mr. Presiding Officer, I'd like to go back to you for a moment, sir, and, if I can, ask you under Rule Twenty-two to direct the witness to answer my question on Lieutenant Beau Johnson."

Leonard rose and said, "Mr. Presiding Officer, may we have a short recess to consult with our client?"

Raucous laughter rolled down from the gallery.

Gordon admonished the spectators. "I would appreciate the gallery not entering into laughter when questions are directed to the chair. . . . I had hoped we would not be brought to this point. . . ." Gordon said he had the authority to direct an answer to a question but believed in this case a vote of a majority of the senators would likely be called upon. "I would like to have you think strongly about that."

"Mr. Presiding Officer," West said, "at this time . . . I will back off of that request. Certainly during the lunch hour let all of us reflect on whether or not that is important to the proceedings because I certainly don't want to put the governor, or anybody else, in the position that would not be proper and appropriate. But I am concerned when the governor of the state of Arizona makes serious allegations that will affect the job of a person in the state of Arizona and then not—under oath—and then not substantiate those with the data that he says that he has."

Beau Johnson had handled the security for the house impeachment hearings and was performing the same job in the senate. Just off the gallery was a command post with a bank of telephones for the media and a television monitor. Johnson spent most of his time in that area.

He was standing in that doorway when Evan Mecham called him a thief. Johnson had no idea the accusation was coming. He thought, [Mecham] must be a desperate man.

To protect a man and his family, it is not necessary to like him or agree with his politics. It is necessary to have human compassion for the people you protect. If it cannot be mustered, transfer.

Until that moment, even when Mecham had accused Johnson of perjury, his residual compassion for Mecham lingered. He had sympathized with him during these times and wished him well.

More than once Johnson had thought of just going to Mecham and explaining what had happened, that he had been no part of a conspiracy to get Mecham, that he had been a peace officer reporting what appeared to be a crime to proper channels.

He knew it was not possible, but Johnson wanted desperately for Mecham to know that he had not betrayed him.

Now, hearing this latest attack on his integrity, Johnson lost the last of those feelings. "I didn't care any longer what happened to him. [Mecham] was ruthless and cared nothing for anyone else that day," Johnson later recalled.

Johnson had to stop himself from running down to the senate chamber and denying the accusation. That night was very difficult. He knew he would have a chance to respond, but every moment the slander was unanswered ate at him.

The days were hard after that. Johnson heard his name over the PA system on which the testimony ran continuously. People recognized him and said things, and he was embarrassed by the attention. At night he went home utterly exhausted from the strain—and his loss of innocence.

Following the lunch break Gordon began, "All right, before we proceed with the witness, Governor Mecham, I would ask Senator West if he has a further request or wishes to pursue his request . . . to the presiding officer, to order Governor Mecham to answer the question. . . ."

Leonard rose and explained that Mecham was prepared "to make a statement" with respect to the question.

Mecham returned to the stand. "Yes, Mr. Presiding Officer, with your permission I'll make a statement that perhaps will clarify the thing that sort of had us tangled up . . . relating to Beau Johnson and the report called the Curtis Report. . . . [I] stated that I"—pause—"found and later was verified by some people that he was the one that handed it to the head people at DPS. . . . I have since found out that the report that I had . . . the word that I had is verifiable, which I do not know to be true. . . .

"I did not have the proof then, and I do not have the proof now. It was reported to me by Lee Watkins that Colonel Chilcoat had told him that Beau Johnson was the one that brought the report to DPS. . . . I have not felt that I had proof; there was no, uh, there was no investigation launched into it. I never formally, uh, uh, accused him of that and don't here now accuse him. But I think that the way I used it, it would give the inference that I was using it as a fact, and I certainly want to set the record straight that I am not accusing him. I didn't really mean to accuse him. . . ."

West said he had come back from lunch prepared not to press the issue but stated that they all had an obligation to protect reputations and not malign without proof. He accepted the statement but pointed out Mecham had also accused Skelly without proof and Skelly had been cleared of wrong-doing.

It is unlikely there is in contemporary political history a more damaging exchange in the life of a politician.

# 42

The following day West asked Mecham, "Do you feel to date, and I think that's as far as we can go, but do you feel to date that this trial, this impeachment process, has been fair and impartial? And that you've had a fair and adequate opportunity to vindicate yourself?"

"I've had a opportunity to get my total side of the story, Senator West, to present our side . . . and to have an exchange. And frankly I'm enjoying the relationship in talking back and forth with you more than I do the attorneys. . . . I add one thing if I may," he said with a big grin, turning to Gordon. "May I?" Laughing.

"Certainly, you have already."

Mecham suggested that when men keep lawyers out, events proceed more smoothly.

Lieutenant Colonel Gary Phelps was now called in rebuttal. French began, "Colonel Phelps, during the case . . . certain testimony was presented through Governor Mecham that a certain document referred to by some as the Curtis Report ended up at the Department of Public Safety. Are you familiar with that testimony?"

"Yes."

"There was initial testimony that the governor thought rather strongly that Lieutenant Beau Johnson had taken the report from his office, or Mr. Colter's office, to the Department of Public Safety. Are you aware of that testimony?"

"Yes, I am."

340

". . . In fact, the Department of Public Safety did obtain that report, did it not?"

"Yes, we did."

"Did Lieutenant Beau Johnson have anything whatsoever to do with the Curtis Report being delivered to the Department of Public Safety."

"Nothing whatsoever."

"Would you tell the ladies and gentlemen of this court who delivered the Curtis Report to the Department of Public Safety."

"That report was hand-carried to the Department of Public Safety headquarters . . . by Mr. Lee Watkins."

The gallery laughed and clapped, and again Gordon admonished it.

Now Beau Johnson was called. "There's been testimony which I'm sure you're aware of concerning the so-called Curtis Report."

"That's correct."

"Lieutenant Johnson, did you have anything to do with the delivery of the Curtis Report to the Department of Public Safety."

"None whatsoever."

"Did you at the time it was delivered even know it was delivered?"

"I had no idea, sir."

"You had nothing to do with transporting or the taking of that document from the Ninth Floor?"

"That's correct, sir."

Peggy Griffith was now recalled. The peculiar nature of this proceeding was emphasized time and again by the familiarity demonstrated between individuals. Senator James Sossaman began with Griffith: "Mr. Presiding Officer, Mrs. Griffith, good morning. Peggy"—Griffith smiled broadly at the use of her first name—"you and I have traveled down a lot of political roads together, haven't we?"

"Yes, Jamie." And so it went.

The senators exercised their prerogative under the Rules and called Fred Craft. Normally an attorney for either side cannot be called as a witness. This issue had been explored when Craft was permitted to represent Mecham.

Craft testified to his recollection of the events of Friday, November 13. He acknowledged that he had declined a position on the Ninth Floor. The questioning by the senators was tame. Then Eckstein rose, fulfilling the dream of every attorney to get his opponent on the stand. Eckstein was smiling warmly.

Leonard shot to his feet and objected. Gordon read his ruling indicating that all witnesses called by the senators would then be questioned by counsel. Leonard's and Craft's consternation was an amusing sideshow to otherwise unproductive testimony.

By this time in the trial Judge Gordon was feeling comfortable with his

*Ronald J. Watkins*

role. His two clerks put in long hours preparing memorandums for him on every possible motion he would hear during the following day's proceedings, and he felt very well prepared. He had studied *Robert's Rules of Order* in anticipation of the trial only to learn the senate used *Mason's Rules of Proceedings*, which were more complicated.

It was Gordon's impression that the senators resented his presence at first and that they especially did not care for the rules of evidence he had to enforce. However, within days he felt they had come to appreciate the need for them.

Lundin prepared the instructions to the senate, something that was usually the job of the judge. That removed a considerable chore from Gordon, and he found he was enjoying the final weeks of the trial.

It was apparent to Gordon that Craft was lacking in trial skills. Leonard had good political savvy and was the better of the pair. Gordon found French and Eckstein "an amazing combination."

When the testimony on Article I was complete, the senate reconsidered its decision to vote on each article in turn. Senator Alan Stephens argued forcefully in favor, but the rules were amended to delay the vote on this article while testimony was taken on Article III. Because the second article was the Wolfson loan, there was some support for the governor's position that he could not defend himself against it without jeopardizing his defense in the upcoming criminal trial. As a consequence, Article II was delayed for last, when the senate would decide what to do.

Article III concerned the governor's borrowing of money from the Protocol Fund, and testimony began on March 22, 1988. The picture that soon emerged was of a governor desperate for money with which to meet the monthly obligation of his floundering car dealership. Mecham's claim that he had taken the eighty thousand dollars just so the Protocol Fund could earn a little extra interest was seen to be patently absurd. Without that money the Mecham Pontiac account would have been sixty-six thousand dollars overdrawn.

Jim Colter, now back from Australia, testified that he had told the governor it was stupid to borrow the money. Mecham insisted, and the money was turned over that very day. Colter required the loan be secured, but Mecham instructed that the deed of trust not be recorded. The only entry not listed in the check register was the eighty-thousand-dollar loan to Mecham.

Colter acknowledged that he had told no one of the loan. "Isn't it a fact, Mr. Colter," French asked, "that very soon thereafter, almost simultaneous with [repayment of the loan] . . . the media broke the story of the loan from the Protocol Fund to Mecham Pontiac?"

"I don't remember."

During redirect French asked, "Mr. Colter, since you have started testifying here yesterday, has the governor tried to reach you by phone?"

"Uh, no. My wife told me when I got home last night that he had called and left a message, I believe on our answering machine, saying that I had done a good job, or words to that effect. He did not ask that I call back, and I did not talk to him myself."

"So he's called you at home?"

"Apparently he did. . . ."

Donna Carlson was recalled to testify about her meeting with Colter after learning of the loan, when she told him people went to jail for similar acts. Colter had told her that he *had* to lend the money to Mecham.

A certified public accountant was called to testify that when Mecham hurriedly repaid the Protocol loan on October 23, 1987, he had borrowed the money primarily from his brothers. Mecham still owed the account $142.21. This did not fit with Mecham's presentation that he was a man of substantial means and that repaying the money was no problem.

Dennis Mecham, who was running the car dealership, testified that the business was basically sound and not in urgent need of money. Dennis Mecham was a polite, much taller version of his father. Before testifying, he had asked Paul Eckstein how to pronounce his name properly.

During his testimony he blamed some of the dealership's difficulties on poor bookkeeping by the former office manager. French and Eckstein had been looking for her without success. That weekend she contacted them and indicated her willingness to testify.

The previous week had been the deadline to file for the recall election. Seven had qualified, including Mecham, Carolyn Warner, Jack Londen, Rose Mofford, John Rhodes, a Socialist party candidate, and a private citizen. A poll of those most likely to vote released the weekend following Dennis Mecham's testimony reported Mofford 34 percent, Mecham 34 percent, and Rhodes 18 percent.

Monday, March 28, was the start of the fifth week of hearings. Leonard passionately argued that the impeachment trial be delayed until after Mecham's criminal trial, scheduled to begin on April 22. Following Leonard's volatile exchange with Gordon the presiding officer recessed a half hour early "to give you time to collect yourself."

Mecham now returned to the stand in his defense against Article III. His and his son's claims of solvency are common with many businessman. Moving money between accounts, overextended loans, slow payments, and overcommitted collateral are commonplace even among businessmen generally accepted as highly successful. Mecham had built a thriving business from nothing, and the problems it experienced once he became governor could well have resulted as much from the adverse publicity surrounding his administration and the loss of his hands-on management as from anything else.

On the stand Mecham denied knowing of the arrangement his inaugural committee had made concerning the Protocol Fund. He insisted he had borrowed the money only so it would earn more interest. He had repaid it a few days after extending the original due date only because he had been persuaded the original loan was politically unwise.

French asked Mecham to repeat for what purposes the governor understood the money could be used. Mecham said he was told, "You can use it for any damn thing you want as long as you don't use it to pay off campaign debts or personal living expenses."

"It's true," French asked, "that you viewed this [loan] merely as a secured note that was paid back."

"That is correct."

"Under your theory, then, hypothetically, it would have been proper to loan the money to your wife, so long as it was secured with a deed of trust on your home, correct?"

A suspicious Mecham hedged: "Could be."

"And under your theory, your wife could spend that money on anything, so long as she paid it back with interest."

"I think that's what you say on a loan."

"Let me ask you a question," French casually began. "Assume that a bank official needs to pay eighty thousand dollars in medical bills for his wife. Assume further that instead of applying for a loan, he takes eighty thousand dollars from the vault and leaves in the vault a note and deed of trust to his house. Assume further that ninety days later he pays back the eighty thousand dollars, plus interest." Mecham was looking ill. "Now, Governor, paying the money back, with interest, doesn't make the bank employee any less guilty of embezzlement, does it?"

Leonard objected. Gordon sustained the objection.

Mecham said, "I have to make a statement."

French started to speak.

"I have to make a statement. Let me—"

Gordon cut him off. "Governor, there is no question before you."

Ignoring the presiding officer, Mecham glared at French. "I resent so highly the word 'embezzlement' in my presence, sir. And that was characterized and done before, and I was insulted by it, and I have to tell the people of the state and this body that I'm insulted by it."

Gordon, now a bit flustered, tried again. "I sustained the objection, Senator [*sic*]. It is not going to be answered, and I hope, sir, you believe the rules are for you as well as everybody else."

"No witness has been insulted as I have," a testy Mecham replied.

Montini pointed out for the *Republic* readers that under Mecham's logic, once he had the money he could use it for anything, even the personal living expenses he had acknowledged were improper.

French had witnessed Mecham's similar response to a question in the house and had observed that he "liked to use righteous indignation." French was satisfied that his point had been made.

The next day Mecham sold his dealership. Clearly now his administration was taking a toll on his personal life.

Leila Christman, Mecham Pontiac's former office manager, now took the stand as a rebuttal witness. She testified that the previous July, when Mecham had borrowed the money from the Protocol Fund, she had told Dennis Mecham that the dealership required $497,000 to meet its monthly obligations. Mecham Pontiac "was having a bad year in 1987," she said.

Leonard asked if she had volunteered to testify. "Yes," she said, "when I heard Dennis [Mecham] lie."

Evan Mecham had previously attacked her for causing him to be delinquent in making payments on his Tacoma property. "When I came down and started functioning in my new government job," he said, "I turned everything over to the office manager to look after and [Christman] did not make the payments, the two thousand dollars a month that was due to Sturgeon for about three months. I did not even know that it was behind."

Christman recalled it differently. "We had gotten a letter from [Sturgeon] about our delinquent payments on the Tacoma property, and I asked [Evan Mecham] if he would give me the address, should we mail January and February payments. And [Evan Mecham] said, 'No, let 'em sue.' "

The brassy, straight-talking, angry Christman proved to be the most popular witness to Article III.

Following testimony on this much shorter article, one of the governor's staunchest allies, Senator Wayne Stump, rose to make a perfunctory motion to dismiss Article II with prejudice. His argument was simply that if the governor had to defend the accusation before them, it could very well fatally flaw his criminal defense on the same allegation.

Article II was the Wolfson loan and was the heart of the impeachment. Estimates were it would take upwards of six weeks to hear since it was by far the most complicated. Under that scenario the vote on all three articles would fall in mid-May, at almost the precise moment of the recall election scheduled for May 17.

Democratic Minority Leader Alan Stephens all along had wanted a vote on each article as it was completed. He was suspicious of a protracted trial. He believed a number of Republicans were unwilling to vote. They wanted the trial to drag to the recall election in hopes a Republican would win. If they voted and convicted Mecham, then these Republicans would have to face the Mechamites in the fall and also explain why they had handed the governorship over to Democrat Rose Mofford. If they did not vote, there was less political risk; they could use the trial to knock Mecham out of the running and still have a chance to retain the governor's slot with John Rhodes. Dismissing Article II would force an immediate vote on I and III.

Following Mecham's attack on Beau Johnson, Stephens believed Mecham would be convicted, especially on the Protocol Fund, but from his point of view, even if the senate declined to convict Mecham, the chances of a Democrat's winning the recall were excellent. Stephens had alerted the Democrats in the senate to the possibility of forcing a vote.

As Stump argued and the senators debated the technicalities, Stephens seized the opportunity. He looked at Senator Peter Rios and indicated this might be their chance.

From his desk toward the rear of the chamber, Senator Greg Lunn watched Stephens moving "as if in slow motion" from desk to desk, speaking quietly to his Democratic colleagues. Eckstein knew the Democrats wanted a vote. When he spotted Stephens, he whispered to French, "Something's happening."

Democratic Senator Carolyn Walker saw the possibility as well. Senator Chuy Higuera walked by her desk, and she told him she was voting to support dismissal. Higuera, who had been reading a Spanish-language Book of Mormon during the trial, nodded his head and said, "Good idea."

Walker went to Senator Jaime Gutierrez to solicit his support. He was hesitant, then agreed. Only a majority—sixteen votes—was required to dismiss Article II.

When Stephens sat down, Eckstein saw the smile on his face. Eckstein spontaneously turned to Senator Bob Usdane and said, "This motion's going to pass." Usdane shook his head.

It is one of the rarely considered but obvious realities of any legislative body that personal friendships exist even among those who hold opposite political philosophies. Republican Senator Jan Brewer, a Mecham supporter, sat immediately behind her friend, the Democrat Walker. Walker turned to Brewer and said, "Jan, this motion's going to pass." Brewer was startled.

The senate vote was by roll call. First was Senator Lela Alston, a Democrat. Brewer nearly always voted the opposite of Alston. Alston voted aye. Brewer gasped and in reflex voted no. The voting proceeded with every Democrat supporting the motion along with the Republican Mecham supporters.

Walker asked Brewer why she was not supporting the motion. Brewer said, "But Lela voted aye!" Walker explained that Stump was a supporter of the governor. Brewer said she understood, but Alston had voted in favor of the motion! Walker told her, "It's the governor's own man. You have to vote aye." Brewer recalls that she believed the impeachment was ill-advised, and when she saw the motion would carry, she decided to switch. When the roll call was complete, Brewer rose to change her vote.

Instead of fifteen for dismissal, raising the possibility of a challenge, that made it sixteen, and Article II was dismissed with prejudice, meaning it could not be raised again.

As they were leaving the senate chamber, Eckstein said to Stephens in an aside, "I hope you can count."

Leonard and Craft declared the dismissal a victory.

Following the vote an angry Usdane exchanged harsh words with Stephens. Partisan squabbling broke out the next day, a Thursday, as some Republicans attempted unsuccessfully to engineer another vote on the motion. When it occurred to Eckstein that the following day was Good Friday, he "was sick to [his] stomach." With all the Mecham supporters making references to crucifying Mecham he thought it foolish to take a vote then. He mentioned it to French. Kunasek understood immediately. Closing argument and a possible vote were set for Monday, April 4, 1988.

# 43

Bill French, for one, was not unhappy when the senate voted to dismiss Article II. When Lela Alston had voted in favor of it, he knew it was gone, and he had thought, "Fine." Both he and Eckstein were tired, and they believed there was enough evidence before the senate for conviction. French had never been "enthralled" at the prospect of prosecuting the Wolfson loan article because there were so many contradictory statements in the record. He had considered it the weakest article and for that reason had not opposed presenting it last.

Eckstein's first thought had been "Terrific" when the article fell. It was not a "sexy" count, and he did not relish prosecuting it. But from a purely legal point of view he thought it established a terrible precedent. The impeachment of a governor should always go forward regardless of the status of any criminal charges.

During the trial Eckstein had experienced the unusual situation of watching his case growing stronger as it proceeded. The Protocol Fund article in particular was much stronger in the senate than it had appeared in the house.

That Monday French and Eckstein presented Exhibit 98, "Supplemental Trial Memorandum," to the senators. More than one found it persuasive. It began:

> After the Board of Managers filed its Trial Memoranda, the Senate Legal Staff provided the Court of Impeachment with the following instruction on statements of the law:

348

"If you believe that any witness has willfully *testified falsely* as to any material fact or facts in the case, *then you are at liberty to disregard the entire testimony* of that witness, except insofar as it may have been corroborated by other credible evidence in the case." [Legal Filing No. 96 at 2 (emphasis added)]

During the course of these impeachment proceedings, it has become evident that Governor Mecham has not been truthful in his statements to the Arizona Senate, the Arizona House of Representatives, or the citizens of Arizona. Indeed, Governor Mecham has made false statements in connection with both of the Articles of Impeachment being considered. With that statement of the law in mind, this supplemental memorandum is being filed to present a sample of Governor Mecham's false statements to "be of help to you in evaluating the evidence and applying it to the law." [*Id.* at 1]

What followed were side-by-side comparisons of Evan Mecham's misstatements relating to the two remaining articles. His conflicting statements concerning Beau Johnson and the Curtis Report were there, side by side, along with thirteen other areas of substantial disagreement. One page read:

### B. *Not Looking to Borrow Money in July 1987*

| *Mecham's Initial Testimony:* | *Subsequent Evidence:* |
|---|---|
| In response to questions posed by Representative Killian: | (a) *Christman*: Mecham Pontiac needed approximately $497,000 in cash in July 1987. [TR 23 (Christman) at 5027/1–3] |
| "**Q.** [Y]ou weren't or Dennis [Mecham] wasn't out looking to borrow any money at that time was he? | |
| "**A.** No, he wasn't. | (b) *$150,000 loan*: Evan Mecham was aware that the company needed money at that time of the $150,000 loan in early July from Farmers & Merchants Bank. [TR 20 (D. Mecham) at 4463/22–4464/7; TR 21 (E. Mecham) at 4653/15–18] |
| "**Q.** So Governor, what you're saying is that Dennis or yourself were not in the position of going out and looking for money at this time? | |

| *Mecham's Initial Testimony:* | *Subsequent Evidence:* |
|---|---|
| "**A.** That's correct." [Trial Ex. 64 (Mecham) at 81/10–16] | (c) *$250,000 loan:* Evan Mecham arranged the $250,000 (on 7/28/88) from the Paulin Trust [TR 20 (D. Mecham) at 4462/ 25–4463/31], because of Dennis Mecham's "discussion with him that the business needed $250,000 at that time." [TR 20 (D. Mecham) at 4463/13–21; TR 21 (E. Mecham) at 4653/19–21] |
| | (d) *$80,000 loan:* The $80,000 protocol fund loan pulled Mecham Pontiac out of a critical cash flow situation. [TR 23 (Christman) at 5096/17–19] |
| | (e) *$480,000 borrowed:* Although they supposedly were not "out looking to borrow any money at that time," they borrowed at least $480,000 in July, 1987. |

The document concluded:

Throughout the impeachment proceedings, Respondent has demonstrated repeatedly his inability to tell the truth. Pursuant to the recent instructions on the law provided by Senate Legal Staff, the Court of Impeachment is "at liberty to disregard the entire testimony" of Governor Mecham. Indeed, the cumulative effect of his false statements—made under oath before both chambers of the legislative branch of government—cries out for an immediate vote of impeachment. A person without integrity, without the capacity to tell the truth, and without the ability to engender basic trust to the citizens, has no business holding any office in this state, let alone to serve as the head of state government.

Evan Mecham attended the court of impeachment that morning for the first time as an observer. He took a seat between Craft and Leonard just a few feet from French and Eckstein. When the attorneys for the Board of Managers assumed the podium to argue, they looked past Mecham to the senators.

As Bill French was waiting for the court to convene, he noticed that senators were taking their personal court of impeachment rule books up to Mecham to autograph. It reminded him of the high school signing of yearbooks. French was troubled because it seemed so out of place. A moment later he summoned a page and asked that his book be taken to Mecham for signature.

Mecham appeared a little startled at first but soon joined in the spirit and warmly signed the small books as they were brought up to him. Throughout the vote to come, however, Mecham sat virtually immobile at his place with his ever-present notebook, in which he diligently took notes.

Eckstein argued that it was not necessary to find that Mecham broke the law in order to convict him. Acts that were "positively wrong" or "serious abuses of official power" were sufficient. He characterized the governor as having engaged in a "lifetime of reckless disregard for the reputations of anyone who stood in his political path." He reminded the senators that they were here to protect the state, not to punish Evan Mecham.

Eckstein said, "[Mecham]'s demonstrated for all the world to see his inability to tell the truth."

Eckstein concluded with "I urge you to consider that by allowing [Mecham] to return to office to wreak havoc once again upon this state, you will have redefined in the most shameful way what is acceptable conduct for a public official."

French in a measured, calm voice said, "It's time for an ending, and it's time for a beginning. The chaos and tumult during the Mecham administration has [sic] done irrefutable harm to the state."

Craft said, ". . . We can certainly be part of an episode that can bring disrepute on our system. I submit to you that Governor Evan Mecham is not the only one on trial here today; we all are."

An impassioned, frequently shouting Leonard said, "[Mecham] doesn't resign because he's not guilty of these charges." He begged the senators to let the people speak in the recall election just forty-four days away. Perhaps forgetting himself for a moment, he blamed in part the senate for having failed to pass a law that would have allowed Mecham to use legal counsel other than the attorney general: "It is the fault of this legislature."

Outside three hundred Mecham supporters had gathered for a mock funeral. They paraded about the mall, carrying a coffin labeled "The Arizona Constitution."

The testimony finished, the arguments complete, the senators filed into the chamber that afternoon to cast their votes. As before, virtually every television set in the state was tuned to watch.

Senators milled around, quietly speaking, until Judge Gordon entered and gaveled the session to order. He said, "It is now the time to determine the final question of this impeachment proceeding." He explained that the rules required a vote, no abstentions, and that the standard was "clear and convincing" evidence. Two thirds of those elected, twenty votes, were required for conviction. They would vote first on Article I; then, regardless of the outcome, they would vote on Article III.

"If any of the facts were proved by clear and convincing evidence to constitute one or more high crimes, misdemeanors, or malfeasance in office," they would then "vote to determine if Evan Mecham should be disqualified from holding any office of honor, trust, or profit in the state."

Gordon paused. "Rule 27A requires a roll-call vote. Will the clerk please call the roll?"

Senator Lela Alston rose to explain her vote. She said that this was "a decision thrust upon us unwillingly. . . . The facts are the basis of my vote." She said this "has not been easy" and called attention to the conflicting testimony. She said the votes this day were not votes of courage or partisan politics; rather they were an "act of responsibility." Hers was "a decision I am comfortable with . . . the facts are undeniable.

"I have made my judgment," she concluded. "I cast my vote on Article One as guilty."

The senate pages had distributed an inordinate number of tally sheets that day, and most of the senators recorded the first vote.

Jan Brewer, looking physically ill, rose. Mecham's opponents had not been the only ones to receive threats. During the trial Brewer had received a number of telephone threats for her support of the governor. One evening a pipe bomb had exploded in her front yard.

Now Brewer said she found "a pattern of acting. . . . I find shameful and disappointing." She had concluded that there was no complete cover-up by Mecham, that he had ordered at least some type of investigation, and that his conduct was "not obstruction. . . . The positions by the governor and his top aides [had been] shockingly self-centered." She drew a deep breath and released an audible sigh. Mecham's conduct was not, however, sufficient to justify removal, and "I vote no."

Senator Peter Corpstein, a vote Mecham was counting on, now voted aye without comment. Senator Bill De Long did as well.

Senator Tony Gabaldon rose. "Only one person did not tell the truth, and that was Governor Mecham." He said that Mecham had been "described as an ethical pygmy by former president of the senate, Stan Turley, a man we all deeply respect. I think his description has been definitely proven here, and I vote aye."

Senators Gutierrez, Hardt, and John Hays voted aye without comment.

Senator James Henderson, from Window Rock, rose and spoke with his mild Navajo accent. "No man is above the law. . . . I have personally been threatened, just as other members of this court have been threatened. I will not be part of any effort to secure jobs for lawless characters who might threaten again." Citing Mecham's "evil insensitivity," he voted aye.

Senator Chuy Higuera voted aye. Senator Jeff Hill, who had passed his time answering constituent mail and completing tax returns, voted no.

Senator Peter Kay had hurt his image with his rambling comments on every issue and now delivered a mind-numbing discourse that was virtually a running stream of consciousness before at last voting no.

A grim Senator Carl Kunasek stared at his desk as he voted no.

Senator Greg Lunn had viewed this article not so much as a violation of law as unseemly conduct for the governor. Governors do not order policemen not to investigate alleged crimes. With so much to say, so much already said, he looked up, then grimaced and quietly said, "Aye."

Senators Carol MacDonald and John Mawhinney voted aye without comment.

Senator Jones Osborn, who had asked insightful technical questions, pointed out that even Mecham's version of his conversation with Milstead established the violation. "I must therefore vote aye."

Senator Manuel Pena voted aye.

Senator Peter Rios, bright, perceptive, articulate, rose to speak. "I have not . . . found Governor Evan Mecham to be an evil person, for I do not believe he is. . . ." Mecham had shown, however, that he was "poorly equipped to serve as governor," and Rios voted aye.

Senator Hal Runyan had been wheeled in to be in attendance. He was assisted in lifting his microphone. He could scarcely speak, and his voice was never more than a whisper as he said he had spent "long hours" reviewing the videotapes. "I have searched my conscience. . . . The governor is guilty."

Senator James Sossaman, a Mecham supporter, said to "negate an election requires great reflection on my part." He voted no.

Senator Jacque Steiner explained that she did not believe she had enough information and voted no.

Senator Alan Stephens had received many calls during the three-day break. A number of Democrats were critical because they felt he had pushed the Republicans too far. He voted aye.

Senator Wayne Stump commented that a court of impeachment is a court of "common law," and "ignorance definitely is an excuse." He voted no.

Senators Taylor and Todd voted aye.

Senator Bob Usdane voted no.

There were now nineteen votes for conviction. Senator Carolyn Walker, the only black lawmaker in the Senate, had been there the day Mecham had proclaimed that some of his best friends were black. She had watched his administration in horror. Walker did not believe it appropriate "to turn the knife." Without rising she said simply, "Aye," and convicted Evan Mecham. "There was," she later said, "too much to say."

Senator Tony West voted aye.

And last, Senator Patricia Wright, a firm Mecham supporter, rose and said, "It appears the votes are here for impeachment," and branded the vote an "amoral judgment." She spoke of "flawed decisions" and said that the public would hold them accountable. If this were the only way, she "could be tempted." Then Wright voted no.

Sitting just a few feet from Mecham, Eckstein had watched the governor closely. He could tell that Mecham "was surprised by the vote." Sam Stanton was also watching Mecham closely. The governor had been tallying the votes, and Stanton saw his hand hesitate before marking that twentieth vote; then it seemed "a sense of relief" came over the governor.

The clerk for the court of impeachment, Shirley Wheaton, handed Gordon a slip of paper with the totals. Before reading it, Gordon looked up briefly at the senators. "By your vote of twenty-one ayes, and nine noes, Evan Mecham is convicted of high crimes, misdemeanors, or malfeasance as contained in Article One of the articles of impeachment."

Mecham looked nearly in tears.

Now Gordon read the same instructions for Article III which concerned the Protocol Fund that he had for the first article before saying, "Rule 27A requires a roll-call vote. Will the clerk please call the roll?"

Brewer and Hill voted no. Now Senate President Carl Kunasek switched and voted aye. Senator James Sossaman voted aye.

Senator Jacque Steiner, citing Mecham's "ethical" lack of judgment, voted aye. Senator Wayne Stump voted no.

Then Senate Majority Leader Bob Usdane rose to explain his vote. There was "no question, it's clearly malfeasance, plainly wrong, a betrayal of the public trust, abuse of official power." He voted aye.

Senator Carolyn Walker spoke briefly this time, thanking even those who wrote nasty letters. "My mother always told me, 'Your word is your bond. And if you can't give your word and if your word can't be believed, you have nothing.' When I was elected to the house of representatives, Art Hamilton also told me, 'Your word is your bond. When you tell people something, you have to tell them the truth because if you lie to them, they will never believe you again.'

"In this article the deciding factor for me was the day the governor walked in and deliberately attempted to mislead this body. . . . If we can't trust you on one small thing, I can't trust you on anything. Mr. Presiding Officer, I vote aye."

During the voting Senator Tony West had been reading portions of a book he had read during the past two days called *People of the Lie* by M. Scott Peck. As he read it, so much seemed to fit Mecham. He had passed the book over to Senator John Hays to look at. Hays would mark a portion for West to read; West would mark a spot and pass it to Hays.

West knew that all of them had imperfections. As the voting proceeded, West prayed about what he should do. He thought the true tragedy here was that Evan Mecham "didn't even know what he had lost." He wanted people to understand Mecham as West had come to know him. So this time he rose to explain his vote.

He said that for a conservative Republican this was an especially difficult moment. "My words, I hope, do not come with any malice or with any rancor, but I hope they come as intended from one human being . . . who has a constitutional obligation and an oath of office to make a decision and to share with you some of my thoughts.

"Because it is obvious now, as we leave here this evening, that you will no longer be the governor of the state of Arizona and that you have abrogated your responsibilities to the people of the state of Arizona, particularly those who, like myself, voted for you, who, like myself, put the care and the custody of the ship of the state in your hands.

"Many people across this state believe in you and believe in you passionately, and I think it is unfortunate that you have abrogated that responsibility to those who so passionately believe in you. . . . I would like to give you something to look into your soul, as I have had to read this, to look into my own soul. So it is not that I read this and have learned this, through trying to understand the Mecham administration, although that has been part of the payoff.

"It comes from *People of the Lie* written by M. Scott Peck. It is hope for healing human evil.

"I particularly point out to those historians who may want to review what we have been through pages sixty-nine through pages eighty-four and pages one hundred twenty through pages one hundred thirty [*sic*], which I think have a direct effect.

"Starting on one of the paragraphs on page seventy-six, it says:

> Evil originates not in the absence of guilt, but in the effort to escape it. It often happens, that the evil may be recognized by its varied disguise. The lie can be perceived before the misdeed it is designed to hide—the coverup before the fact. We see the smile that hides the hatred, the smooth and oily manner that masks the

fury, the velvet glove that covers the fist. Because they are such experts at disguise, it is seldom possible to pinpoint the maliciousness of the evil.

"Another paragraph from page seventy-seven:

> Since they will do almost anything to avoid the particular pain that comes from self-examination, under ordinary circumstances the evil are the last people who would ever come to psychotherapy. The evil hate the light—the light of goodness that shows them up, the light of scrutiny that exposes them, the light of truth that penetrates their deception.

"On page one hundred twenty-nine where the author was talking about ambulatory schizophrenia, [he] says:

> In addition to the abrogation of responsibility that characterizes all personality disorders, this one would specifically be distinguished by:
> A: Consistent destructive, scapegoating behavior, which may often be quite subtle.
> B: Excessive, albeit usually covert, intolerance to criticism and other forms of narcissistic injury.
> C: Pronounced concern with a public image and self-image of respectability, contributing to a stability of life-style, but also to pretentiousness and denial of hateful feelings or vengeful motives.
> D: Intellectual deviousness, with an increased likelihood of a mild schizophrenic-like disturbance of thinking at times of stress.

"Governor Mecham, I don't know what the future holds for either one of us, but as one human being to another, at the proper time, I extend to you the handshake of reconciliation, if and when you would like to have that.

"And it is with a heavy heart that I have found through the testimony and the facts . . . that your veracity and your ethics, particularly in government, are in a state of bankruptcy. . . .

"I pray that you will . . . work your way through, but the consequences of your behavior have been heavy on all of us. This day it is unfortunate that we have come to this conclusion, but I, like my colleagues, have found you guilty of Article Three, and I vote aye."

Senator Patricia Wright briefly explained her no vote.

Then Gordon spoke. "By your vote of twenty-six aye, and four no, Evan

Mecham is convicted of high crimes, misdemeanors, or malfeasance in office as contained in Article Three of the articles of impeachment.

"I think it is appropriate at this time that we take about a fifteen-minute recess, and I would like to suggest to counsel—"

"No!" Mecham called out.

Leonard shouted, "Mr. Presiding Officer, I object to that."

Gordon agreed to proceed. "There is one remaining vote that the members of this court must decide because this court has voted to sustain Articles One and Three of the articles of impeachment." The senators were now required "to decide if Evan Mecham should be permanently disqualified from holding a position of honor, trust, or profit in this state. Do counsel wish to argue on this issue? No request for argument." Gordon read the instructions.

This portion of the vote was generally referred to as the Dracula Clause since it would effectively drive a wooden stake through Mecham's political heart. There was some uncertainty about the outcome, but most observers were of the opinion the senate would not dare let Mecham remain a viable political figure once it had convicted him.

Gordon had misgivings that this vote even had to be taken. A plain reading of the state constitution seemed to say that once the governor had been found guilty, he was automatically excluded from holding further state public office. There was, however, a conflicting statute, and the senate's counsel had decided on a two-tier vote. Twenty votes were necessary.

Some Democrats, willing to let Mecham remain the scourge of the Republican party, voted no; some Republicans, extending an olive branch to the impeached governor, also voted no.

When the quick vote was concluded Gordon said, "By your vote of seventeen ayes, thirteen noes, Evan Mecham is *not* permanently disqualified from holding any office of honor, trust, or profit in this state." He paused before explaining that Arizona statutes now required that a formal resolution be passed. Usdane said that none had been prepared in advance. The court of impeachment stood in recess while one was made ready.

Mecham was ushered to an adjoining room along with his attorneys. In private he was visibly shaken. He wanted immediately to dismiss his treacherous DPS security detail. Craft insisted forcefully that he not, considering the public mood at the moment.

Mecham cried. Within a few minutes the attorneys returned without him for the resolution vote.

Afterward Mecham, who could easily have avoided the press, "waded into them," answering questions. Mike Murphy, up in the gallery, had found the senate vote to be "beyond belief." Now Mecham was with them the way he always was, gutting it out. "Well," Mecham said, "they don't like my politics, so we've finished a political trial. It's as simple as that."

Senator Greg Lunn does not consider himself a religious man, but as he witnessed these events, it came to him with absolute certainty that Mecham "had been punished for his sins in a very direct way."

There had been scarcely any mention in the press of the significance of this day, April 4, 1988. No one said anything about it in any of the speeches delivered from the floor of the senate, that this day had also been the twentieth anniversary of the murder of Dr. Martin Luther King, Jr.

# PART FIVE

*[Burt Kruglick] got his tail twisted by that Jewish group.*
    —EVAN MECHAM, *explaining why the
    state Republican chairman who
    was Jewish would ask Mecham not
    to run again for governor*

# 44

The afternoon of the impeachment verdict Gordon, Eckstein, Craft, Leonard, and others met at Oaxaca to share a drink. They knew they had been through a never-to-be-repeated experience, and for a short time the five lawyers shared the experiences common to their profession. At one point Gordon told the gathering, "If they make a movie, I want to play Milstead."

The day following Evan Mecham's removal from office Fred Craft and Jerris Leonard met with Attorney General Bob Corbin, Steve Twist, John Shadegg, Michael Cudahy, and Barnett Lotstein. They were meeting with the attorney general with the approval of Michael Scott, Mecham's criminal defense attorney, and had a letter to that effect. Craft believed that to proceed with the criminal trial at this point would be a "travesty." Craft said that the state would welcome an end to the turmoil.

Therefore, Craft was suggesting that though Mecham knew he had done nothing wrong, he would be willing to absent himself from state politics and leave the state for a period of time. He said that Mecham would perhaps be willing to plead guilty to a misdemeanor. "He's suffered enough," Craft said. Craft was agitated and both he and Leonard appeared "disgusted" with their client, according to one observer.

The former governor's lawyer reviewed the facts of the Wolfson loan and believed he demonstrated that the attorney general would be unable to secure a conviction. He tried to persuade the men that a plea such as he was suggesting was also the wise political move. Craft told them that in the absence of such an agreement Mecham would reassert himself in state politics.

According to Craft, Corbin said that he was willing to make an offer but that he would not agree to anything less than an undesignated offense. This meant that Mecham would serve some period of probation, with no guarantee the court would not sentence him to jail, that during the term of the probation the offense would be a felony, but that if all went well, it could later be designated a misdemeanor.

Craft said, "No way." He said again that he believed Mecham would accept a misdemeanor in the interest of saving the state the cost of a prosecution. It seemed to Craft that Twist was leading the attorney general's response. He also thought that Lotstein and Cudahy were being a bit sanctimonious in describing how evil Mecham was. Craft also believed that they were using Willard Mecham to force a plea from Evan Mecham.

Craft reminded them that he was going to return to Washington, D.C. They were going to remain in Arizona and have to face the consequences. He told Corbin that no one had ever been jailed before for violating the statutes under which Mecham was charged. The refusal of the attorney general to accept his offer convinced Craft that they wanted to throw the former governor in jail. He found the effort "sick and sleazy." One observer recalls Craft returning from the meeting "outraged."

Lotstein and Cudahy recall this meeting differently. According to them Craft and Leonard had not as yet discussed any possible plea with Mecham and they were uncertain what the point of this meeting was. They recall that the proposal from Mecham's lawyers was that all charges would be dropped, that Mecham would plead to nothing, and that he would leave the state, possibly on an LDS mission, for an undetermined time. The state's response was that Mecham had to plead to some crime and that the sentence would be up to the court. Lotstein and Cudahy recall that Craft and Leonard said they did not think things would go well for Mecham if he testified in his criminal trial as he had in the senate. The assistant attorney generals deny characterizing Mecham in unsavory terms.

The recall election was scheduled for May 17, and Mecham was busy campaigning to reclaim his seat. In the weeks following the filing of the petitions the recall committee was organized to protect the process and prepare for the legal challenges that never came. Once it appeared that Mecham might be removed from office by impeachment, the opponents of the recall, including Mecham himself, demanded the election to vindicate the governor and, after his removal, to restore him to office. An effort they had branded as immoral was now seen as Mecham's salvation. "Let the people decide" became the battle cry of the Mechamites.

Once Mecham had been removed from office, the recall election appeared superfluous. It raised very interesting questions. In a quiet ceremony the day following his conviction, Rose Mofford had been sworn in as governor. How could she now be removed? For a time it appeared she would have to resign as governor for her name to appear on the recall ballot. In that case Bob Corbin would become governor.

No one was certain if Mecham could even run and, if he ran and won, if he could serve. He had been impeached for the period of his term. Did the winner of the recall election start a new term or finish the old? No one knew.

A Phoenix couple had filed an action to have the recall election voided now that Mecham was removed. The dilemma the state supreme court faced involved two conflicting provisions of the state constitution. One of them called for the secretary of state to become governor upon the conviction of the governor; the other mandated a recall election when sufficient signatures had been filed.

In fact, with so many candidates, the winner of the recall election would likely assume office with a plurality smaller than Mecham's.

On April 12, 1988, just eight days following Mecham's removal, the state supreme court with Chief Justice Gordon not participating voided the recall election. The court stated it was unjust to oust Rose Mofford, who had lawfully succeeded to the governorship. Most of the state's politicians were relieved.

Mecham called the decision "a demonstration of raw political power."

Asked to comment, Ed Buck said, "It's over now." As the time neared for the criminal trial of Evan Mecham in the Maricopa County Superior Court, Buck ceased paying attention to the process. He, like everyone else, knew Mecham would be convicted. A Maricopa County poll taken in mid-May showed that 65 percent of the people believed Mecham was either definitely or probably guilty. The only real question was whether or not the former governor would be sent to prison.

That was just one of the questions troubling Michael Scott as he prepared for the criminal trial, now set for June. Scott, a former rodeo cowboy with battered knees, is a handsome man, with a cocksure manner and a zest for life. Joe Keilp, who had worked at the U.S. attorney's office with Scott, took over Willard Mecham's defense and the two attorneys worked in tandem.

Mecham had first instructed Scott to secure an early trial date with an eye to a quick acquittal that would stop the impeachment in its tracks. Superior Court Judge Michael Ryan had been assigned to the case in February. He had, in fact, done some work on the matter during its state grand jury phase.

Scott was convinced that Mecham had been unjustly indicted. "The case was not there," he says, "and should not have been brought." He thinks there is no question that Lotstein and Cudahy manipulated the grand jury process to obtain the indictments. He also sees no coincidence in the timing of the indictment and the articles of impeachment. Scott was faced with taking an impeached client into court.

The issue of an improper indictment was argued before Ryan. Scott had access to the transcript of the state grand jury proceedings and all the evidence the grand jury considered in deciding to indict. Ryan was not persuaded of any impropriety, and the motion to dismiss the indictment was denied.

Ryan had initially thought this would be a historic confrontation between the rights of the trial court and the prerogatives of the senate. By the time of the senate conviction that possibility had disappeared, and it became essentially another case, albeit one with inordinate media attention.

Ryan had also been concerned about the governor's right to a fair trial if the senate had proceeded with the Wolfson loan article. His job was made much easier once that had been dismissed.

The cancellation of the May recall election cleared the way for the trial in superior court. Had that not occurred Ryan would have been disposed to continue the trial until the fall to allow Mecham time to campaign and then a period to prepare his defense. As it was, the governor's attorneys had argued for an early trial and, when they were unable to delay the impeachment proceedings, were stuck with it. In consequence, the criminal trial of Evan Mecham occurred a month or two earlier than average and much earlier than would reasonably be expected.

Ryan found himself having to make accommodations to the media. Once the firm trial date had been established, Ryan met with their representatives to determine the ground rules. Besides his obvious concern that television coverage not interfere with the proceedings he was concerned that the jury's anonymity be protected.

The superior court building where the trial was being held already had excellent security, including metal detectors and security personnel. In addition, the Sheriff's Office placed uniformed officers outside the courtroom, and one or two plainclothesmen among the spectators.

Lotstein did not view this as a complicated trial. He anticipated about one week for the state to present its case. When Mecham was convicted by the senate and removed from office, Lotstein said to Cudahy, "Our job has just been made ten times tougher." It was their feeling that Mecham would now benefit from a sympathy vote.

The ace in the hole for Lotstein and Cudahy was Mecham's inability to refrain from speaking in his own behalf. Mecham was convinced that he could persuade others to his version of events. When Mecham took the stand, Lotstein expected the former governor to assure his conviction. As the trial neared, however, Lotstein became convinced Mecham would not testify. He made a bet with Cudahy, who disagreed.

The most sensitive part of the trial was the jury selection. Every aspect of the Wolfson loan had received microscopic coverage for nearly eight months. Many of the key documents had been reproduced in the press. Also, an impeachment by its nature tends to polarize the electorate, and it was from that polarized pool the court had to select an impartial jury. It meant, in essence, that any jury in which no member had signed the recall petitions, watched the house or senate proceedings, or followed the course of the Mecham administration in the press was going to be apolitical. The charges against Mecham concerned his filing of public documents during a political election. The kind of jury likely to emerge was one that would ask, "What's the big deal?"

The selection process was one Ryan had followed previously in extraordinary cases. Each side presented a list of questions it wanted to ask prospective jurors. Ryan narrowed the questions down to those that were relevant. During the weekend before jury selection he reviewed the answers from the pool of one hundred jurors and eliminated forty-eight of them. To assure an appearance of fairness, the state moved to strike any who had signed recall petitions, eliminating ten more. Ryan and opposing counsel then questioned the remainder.

The week prior to the actual trial Scott conducted a mock trial in secret. Jurors were randomly selected, given the facts of the case, and then offered opposing arguments. Scott first presented the standard Mecham conspiracy defense with some attention to the alleged death threat. The jury was not receptive. Scott changed his approach, emphasized the facts as he saw them, and this time the jury gave a favorable critique.

Scott found Mecham to be a pleasant client. Clearly Mecham wanted to testify and vindicate himself. Scott knew Lotstein and Cudahy were counting on it. It is not good form for a client's lawyer to talk him out of testifying; it implies a lack of faith, so Scott had one of the other attorneys raise his concerns.

The night before the start of the trial Lotstein and Cudahy contacted Scott and "solicited an offer," according to Scott. If Mecham would plead to three misdemeanors, there would be no jail and Willard Mecham would walk.

According to Lotstein, Cudahy spoke to Scott for the attorney general. Scott proposed that Mecham plead no contest to one count involving an act that did not require an admission of intent and that the ex-governor receive no jail. The state countered with an offer that he plead to at least one count that involved an act with an admission of intent and that the sentence would be up to the court. Negotiations never reached the point where they discussed an undesignated offense or a misdemeanor since Scott soon made it clear his client would not plead under those conditions.

Scott contacted Mecham and told him of the offer. Mecham asked, "Well, Mike, are you ready?"

Scott said, "If you take it, you're dead politically."

"Ah, let's just go to trial," Mecham said.

As Scott later said, "Mecham never expressed any fear to me."

Ryan did not know until the last minute that the trial would be covered live, gavel to gavel, the first criminal trial to be publicly broadcast in such a fashion in the nation. He acknowledges he found the experience "a little unsettling." Ryan occasionally had the feeling that some of the events in the courtroom were affected by the television coverage and especially that the state's attorneys were playing the trial to the television audience. It seemed to Ryan that in their attempt to present an "image of extraordinary fairness" the assistant attorneys general went perhaps "too far." For instance, it was they who decided that prospective jurors who had signed the recall petitions be automatically excluded.

Lotstein and Cudahy acknowledge that they were sensitive to public perceptions of the trial. Lotstein made objections that he would not usually have made in a closed courtroom. Lotstein says he was pleased at the coverage because he wanted people to see how fairly the former governor was being treated.

The jury selected consisted of seven men and five women. The actual jury was eight; four were alternates but would not know that until the last moment when their names were selected at random. Those with conspicuously negative attitudes toward Mecham were eliminated, but a surprising number with positive feelings toward him made it on the jury. One thought Mecham was a truthful man. Another, who belonged to the Daughters of the American Revolution, was uncertain Mecham should have been impeached. A third said Mecham had been impeached for rescinding the Martin Luther King holiday.

In addition, at least two of the jurors showed an appalling lack of interest or understanding of events. One man said he had tried to read a *New Times* article about the impeachment but had quit because he became confused. Another man said he did not have a radio in his car and watched local news only for the weather. One juror claimed he had never heard of Evan Mecham. Sam Stanton wrote an article in which he said "the good people of Arizona" who Mecham claimed supported him had landed on his jury.

During the opening Cudahy attacked Mecham's integrity and cited his "ill-fated bargain" with Wolfson.

Scott said, "These men have been dragged from bumper sticker to legislative hall, from forum to forum, without one ounce of justice."

Keilp suggested that Willard Mecham was the victim of his own "primitive bookkeeping."

The afternoon of the first day of the trial, June 2, 1988, Lotstein noticed that the two Mecham wives had moved close to their husbands, where they would be conspicuous to the jury. Periodically they read Bibles. Ryan declined to make them move, and the next day Evan Mecham was holding his wife's hand in the presence of the jury. This time Ryan instructed the wives to move.

As it happened, the women were being told by Mecham at the time the jury filed in. Mecham immediately raised his voice and said, "Mr. Lotstein doesn't want you sitting near us." Lotstein discreetly objected, but Mecham had made his point. Moving the women did little good. During breaks, often in the presence of the arriving or departing jury, Mecham would stand at the rail and hold hands with his wife while they locked eyes in adoration.

The state elected to go with a bare bones case. The various documents relating to the Wolfson loan were introduced. It called a certified public accountant to testify that the Mecham campaign was $137,000 in debt, with checks written for the media in the amount of $177,000 when Mecham borrowed the Wolfson money. Donna Carlson testified briefly about signing a promissory note and to the fact that the loan was kept secret from those working on the campaign. Vern Gasser took the stand to testify that yes, he had taken some notes, and no, he had had no idea what they meant. Willard Mecham's testimony from the grand jury was read to the jury.

And the state rested.

On June 8 Scott and Keilp began the defense. Barry Wolfson testified that he did not want to be identified as a "fat cat," and no, he had not expected any favors from Mecham for the loan. Edith Richardson testified the loan had been "common knowledge" to the campaign staff. Vern Gasser was recalled to emphasize still again that he did not know what any notes meant. The new secretary of state, Jim Shumway, then testified to campaign finance law.

On Friday, June 10, following Shumway's testimony, the trial broke for lunch. Scott still had four character witnesses to call that afternoon.

Scott had one of his firm's partners, Thomas Crowe, talk to Mecham about the former governor's desire to testify. Mecham was told that the state had not done a good job and that the defense witnesses had made the necessary points for the jury. The jury already had the entire story. Mecham's testimony was not needed.

Mecham, his brother, and their wives met alone to talk about it. Mecham came out and told Scott he would rely on his advice and not testify.

At 1:45 P.M. Scott informed the stunned courtroom that the defense rested. Keilp followed suit. Ryan had not expected the trial to end this quickly and as a result jury instructions had not been prepared.

Closing arguments were set for the following Tuesday, June 14. During his presentation Scott asked the jury to deny Lotstein and Cudahy Mecham's "scalp [to take] back to the attorney general's office to hang in their trophy case." His rambling, impassioned speech was given to excess, and at times he seemed to be begging for a hung jury. He admits as much.

Cudahy said, "[A]long came a pot of gold in the form of Barry Wolfson" when the Mecham campaign needed money.

Keilp argued, "It's quite clear that Willard, finally, didn't know what the hell he was doing."

In one moment of intemperance Scott said, "Maybe I shouldn't be so hard on my colleagues; like the guards at Auschwitz, they're just doing their jobs."

The audience winced at the words. Lotstein acknowledges he was "offended" by the remark. He and Cudahy exchanged glances. Immediately Lotstein calculated how he could turn it to their advantage. Scott finished with about fifteen minutes remaining in the day. Lotstein asked to be allowed to proceed. He wanted to take maximum advantage of the tasteless remark.

"Why the attack?" he asked. "Why the attack?" Because they wanted to make the assistant attorney generals the issue rather than Mecham's conduct, Lotstein said. The following day Lotstein completed closing.

Toward the end of the trial three men approached two jurors in what appeared to be attempts to influence them in the governor's favor. The jurors were allowed to remain, though one was selected as an alternate and was excused.

The jury met for deliberations that afternoon. It resumed the next morning. During the lunch hour the word came from the jury foreman that read, "We are ready to announce our verdict at 1:30 P.M." Once again the state came to a standstill as everywhere citizens turned to radios and televisions.

Once before Scott had kept a client he believed to be innocent off the stand and watched him get convicted. Ever since he had dreaded jury verdicts. This day he was "queasy" in his stomach and genuinely feared he had lost. Mecham asked what he thought, and Scott replied, "I don't know, Governor. I hope we're there."

Indictments by the state grand jury have a 98 percent conviction rate. Both Lotstein and Cudahy were confident. Sam Stanton was there with Mike Murphy, Laurie Asseo, and John Kolbe.

After Judge Ryan took his place, he looked to the jury and asked, "Ladies and gentlemen, have you reached a verdict?"

"Yes, sir, we have." The jury could not be seen by television, and for the viewers watching KAET the sound came from out of sight.

"Will you please hand all forms of verdict to the bailiff?" The bailiff collected the papers, then handed them to Ryan. At this point Ryan was most concerned with not revealing anything of the verdict as he checked each form to be certain it had been properly completed and signed. He now admonished the court that he would stand for no demonstrations, that he would clear the courtroom if necessary.

"The clerk will please read and record the verdicts, omitting the formal caption," he said as he handed the forms to his clerk, a handsome woman of middle years, dressed in a white summer suit with a mauve blouse.

She rose. "We the jury duly impaneled and sworn in the above entitled motion upon our oaths do find the defendant, Evan Mecham, not guilty of count one."

A woman sitting beside Florence Mecham exclaimed, "Jesus!"

The clerk continued. "Ladies and gentlemen of the jury, is this your true verdict, so say you all?"

The jury responded in unison, "Yes."

The clerk then read counts two and three, which also included Willard Mecham, repeating exactly the same words. Willard Mecham did not move at all. For the first count Evan Mecham moved his hand to his face and rubbed his brow. For the second count he appeared nearly overcome with emotion as he ran a finger across his mouth. For the third count, which meant his brother was entirely cleared, he began to blink severely.

Scott was apprehensive as the clerk began the verdict for count four. This one and the last two charged Evan Mecham alone. It was possible the jury had cleared the brothers of the first three but had convicted Evan Mecham alone of the last three. "The governor was hanging out by himself," he later said as the clerk announced "not guilty" to count four. Scott knew they had won.

For the verdict to count four, Mecham pulled at the skin on his face; for count five Scott said something to Mecham, who leaned over to hear it. As the clerk asked, ". . . so say you all?" Scott placed his arm across Mecham's shoulders. For count six Mecham had his hand to his brow, then at the last moment covered his mouth. He was motionless, not even blinking. With the words "not guilty," Scott slapped Mecham on the back. The men embraced awkwardly. Scott had tears in his eyes. The crowd behind the governor let out an exclamation. A spectator in a dated electric blue suit leaned over to congratulate Mecham, who went immediately to the rail and embraced his wife.

Scott asked Judge Ryan if his client could address the jury. "No," Ryan said, "[this is a] court of law."

Before ending the trial, Judge Ryan spoke to the courtroom and to the television viewers as he reminded them that there had been many who did not believe Evan Mecham could receive a fair trial "under intense and high publicity situation." He thanked everyone and told the jurors they were free to discuss their verdict if they wished. With that Evan Mecham's trials ended.

> *There was some things [in Arizona] that was really stinko.*
> —EVAN MECHAM *to author*
>
> *I think [Mecham] is perhaps the best demonstration that Darwin was wrong.*
> —BRUCE BABBITT

# 45

Barnett Lotstein had thought the worst that would happen was a hung jury. He had found the jury to be attentive, and he "had no quarrel" with the verdict. Because of the relentless attacks by Mecham and his supporters on the attorney general's office, Lotstein and Cudahy had decided they would not slink away if the verdict went against them. They went to the herd of reporters and took all the questions. That night both of them appeared on *Horizon*. They made appearances on the talk radio stations as well.

They believed the indictment had been properly brought, the trial had been fair, and the system was vindicated. They had no apologies.

Mecham fielded only a few questions from reporters at the scene. He said he would have a full comment the next day. He did tell them, "We haven't broken any laws, and now we have at least eight people who believe us." His wife, Florence, never one to make a public statement, said, "I feel a heart full of gratitude."

Interviewed by reporters, Bob Corbin said that in early April he had offered Mecham pleas to misdemeanors, but Mecham had refused them. Commenting on the verdict, Corbin said, "You win some and you lose some."

Back at the Capitol, Joe Lane was watching the verdict on television. When the "not guilty" verdict was announced for the first count, he said, "That's terrible." When the entire verdict was in, he had no comment and retired to his office.

Lane was puzzled that the jury had been unable to see it the way those in the house had. He knew the upcoming elections would be rough for him and for the others who had supported the impeachment.

When Evan and Florence Mecham returned to their house in Glendale, a small crowd of cheering supporters was waiting. They had decorated his door with signs and a banner. Mecham said as he entered his house, "I didn't expect this."

The next day Steve Benson's cartoon pictured Abraham Lincoln, Mecham's favorite president, reading the results in a paper and saying, "You can fool 8 of the people all of the time."

The same morning at his Glendale office Mecham held a press conference. Yes, his new political action committee, Forward Arizona, would be busy in the upcoming elections and would be supporting candidates in the primary against incumbent Republicans. He set as his goal ridding Arizona of its corruption and its "obsessed attorney general." He denounced his impeachment as a "political lynching." He announced his plans to start a competitive paper against the *Arizona Republic* and the Phoenix *Gazette.*

Willard Mecham at last publicly commented on the trial. He called his indictment and trial an "evil experience." He said, "I think yesterday was the happiest days [sic] in Arizona."

Following the impeachment conviction of Evan Mecham in the state senate the legislature still had to attend to the business of government. Joe Lane found it "hard to work in a poisoned atmosphere." Still, legislation and a budget were passed, and on July 1, 1988, the 173d day of the Second Regular Session, at 1:56 A.M the house of representatives adjourned, concluding the longest session on record for the state legislature.

There was a poignant moment in the last days when a clearly moved Speaker Lane addressed his colleagues and remarked that he did not know if he would be returning following the elections, but he wanted them to know how proud he was to have served as their speaker.

During the last weeks of the session Lane had put thousands of miles on his car driving to his home district, campaigning for reelection. Now he and his wife moved back to the ranch home outside Willcox and began campaigning seven days a week. Both of them were surprised at the lack of understanding the people to whom they talked showed for the tumultuous events they had just experienced in Phoenix. Lane knew he was vulnerable because of the large LDS population in the district and found it difficult to persuade his supporters that they really needed to go to work. The Democrats would support him in the general election; it was the primary that concerned him. Everyone seemed to assume the speaker would be reelected.

Local hometown heroes Rex Allen and Rex Allen, Jr., both recorded commercials for him. All six dailies in the district endorsed him for reelection.

The official kickoff for the speaker's campaign was a Bisbee parade, followed immediately by a parade in Douglas on the Fourth of July. Lane was not booed once in either event, but there were some negative responses to him in the crowds. Some men turned their backs as he rode by, and a few gave him the thumbs-down. Still, he felt better about his chances for reelection than he had in some time.

In the Arizona legislature, in some years, there are no changes at all following elections. Perhaps two senators decide not to run; perhaps one or two are defeated. In the house two or three might not run, and one or two are defeated. In the wake of the Mecham impeachment a number of legislators decided not to seek reelection.

Senator Hal Runyan did not run because of his deteriorating health. Senator Greg Lunn, one of the few lawmakers who actually tried to support a family on his salary, decided to seek a seat on the Pima County Board of Supervisors that paid a living wage. Senator Tony West decided not to run as well. When Mecham was acquitted, he said, "If I had any reservations about what I was doing [in not seeking reelection], I lost them."

In the house Representative Larry Hawke chose to enter law school. Representative Jim Ratliff did not seek reelection for health reasons. Representative George Weisz elected not to run and returned to his job as an investigator for the attorney general. Representative Jim White also did not run, purportedly for financial reasons, but he had voted for impeachment and was from Mecham's home district.

Forward Arizona was active in the campaign. A slate of candidates appeared with its support in a number of districts. Certain conspicuous figures were clearly targeted for defeat. These included House Speaker Joe Lane, Senate President Carl Kunasek, Representative Jim Skelly, and Senator John Hays.

Kunasek was not particularly concerned as primary day approached. His personal polls showed him with a substantial lead over his Mecham-backed supporter. In the last days of the primary Forward Arizona issued tabloids, one of which viciously attacked Kunasek. With the large Mormon population in his district, he grew less certain of his chances.

As the results came in on September 13, 1988, it was clear that some of those who had supported the impeachment were in trouble. Despite all the publicity it was another low voter turnout. Representatives Bob Hungerford, Bob Broughton, Betty Rockwell, and Don Strauch, all of whom had voted for impeachment, were defeated. Representative Jim Skelly however was reelected, as was Chris Herstam.

The only Mecham supporter to suffer a loss was Representative Gary Giordano. Ron Bellus, running for Tony West's senate seat, was soundly defeated by the former Senate president Leo Corbet. Mecham supporter Trent Franks was defeated for the house.

Senator John Hays was given a tough fight but won, as did Senator Jacque Steiner. Senators Peter Kay and Jack Taylor, who both had voted for impeachment, were defeated. And Carl Kunasek in an upset was defeated.

In District 8 Joe Lane had heard the stories of Mormons reregistering as Republicans just to vote against him. Three television stations and one newspaper reporter were in his home to cover the returns. In the past he started low, but as the rural precincts were counted, he would pull ahead around midnight. By 2:00 A.M. he knew it would come down to a few votes.

Lane had always been lucky in politics and had profited many times from it. That night his luck ran out. At 8:00 A.M. he learned he had lost the election by 127 votes out of 9,932 cast.

John Kolbe wrote, "The next time you start griping about a politician's unwillingness to stand up boldly for what's right, keep Lane's example in mind. Politicians are timid because we voters insist upon it. In politics, no good deed goes unpunished."

Joe Lane was a man with no regrets. Later he said, "The system worked, and we cleaned up our mess in Arizona. How many states can say that? Nobody died in this, and I'm very proud of all of us, proud of Arizona for that." He added, "There are worse things in life than being known as the man who impeached Evan Mecham."

Others who had voted for impeachment were defeated in the general election. Senator Carol Macdonald lost. Representative John King was also defeated and replaced by a Mecham supporter though Mecham supporter Ted Humes was defeated. Joe Lane's District 8 returned to Democratic control as the two Mecham Republicans were defeated.

In the general election of November 8, 1988, Arizona voters passed Proposition 105 as a direct result of the Mecham administration. Beginning with the gubernatorial election of 1990, candidates for governor and four other state positions are required to win with a majority of the vote. In the event of a multicandidate general election in which no one obtained a majority there would be a runoff election.

At the Republican State Convention of January 1989 the Mecham forces closed ranks with supporters of Pat Robertson and gained control of the party. Longtime supporters of the party were booed while Mecham loyalists with scant party credentials were treated to ovations. In the waning moments of the convention Mecham and Robertson supporters proposed, then passed a resolution declaring the United States "a Christian nation . . . a republic based upon the absolute laws of the Bible, not a democracy."

# EPILOGUE

The 1988 elections have been over for months. Each day Evan Mecham reports to his Glendale office, vacant except for himself and a handful of the faithful. He wears a crisp suit and sits in his small office, making and receiving calls. "I have to work hard," he says. "There is so much to do." He says he accomplished a great deal this week, but "I'll need to live to be one hundred and twenty to accomplish all I want."

There are plans, a new newspaper, the pending elections in 1990, 1992. "I have learned it takes time," he says. There is the conspiracy to fight, the scores to settle. The telephone rings. "Thank you for your help," he says soothingly. "We'll get there. We'll get there," he says as he hangs up.

Who is behind the conspiracy? he is asked. He does not know, just as he did not know in 1964, when he declined to tell the reporters who the secret power brokers were.

What does all this mean? he is asked. "You cannot allow people in government to get so cozy they serve the wrong people. All you have then is incestuous corruption. There needs to be competition in the news field, someone to keep them honest." He pauses. "I have a high regard for people. If you give the public the facts, they'll choose properly."

In at least one regard Evan Mecham's administration has been a personal triumph. No significant political event occurs in Arizona now without his comment being solicited. From the perennial loser to whom no one listened, he is now a man the state is afraid to ignore.

Across the street, though it is midafternoon, a rooster crows. The barn looks as if any gust of wind would send it crashing down. It is a beautiful day, the kind of magical day for which thousands every year come to Arizona. It is a day when all the state's shortcomings are insignificant and you wish it could be like this forever even as you know it cannot be.

Inside the dark office Evan Mecham scratches notes on his pad and plans.

Mecham called the press conference of April 4, 1989, for 7:00 P.M. at the Crescent Hotel just off the freeway in northwest Phoenix. It is the anniversary of his removal from office and coincidentally the twenty-first anniversary of the assassination of Dr. Martin Luther King, Jr.

The conference is more like a pep rally. The press and television crews are out in force. KFYI is covering the event live. Mike Murphy is bored beyond belief. He cannot believe how lucky Stanton has been to be assigned to Washington, D.C., and escape this.

What if it starts all over? he asks. He cannot fathom another period like the one he has just experienced.

The crowd is not large enough to fill the room. There are perhaps four hundred people there. A group of teenage girls dressing and acting like cheerleaders does several routines. Mormonettes, someone says. It is not likely he has ever heard of the Mechamettes, who gave similar performances for Mecham in 1962. Barbara Blewster, fellow Mormon and longtime Mecham supporter, leads several singers in a poor rendition of "When Johnny Comes Marching Home Again" set to new words.

When Evan comes marching home again,
Harrah, harrah,
We'll give him a hearty welcome then,
Harrah, harrah.

The reporters groan. MECHAM FOR GOVERNOR bumper stickers are everywhere. The Mecham supporters cluster together, as does the press. The two groups look at each other from time to time. The looks are difficult to decipher. Clearly the supporters do not like the press, but they also want it to cover the occasion. Love, hate.

Max Hawkins is giving Don Harris with the *Republic* an interview. The next day he is quoted as saying he hopes for a low voter turnout in 1990, so Mecham can win again.

Other familiar faces are in the crowd. Todd Sprague, head of Mecham's fan club, is in the front row. Apparently he has nowhere else to go. Horace Lee Watkins is seated toward the rear. He glares at Mike Murphy with malice.

There are some speeches to warm up the crowd. Evan Mecham is seated in the front row with Florence Mecham. He is enjoying himself. The most impassioned speech comes from Donald "Mac" MacPherson who identifies himself as Mecham's new lawyer. He talks about the appeal he is filing and how he hopes to put Mecham back into the governor's chair.

MacPherson believes in conspiracies. He also represents James Earl Ray, Martin Luther King's murderer, *pro bono*.

As Mecham assumes the podium, an assistant places a box for him to stand upon to reach the microphones. The former governor's speech is surprisingly flat. He announces that he is a candidate for the office of governor. He makes fun of Joe Lane's losing his election, and the crowd has a good laugh at Lane's expense.

Afterward the reporters ask a few questions, then leave to file their stories. The cameras are taken down. Mecham is holding his speech notes, and they are just scraps of paper, a collection of ideas. Much of the speech was apparently extemporaneous.

The crowd closes around to touch him and shake his hand. One man in a cowboy hat tells Mecham that he is new to the state but he believes Mecham was railroaded out of office. A woman is sitting on the stage. She says that a friend brought her to the affair. She is new to the state and confesses she knows little about the man. He's a politician, though, she says; aren't they all alike?

Horace Lee Watkins is moving slowly down the wall. All the media appear gone now. He approaches Mecham and says, "Hello, Boss." As they speak, a journalist thrusts his tape recorder up to them. They stop speaking and appear startled. Watkins shakes Mecham's hand and with a glare to the journalist moves off. Mecham turns to the next well-wisher. His 1990 campaign is off and running.

# Aftermath

Jane Dee Hull was elected Arizona's first woman speaker of the house in January 1989. Chris Herstam became house majority whip. In the Fall of 1989 he announced his intention not to seek reelection in 1990. Bob Usdane was elected president of the senate.

In January 1989 Jim Ratliff returned home from the Phoenix Open. He collapsed and died. Neither Evan Mecham nor anyone representing him appeared at the funeral.

Sam Stanton was a finalist for the Pulitzer Prize. He, Mike Murphy and Laurie Asseo were assigned to the Washington bureaus of their respective organizations.

Pat Murphy resigned as publisher of the *Arizona Republic* and the Phoenix *Gazette* on August 8, 1989, after forty years in the newspaper business to lecture and write. Ralph Milstead was appointed a special assistant to Governor Rose Mofford.

Two members of the LDS Church petitioned Salt Lake City to have Steve Benson stripped of his church positions because of a cartoon he ran in response to Mecham's announcement that he was again running for governor. The cartoon pictured Mecham holding the "Book of Moron by Ev Mecham" as rats filling in for angels trumpet his candidacy. It was entitled "The Second Coming."

Max Hawkins contacted the administrator for the Phoenix Bishops and Executives Round Table and requested the group take action. Twelve valley religious leaders, including the Roman Catholic bishop, signed and sent to a representative of the LDS Church a letter protesting Benson's use of religious symbols in his cartoons. Shortly after this latest Mecham cartoon Benson was stripped of his church positions for having published it. In January 1990 Benson resigned from the *Republic* and joined the *Tacoma News-Tribune* in Washington.

Horace Lee Watkins was last reported to be operating a tow truck in Mesa. Some months after the impeachment his wife accused him of trying to strangle her. Watkins retained Barry Wolfson for his divorce. No charges were filed in the alleged assault.

Ron Bellus became director of advertising sales for the *Latter-day Sentinel* which then went out of business. Ken Smith turned to selling real estate in the Valley of the Sun and published an occasional magazine article.

Donna Carlson relocated to California, where she worked for the Hol-

378

lywood Chamber of Commerce in charge of economic development. She abandoned her attempts to market a book-length account of her period in the Mecham administration.

Fred Craft and Jerris Leonard share offices in Washington, D.C. Bill French left Storey & Ross for another firm. As a result of exposure on C-SPAN, his practice has improved dramatically. Paul Eckstein continues to be active in Democratic party politics. Ed Buck purchased an auto body shop in Scottsdale and devotes time to occasional civic crusades.

Beau Johnson never returned to the governor's security detail. He was named the local Fraternal Order of Police Officer of the Year. He was also promoted to DPS captain and assigned as commander of its human resources section. Officer Frank Martinez was reassigned to the Ninth Floor on Governor Rose Mofford's security detail.

On September 21, 1989, the Arizona State Legislature meeting in special session passed a state holiday honoring Dr. Martin Luther King, Jr.

Late in the summer of 1989 the Pinal County Republican party chairman, who had won passage of the Christian nation resolution, described his common practice at party meetings, saying, "We just get right down into it. In fact, we start praying in tongues. . . . There are some people very nervous with that. . . ."

Later in the interview he said, "We wanted things to settle down without alienating the Jews. They're the ones who carry the purse strings for the party."

# About the Book

This book is based on more than 175 interviews with most of the key participants, review of grand jury transcripts and court documents, news accounts, and video recordings of the various proceedings. Though some who have assisted spoke on condition of anonymity, nearly everyone commented on the record. Conversations have been reconstructed from the memories of participants or a participant. In some cases these were supplemented with written accounts or from testimony. The memories of others who were present may be different. Thoughts and emotions attributed to participants are based on their reporting of them and have not been construed.

The events have been portrayed as they occurred. In any book of this type the author exercises control over what portion of the events will be depicted. The author has sought in his selection to present an accurate picture of the total event. He may have omitted some occurrences that others will consider more relevant than the ones used.

In some places in the text there is disagreement on what took place. Those disagreements have been presented, and no attempt has been made to resolve them. Readers may judge for themselves or withhold judgment.

The names used are those of the participants as they choose to use them in public life. Todd Sprague is the only name that has been changed. During the period covered by this book the participant identified as Sprague was sixteen and seventeen years old. He actively sought publicity and subsequently self-printed his account of some of the events. Since he was a minor at the time and may someday wish to distance himself from his juvenile past, the author leaves it to him to publish his true name. Except for the name, everything else concerning Todd Sprague is correctly portrayed.

The author is not related to either Ralph Watkins or Horace Lee Watkins.

Those who cooperated with the author are self-evident from the text, and the author wishes to thank them at this time. Special thanks must go to Joe and Sue Lane, Rick Collins, Donna Carlson, Sam Stanton, Mike Murphy, and Steve Benson.

Thanks to the many reporters and columnists on whose work the author has relied so heavily. Unfortunately the narrative style did not always permit attribution.

Thanks also to Pat Murphy, publisher of the *Arizona Republic* and the

Phoenix *Gazette* during the period of research, who made himself available for every question and provided total access to his staff and archives, all without preconditions.

The author thanks former Arizona Governor Evan Mecham for his co-operation and especially for waiving attorney-client privilege which made detailed interviews with his lawyers possible.

A number of participants entrusted their personal diaries, notes, correspondence, and documents to the author's care for many months. Thanks and deepest appreciation to each of them.

A special debt of gratitude is owed to those portrayed here who trusted the author with their personal and at times very painful life stories. While remaining true to events, the author has sought to return that trust with a discreet handling of sensitive matters not relevant to the main narrative.

Thanks also to the many secretaries who tolerated the author's insistence and to the staffs of the state archives at the Arizona State Capitol, the Arizona Senate, and the Arizona House of Representatives for their professional response to unusual requests.

No work such as this is written without assistance. This book has benefited from the inspiration of the author's agent, Mike Hamilburg, and the gifted editing of Lisa Drew, vice-president and senior editor with William Morrow.

Words in an acknowledgment such as this cannot adequately convey the author's debt to his daughters, Theresa and Elizabeth, for accepting his absences with good cheer; to his son, Stephen, for originating the title, making the word processor work, and spending so many hours proofreading; and to his friends Steve and Lisa Tufts for listening to his ramblings for so many long months. Thanks to Allen Reed for his forbearance and shared joy in the project.

And last, the author's profound gratitude to his wife, Jo Ann, who was more than a supporter and companion. Without her tireless research and unflagging assistance this work would not have been completed. Mere words can never repay the debt. It will take at least a diamond.

# INDEX

Adams, Bill, 199
Adams Hotel, 29
Ahavat Torah Congregation, 231
AIDS, 127
Allen, Rex, 372
Allen, Rex, Jr., 65, 372
Alston, Lela, 346, 348, 352
Altamont High School, 23
Anderson, Dale, 324
  senate impeachment trial and, 327
Anti-Defamation League of B'nai B'rith,
    232, 233
Antidrug task force, 84
Antonino, Mariel, 133
Apacheria, 37, 38
Apaches, 37, 38
Arizona
  apathy of population toward politics in,
    41, 48, 57
  conservatism of, 41
  early history of, 37–39
    animosity toward federal government,
      37, 38
    racial mixture of settlers, 39
    statehood, 39
  mineral wealth of, 38, 39
  Old West mystique of, 14–15

  population explosion in, 40, 41, 60
  post–World War II growth of, 40, 41
  recall elections in, 11
  state government of
    political "system," 29
    Republican Party domination, 38,
      40–42
    senators and representatives, 28–29
    voting districts, 29$n$
  tourist industry of, 40, 41
  transitory nature of population, 41
Arizona, University of, 69, 122
Arizona Automobile Dealers Association, 56
Arizona Chamber of Commerce, 104
Arizona Commission on the Bicentennial
    of the Constitution, 72, 115
*Arizona Daily Star*, 102
  recall election drive and, 177
Arizona Department of Liquor Licenses
    and Control, 74
Arizona Drug Control Service, 84
Arizona Eagle Forum, 99
*Arizona Journal*, 31
Arizona National Guard, 65
Arizonans for Traditional Values, 295
Arizona Prosecuting Attorneys Association,
    110